The One Year® Father-Daughter Devotions

THE ONE YEAR®

FATHER
Daughter
DEVOTIONS

Jesse Florea
Leon C. Wirth
Bob Smithouser

TYNDALE HOUSE PUBLISHERS, INC.
CAROL STREAM, ILLINOIS

Visit Tyndale's website for kids at www.tyndale.com/kids.

TYNDALE, Tyndale's quill logo, *One Year*, and *The One Year* are registered trademarks of Tyndale House Publishers, Inc.

The One Year Father-Daughter Devotions

Copyright © 2012 by Jesse Florea, Leon C. Wirth, and Bob Smithouser. All rights reserved.

Cover photograph of denim copyright © Oleksiy Maksymenko/Getty Images. All rights reserved.

Cover photograph of dot fabric copyright © Datacraft Co. Ltd./Getty Images. All rights reserved.

Interior photograph of popcorn pattern © 100kers/iStockphoto. All rights reserved.

Designed by Mark Anthony Lane II

Edited by Erin Keeley Marshall

Unless otherwise indicated, all Scripture quotations are taken from the *Holy Bible*, New Living Translation, copyright © 1996, 2004, 2007 by Tyndale House Foundation. Used by permission of Tyndale House Publishers, Inc., Carol Stream, Illinois 60188. All rights reserved.

Scripture quotations marked NIV are taken from the Holy Bible, *New International Version,*® *NIV.*® Copyright © 1973, 1978, 1984 by Biblica, Inc.™ Used by permission of Zondervan. All rights reserved worldwide. www.zondervan.com.

Scripture quotations marked HCSB are taken from the Holman Christian Standard Bible®, copyright © 1999, 2000, 2002, 2003, 2009 by Holman Bible Publishers. Used by permission. Holman Christian Standard Bible®, Holman CSB®, and HCSB® are federally registered trademarks of Holman Bible Publishers.

Scripture quotations marked CEV are taken from the Contemporary English Version, copyright © 1991, 1992, 1995 by American Bible Society. Used by permission.

Scripture quotations marked NKJV are taken from the New King James Version.® Copyright © 1982 by Thomas Nelson, Inc. Used by permission. All rights reserved. NKJV is a trademark of Thomas Nelson, Inc.

For manufacturing information regarding this product, please call 1-800-323-9400.

ISBN 978-1-4143-6486-5

Printed in the United States of America

18	17	16	15	14	13	12
7	6	5	4	3	2	1

To my daughter, Shelby; my son, Colin; and my amazing wife,

Julie. Your transparency, playful spirit, and godly curiosity

during our own family devotions inspired this journey more

than you'll ever know. You are my greatest blessings.

—BOB

To my daughter, Amber. Watching you grow and blossom into

a caring young woman has been one of my greatest joys as a father.

Being a follower of Jesus Christ is a lifelong adventure, and I pray

you and your brother, Nathanael, will walk the path God has for

you. Special thanks to my wife, Stephanie, for your patience and

encouragement during late nights and busy weekends. I love you all.

—JESSE

To my incredible daughters, Hannah, Rebecca, Emma, Olivia,

Leah, Clara, Alicia, and Jenna. You have brought me more joy,

love, and life lessons than I could've ever anticipated when I first

became a daddy. I love you all dearly. I pray you'll grow in your love

for the Lord, for the Word, and for others, just like your beautiful

mommy, Michelle. I am forever honored to be hers and yours.

—LEON

PROMISES, PROMISES

WELCOME to a new year. *Woo-hoo!* Time for new beginnings, new calendars, and new promises. Some people call them New Year's resolutions. And they're not such a bad idea. Sometimes they inspire people to try new things, learn a new skill, create new habits, or develop new disciplines. But many, many times these promises are quickly broken, disappointing the promise makers until they forget about it. One researcher found that about eight out of every ten people who make New Year's resolutions break them before the month is over. *Time* magazine once published a list of the most commonly broken resolutions, which included

> lose weight and get fit;
> eat healthier and diet;
> get out of debt and save money;
> spend more time with family;
> be less stressed; and
> volunteer.

Sounds like a good list of promises. So why do many people break them? The most common reason for failure is that people think too much about failing. Weird, huh? By focusing on the consequences of failing, instead of looking at the benefits of success, people fail. In addition, most people try to accomplish these goals through individual effort. They don't pull in a friend to help, and they don't rely on God.

Jesus made an important point about our futures and our promises. In Matthew 6, he ends with these words: "Seek the Kingdom of God above all else, and live righteously, and he will give you everything you need. So don't worry about tomorrow, for tomorrow will bring its own worries."

Today might be the start of a new year filled with new resolutions for you and your dad. If so, that's terrific! Pray that this year will draw the two of you closer to God and each other. Just remember that seeking God is not just a resolution . . . it's a lifelong pursuit. Go for it together!

DADDY-*Daughter Time*

Does your family make resolutions? Talk together about some things you would like to achieve this year. Figure out how you might work together and encourage each other in those pursuits.

Now look at your list of resolutions and see how it compares to Matthew 6:33-34. Are there any resolutions you could make that are more important than seeking God this year? Make a plan on how you'll grow closer to him. (This book can help!) And don't forget to ask God to help you both.

WHAT'S THE WORD?

Seek the Kingdom of God above all else, and live righteously, and he will give you everything you need. So don't worry about tomorrow, for tomorrow will bring its own worries. Today's trouble is enough for today. MATTHEW 6:33-34

A FAMILY PRIORITY

FOOTBALL fans are pretty excited this time of year. College football bowl games are being played, the National Football League play-offs are under way, and the Super Bowl is a few weeks away. Each game is important, but to some people they can become too important.

A credit-card company once produced a series of television commercials about a unique group of football fans. They had been to every single Super Bowl. One commercial featured a man named Larry. The Super Bowl was so important to him, he said, "I've missed weddings; I have missed babies being born; but I have no intention of missing a Super Bowl—ever."

A 2011 newspaper article featured a story about Ben. He loved his football team and had a ticket to the final regular season game. A win meant his favorite NFL squad would make the play-offs. Ben couldn't wait for the game. But the day before the contest, Ben's wife went into labor. Their baby was born on the day of the game. Where was Ben? Right there with his wife and baby girl, Aubrey. His team made the play-offs without Ben cheering them on. He had no regrets, calling Aubrey's birth "a better surprise."

Two men . . . two different priorities.

God told his people long ago how important family is. He told parents to love him, then pass their knowledge of his love to their children every day (see Deuteronomy 6:1-9).

Later in that same book, God explained that each family had a choice: to choose life or death, blessings or curses, for their family. By choosing life and focusing on him first, God said it would help future generations to live with him. The choices we make about our families now can affect generations of family members to come.

DADDY-*Daughter Time*

How do others know if your family is important to you? List what evidence people can see in your everyday life that shows your family is a priority. Discuss if you would be willing to miss an important family event for something else. What would that be?

Pick a father you know who shows that his family is a priority. Together, choose a little card and "prize" to share with him, honoring his commitment to his family.

WHAT'S THE WORD?

Today I have given you the choice between life and death, between blessings and curses. . . . Oh, that you would choose life, so that you and your descendants might live! . . . This is the key to your life. DEUTERONOMY 30:19-20

BAD TIME FOR
A DEAD BATTERY

HAVE you ever been in a car when the engine won't start? The key turns—*click, click, click*—nothing. Usually that happens at the worst time. Late for school. Late for work. In a hurry to get somewhere.

Many times when a car won't start, the problem is a dead battery. It's a common issue with an easy solution. To make a dead battery come to life, all you have to do is connect it to a battery with plenty of power. Maybe you've seen two cars with their hoods up attached by jumper cables. By linking the batteries together, the weak battery gets the juice it needs to fire up the engine.

King David once had a dead battery of sorts. After God's prophet confronted David for serious sins and enduring the death of his baby boy, David realized his heart had not only drifted away from God . . . it was on empty. No spark. No energy. No power.

So what did he do? He asked God to "jump-start" his heart. David repented, asked for forgiveness, and acknowledged his bad choices (see Psalm 51). He didn't sugarcoat things with God. He honestly admitted his faults. But he didn't just beat himself up. He realized God had an everlasting battery that could recharge him. So David humbly asked God to do for him what he couldn't do for himself.

> *Purify me.*
> *Wash me.*
> *Give me back my joy again.*
> *Let me rejoice.*
> *Remove my guilt.*
> *Create in me a clean heart.*
> *Renew a loyal spirit within me.*
> *Restore to me the joy of your salvation.*

God answered David's humble, honest prayer. God reignited David's spark, and the battery of David's heart became so strong that he is remembered as a man after God's own heart. Now that's real cranking power.

DADDY-*Daughter Time*

Ask your dad to pop the hood and show you where the battery is in your family car. Ask him to explain how the battery is vital to the car, to the computer in the car, to the radio, etc. If neither of you is familiar with how a car battery works, go online and search for videos to learn about it together.

Are there things sapping your energy? Is your battery empty? Pray together a prayer similar to David's. Ask God to show you what you need to recharge with his help. He'll do it!

WHAT'S THE WORD?

Restore to me the joy of your salvation, and make me willing to obey you.
PSALM 51:12

DADDY'S HOME!

HAVE you heard the saying "Home is where the heart is"? That seems especially true when you're a father who has been away from your family for a long time. Some dads travel a lot for their jobs. They can be gone days or weeks at a time. Military fathers might be gone even longer—for over a year. Maybe that's what makes the reunions of military families so special. It's not hard to find videos online of returning soldiers who surprise their children by getting home earlier than expected. By the time the video ends, most people find themselves dabbing tears from their eyes.

What is it about these scenes that makes them so powerful? Maybe it's the fact that the wait is over. The soldier has safely returned. They are, simply and beautifully, together again. Reunions like these melt our hearts, but they absolutely thrill God. His heart longs for families to be together, for hearts to be turned toward each other, especially between dads and their children.

Did you know God talked about this in the Bible? In Malachi, God told his people that another prophet would be coming soon to do something very special: "His preaching will turn the hearts of fathers to their children, and the hearts of children to their fathers" (Malachi 4:6). God really cares about the love between a father and his daughter! He wants dads to see their girls as special treasures, worthy of their time, attention, and love. He wants girls to turn away from other distractions in life to honor and respect their dads. It's beautiful and powerful when God's people have their hearts turned toward home.

DADDY-*Daughter Time*

Do you ever have to spend long amounts of time away from each other? If so, how do you spend time together when you're reunited? Search for videos on the Internet that show military dads surprising their kids. Pick a favorite and discuss what makes it so special and interesting to you.

Plan how you might set aside some special daddy-daughter time the next time you have to be apart. Think of ways to surprise each other with a little note, poem, or other little gift. When you give your gift, start by saying something like "I want you to have this to show you that my heart is with you, because . . ." and explain what you've missed most about the other person.

WHAT'S THE WORD?

His preaching will turn the hearts of fathers to their children, and the hearts of children to their fathers. MALACHI 4:6

YESTERDAY'S INTERESTS

WHAT did you receive for Christmas this year? We're only a handful of days into the new year, but chances are a majority of your Christmas presents are already being unused or ignored. It happens every year. Something you wanted so badly winds up being boring way before you thought it would be. Even your all-time most-loved, well-used toys and gifts eventually lose their shine. They break. You outgrow them. And soon your favorite gifts are discarded.

Ask some adults what their favorite toys, videos, music, video games, or hobbies were when they were younger. You'll get some fun answers. Occasionally, you'll find someone who discovered a lifelong passion from that time in his or her life. But more often you'll get stories of nearly forgotten toys. Disney's *Toy Story* movies show this. The plots often center on the toys' desire to be played with versus an aging child who's discovering new interests. First Corinthians 13 explains this natural part of growing up. The writer, Paul, points out that when we mature, we naturally think, talk, and play less like children. "When I was a child," Paul writes in verse 11, "I spoke and thought and reasoned as a child. But when I grew up, I put away childish things." It's not that being young is bad. But as we mature in our love for God, his Word, and each other, we'll naturally see the world in a different way, and that change will impact how we live.

So next time you find yourself less interested in a toy or game you used to love, think about this passage. When we make God most important in our lives, the joy we find in other things will be replaced by the joy and love we feel for him and others!

DADDY-*Daughter Time*

Daughters, make some guesses about what your dad's favorite gifts, toys, and games were when he was your age. Were you right? Which things still interest him? Now share with him some of the things that used to be your favorites but aren't anymore. Any recent Christmas gifts on that list?

Pray together and encourage each other in gaining clarity to let go of things that aren't as important as your relationship with God and others.

WHAT'S THE WORD?

When I was a child, I spoke and thought and reasoned as a child. But when I grew up, I put away childish things. Now we see things imperfectly, like puzzling reflections in a mirror, but then we will see everything with perfect clarity. All that I know now is partial and incomplete, but then I will know everything completely, just as God now knows me completely. 1 CORINTHIANS 13:11-12

YOU WANNA WHAT?

HAVE you ever realized as you were speaking that your brain and your tongue weren't working together? Sometimes a misfiring synapse can cause you to say something really silly. Other times it allows words to escape that you immediately regret. Our words can be powerful—for good or for bad—especially in our families.

One evening, after a particularly long, tiring day, a dad realized he must've left his brain at work. He arrived home to eat dinner with his family. His wife had other commitments, so Dad served the meal and sat down to eat. However, his five-year-old started complaining. Usually not a picky eater, she fought against eating her dinner, which was usually one of her favorites. The dad tried again and again to explain that she was complaining about something she usually liked! Finally, his patience wore thin. He stood up, raised his voice, and said, "Do you wanna *fight* me about *this*?" What he *meant* to say was "Do you wanna *argue* with me about *this*?" But his brain and his tongue weren't cooperating. His daughter stared silently, too stunned to speak. Her fear, which was not the response Dad was expecting, forced him to rewind the words in his brain. Once he realized what he had said, his daughter's response melted him. He faced a choice: apologize for his carelessness, or pretend that her stubbornness caused him to lose his temper.

He apologized.

Today, his family laughs about this story, knowing that what he said and what he meant were two different things. The Bible warns fathers not to aggravate their children (see Colossians 3:21). Some versions of that verse say not to "embitter," "provoke," or "make your children resentful."

The words a dad uses can build up or provoke his children. We have to be willing—dads and daughters—to apologize and make things right when our mouths and minds don't work together. There may be nothing more important than for a family to learn repentance, grace, and forgiveness with each other.

DADDY-*Daughter Time*

Daughters, now would be a good time to share if you have any past hurts that have not been settled between you and your dad. The Bible says in Ephesians 4:26 that we shouldn't let the sun go down on our anger. It's better to deal with these hurts as soon as possible.

Dads, ask God to give you a heart willing to say, "I'm sorry." Without your willing heart, some hurts can last far too long.

WHAT'S THE WORD?

Fathers, do not aggravate your children, or they will become discouraged.
COLOSSIANS 3:21

BUT I WAS DOING IT FOR GOD!

IS it possible to do the wrong thing for the right reasons? The answer's not as simple as you think. For thousands of years, people have blamed their sins on having good intentions.

Of course, sometimes our disobedience is blatant. In the Garden of Eden, Adam and Eve basically had one rule: Don't eat the fruit on the tree of the knowledge of good and evil. What'd they do? Ate the fruit. Adam blamed Eve. Eve blamed the serpent. The serpent hissed—well, probably. But other times in the Bible, people tried to reason away their wrongdoings, saying, "I was doing it for God."

- Abraham was promised more descendants than all the stars. But he was getting old and didn't yet have a child. So he started a family with his wife's servant. That did not go well.
- God told Moses specifically to *speak* to a rock to make water come out for the thirsty, desert-wandering Israelites. But whether out of anger or pride, Moses *struck* the rock. That did not go well, either.
- Then there's the disciple Peter. When Jesus was arrested, Peter, wanting to protect Jesus, drew a sword and cut off a servant's ear. (Jesus quickly healed the man.)

What do these stories show us? Our good intention to do something for God doesn't make a *wrong* action *right*. God is not honored when we sin, no matter our intentions. Just like it says in Psalm 139:23-24, we should ask God to test our motivations and to lead us "along the path of everlasting life."

DADDY-*Daughter Time*

The popular radio drama *Adventures in Odyssey* featured a great game that showed this concept. In the episode "Rights, Wrongs & Reasons," Whit, Connie, and Jenny discuss real or pretend situations and see if they agree if there's both a right action and a right motive. If you'd like to hear that show, you can download it at whitsend.org. Just search for "Rights, Wrongs, Reasons."

Our goal in life should be to honestly assess when an action and a motive are both right. If not, you may end up doing the right thing for the wrong reason or the wrong thing for the right reason. Then there's the wrong thing for the wrong reason—but that should be obvious.

WHAT'S THE WORD?

Search me, O God, and know my heart; test me and know my anxious thoughts. Point out anything in me that offends you, and lead me along the path of everlasting life. PSALM 139:23-24

January 8

BOYS will be boys . . . because they're boys. If a boy likes a girl, he might show his interest in a number of ways—none of which include actually telling her. Instead he might act goofy, be gross, show off, pull her hair, trip her, or generally be childish. Not exactly Mr. Suave.

On one particular day, a dad walked into his house to find his oldest daughter waiting for him. "Why are boys so immature?" she asked.

There's not enough time to answer that question! Dad thought. Then his mind wandered back to his elementary years. *Sardines for lunch in fifth grade, not because I liked them, but because I'd seen another boy gross out the girls with them the week before. Starting a club for my buddies called the "Iguana Club." Throwing a dodge ball as hard as I could at a girl's feet, hoping to impress her, but causing her to fall awkwardly and gash her left hand.*

"Uh, Dad," his daughter said, interrupting his thoughts. "You haven't answered my question."

The truth is, boys typically develop more slowly than girls—physically, mentally, and emotionally. It's an awkward but real fact of life. As a boy enters his teen years, he's often trying to figure out how to be a man while feeling like a boy, and looking for respect. But whether it's a boy who bothers you or someone else who tests your patience, there's one important response followers of Jesus should have: patience. Titus 3:3-5 reminds us that we were all foolish at one time, until Christ saved us through his kindness and love.

The next time someone really annoys you, consider what it might look like if you showed that person gentleness and humility—like God does for you. With God's help, he or she might even grow out of it someday . . . even a boy.

DADDY-*Daughter Time*

Dad, tell your daughter about times when you were really silly or annoying as a boy. Discuss the best way to respond to people who annoy you or seem immature. Praying for them and showing some kindness can do a lot to help them. Resolve together to pray for each other for specific situations where you know you'll be around some people who challenge you.

WHAT'S THE WORD?

Once we, too, were foolish and disobedient. . . . But—"When God our Savior revealed his kindness and love, he saved us, not because of the righteous things we had done, but because of his mercy." TITUS 3:3-5

TIME FLIES . . .
AND DRAGS ON

THE girl couldn't believe it. After she'd prayed for years to hear God's voice, his Spirit showed up in her room one night.

"Lord, I've always wanted to ask you a question," she said. "Lord, I know you're not bound by time. What is a thousand years like for you?"

"For me a thousand years is like a second," God answered.

"What about money?" the girl said. "What would a million dollars be to you?"

"For me a million dollars is like a penny," God said.

Hmmmm, the girl thought. "Lord, I have just one more question: Can you give me a penny?"

"No problem," God said. "But you'll have to wait a second."

Obviously, that story is a joke . . . and not a very good one. But it illustrates an important point. We relate to time very differently from God. We're so impatient that it bothers us to wait for microwave popcorn to pop. God can patiently wait thousands of years for his plans to come to fruition. God is beyond time. But in 2 Peter 3, the apostle Peter explains that in spite of how slow God seems to be, he can always be trusted to do what he says. Peter knew people would mock God because Jesus hadn't come back yet. Even the early Christians thought Jesus would be coming back *really soon* . . . and he is.

Peter knew that God doesn't view time the same way we do. To God, a day is like a thousand years, yet a thousand years would be like a day. Time doesn't affect God the same way it affects us. When we get impatient, we need to keep trusting God, regardless of how long he takes to bring about his plans.

DADDY-*Daughter Time*

Talk about the weeks leading up to and since Christmas. Did the days go faster before or after Christmas? Ask your dad if that feeling was the same when he was a boy.

The next time you get impatient about one of God's promises, remember that he always has a plan. Maybe he's just waiting for somebody else to follow him.

WHAT'S THE WORD?

You must not forget this one thing, dear friends: A day is like a thousand years to the Lord, and a thousand years is like a day. The Lord isn't really being slow about his promise, as some people think. No, he is being patient for your sake. He does not want anyone to be destroyed, but wants everyone to repent. 2 PETER 3:8-9

CARE PACKS FOR THE ROAD

YOU can't miss them: people holding signs at the entrances to highways or shopping malls. The cardboard signs look similar, but the messages can vary:

> *Looking for work. Please help. God bless.*
>
> *Ran out of gas. Trying to get home. Change appreciated.*
>
> *Homeless and hungry.*
>
> *Family to feed. Need help.*

Different families have different attitudes and convictions about how to respond to people on the street looking for help. Money is not always the best solution, because it can be used for anything . . . even purchasing drugs or alcohol. Instead of handing out cash, one family came up with a very practical idea. After considering what Jesus says in Matthew 25:35 about caring for people in great need, this family decided to try to meet the temporary and eternal needs of the people they encountered as they drove around town. First, they bought gallon plastic bags. They filled each one with a bottle of water, a granola bar, a copy of the Gospel of John from the New Testament, a package of beef jerky, a pack of gum, a toothbrush, a tube of toothpaste, a packet of mints or candy, a gospel tract, and a meal ticket to a local homeless shelter. When the weather turned cold, they added little hand-warmer or foot-warmer pads.

The family kept a small quantity of these "blessings bags" in the car. When anyone spotted someone looking for help, they would stop and hand one of the bags out of the car, saying, "Jesus loves you. God bless you."

When you help "the least of these" in our world, it's like you're serving the Lord himself.

DADDY-*Daughter Time*

Has there been a time when your family needed help? If so, talk about those times with your dad. What did receiving help feel like? How did it give you hope and strengthen your faith?

Think about some ways your family can help those who need it. Maybe you can make your own blessings bags. Look into what local ministries are doing, and find out how you can support them. You'll be amazed by how great it feels to give.

WHAT'S THE WORD?

I was hungry, and you fed me. I was thirsty, and you gave me a drink. I was a stranger, and you invited me into your home. MATTHEW 25:35

BEING WATCHED IN
TROUBLED TIMES

THE family bike ride started out fun for Kylee. The trail twisted along a neat path near their home in Canada. Kylee had just received a new bike. It was bigger and faster than her old bike, and she was still adjusting to it. Pretty soon Kylee zoomed well ahead of her family. As she started down a steep hill bordered by a row of trees that guarded a deep ravine, Kylee found herself going too fast. Her mind raced. *How do I use these brakes?* she thought as her bike picked up speed. *God, help me.* She was about to run into one of the trees and maybe fly into the ditch when an old man came out of nowhere, grabbed onto her bike, and saved her. As the man helped Kylee off her bike, he said, "God bless you," smiled, and walked away. By the time Kylee's family caught up with her, the man was gone.

What does Kylee's true story do for your faith? We love to hear how God rescues people who call out to him. In the book of Psalms, David often cries out to God for help, for understanding, or for hope. David was brave, noble, and wise. He was also hunted, despised, and sinful. David recognized that people watched him to see how he handled difficulties in his life. He knew that when others witnessed God rescue him, their faith would be helped as well. Like David writes in Psalm 40:3, "Many will see what he has done and be amazed. They will put their trust in the LORD."

Whenever God does something amazing in your life, don't hide it. Tell your friends, speak about it at your church, or write your story to a magazine. Kylee's story appeared in Focus on the Family's *Clubhouse* magazine, so thousands of kids could be encouraged about what the Lord had done.

DADDY-*Daughter Time*

Are you wrestling with difficult times? Add the end of Psalm 40:3 to your prayers about those situations. It's a great idea to keep track of your prayer requests and how God answers them. Then you can tell others how God works in your life.

WHAT'S THE WORD?

I waited patiently for the LORD to help me, and he turned to me and heard my cry. . . . He set my feet on solid ground and steadied me as I walked along. He has given me a new song to sing, a hymn of praise to our God. Many will see what he has done and be amazed. They will put their trust in the LORD. PSALM 40:1-3

TWO ARE BETTER THAN ONE

MOST people don't like to be alone. It's been that way from the beginning of time. When God made Adam, he paused before creating Eve to say, "It is not good for the man to be alone" (Genesis 2:18). Our relationships with others are a big part of who we are.

King Solomon understood the value of friends. As he wrote the book of Ecclesiastes, he explored the meaning of friends, among other things. What he found over and over again is that life can feel meaningless when we live for ourselves. Whatever the gain, whatever the pleasure, when we live for ourselves, life feels empty. But in chapter four, Solomon shifts to the special advantages of friendship.

"Two people are better off than one, for they can help each other succeed," he begins in verse 9. He then notes that a companion provides strength in work, in survival, and in defense. A friend can give us the strength to battle sin. When we're alone, the temptation of sin can overwhelm us. We're more likely to stumble. But when we share our struggles, a friend can lend support. She can help us realize we are not alone and give us a hand if we fall (see Ecclesiastes 4:10).

Perhaps you have a friend who deserves more appreciation. Perhaps you long for a friend unlike any you've ever had. Or maybe you miss a friend who has not been near for some time. Companionship can also be an important part of our families. Don't miss the chance to build relationships with siblings, cousins, and other family members. God cares about relationships, and he wants us to rely on good friends along life's journey.

DADDY-*Daughter Time*

A good friend can make a big difference in life. You can find friends in unexpected places. Make plans to watch the movie *Because of Winn-Dixie* together. How did the main character make friends, and what were the benefits? Look for more discussion topics for this movie in the Father-Daughter Movie Nights appendix at the back of the book.

If you haven't had a close friendship for a long time, understand that this is a common desire. Commit to pray together that God will provide a godly friend.

Talk with your dad about some friendships that have meant the most to him. Maybe he needs a good friend too. If so, pray for that, too.

WHAT'S THE WORD?

If one person falls, the other can reach out and help. But someone who falls alone is in real trouble. ECCLESIASTES 4:10

HARD WORDS TO HEAR

ADJECTIVES can be wonderful. Who doesn't want to be a brave, cheerful, dazzling, exuberant, fabulous, hilarious, joyous person? The right descriptor can make even a negative-sounding word better. Think about the word *criticism*. Nobody likes to be criticized. Learning about your faults and foibles isn't fun. But when you add the word *constructive* in front of it, it doesn't seem too bad.

Actually, constructive criticism can be a good thing. Proverbs 15:31 says, "If you listen to constructive criticism, you will be at home among the wise." Constructive criticism isn't negative. Sure, family members or friends might point out weaknesses or blind spots in your life, but their desire is to build you up, make you better, and give you another perspective. The best constructive criticism comes from a humble, loving heart. (See? Aren't adjectives cool?) To properly receive criticism and benefit from it, the key is to not get defensive. And that's not easy. When somebody points out a weakness, it's natural to want to justify our actions and make excuses. Instead we should listen and understand the intent of the person's advice. When we learn from criticism, we become wise.

Often, constructive criticism comes from parents and our closest friends. We also may find criticism in God's Word that convicts our hearts and causes us to want to change. Sure, it's a hard message to hear. But we shouldn't automatically assume that someone is trying to hurt us when they criticize. Those critical words might be just the gift that helps make us better and molds our character closer to Christ's.

DADDY-*Daughter Time*

Have you ever been hurt by someone's criticism? Looking back, do you think that person was trying to be helpful? Get some paper and pencils. Write down a bunch of adjectives that you'd like your life to reflect. Do you need to change any habits or actions to become more like your list? Commit to only constructively criticize each other, and stay away from mean, negative words. Remember that sometimes *how* we say something speaks louder than our actual words. Pray that you'll be able to give and receive constructive criticism with kindness and joy.

WHAT'S THE WORD?

If you listen to constructive criticism, you will be at home among the wise.
PROVERBS 15:31

January 14

HAVE you ever noticed how many people it takes to make a movie? What exactly do the gaffer, key grip, and Foley artist do anyway? In some movies, the credits go on for nearly as long as the film itself. No wonder filmmakers sometimes add special bloopers, extra animations, or deleted scenes while the credits roll: they want you to stay and see all the people who worked on the film.

And what do all those hundreds of people have to show for their creative energies? Usually it's ninety minutes of mindless entertainment. Sure, movies can be fun. But rarely does a movie challenge your thinking or change the world. In an hour or two, the lights come on, and it's done.

When you think about that, movies make what God did at Creation even more astounding. His creative energies didn't only change the world—they created it. He didn't need actors or casting experts. He didn't have a director or a producer. There was no special music, best boy, or stunt coordinator. And he didn't need a marketing team to create a buzz.

All God had to do was speak, and the universe came into existence. "God said, 'Let there be light,' and there was light" (Genesis 1:3). Wow. In the first chapter of John, we learn that God's Son was with him at Creation. The heavenly Father and the Son worked together. So if the credits had rolled after God's amazing display of special effects at Creation, they might have looked something like this:

Maker of the Universe—God the Father, with God the Son.

That's it.

That humbles us in every way possible. Despite all the technology and razzle-dazzle of the best, shiniest, most incredible film, it will never have a credit of one.

DADDY-*Daughter Time*

The next time you watch a movie together, slow down the credits and look at some of the titles and names. By the way, the gaffer is in charge of electricity and lighting a movie, a key grip moves major pieces on the set and works with the director of photography, and a Foley artist creates the sound effects in a movie.

The next time you're outside enjoying God's creation or marveling at the snow or a newborn baby, pause to give God glory for all he has created. Always remind each other that we know a great and awesome God.

WHAT'S THE WORD?

God said, "Let there be light," and there was light. GENESIS 1:3

OXYGEN MASKS AND TIME WITH GOD

HAVE you ever paid attention to the safety procedures when you're waiting for an airplane to take off? Passengers are instructed to pull out a reference card and follow along as flight attendants explain the safety features of the plane.

"There are the doors. . . . No smoking anywhere, anytime. . . . Here's how you use a seat belt, and please keep it buckled. . . . Your seat cushion can be used as a flotation device if we land in water."

Then there's the oxygen mask. If the air pressure drops while the plane is in flight, masks will fall out of the ceiling. The flight attendants explain how to put on a mask, tighten it, and breathe. Of course, they assume everyone will remain calm in an emergency, which is probably wishful thinking. One additional piece of advice is that you should put on your mask before helping someone who needs assistance with his or hers.

Why? Well, if the plane loses pressure, the oxygen in the cabin gets sucked into the atmosphere. That's why the masks are so important. By securing your mask, you receive the oxygen you need to function. If you help somebody before making sure you can breathe, you may pass out from a lack of oxygen. Then you couldn't help anyone else, and you might end up in a world of hurt.

That same principle is seen throughout Jesus' ministry on earth. Time and again, Jesus would go off by himself to spend time with God (see Luke 5:16). You might be wondering, *Why would Jesus need that time if he was the Son of God?* Jesus was setting an example for us. He firmed up his relationship by "putting on his mask" to get the spiritual oxygen he needed. The time Jesus spent in communication with God reenergized him. He wants us to do the same. Spending time alone with God is healthy, not selfish. Building up our own faith makes it easier for us to help others.

DADDY-*Daughter Time*

Have you made spending time with God a priority in your life? Resolve together to fortify your spiritual life. You can start small, but it's important to get life-giving "spiritual" oxygen through prayer and fellowship with your heavenly Father. By helping your own relationship with God, you'll be better able to help others know him as well.

WHAT'S THE WORD?

Despite Jesus' instructions, the report of his power spread even faster, and vast crowds came to hear him preach and to be healed of their diseases. But Jesus often withdrew to the wilderness for prayer. LUKE 5:15-16

FINDING FORGIVENESS FROM DAD

GOD is often referred to as a father. God our Father. God the Father. The heavenly Father. Father to the fatherless. And it's a title God embraces. He refers to himself as our Father in both the Old and New Testaments. Dads and daughters can learn a lot about the purpose of fathers and family relationships by looking at God. One such lesson in the book of Hosea shows us discipline, repentance, and forgiveness in the father-child relationship.

In Hosea, God speaks to his people and refers to them as children. He explains both his love for them and his disappointment and anger at their sinfulness. The Israelites had turned away from God and put their trust in other gods. But the book doesn't end with God as an angry, disappointed father. God ends it with a message of hope and love.

If you'll repent, if you'll acknowledge you were wrong, if you will ask forgiveness, if you will come back to me and stop looking for love and hope and help from others . . . I will heal and love and forgive, like a father.

There are always consequences for sin. But God offers forgiveness and love if his people return to him and confess. That's essentially the statement of a loving father to his children: *Your sin is wrong, but it can all be forgiven and worked out.*

The lesson for daughters is to be humble, to repent, and to ask forgiveness when you mess up. The lesson for dads is to forgive, to nurture, and to heal the relationship.

DADDY-*Daughter Time*

Dads, when you show compassion, you put on the heart of God for all to see. Plus, you create an environment for your daughter to be completely open with you.

Daughters, talk with your dad about what he does that makes you feel loved and accepted, and what he might do that would make you feel safe to ask for forgiveness. Do you find it hard to come to your dad and confess something you've done wrong? He'll want to know how he can better show you that he loves you.

WHAT'S THE WORD?

Bring your confessions, and return to the LORD. Say to him, "Forgive all our sins and graciously receive us, so that we may offer you our praises." . . . The LORD says, "Then I will heal you of your faithlessness; my love will know no bounds, for my anger will be gone forever." HOSEA 14:2, 4

THE BEST SOCIAL
NETWORKING

CLAY tablets. Papyrus paper and ink. Carrier pigeons. Telegrams. Telephones. Greeting cards. Walkie-talkies. Fax machines. E-mail. Text messages. Video calls. Social networks.

Want to send a message to someone? Throughout history, there have been many ways to communicate. Technologies change, but one thing stays the same: people love to feel connected.

In a world where there are so many technological choices on how to communicate, people still get lonely. In fact, some studies show that teenagers are more lonely and self-centered today than at any other point in history. One reason for this loneliness is that nothing can really replace being *together* with someone. Bonds grow best between people, not over the Internet or phone, but when they're in the same room . . . face-to-face.

The book of 2 John is one of the shortest in the Bible. In this thirteen-verse letter, John writes "to the chosen lady and to her children, whom I love in the truth" (v. 1). There is no clear consensus among Christian scholars as to who the "chosen lady" and her children are. Some think it was a personal letter to a family, while others believe John was writing metaphorically about a church of believers. In either case, the ending of the letter remarkably demonstrates an understanding of the power of personal presence in building relationships. John finishes the letter by saying, "I have much more to say to you, but I don't want to do it with paper and ink. For I hope to visit you soon and talk with you face to face. Then our joy will be complete" (v. 12).

As we use all the great communication tools that exist today to stay in touch, we should never forget the simple lesson of this statement. The joy of being with each other should never be taken for granted.

DADDY-*Daughter Time*

Who are some people in your life that are important but not close by? Do you have a way of staying in touch with them regularly using current technologies? Face time is so important in a relationship. If you can, try to surprise a close family member or friend with a personal visit sometime this year.

As you interact with family members and friends nearby, try to see them as much as possible. Facebook and phones are fine. But nothing's better than a face-to-face visit.

WHAT'S THE WORD?

I have much more to say to you, but I don't want to do it with paper and ink. For I hope to visit you soon and talk with you face to face. Then our joy will be complete.
2 JOHN 1:12

WHAT A DIFFERENCE A NAME MAKES

HOW would you like to go on a tropical vacation to the Sandwich Islands? *Mmmmmm.* Sandwiches. Okay, what about Hawaii? Would you want to walk the sandy beaches of that island paradise?

If you're a history buff, you'll know that the Sandwich Islands and the Hawaiian Islands are actually one and the same. When Captain James Cook discovered the Hawaiian Islands on this day in 1778, he named them the Sandwich Islands to honor John Montagu, who commanded the British Navy and was the fourth Earl of Sandwich. But that name only lasted about forty years, because by 1819, King Kamehameha had united the islands as the Kingdom of Hawaii.

Names have special meaning and significance. Just hearing a name can conjure up strong feelings and images. When you say the name *Hawaii*, you might immediately think of beautiful beaches, surfing, and hula dancing. But when you hear the word *sandwich*, you might think of a delicious meat-filled treat between two pieces of bread. In the Bible, names often describe a person's calling or position. For instance, the name *Adam* means "earth" or "man." Sometimes God would even change a person's name to describe a new story or promise for the future. Abram became Abraham, and Sarai became Sarah, to remind them of the promise that many nations and descendants would come from their family (see Genesis 17:1, 4-5). Jacob became Israel as a reminder of the strength he showed when he wrestled with God, and as a blessing to him (see Genesis 32:28-29). And Saul, a persecutor of the early church, became Paul after his conversion.

Incidentally, the sandwich *is* named after John Montagu. As the Earl of Sandwich, he made putting meat between slices of bread famous—and the name stuck!

DADDY-*Daughter Time*

You've probably had the same name since birth—unlike Hawaii. Look up the meanings of your first and middle names on the Internet. Many books and websites can help you in your search. Talk about the meanings of your names and what they say about God's calling on your life. Do you see a connection? Fathers, tell your daughter how you chose her name. Hopefully, you didn't name her after the inventor of the sandwich.

WHAT'S THE WORD?

When Abram was ninety-nine years old, the LORD appeared to him and said, "I am El-Shaddai—'God Almighty.' Serve me faithfully and live a blameless life. . . . This is my covenant with you: I will make you the father of a multitude of nations! What's more, I am changing your name. It will no longer be Abram. Instead, you will be called Abraham, for you will be the father of many nations." GENESIS 17:1, 4-5

ATTENTION TO DETAILS

SOME people go through life enjoying all the little details around them. They saunter through situations and often stop to smell the roses. Others go through life in a whirlwind of activity. These people often miss the finer nuances of their surroundings. To these people, life can seem like a blur. They might miss the beauty around them as they get lost in an ocean of distractions.

What kind of person are you? There's no right or wrong answer.

The "smell the roses" people are important to our world because they love digging into details. These people carefully inspect things to make sure products are precisely crafted and safe. They also might discover scientific breakthroughs, because they explore every aspect of their experiments. These people are often the storytellers who spend countless hours writing books, crafting props, or building scenery for movies.

The hard-charging go-getters are often leaders. They run companies, build businesses, or lead nations. They get an idea and go for it. Their passion helps their dreams come to life, often overcoming difficulties with a get-'er-done attitude.

The cool part about God is that he embodies both characteristics. We can see his incredible attention to detail in the Scriptures. For example, he lists generations of families to show precisely how key figures in biblical history are related to each other and fulfill prophecy. He demonstrates that he's a God of order, not a God of random chaos, in the way plants, animals, and natural systems work. But God also gets things done. He judges nations, overturns kings and other leaders, and demonstrates his power on many occasions.

No matter what kind of person you are, you can count on God to understand your thoughts and actions every day. You can use your strengths to glorify him.

DADDY-*Daughter Time*

Talk about the similarities or differences you and your dad have regarding attention to detail. Sometimes people notice detail but don't think or work with great detail. That's okay . . . we're all made differently.

Think about some of the littlest details you see in the life of Jesus. He said even the tiniest details of God's law would be around until their purposes were achieved (see Matthew 5:18). That shows God's into details *and* getting things accomplished.

WHAT'S THE WORD?

[Jesus said,] "I did not come to abolish the law of Moses or the writings of the prophets. No, I came to accomplish their purpose. I tell you the truth, until heaven and earth disappear, not even the smallest detail of God's law will disappear until its purpose is achieved." MATTHEW 5:17-18

A CHANGE OF HEART

IS your school backpack at home right now? If so, go pick it up. For many students, their backpacks are a lifeline to their education. They hold all their books, assignments, and supplies, which is why they're so heavy. But when Marcela Padilla walked out of a Tucson, Arizona, hospital on this day in 2011, her backpack was her lifeline—literally. That's because the twenty-year-old became the first woman in the United States to leave a hospital wearing a Freedom portable driver to power her temporary Total Artificial Heart. The battery in her backpack connected to an artificial heart that kept her alive. Amazing, huh?

Normally, patients who wait for heart transplants have to be connected to a 418-pound machine called "Big Blue," which keeps them stuck in the hospital. Companies are experimenting with lighter machines that allow patients to be at home with their families until they can receive a suitable replacement heart. Marcela was the first woman to try out the portable power device, which allowed her to celebrate her twenty-first birthday at home and be with her husband and young son. For Marcela, getting a new heart was key for her life.

Similarly, God wants to give his children a new heart. God's not talking about a physical heart transplant. But he desires that his followers have a tender heart that responds to God's leading and wants to help others. The prophet Ezekiel delivers this message from the Lord: "I will give you a new heart, and I will put a new spirit in you. I will take out your stony, stubborn heart and give you a tender, responsive heart" (Ezekiel 36:26).

Who would want a stony, stubborn heart anyway? Our hearts should be soft and pliable, so they can be used powerfully for God.

DADDY-*Daughter Time*

How would you describe your heart? We all have areas of stubbornness. Where are your "harder" areas? Fathers and daughters, commit to hold each other accountable to softening your hearts in all areas to God. Has God laid a special passion on your heart? If so, give all your efforts to accomplish his will in your life.

WHAT'S THE WORD?

I will give you a new heart, and I will put a new spirit in you. I will take out your stony, stubborn heart and give you a tender, responsive heart. EZEKIEL 36:26

HEALTHY HABITS

STATISTICS show that sales for gym memberships and diet plans skyrocket this time of year. But being healthy is a year-round decision, not a simple resolution. Answer these questions together to rate your healthy habits.

1. Doctors say breakfast is the most important meal of the day, so every morning I eat
   a) Choco-Coco crunch cereal. b) coffee. c) oatmeal or fruit.

2. When I have free time, I enjoy
   a) watching TV. b) dancing around to music. c) hanging out with friends.

3. I love to sleep, so every night I get
   a) five hours. b) seven hours. c) ten hours.

4. I know my body needs food to work properly, so I eat
   a) when I'm sad, bored, or excited. b) all the time; I'll snack on anything. c) only when I'm hungry.

Now check your answers. If you said mostly *a*'s, then you may be on a potentially dangerous path when it comes to your health. Look for ways to introduce more whole grains and vegetables in your diet. And remember that sleep is important for a healthy body. If you answered mainly *b*'s, your body may be doing okay, but there's still room for growth. Food is fuel, so try to stay away from sugary snacks. Finally, if you fell in the *c* category, keep up your activity level. A healthy body takes work, but the benefits are worth it.

There's a great story about Daniel and his friends in the Bible. When King Nebuchadnezzar attacked Jerusalem, his officials took some of the best and brightest young people—which included Daniel and his pals—to a Babylonian palace. They were offered rich and decadent foods. However, Daniel humbly refused and asked if he and his friends could eat vegetables and water. At the end of ten days, "Daniel and his three friends looked healthier and better nourished than the young men who had been eating the food assigned by the king" (Daniel 1:15).

DADDY-*Daughter Time*

What did you pick up from Daniel's story? Get some paper and pens and write down everything you eat for one day. Look at your food choices. Do you need to make any changes? Being healthy isn't about being rail thin. It's about taking care of your body and treating it like a temple (see 1 Corinthians 6:19-20). Commit to come up with a plan to be healthier over the next month.

WHAT'S THE WORD?

At the end of the ten days, Daniel and his three friends looked healthier and better nourished than the young men who had been eating the food assigned by the king.
DANIEL 1:15

GREAT SKATER

CINDY Klassen grew up with a pair of skates on her feet . . . hockey skates, that is. When she was two, her dad gave her a hockey stick. At four, she started playing hockey with the boys, because there weren't any programs for young girls where she lived. During her teen years, Cindy's parents read that the 1998 Winter Olympics would feature women's hockey for the first time. Immediately, Cindy dreamed of playing for Team Canada in the Olympics. When she was sixteen, she made the Canadian Junior National team. But at the tryouts for the Olympic team a couple of years later, Cindy failed to make the roster.

Cindy was certain it was God's plan for her to play hockey. But that dream seemed dead. Cindy's parents suggested she try speed skating. At first Cindy looked like a baby horse just learning to walk. The skates and equipment were so different. But her feel for the ice and natural athleticism and drive allowed her to improve quickly. By 2001, she placed near the top in the world championships. Then in 2002 her Olympic dreams came true when she won a bronze medal in the 3,000-meter race in Salt Lake City. But Cindy wasn't finished on the ice. Four years later she won five medals at the Winter Games in Torino, Italy. She placed third in the 3,000- and 5,000-meter races, earned silver medals at 1,000 meters and in the team pursuit (like a relay race on ice), and took home gold in the 1,500. Her five medals in one Olympics set an all-time record for Canadian athletes.

Do you think Cindy missed hockey? Well, maybe a little. But when one dream ended, she didn't give up and quit skating. Instead she tried a new sport, developed a new passion, and made history! During the hard times, Cindy said she relied on her faith in God and the truth of her favorite Bible verse, "I know the LORD is always with me. I will not be shaken, for he is right beside me" (Psalm 16:8). She knew she didn't have to worry about success on the ice, because God was always with her.

DADDY-*Daughter Time*

Do you have a favorite Bible verse? What is it? Both of you write the reference for your favorite verse here: _____

If you haven't memorized your favorite verse, commit to setting it to memory. And if you don't have a favorite verse, find one. The truth of God's Word can help carry you through difficult times.

WHAT'S THE WORD?

I know the LORD is always with me. I will not be shaken, for he is right beside me.
PSALM 16:8

INFESTING THE WHOLE

WHAT'S the largest living thing in the world? A blue whale? An elephant? A giant sequoia tree? Those are all pretty impressive. But when it comes to massive living organisms by area of size, you won't find anything bigger than a huge mushroom in the woods of eastern Oregon. No kidding. Although it is a fun-guy. *Ha!*

This fungus, the honey mushroom, extends over 2,384 acres, or about 1,665 football fields. The mushrooms are interconnected, genetically identical, and some would say, incredibly gross. The fungal jungle of mushrooms is estimated to be over 2,400 years old, based on its natural rate of growth. The fungus started small, but then grew unchecked in this remote area, eventually taking over the ground and damaging and killing trees.

If you think about it, sin can be like that mushroom growth. It can start small, spread wildly, and leave a path of destruction. In the Bible, sin is sometimes compared to yeast. Bread dough often requires yeast for the bread to rise. It takes only a little yeast to affect the whole loaf. Similarly, only a little sin, when left unchecked, will spread rapidly among a church.

In the New Testament, Paul rebuked the church in Corinth for letting sin spread like yeast through a batch of dough (see 1 Corinthians 5:6-7). Apparently, one man in particular was living rebelliously while the church did nothing. Paul's advice was to treat him like unwanted yeast in bread. The man needed to be put out of the church. That might sound harsh, but at critical times we need to trust our church leaders to make the right decision for the whole body.

DADDY-*Daughter Time*

Talk about why Paul's direction to the church at Corinth was important. If the church did what Paul asked, what would be the message to the rest of the body? As we see often in Scripture, Christians who battle sin (and that's all of us) need to be humble and repent. Is there anything in your heart that's keeping you from good fellowship in your family or church? Do you have any yeast in your life that needs to be removed? Ask God to help you deal with it.

WHAT'S THE WORD?

Don't you realize that this sin is like a little yeast that spreads through the whole batch of dough? Get rid of the old "yeast" by removing this wicked person from among you. Then you will be like a fresh batch of dough made without yeast, which is what you really are. 1 CORINTHIANS 5:6-7

BRAVEST WORDS

"GIVE me liberty or give me death!" Historians feel Patrick Henry's bold words at the Virginia Convention in 1775 were some of the bravest spoken during the American Revolution. What are the bravest words you've ever heard? Maybe they were spoken in a movie, in a book, or by someone you know.

The Bible is full of brave words. Throughout history, God's people have made bold declarations, risking their lives to declare God's power or to call out sin in the lives of powerful people. Of course, the Bible contains stories of cowardly words as well. Peter boldly declared that Jesus was the Messiah. But later he denied even knowing Jesus, because he was scared of what people would think or what they would do to him.

We cheer for courage. We love to see bold men and women laugh in the face of danger. Two incidents in the Bible show incredible bravery. The first can be found in Daniel 3. It's a familiar story: Shadrach, Meshach, and Abednego refused to bow down to an idol because they worshiped only God. Instead of caving in, they said to the king, "If we are thrown into the blazing furnace, the God whom we serve is able to save us. . . . But even if he doesn't . . . we will never serve your gods or worship the gold statue you have set up" (Daniel 3:17-18). Those three young men showed great bravery. They had such confidence in God that they said they would obey him even if God decided *not* to save their lives. The other example came near the end of Jesus' life. After agonizing in prayer before God the Father in the garden of Gethsemane, Jesus saw the arresting mob coming and said these brave words: "Up, let's be going. Look, my betrayer is here!" (Matthew 26:46).

Jesus didn't say, "Run away!" He got up and went to the trial and to the cross to pay for all of our sins.

Brave words indeed.

DADDY-*Daughter Time*

Have you ever been provided the opportunity to speak brave words? How did you respond? Ask your dad to share a time or two when he either spoke up, or when he didn't speak up and wished he had.

As you study speeches, read stories, or watch movies, look for examples of brave words. Make a collection of them together in a notepad or journal. Let them inspire you!

WHAT'S THE WORD?

[Jesus] came to the disciples and said, "Go ahead and sleep. Have your rest. But look— the time has come. The Son of Man is betrayed into the hands of sinners. Up, let's be going. Look, my betrayer is here!" MATTHEW 26:45-46

HOW TO BE A STAR

DID you know the Bible contains the key for anyone who wants to be a star? You should be aware that this advice may not get you on a nationally televised singing contest. It may not land you your own reality show. You might not tally millions of views on an Internet video site. And it doesn't guarantee a movie contract for millions of dollars.

But you'll be a star.

How? Simple . . . just stop complaining and arguing. Paul wrote to the Christians in Philippi with some star-making advice. In Philippians 2:14-15, he says, "Do everything without complaining or arguing, so that you may become blameless and pure, children of God without fault in a crooked and depraved generation, in which you shine like stars in the universe" (NIV).

That's the formula.

But does it work? That's a good question. And the best answer is to give it a try. You've probably noticed that many people love to grumble and argue. Whether it's about sports or clothes or politics or religion or work or schools, they (and, often, we) love to complain. Now, imagine if we, as Christians, went about our daily lives without giving in to the temptations to argue and complain. Do you think you'd be recognized? Quite simply, your actions would be totally unexpected and refreshing!

That's the point Paul was making. When our lives in Christ make us act differently from everyone else, it gets noticed for all the best reasons. We can shine like stars in a dark world. God's truth and the impact of his truth in our lives always create a light. And light doesn't get swallowed up by the darkness. Light always wins. You may not get famous, but you can be a star shining brightly for God.

DADDY-*Daughter Time*

What are some things the two of you complain about? Help each other make lists, because sometimes we can complain without realizing it. Have fun with it . . . this isn't meant to make you feel bad. Then the next time you or your dad start grumbling, quietly whisper, "Be a star!" as a gentle reminder to refrain from complaining or arguing.

WHAT'S THE WORD?

Do everything without complaining or arguing, so that you may become blameless and pure, children of God without fault in a crooked and depraved generation, in which you shine like stars in the universe as you hold out the word of life.
PHILIPPIANS 2:14-16 (NIV)

SPECIAL TREASURES, SPECIAL COLLECTIONS

THINK of an item . . . anything. Whatever you're thinking of right now, chances are good that someone in the world collects it. New York native Michael Zarnock may have the largest collection of Hot Wheels cars—over eight thousand of them. He'll often take parts of his fleet to show at schools and toy conventions in the United States and Canada. Edmond Knowles of Alabama liked to collect pennies—lots of them. In 2005, he cashed in his penny collection—all 1,308,459 of them—for more than $13,000! Dan Brown had so many LEGOs—over four million—that he opened an unofficial LEGO museum in Ohio.

It's amazing what people treasure. Having a collection can be fun. But if collecting things is our greatest passion, then that's a problem. God is concerned with the place *things* have in our hearts. He's a "jealous God," who wants to be the greatest desire of our hearts and love in our lives. If we treasure our collections above living for God, what are we revealing about our priorities?

We find an interesting example of what one man did with his treasures by reading about King David. He wanted to build a great temple for God. But God told him he couldn't build it and that his son Solomon would be the builder instead. Disappointed, David didn't fight with God. He accepted God's decision and sacrificed what he had to make sure the project would be a success.

In 1 Chronicles 29, David told the people that Solomon would build the Temple. Then he added, "I am giving all of my own private treasures of gold and silver to help in the construction" (v. 3). That sacrifice showed the true priority God held in David's heart. He was willing to give up his treasures for God.

DADDY-*Daughter Time*

Think about your earthly treasures or collections you might have. Are these things becoming idols in your heart? Talk together about things you've collected over the years. What do you think your collections say about what's important to you?

The next time you hear of a need, think about your collection. Is God prompting you to give up some of your "private treasures" to honor him and to show the world that people are more important than things?

WHAT'S THE WORD?

[King David said,] "Using every resource at my command, I have gathered as much as I could for building the Temple of my God. . . . And now, because of my devotion to the Temple of my God, I am giving all of my own private treasures of gold and silver to help in the construction." 1 CHRONICLES 29:2-3

THE PRIDE AND
JOY OF FAMILY

YOU can spot new grandparents a mile away. They usually grin from ear to ear and have a photo or two—or twenty—handy that shows their pride and joy. One of the beautiful things about family is the power it has to be a source of pride. As a grandchild, you don't have to do anything to earn your grandparents' affection. They're going to love you and try to spoil you (in a good way) no matter what.

In Proverbs 17:6 we read that "grandchildren are the crowning glory of the aged; parents are the pride of their children."

The first part of that verse makes sense, but the second part makes you think, *Didn't Solomon mean to say, "Children are the pride of their parents"?*

To understand the first part, think about it from your parents' perspective. They have a lot of responsibility. Parents have to provide food, clothing, shelter, and education. Parents teach their kids how to live well, how to learn from mistakes (including a parent's mistakes), and how to have a relationship with God. Parents want their kids to have a better life. Parents also want to please their own parents. You'll always be your father's daughter, even when you're fifty. So when a grandchild comes along, the whole family is blessed. Because family is so important to God's heart, he wants to see families grow and thrive. A grandchild guarantees a family will continue into the next generation.

For the second part, think how parents bear the family name before the kids do. A parent's character and integrity reflect on their children. So naturally, parents have the opportunity to bring pride, or shame, on their kids.

Both parts of this verse remind us that we can make a difference to every generation in our family by the way we live. When we look back, wouldn't it be nice to say that our words and actions brought our family a lot of pride and joy?

DADDY-*Daughter Time*

Talk together about past generations of your family. Did they follow the Lord? What made them special and honored? Tell each other about things the other does that make you proud. Dads need to know that their daughter is proud of them, just like daughters desire to know the same thing. Always seek to build up your family with your words and actions.

WHAT'S THE WORD?

Grandchildren are the crowning glory of the aged; parents are the pride of their children. PROVERBS 17:6

January 28

MOST third-grade boys could be described as childish. But this particular third grader may have crossed the line into foolish. He loved grossing out the girls. Maybe it was the reaction—the screams of repulsion—that the boy enjoyed. Or perhaps it was merely the attention. He constantly looked for ways to get a rise out of the fairer sex. So when he got a nasty cut on his finger that required stitches, he didn't think about the pain. He thought about the opportunity. The next day at school, he whipped off the bandage on his finger to show the stitches to his entire class . . . while they were eating lunch. Before standing up, the boy proudly told his buddy, "Watch me gross the girls out!"

Mission accomplished. Unfortunately for the boy, a teacher was grossed out as well and discipline soon followed. It wasn't the first time the boy had been punished for his gross-out antics, and it wouldn't be the last.

The book of Proverbs has a lot to say about foolish people. In one of the grossest verses, it says, "As a dog returns to its vomit, so a fool repeats his foolishness" (Proverbs 26:11). Talk about a remarkably graphic illustration!

Dogs can be cute and cuddly, but "man's best friend" also has some peculiar habits. Among them is the desire to eat what it just threw up. Seems absurd, right? Especially when you understand that sometimes a dog throws up something it ate that was toxic or poisonous. Yet the dog goes back for more.

Do you see how this relates to a foolish person? A fool isn't someone who merely makes a mistake or a bad decision. Fools refuse to learn from the past, even when there were negative consequences. They'll do the same foolish action again and again, even if it's dangerous or bad for them . . . just like a dog returning to its vomit.

DADDY-*Daughter Time*

Discuss together some well-known celebrities, politicians, or sports figures who keep making the same bad decisions in their lives. Why would those actions be signs of foolishness? Some people are addicted to certain behaviors—such as using drugs or alcohol—but still act foolishly by not seeking help.

Do you show any foolish behaviors in your own life? Many of us repeat our mistakes. Ask God to give you the strength to overcome your dogged tendencies.

WHAT'S THE WORD?

As a dog returns to its vomit, so a fool repeats his foolishness.   PROVERBS 26:11

SERVING TO
SAVE AN ENEMY

THE Bible has been called the "greatest story ever told." The coolest thing is that every story in the Bible is true. Noah's ark, Daniel in the lion's den, Elijah outrunning a chariot, Jesus walking on the water—you know the names and achievements of many biblical heroes. However, in one of the remarkable stories in the Bible, we never learn the heroine's name.

In 2 Kings 5, we read about a powerful Aramean commander named Naaman. He was a mighty warrior who won many battles, but he couldn't win his battle against the disease leprosy. During one of Aram's invasions of Israel, the Arameans captured a young girl and forced her to be a servant for Naaman's wife. We never learn the servant girl's name. But we do hear her speak. In verse 3 she says, "I wish my master would go to see the prophet in Samaria. He would heal him of his leprosy."

In those days leprosy meant death. Since Aram constantly fought with Israel, it'd be hard to blame the young girl if she had stayed silent and watched Naaman die. But this girl trusted in God's power. She knew about God's prophet Elisha, who could do amazing things in God's name. Instead of watching an enemy die (an enemy who had ripped her away from her family and enslaved her), she wanted to introduce Naaman to God's healing power.

The rest of the story is well known. Naaman went to Israel and found Elisha. Elisha ordered Naaman to wash seven times in the Jordan River, which he did, and he was healed. When Naaman climbed out of the river, he told Elisha, "Now I know that the God of Israel is the only God in the whole world" (2 Kings 5:15, CEV).

The kindness, courage, and grace of a young servant girl turned a powerful enemy into a child of God . . . and we still don't know her name.

DADDY-*Daughter Time*

How does it feel to help somebody? Have you ever helped someone who treated you poorly? It's easy to help a friend, but it takes true mercy and grace to reach out to an enemy. Read the whole story in 2 Kings 5. Talk about what the girl might have felt when she first heard of Naaman's sickness. Who got the glory for her actions in the end?

WHAT'S THE WORD?
One day the girl said to her mistress, "I wish my master would go to see the prophet in Samaria. He would heal him of his leprosy." 2 KINGS 5:3

AN UNEXPECTED PEACE

HAVE you ever felt an intense rivalry with someone? It may seem that peace can only be found with that person by defeating him or her or by winning an argument. If you've studied history, you know that's how most wars end. The victorious nation wins a battle and accepts the surrender of the defeated. The winner decides the terms of peace, while the losing country has to pay a great cost.

But in the peace between humankind and God, the opposite is true. God won by "losing." We win by giving up everything to follow him. What is remarkable about our relationship with God through Jesus is that we find peace not by us winning anything over God, but by him losing everything for us. We didn't defeat God in some battle. We didn't force him to accept our terms. If anything, we were vulnerable to being defeated by God because our sinfulness couldn't be overcome. If he chose to, he could have wiped out humanity as his sinful enemies. But he loved us and brought peace by flipping it all upside down.

We can now "have peace with God because of what Jesus Christ our Lord has done for us" (Romans 5:1). That peace means no war with God. It means comfort and rest from the weariness of a sin-filled world. It means hope for eternal life instead of death.

Peace usually comes by strength of will, determination, and dominance. Yet our peace with God comes from the sacrifice of his Son for us. Unexpected? Yes. To us, it seems backward. But to God, it's the only way a lasting, eternal peace could have been won. And our God is always victorious.

DADDY-*Daughter Time*

Can either of you think of a war that ended with the losing side gaining more than the victor? Isn't it amazing that Christ's victory over death gives us victory in a battle over sin that we never could've won? Are there areas of your lives where you would like peace . . . an end to fighting, to conflict, to anger, or to damaged relationships? What can we learn from Christ's example of how he earned peace for us with God? Talk about how that might apply to your situations.

WHAT'S THE WORD?

Since we have been made right in God's sight by faith, we have peace with God because of what Jesus Christ our Lord has done for us. Because of our faith, Christ has brought us into this place of undeserved privilege where we now stand, and we confidently and joyfully look forward to sharing God's glory. ROMANS 5:1-2

BETTER THAN
SEVEN BOYS

"ANYTHING you can do I can do better. I can do anything better than you." If you're a fan of musicals, you'll know those lyrics come from *Annie Get Your Gun* as Annie Oakley and Frank Butler have a sharpshooting contest. More recently a popular drink company launched an advertising campaign using this song as two athletes, a male and a female, competed against each other in basketball, soccer, fencing, tennis, running, and martial arts.

Since time began, people have debated who's better—men or women, boys or girls. In ancient cultures, men were valued for strength and manual labor. Women were often treated like property. In modern Western cultures, women are now viewed as being able to do anything they want. But in some parts of the world, a boy is a must-have in a family, while a girl is seen as a burden.

How this messed-up view must grieve the heart of God, who made humanity in his image—both male and female (see Genesis 1:27)! In God's eyes, both boys and girls are ultimately important. Both are essential for humanity to thrive and survive. And both can do incredible feats that are often honored throughout history.

One example is Ruth. After her mother-in-law, Naomi, lost her sons and husband, she told Ruth to go away. Ruth stuck with Naomi and ended up marrying Boaz, a relative who reclaimed Naomi's family and provided for them. Ruth showed nobility, courage, hard work, obedience, loyalty, honor, and self-sacrifice. And for this, God honored her. The ladies of the town acknowledged that Ruth was more valuable than a houseful of boys (see Ruth 4:15).

No matter how you feel about the age-old question of "Who is better?" know that by living a godly life, you can build a great reputation that could be remembered for generations.

DADDY-*Daughter Time*

Ask your dad who he thought was better—boys or girls—when he was your age. Does he feel differently about that question now? Make lists of things God has uniquely gifted boys/men or girls/women to do, and the things that both can do well. That third list is going to be pretty long. Talk about how important it is to understand the unique strengths that you bring to your family, your church, and your community.

WHAT'S THE WORD?

The women of the town said to Naomi, "Praise the LORD, who has now provided a redeemer for your family! May this child be famous in Israel. May he restore your youth and care for you in your old age. For he is the son of your daughter-in-law who loves you and has been better to you than seven sons!" RUTH 4:14-15

WELL, WELL, WELL

TELLING time. Identifying shapes. Learning how to hold a pencil. That's what most first graders spend their days mastering. But when Ryan Hreljac was six years old, he discovered how he could provide clean water to strangers halfway around the world.

In 1998, Ryan's first-grade teacher explained that people were dying because they lacked sanitary drinking water. That didn't seem fair. So Ryan did odd jobs and extra chores to earn enough cash to build a well in Uganda. And that was just the beginning. Before long, the Ryan's Well Foundation was raising big bucks for wells and latrine projects in developing countries. Ryan even spoke at international conferences and events, inspiring others to get involved.

"I don't have a smile that lights up on my face in the morning just because I can have a drink or a shower," Ryan said ten years and three hundred wells later in a Get Involved! video (www.getinvolved.gov). "And to see other people having this huge celebration because they have clean water, it just helps you put things in perspective."

Ryan saw a need and met it. His heart was touched, and he made a difference. Sometimes it's easy to get so overwhelmed by all the problems in the world that we don't know where to begin. But God wants to use you to make a difference. Are you willing to help with the cause he puts on your heart?

In Isaiah 6, God had a message but needed a mouthpiece. The prophet Isaiah didn't know what the job was yet, but he eagerly made himself available, saying, "Here I am. Send me" (v. 8). That's all God wants—a willing partner. He doesn't expect you to solve every crisis, but he may want you to help him out with one. Which one? Ask him to show you and give you a passion for it. In Ryan's words, "Whatever you feel strongly about, do your part, or do what you think is your part to make the world a better place in your own way." He's right. Then people will see your good works and glorify the God you serve!

DADDY-*Daughter Time*

Has God fired you up to tackle a particular problem? What concerns you? If the world seems dark and cold, light a candle . . . literally. Some snowy night, stack rings of snowballs around a candle, eventually forming a dome (with small openings between the snowballs so the flame can breathe). Let this wintry luminary symbolize your availability to God.

WHAT'S THE WORD?

I heard the Lord asking, "Whom should I send as a messenger to this people? Who will go for us?" I said, "Here I am. Send me." ISAIAH 6:8

THE LAST GREAT RACE ON EARTH

A vicious wind whistled across the Alaskan tundra. Swirling snow all but blinded the musher and his intrepid team. Despite paws matted with ice and snow, the huskies pressed on. They had to. Lives hung in the balance. It was the dead of winter, and a diphtheria epidemic had left the city of Nome desperate for vaccine. With the nearest supply 1,200 miles away, the only hope of transporting the lifesaving drug across the vast, white wilderness was via dogsled. And on this date in 1925, they succeeded.

Did you know that Alaska still honors that heroic trek every March by repeating the feat? You may have heard of the Iditarod. It's a grueling dogsled race that begins in Wasilla and ends in Nome. It takes anywhere from nine to fifteen days, and competitors pack only essentials in an effort to keep their sleds light and swift. The teams must contend with violent winds, long hours of darkness, below-zero temperatures, and treacherous climbs. But at the end of the trail, each finisher receives a true hero's welcome.

It's cool that all the glory isn't reserved for the one who comes in first. Just finishing is a major achievement, considering the danger and distance involved. It's no wonder the Iditarod has been called the "Last Great Race on Earth."

The Christian life is a lot like that. Even with God on our side, each of us faces a long journey full of challenges and uncertainty. That's why Hebrews 12:1 encourages us to unload any unnecessary weight—especially sin—that could slow us down as we run our race. You may get tired. You may be tempted to quit. But if you run with endurance, much like the Iditarod, there's a hero's welcome in store for everyone who crosses the finish line.

DADDY-*Daughter Time*

At this stage of your life's race, what challenges are you experiencing? Is something weighing you down? Who's cheering you on? Discuss ways you can support each other.

Consider setting aside an evening to watch the animated movie *Balto* together. This exciting, touching, G-rated tale is loosely based on the lifesaving trek that inspired the Iditarod. You can find lots of other fun movies to watch together in the Father-Daughter Movie Nights appendix at the back of this book.

WHAT'S THE WORD?

Since we are surrounded by such a huge crowd of witnesses to the life of faith, let us strip off every weight that slows us down, especially the sin that so easily trips us up. And let us run with endurance the race God has set before us. HEBREWS 12:1

NOBODY'S PERFECT

IF your favorite football team ended the season with eighteen wins and one loss, chances are you'd be pretty satisfied. After all, that's quite an accomplishment. But don't tell that to the New England Patriots or their fans, who have bitter memories of going 18–1. That's because their only defeat—the sole blemish on an otherwise perfect record—came in the championship game.

On this date in 2008, the New York Giants beat the previously undefeated Patriots in Super Bowl XLII by a margin of 17–14. More than just a game, it was a devastating disappointment for a team that had squashed the competition all year long and had actually beaten the Giants in the final game of the regular season. Everyone expected them to do it again on football's biggest stage. The Patriots were twelve-point favorites. Perfect. Unstoppable.

Apparently somebody forgot to tell the players from New York. When the game clock expired, the Giants were champs. Eli Manning was named MVP. Parties for the Patriots from Connecticut to Maine turned quiet and ended early. And hundreds of shirts and caps that had already been printed honoring the Patriots' sure-fire victory were boxed up and shipped to poor children in Nicaragua. Heartbroken fans stateside didn't want to be reminded of going 18–1 when they were expecting perfection.

Have you ever expected something or someone to be perfect—including yourself? Maybe an important event? Your GPA? A relationship? That creates a lot of pressure, doesn't it? And anything short of that mental picture becomes a huge disappointment. The author of Psalm 119 writes in verse 96, "Even perfection has its limits." There's nothing wrong with having high hopes. God wants us to strive for excellence. Still, we should always maintain perspective, doing our best to see beauty in things and people as they are. Only God's commands and Jesus himself are perfect.

DADDY-*Daughter Time*

Would you consider yourself a perfectionist? Why or why not? Talk about a time when you were disappointed by unmet expectations, how you responded, and what you learned from that experience. If this area is a challenge for you, pray that God will help you extend grace to yourself and others. Tell that imperfect person next to you something you find beautiful about him or her.

WHAT'S THE WORD?

Even perfection has its limits, but your commands have no limit. PSALM 119:96

PLEASE HEAL
MY DAUGHTER

February 4

HOW far would you go to heal your sick child? Some parents risk everything. Just ask Megan Crowley. In 1998, when Megan and her brother were diagnosed with a rare, fatal neuromuscular disease, her father quit his job and spent all of his time raising money—more than $100 million—to launch biotech companies in hopes of finding a cure. No wonder they called the movie about their experience *Extraordinary Measures.*

Another dad desperate for a remedy was a man in the Bible named Jairus. In Mark 5, this synagogue leader searched for Jesus, fell at his feet, and pleaded with the Lord to follow him home and heal his dying twelve-year-old daughter. But before they could reach her, news arrived that the girl had breathed her last. Imagine the wave of grief that swept over Jairus, only to hear Jesus tell him seconds later, "Don't be afraid. Just have faith" (v. 36). What do you think this father felt at that moment? What thoughts raced through his mind? And how do you suppose he reacted when, upon arriving home, Jesus miraculously raised his dead child to life right before his eyes?

These dads went to great lengths to rescue their children from death. Yet even a multimillion-dollar fund-raising campaign can't compare with the extreme measures our heavenly Father took to rescue us from a godless eternity. He sent his Son, Jesus, who left his rightful home in heaven. Clothed in the humility of humanity, Christ came to earth as a servant. He allowed himself to be nailed to a cross as the penalty for our sin, then conquered death through his resurrection. Because of Christ's sacrifice, we can be confident of the truth found in 1 Corinthians 15:54-55: "When our dying bodies have been transformed into bodies that will never die, this Scripture will be fulfilled: . . . 'O death, where is your victory?'"

Just as he was the only hope for Jairus's daughter, Jesus Christ remains our only hope of rising again.

DADDY-*Daughter Time*

Has your family been touched by serious illness? If so, talk about the ways God has revealed himself to you in the midst of that challenge. If not, share a hug and give thanks for your health, praying together that the Lord will reveal a way that you can reach out to a family struggling in this area.

WHAT'S THE WORD?

When our dying bodies have been transformed into bodies that will never die, this Scripture will be fulfilled: "Death is swallowed up in victory. O death, where is your victory? O death, where is your sting?" 1 CORINTHIANS 15:54-55

INCREASE YOUR WORD POWER

DO you have a favorite magazine? It may arrive weekly or just once a month, but it always makes your day brighter when you find it in the mailbox. One popular monthly has been brightening readers' days since it debuted on this date in 1922. It had no illustrations or ads back then. It simply reprinted condensed versions of articles appearing in other publications. Maybe that's why husband-and-wife publishers DeWitt and Lila Bell Wallace called it *Reader's Digest*.

Over the years, *Reader's Digest* has become well known for features such as "Laughter, the Best Medicine," "Humor in Uniform," and the brainteaser "Word Power," guaranteed to improve even the best vocabulary. Have you ever tried that one? You get a list of challenging words and have to pick the correct definition from several possible answers. Sort of like this:

1. propitiate
   a) to empty of malice or deceit
   b) to exact retribution or punishment
   c) to appease or turn aside wrath

2. selah
   a) profound grief or sadness
   b) musical term, possibly indicating an intended pause
   c) sluggish, not hasty

3. expiation
   a) purification or cleansing, atonement
   b) charging excessive interest on money lent
   c) a proclamation of good news

You may recognize those tricky terms from the Bible. So how did you do? If you guessed *c*, *b*, and *a*, congratulations! As Christians, it's important to increase our word power, not just in our spiritual vocabulary, but also by understanding and applying the power that comes from God's Word. That may seem like a lot for readers to digest, but most of the time the Bible is very straightforward and easy to grasp. As it says in Psalm 119:130, "The teaching of your word gives light, so even the simple can understand."

DADDY-*Daughter Time*

Talk about the magazines you enjoy reading and why. Then try "Word Power" and see if you can make three new words a permanent part of your vocabulary. If you don't subscribe to *Reader's Digest*, you can find back issues at the library. You can also try to stump each other by creating your own quiz (like the one above) with the help of a Bible dictionary or concordance.

WHAT'S THE WORD?

Your laws are wonderful. No wonder I obey them! The teaching of your word gives light, so even the simple can understand. PSALM 119:129-130

DREAMING
GOD-SIZE DREAMS

NOTHING compares to a roaring fire and hot cocoa after a day on the slopes. The rest of the family was still turning in their skis and snowboards, which gave Olivia and her dad a few quiet minutes alone. She leaned back and scanned the room, drinking in the rustic, woodsy charm of the architecture and wrought-iron accents.

"I love it here. It's so cozy," she said, "though when I design my ski lodge, I won't have any lamps or chandeliers made out of antlers."

"Your ski lodge?" her father asked. "Since when has that become a dream of yours?"

Oops. Truth be told, it was a desire Olivia had kept to herself because she didn't figure a Christian's plans should be so frivolous. Living for Jesus meant being ready at a moment's notice to jump on a plane and eat bugs in the jungle somewhere. It was about doing something you didn't like for a good cause . . . , wasn't it? Then her dad shocked her. "Well, if that's the dream God put on your heart, and you're willing to work hard at it, I'm sure he'll use you to do great things."

"Huh? Really?" Olivia asked. "I can serve God by designing lodges?"

"Why not? Someone designed this one for the Christian businessman who hosts retreats here. That's ministry. Did you see the Bible verse in that frame?"

Olivia walked over to the passage hanging on the wall. Her father took another sip of cocoa and continued, "God wants us to dream big dreams yet always keep him first and be open to his leading. If he wants you to be something else, he'll get you excited about that. Sweetie, if I've learned anything, it's that he knows best what will satisfy our deepest desires. He created us. He loves us. God's not out to make us miserable."

Olivia's sister and grandmother walked in and started knocking the snow off their boots. Grandma Lucía asked what she was looking at.

"Psalm 37:4," she replied.

"So what does it say?"

Olivia smiled. "It says if I keep God first, it's okay to dream about designing ski lodges."

DADDY-*Daughter Time*

What's your God-size dream? Have you ever worried that he has plans for you that you won't like? Read Jeremiah 29:11 together. Although this promise is specifically for the nation of Israel, it suggests that it's within God's nature to bless those he loves. Pray for the ability to trust him and be completely open to his leading.

WHAT'S THE WORD?

Take delight in the LORD, and he will give you your heart's desires.   PSALM 37:4

February 7   # TO GOD BE THE GLORY . . .

HAVE you ever wondered where the expression "fifteen minutes of fame" comes from? Or what it really means? In February 1968, pop art pioneer Andy Warhol's work appeared at an exhibition in Stockholm, Sweden. His catalog contained the line "In the future everybody will be world famous for fifteen minutes," which got the media's attention and became part of the public consciousness. Warhol's point was that, with the rise of mass media, the common man would be more likely to experience widespread but fleeting glory. It turns out he was right.

Isn't it amazing how many people are desperate to get attention on the Internet or reality TV these days? And many of those fame seekers seem hungry for more than just fifteen minutes. They want celebrity. They want glory. They want adoration. Some will even do foolish, humiliating things if that's what it takes to get noticed. Fortunately, the Bible gives us a rule of thumb for "glory" that will help us avoid falling into that trap: God gets all of it!

Too bad Herod Agrippa didn't realize that. In the book of Acts, this king who persecuted the early church made a stirring speech that inspired a crowd to treat him as if he were godlike. Because he didn't redirect the glory to God, an angel of the Lord took his life (see Acts 12:23).

The prophet Isaiah writes that *our* glory is as fragile and temporary as a flower (see Isaiah 40:6-7). On the other hand, the glory God receives has lasting value, which is why the apostle Paul says, "Whether you eat or drink, or whatever you do, do it all for the glory of God" (1 Corinthians 10:31). That sort of takes the pressure off, doesn't it? If we're focused on God's glory and not our own, we're less likely to compromise our principles or do something foolish just to get attention. And when success does find us, we won't make Agrippa's mistake of getting too full of ourselves.

DADDY-*Daughter Time*

A fantasy on many kids' TV shows is to be a superstar. Why do you think that is? Discuss the difference between fame that's a result of excellence and fame that is pursued just for the sake of being famous. Do you know someone at work or school whose sense of self-worth is wrapped up in receiving glory? How might that rob him or her of peace? How do you sometimes struggle with the same thing?

WHAT'S THE WORD?

Whether you eat or drink, or whatever you do, do it all for the glory of God.
1 CORINTHIANS 10:31

GREAT THINGS
HE HAS DONE

THESE days we have plenty of ways to capture moments and preserve them for future generations. Take YouTube, for example. From a baby's first steps to a crazy BMX stunt to a girl lip-synching into her hairbrush, people can record and post just about anything for the whole world to see. And it'll be there forever! But immortalizing slices of life hasn't always been that easy. In fact, the Israelites had a low-tech version of YouTube called "stack of rocks."

Early in the book of Joshua, God decided it was time for his people to enter the land promised to them. First stop: Jericho. But they had to cross the Jordan River to get there. Following God's instructions, the priests who carried the Ark of the Covenant stepped into the swollen river, and the water stopped flowing downstream. Those priests stood in the middle of the dry riverbed as the entire nation of Israel passed through.

Before restoring the waters to normal, God told Joshua to have twelve men (one per tribe) grab twelve large stones from around the priests' feet and carry them to their camp. Joshua stacked them as a memorial to what God had just done (see Joshua 4:20-22). God wanted that moment captured for memory. For generations to come, whenever kids asked, "Hey, what's with the stones?" parents were reminded to replay the story of how the Lord protected Israel and guided the nation to a new home.

There's a lot of silly stuff on YouTube, isn't there? Practical jokes. Wedding cake disasters. Large people crawling through doggie doors. It's enough to make you wish that folks in the Bible had owned helmet cams for capturing the good stuff. No one's sure how many "views" Joshua's stack of rocks received over the years, but we can confidently say that God got the glory, which is what the best memorials are all about.

DADDY-*Daughter Time*
Talk about times you knew that God was looking out for you, personally or as a family. Did you record those experiences in a scrapbook or a journal? Consider doing that. Or, like the Israelites, each of you can find a special stone and paint it as a memorial to the Lord's goodness (put small stones in a planter, larger ones in a garden).

WHAT'S THE WORD?
It was there at Gilgal that Joshua piled up the twelve stones taken from the Jordan River. Then Joshua said to the Israelites, "In the future your children will ask, 'What do these stones mean?' Then you can tell them, 'This is where the Israelites crossed the Jordan on dry ground.'" JOSHUA 4:20-22

A QUEST FOR CLARITY

HOW do you listen to your favorite music? Do you slide a black vinyl record out of its paper sleeve, carefully placing it on a turntable and setting the needle on the edge? Probably not. Although Thomas Edison's phonograph set the standard for audio excellence for nearly a century, humanity's quest for the crispest, clearest, most lifelike music has led to big changes.

Vinyl records crackled and skipped. So you can imagine the rejoicing when audiocassettes came along. Throughout the 1970s, a famous ad campaign for one brand even asked, "Is it live, or is it Memorex?" Music fans loved the improved sound quality and portability. After all, have you ever tried to boogie on roller skates while carrying a forty-pound turntable? But wait . . . that wasn't good enough.

Cassette tapes and other "magnetic media" had their own limitations, so in the mid-80s, we went digital with compact discs. Sharper. Cleaner. Even more lifelike. But once again, the format would become a stepping-stone. To enhance sonic clarity, the recording industry came up with digital downloads. Short of piping a playlist directly into your brain, music can't get much clearer or more convenient than that.

As much effort as people have put into hearing music more clearly, we don't seem nearly as interested in getting a pure, clear signal from God. That's a shame, because he wants to connect with us, and he places high value on our hearing and obeying him. First Samuel 15:22 says, "What is more pleasing to the LORD: your burnt offerings and sacrifices or your obedience to his voice? Listen! Obedience is better than sacrifice." Spiritually, are things a little muffled or scratchy in your life? If so, strive for something better. Spend more time praying and reading the Bible. Listen more closely. The difference could be like going from vinyl records to digital downloads.

DADDY-*Daughter Time*

On a scale of one to ten, how clearly are you hearing from God right now? Where on that scale would you *like* to be? Discuss practical things you can do to enhance the quality of interaction with your heavenly Father.

If you own music in the various formats mentioned above, listen to the differences in audio quality together. Did you know The Beatles first appeared on *The Ed Sullivan Show* on this date in 1964? That event, viewed by nearly half of all Americans, changed music forever. Watch it on YouTube.

WHAT'S THE WORD?

Samuel replied, "What is more pleasing to the LORD: your burnt offerings and sacrifices or your obedience to his voice? Listen! Obedience is better than sacrifice, and submission is better than offering the fat of rams." 1 SAMUEL 15:22

ARTIFICIAL INTELLIGENCE   *February 10*

WHAT does GIGO mean to you? No, it's not the name of a bounty hunter in one of the *Star Wars* movies. Nor is it the insurance company whose advertising features that cute gecko. If you're handy with computers, you know that GIGO stands for "garbage in, garbage out." In other words, if invalid data gets entered into a computer program, you can count on the output being just as messed up. That's because a machine is only as smart as the intelligence put into it by its designer.

For that reason, using the term "artificial intelligence" to describe supersmart technology is sort of misleading. There's nothing artificial about it. It takes genuinely sharp, gifted people to develop a computer that can navigate physical space, interpret spoken language, or answer more trivia questions than *Jeopardy!* champ Ken Jennings. These brainy contraptions simply do what they've been programmed to do. So who really deserves the credit?

Before you applaud some MIT grad with a pocket protector, keep in mind that Proverbs 2:6 tells us, "The LORD grants wisdom! From his mouth come knowledge and understanding." And not just in spiritual things. God allows us insight into his creation and how things work, from astronomy to medicine to technology. So instead of calling it "artificial" intelligence, maybe we should call it "third-hand" intelligence: first revealed by God to man, then programmed by man into machines, and finally applied by those well-schooled gadgets.

Did you know that a major test of thirdhand intelligence occurred on this date in 1996? That's when IBM's chess-playing computer Deep Blue beat Garry Kasparov in the first game of a historic match eventually won by the reigning world champion. Kasparov got bragging rights. The engineers behind Deep Blue got pats on the back. Yet there's no record of anyone pausing to praise God, the source of all intelligence. Why don't you take a moment to thank him yourself?

DADDY-*Daughter Time*

In what ways do people take credit for knowledge, talent, or wisdom for which God really deserves glory?

An amazing example of the Lord's craftsmanship is the uniqueness of each snowflake. To get a better look at some snowflakes, staple black velvet to a firm, flat surface and place it in the freezer. Next time you see flurries, catch snowflakes on it. They should retain their shape on the soft, cold velvet—perfect for a closer look under a magnifying glass!

WHAT'S THE WORD?

The LORD grants wisdom! From his mouth come knowledge and understanding.
PROVERBS 2:6

THE COZY CORNERS COOKIE CRISIS

WHO knew that cookies could cause such trouble? It all began when a junior-high youth group decided to spend one afternoon a month at the Cozy Corners nursing home. Well, Jamie loved to bake, so she decided to make gingersnaps for the elderly folks they'd be visiting. It was a thoughtful gesture. And her cookies were a huge hit. In fact, after three or four visits, Jamie started getting special attention for her tasty treats and the distinct aroma that entered the room just seconds before she did.

Everything went smoothly until Colleen showed up one day with chocolate chip cookies and milk. The residents got so excited! Best of all, Colleen's cookies were still hot. But not nearly as hot as the temper of the one who had the idea first. Jamie was so angry that she considered not coming back to the nursing home anymore.

"I can't believe she would do this to me!" Jamie complained to her youth pastor. "It's not fair. Cookies were my ministry."

Believe it or not, Jamie isn't the first Christian to be jealous of someone encroaching on her turf. In Mark 9:38, John told Jesus, "Teacher, we saw someone using your name to cast out demons, but we told him to stop because he wasn't in our group." Elsewhere, John the Baptist's team resented the sizable dip in traffic when people began flocking to Jesus to be baptized instead (see John 3:26).

It's natural to feel a little threatened when people step into roles we view as our own. Even in ministry. But if we're really out to serve others and glorify God rather than ourselves, we need to set aside emotions and focus on the good that could come of our "rival's" efforts. That's what Jesus told his disciples to do. Is the gospel spreading? Are people being helped? Will it honor God? Those are the things that really matter.

DADDY-*Daughter Time*

Have you ever run into a situation like Jamie did? Talk about that. Do you think she had a right to get upset? Why or why not? If you were the girls' youth pastor, how would you have handled the situation? Instead of stirring up trouble, stir up some cookies together. As they bake, decide who to give them to: your pastor, an elderly neighbor, a homeless shelter.

WHAT'S THE WORD?

John's disciples came to him and said, "Rabbi, the man you met on the other side of the Jordan River, the one you identified as the Messiah, is also baptizing people. And everybody is going to him instead of coming to us." JOHN 3:26

HONEST ABE,
HONEST BOBBY

ON this date in 1809, the sixteenth president of the United States was born in a log cabin in rural Kentucky. Abraham Lincoln would eventually end slavery, unite a nation torn by civil war, and deliver some of history's most memorable speeches. Of course, the virtue most often ascribed to the man on the five-dollar bill is honesty. "Honest Abe" we call him. A man of integrity.

Speaking of great Americans with a reputation for honesty, do you like golf? Even if you're not a big fan, you've got to love what happened during the first round of the 1925 US Open. Legendary golfer Bobby Jones was preparing to hit out of the rough. While setting up the shot, he accidentally touched the ball with his club. Its movement was so imperceptible that no one noticed but him. Bobby could have ignored it. Instead, he summoned the officials and gave himself a penalty stroke. And wouldn't you know, he went on to lose the tournament by one stroke! Yet while that self-imposed penalty cost Bobby a championship, his display of honesty and sportsmanship has earned him the respect of countless people to this day.

For Bobby Jones, even one stroke of compromise was too much. As Christians, we should sweat the small stuff too, because the big stuff depends on it. Jesus said so. In Luke 16:10, he told his disciples, "If you are faithful in little things, you will be faithful in large ones. But if you are dishonest in little things, you won't be honest with greater responsibilities."

You don't have to look far to find folks cutting corners. You may begin to wonder if that's what it takes to succeed in life. Don't give in! Even if integrity seems to be as rare as people being born in log cabins, it's as important as ever. Choose to be the next great American to make honesty part of your legacy!

DADDY-*Daughter Time*

It's been said, "Integrity is who you are when no one's looking." Do you agree? God watches us all the time. How should that impact our decisions? Have you ever paid a price for doing the right thing? Talk about that. Why do you think a modern athlete would or wouldn't do what Bobby Jones did? Make a date to play miniature golf together (watch out for the windmill!). As you play, be sure to follow all the little rules.

WHAT'S THE WORD?

If you are faithful in little things, you will be faithful in large ones. But if you are dishonest in little things, you won't be honest with greater responsibilities. LUKE 16:10

BELIEVE IT OR NOT

BOB was a sports columnist who liked to draw. One slow sports day, he submitted a series of cartoon-style drawings of athletes performing strange-but-true feats. Broad-jumping on ice. Spending more than six minutes underwater without a breath. Walking across the continent . . . backward. It was such a hit that it became a regular feature in the *New York Globe*. Syndication followed in 1929, and several years later "Ripley's Believe It or Not" made Robert Leroy Ripley the world's first millionaire cartoonist.

The public's appetite for the unusual quickly expanded beyond sports. So Ripley traveled the globe in search of odd facts, peculiar people, and curious customs. Even so, a lot of his material found him. Ripley received more than a million letters per year and employed a full-time fact-checker to make sure people weren't pulling his leg. Here are a few examples that appeared in print:

- A sideshow performer chews and swallows lightbulbs.
- A woman proves she can recite more than two hundred words in just twenty-four seconds.
- A marshal wins a duel with an outlaw by shooting a bullet into the muzzle of the bandit's gun.

In time, Ripley created radio and television shows, produced short films, published books, and opened museums called "Odditoriums." All of this from a man who sold his first drawing to *LIFE* magazine at the age of fourteen.

The Bible is full of "believe it or not" moments. But unlike a one-legged tightrope walker or the lady with 1,903 body piercings, the miraculous events recorded in Scripture do more than amaze or amuse us. They reinforce our faith (see John 20:30-31). From the parting of the Red Sea to the resurrection of Jesus Christ, they give us confidence that God is holy, powerful, gracious, and sufficient to meet our every need . . . in this life and the next.

DADDY-*Daughter Time*

Can you think of three miracles recorded in Scripture that really impress you? The apostle John said a lot of other cool things happened, but only a few were written down (see John 20:30-31). Write some down now that you have read about in the Bible or heard about in sermons. Then compare notes and discuss your choices, including what each incredible event reveals about God's character.

Visit your local library to see if it has any of Ripley's volumes of strange facts, which continue to be published today.

WHAT'S THE WORD?

The disciples saw Jesus do many other miraculous signs in addition to the ones recorded in this book. But these are written so that you may continue to believe that Jesus is the Messiah, the Son of God, and that by believing in him you will have life by the power of his name. JOHN 20:30-31

GOD = LOVE

IF you ask around for definitions of the word *love*, you'll get lots of different answers. Try it sometime. Especially around Valentine's Day, we tend to think of love in a romantic sense. Red roses. Boxes of chocolates. Hearts trimmed with lace doilies. However, from Hollywood to Hallmark, any definition of love that doesn't feature God at the center is incomplete. That's because God *is* love.

We don't simply say God is love because he fits our understanding of the term. He came first. It was his nature to love before a human ever uttered the word. Did you know that Christians are called to be love—not just to respond in love, but to *be* love to those around us? Check this out: God is love (see 1 John 4:16). Jesus is God (see John 8:19; 10:30). We are called to be like Jesus (see 2 Corinthians 3:18). Which brings us full circle. As we become more like Christ, qualities of true, godly love will be more deeply ingrained in our character. So what are those qualities? Glad you asked!

You'll often hear 1 Corinthians 13:4-8 quoted at wedding ceremonies for its beautiful, practical explanation of love. Since our goal is to be love to others, just replace the word *love* from verses 4-7 with your name to see how you're doing:

"_____ is patient and kind. _____ is not jealous or boastful or proud or rude. _____ does not demand [his/her] own way. _____ is not irritable, and [he/she] keeps no record of being wronged. _____ does not rejoice about injustice but rejoices whenever the truth wins out. _____ never gives up, never loses faith, is always hopeful, and endures through every circumstance."

Does that describe you? Odds are you have a thing or two to work on. That's perfectly normal. Ask God for help. Then repeat this exercise every few months to check your progress. By the way, happy Valentine's Day. God really loves you!

DADDY-*Daughter Time*

As you read 1 Corinthians 13:4-7 with your name in place of the word *love*, which of those virtues would you consider strengths? Which need a little extra attention? Encourage each other by recalling times the other demonstrated love in one of these ways.

Visit a store and read through some Valentine cards together, rating each on a scale of one to ten. See who finds the best one, and give it to someone you love.

WHAT'S THE WORD?

We know how much God loves us, and we have put our trust in his love. God is love, and all who live in love live in God, and God lives in them. 1 JOHN 4:16

IT'S A MASTERPIECE!

IMPRESSIONISM. Symbolism. Cubism. If you're a fan of modern art (and who doesn't love a good abstract now and then), you can thank the organizers of the Armory Show of 1913. It was the first major US exhibition of works from that experimental period, which lasted from the 1860s to the 1970s. This landmark event opened in New York City on February 15 and featured paintings and sculptures by soon-to-be famous artists such as Renoir, Monet, Cézanne, van Gogh, and—for the first time in the United States—Pablo Picasso.

You may be surprised to know how much some of Picasso's paintings have fetched at auction or private sale. *Femme aux Bras Croisés*: $55 million. *Dora Maar au Chat*: $95.2 million. And for his *Garçon à la Pipe*, a collector paid $104.2 million! Is any painting worth that much money? One thing's for sure: if someone discovered an ashtray Picasso made for his mom in third grade, it would sell for a fortune too. Not because it was a masterpiece, but because it was made by Picasso!

Indeed, we tend to assign value to art based on the one who created it. Think about that. Who is the greatest artist ever, the one whose work has inspired every artist to come after him? Here's a hint: he set the universe in motion, created birds and trees, and continues to do miracles today. A gallery is too puny to showcase his marvelous works. More incredible than any mere rendering of nature, God designed the universe from scratch and continues to reveal himself as the grand artist to this day. That makes everything he creates of infinite worth . . . including you, which he describes as "very good" (Genesis 1:31)!

Sometimes we can question our value. Things happen to us. Someone makes a rude comment. We make mistakes. But you are a precious masterpiece worth more than any Picasso. You are God's creation. As David says in Psalm 139:14, "Thank you for making me so wonderfully complex! Your workmanship is marvelous—how well I know it."

DADDY-*Daughter Time*

Dads treasure the drawings and crafts made by their children. Reminisce about special projects or refrigerator art you've shared over the years. Does one piece stand out? Why? Have you ever created a unique work of art? Why is it so meaningful?

Get artistic together and make something for Mom. It could be as simple as a bookmark, as practical as jewelry, or a masterpiece of your own design.

WHAT'S THE WORD?

God looked over all he had made, and he saw that it was very good! GENESIS 1:31

WHEN you're having a rough day, what do you do to turn things around? Go for a walk? Catch a movie? Grab a spoon and a pint of ice cream? Or maybe, like Paul and Silas, you've discovered the power of lifting your voice to God. Once, after being severely beaten, these early missionaries had a midnight hymn-sing in jail that really brought down the house. Acts 16 says an earthquake shook the very foundations of the prison. Doors flew open. Chains fell loose. *Woo-hoo, freedom!* Can't you just picture Paul and Silas praising God while making a run for it? The weird part is, they didn't flee.

Awakened by the earthquake, the jailer noticed the doors were wide open. He feared that the prisoners had escaped, and he was about to take his own life when Paul called out, "Don't kill yourself! We are all here!" (v. 28). Next thing Paul and Silas knew, the jailer was asking to be saved. And before dawn, his entire family received Christ! Were prisoners freed that night? You bet. Spiritual prisoners.

It's interesting that Acts 16:25 says Paul and Silas were also praying while they were singing. Though the Bible doesn't tell us the nature of those prayers, it's safe to assume they were *not* along the lines of "Dear God, please deliver us from this crummy situation." Rather, their response suggests that they may have been praying for an opportunity to share God's Good News. They didn't run; instead they viewed this miracle as God's way of creating an opportunity.

Paul and Silas knew freedom isn't about roaming around outside a jail cell as opposed to being locked up *in* one. Real freedom comes from being secure in Jesus Christ (see John 8:36). Are you truly free? If so, next time you have a rough day, try singing and praying. Who knows, God may take your eyes off your own problems and, like Paul and Silas, use you to meet someone else's needs.

DADDY-*Daughter Time*

If you were Paul or Silas, would you have been tempted to escape? What might have happened had they not been so committed to prison ministry? You can get involved in prison ministry right now. Prison Fellowship reaches out to inmates and their families. You can find out more together by going to prisonfellowship.org. You can pray for prisoners or even buy gifts for kids who have a parent in prison through its Angel Tree ministry during Christmastime.

WHAT'S THE WORD?

Around midnight, Paul and Silas were praying and singing hymns to God, and the other prisoners were listening. Suddenly, there was a massive earthquake, and the prison was shaken to its foundations. ACTS 16:25-26

February 17   PLAYING A SMALL PART

DUCKING into the lobby of the local TV station, Melissa stomped her feet on the mat. Hard. To the receptionist, the tween was simply knocking snow off her boots. But each vicious stomp released a little anger, too. And the icy wind was only partially responsible for the red in her face, which was still quite rosy when she reached her dad's cubicle. He knew right away something was wrong.

"Want to talk about it?" he asked.

"No, this is your big night covering the president's speech and everything. I don't want to spoil it with my problems." Her father insisted, so she continued: "The cast list for the spring musical came out today, and all I got was a stupid chorus part. It's so unfair! My audition was so much better than the girl who got the lead. Now I'm stuck wandering around the stage with five other nameless villagers without lines. I'm not even sure I want to be in this play anymore."

"I'm sorry, Melissa. I know you're disappointed—and certainly talented enough to handle a bigger part. No question." He paused. "But supporting roles are just as important as starring ones. Every member of the team has a job. Some may be a little more glamorous than others, but you're all working toward the same goal, right? Things happen for a reason. Sometimes God uses situations like this to humble us and teach us things."

Suddenly, a producer for the evening news poked his bald head into the doorway. "Hey Jim, last-minute change for tonight. Since the weather's so nasty, we're gonna have you wait outside for the president's motorcade and let Pam work the ballroom instead. After all, she's eight months pregnant and, well, I knew you'd understand." The bald head vanished as quickly as it had appeared, leaving Melissa's father . . . speechless.

"Sorry, Dad. So what were you saying about supporting roles?"

DADDY-*Daughter Time*

Have you ever been denied a cool opportunity and given a supporting role instead? What happened? Read 1 Corinthians 12:12-31 together. What is that passage saying, and how could it apply to Melissa and her dad? What's the difference between temporary disappointment (as in the story) and coming to terms with the fact that we all can't be eyes, simply because we're gifted in different areas?

WHAT'S THE WORD?

If the whole body were an eye, how would you hear? Or if your whole body were an ear, how would you smell anything? But our bodies have many parts, and God has put each part just where he wants it. How strange a body would be if it had only one part!
1 CORINTHIANS 12:17-19

TAKE IT TO THE BANK

HOW far would you go to rescue your life savings? Let's hope you're never in Louis Remme's shoes. On February 18, 1855, the cattle dealer deposited $12,500 in the Sacramento branch of the Adams & Co. bank. That's still a lot of money today, but back then people earned about thirty dollars a month. So you can imagine how Louis felt when, just days later, news arrived that the largest financial institution west of the Alleghenies had gone belly up. People panicked. They raced to withdraw their money. And by the time Louis got back to Sacramento, he was too late. Nothing was left.

What would you have done? Keep in mind that news traveled slowly in 1855. No Internet. No telephones. No radio. In fact, Louis realized the bank branch in Portland, Oregon, had no telegraph or Pony Express, either. *They didn't know yet!* If he could reach Portland ahead of the news-carrying ocean steamer, he could cash in his receipt while it was still worth something. So he borrowed a fast horse and began riding. And riding. He covered 665 miles in 143 hours, trading exhausted horses for fresh ones and sleeping just ten hours along the way. Louis barely beat the steamer, but he collected his $12,500 in fifty-dollar gold pieces.

Some people will go to great lengths to preserve worldly wealth. One guy in the New Testament was so worried about losing his stuff that he was willing to trade something far more valuable: heaven. One day, a rich young man asked Jesus how to be saved. The Lord told him to sell everything he had, give the money to the poor, and follow him. That price was too steep. The young man valued earthly treasures more (see Matthew 19:21-22). Was Jesus saying we have to sell everything we own in order to be Christians? No. He does, however, want the things we value most to be completely surrendered and available to him. It's the wisest investment we'll ever make!

DADDY-*Daughter Time*

Consider Jesus' words to the wealthy young man in light of his parable about investing God's resources wisely (see Matthew 25:14-30). What's a healthy balance? How do you and your family attempt to honor God by managing money wisely? Think of creative ways you can invest in heavenly things.

WHAT'S THE WORD?

Jesus told him, "If you want to be perfect, go and sell all your possessions and give the money to the poor, and you will have treasure in heaven. Then come, follow me."
But when the young man heard this, he went away sad, for he had many possessions.
MATTHEW 19:21-22

SPECIAL DELIVERY

WHAT are some ways your family tries to save money? These days, it's wise to pinch pennies wherever we can. The same was true a hundred years ago, when a penny had a lot more value than it does now. But wait until you hear how one family chose to save a few cents.

On February 19, 1914, the Pierstorffs of Grangeville, Idaho, sent their four-year-old daughter, May, to visit her grandparents in Lewiston, seventy-five miles away. Train fare equaled a whole day's pay. Way too much. So May's father did a little research and discovered that a forty-eight-and-a-half-pound parcel-post package would only cost fifty-three cents. There were no laws against mailing a person, so Mr. Pierstorff bought the stamps and had them affixed to May's coat. He and his wife waved good-bye as their little girl embarked on her journey in the train's mail compartment.

You might ask, How could a loving parent send a child that way? How dangerous! How humiliating! If they really cared about her, couldn't they find a more suitable means of getting her where she needed to go? For the record, May was never put in a box. And because she was a "package," the mail clerk on duty in Lewiston delivered her directly to her grandparents' house. In the end, May's dad seemed to know what he was doing. And everything went as planned.

In some ways, that's how God sent his Son to us. Jesus needed to come to earth and be the Savior of the world. You might argue that he should have traveled first-class. After all, even before his heavenly Father waved good-bye, Jesus was already King of kings and Lord of lords. He deserved to make the trip in style. Comfort. Safety. Yet how did he arrive? As a helpless baby in a filthy manger, surrounded by smelly animals (see Luke 2:7). Yet Jesus' Father knew exactly what he was doing. And everything went as planned.

DADDY-*Daughter Time*

What do you think of Mr. Pierstorff's frugality? Could you see yourself doing that? Consider reading about May's story together in the 1997 children's book *Mailing May.* What's the craziest thing you've ever done to save money?

Read what the apostle Paul says in Philippians 2:4-11 about Christ's humble station and how God later exalted him. What is Paul's point in sharing this? How well are you doing in this area?

WHAT'S THE WORD?

She gave birth to her first child, a son. She wrapped him snugly in strips of cloth and laid him in a manger, because there was no lodging available for them.   LUKE 2:7

TARA felt frustrated. Even though she'd roller-skated brilliantly since she was three, the six-year-old couldn't get the hang of ice skates. Her ankles bent in. Her elbows pointed out. She kept landing on her backside. As she picked herself off the ice one more time, she no doubt flashed back to one year earlier, when she sat in her living room, enthralled by the figure skaters at the Calgary Olympic Games. Her dad had built a podium out of boxes, and as Katarina Witt received her gold medal, Tara stepped onto those boxes with visions of Olympic glory swirling in her head. Yet here she was, her first time on ice, as wobbly as a newborn giraffe.

Pretty soon, blades became less of a problem for the talented young roller skater. In fact, she was getting pretty good. *Really* good. She practiced long and hard. Some people wondered if she had enough seasoning to compete at a high level. But on this date in 1998—at the age of fifteen years, eight months, and ten days—Tara Lipinski became the youngest Olympic figure skater ever to win a gold medal. In fact, commentator Scott Hamilton noted, "For one who looks so young, she skates with great maturity." That night in Nagano, Japan, an effervescent, four-foot-ten-inch teen proved that youthful enthusiasm could more than hold its own against experience and "seasoning."

In a letter to his companion Timothy, the apostle Paul encouraged his friend: "Don't let anyone think less of you because you are young" (1 Timothy 4:12). Paul knew that society tends to underestimate youth. He may have been guilty of it himself at times (see 1 Corinthians 13:11). But he also knew that God has plans for the youngest among us. The Lord called out to a boy named Samuel. He helped young David fell a giant. And Jesus relied on a child's lunch to feed thousands of people. It's never too early to partner with the Lord . . . and go for the gold!

DADDY-*Daughter Time*

In addition to encouraging his young friend in 1 Timothy 4:12, Paul challenged him to live a life worthy of respect. To be an example. No lowered expectations because he was "just a kid." How can your life be an example in the areas of love, faith, and purity? In what ways can our culture value or devalue young people?

WHAT'S THE WORD?

Don't let anyone think less of you because you are young. Be an example to all believers in what you say, in the way you live, in your love, your faith, and your purity.
1 TIMOTHY 4:12

GONE IN A PUFF OF SNOW

WINNING gold is the dream of every Olympic athlete. But during the 2006 Winter Olympics, American Lindsey Jacobellis saw a surefire gold medal turn into silver.

In the finals of the first Olympic women's snowboard cross, Lindsey had built a commanding fifty-yard lead. She'd stayed out of the fray—which is key in snowboard cross, where four competitors fly over jumps and around high-banked curves in a race to the finish line. She was just seconds away from taking gold. On the second-to-last jump, Lindsey peeked over her shoulder, saw her huge lead, and pulled a backside method grab in the air. There was just one problem: she styled too long and wrecked on her landing. Switzerland's Tanja Frieden saw the spill and flew past Lindsey to earn the gold medal. Lindsey quickly popped up on her snowboard and finished second.

After the race, sports reporters bashed Lindsey for showing off. They said her pride had gotten the best of her. Lindsey had a different explanation: "I was having fun," she told reporters. "Snowboarding is fun. I was ahead. I wanted to share my enthusiasm with the crowd." Whether it was enthusiasm or showing off, one thing is certain: Lindsey will always be remembered for her Olympic blunder.

Would Lindsey have won gold if she had kept her eyes on the finish line and not tried to pull a fancy jump? Probably. The Bible tells us that "pride leads to disgrace, but with humility comes wisdom" (Proverbs 11:2). Lindsey's coaches said the twenty-year-old made a youthful mistake. It didn't matter that she was the reigning world champion and had breezed through earlier rounds. Lindsey had to settle for second.

What are you really good at? If you're the best at something at your school or in your family, it's easy to get prideful and start showing off. However, God wants you to stay humble. If you show off, you can make your opponents feel bad and even make fans root against you instead of for you. Nobody likes a show-off, but everybody likes a humble winner.

DADDY-*Daughter Time*

Watch Lindsey Jacobellis in the gold medal race by searching for "Winter Olympics 2006 Torino Snowboard Cross Finals." How did watching Lindsey fall make you feel? It's never fun to watch someone's Olympic dreams go up in a puff of snow. After watching the race, talk about how you can stay humble as you try your best at school, at work, and on sports teams.

WHAT'S THE WORD?

Pride leads to disgrace, but with humility comes wisdom.   PROVERBS 11:2

WHO WAS HE REALLY?

WE all know George Washington. He's the guy in the powdered wig and long coat who sells cars and furniture every February. And he's willing to cross the Delaware to bring you the biggest savings of the year! Does it ever bother you that, as we celebrate Washington's birthday, the father of our country has been reduced to an advertising pitchman?

Amid the dollar deals and talk of chopping down cherry trees (while also slashing prices), it's easy to forget who America's first president really was and why we honor him. In addition to leading the Continental army to victory in the American Revolution, Washington oversaw the writing of our Constitution. Did you know that he was also the only Founding Father to free his slaves? There's so much more to Washington than we tend to hear about.

That's true of many historical figures and heroes of the faith. To a lot of people, Daniel was just the guy who hung out with lions. Noah was a glorified zookeeper with a long beard and humongous boat. And Jonah, like Pinocchio, got swallowed by a fish.

Even Jesus can come across as the manger-born carpenter who let little children sit on his lap, rode a donkey, and somehow wound up on a cross. But that's not the full picture of who Jesus is or why he came. Of course, most people missed the point back in our Savior's day too. That's why he asked his disciples precisely who the crowds thought he was. Rumors had been swirling that maybe he was John the Baptist or Elijah. Others believed he was an ancient prophet come back to life. After the disciples explained that to him, Jesus asked, "But who do you say I am?"

That's the multimillion-dollar question. And he asks it of each of us today. Peter knew the answer: "You are the Messiah sent from God!" (Luke 9:20). Only by knowing Christ and sharing that understanding with others can we help a confused world see Jesus for who he really is.

DADDY-*Daughter Time*

Share false ideas you've heard about Jesus' identity. In your own words, who is he? Why is it risky to rely on a mere impression of someone rather than hearing his or her full story and spending time together?

See if you know these facts about each other: (1) best subject in school; (2) favorite TV show; (3) most hated vegetable; (4) preferred style of music; (5) greatest fear.

WHAT'S THE WORD?

[Jesus] asked them, "But who do you say I am?" Peter replied, "You are the Messiah sent from God!" LUKE 9:20

A WELL-MEANING BUT MISGUIDED CRICKET

MOST folks are aware that Walt Disney's first-ever animated feature was *Snow White and the Seven Dwarfs*. But do you know which came second? Here's a hint: "Give a little whistle!" That's right, on this date in 1940, the studio released its second full-length cartoon, *Pinocchio*, the beloved story of a marionette that comes to life and, aided by a cricket, tries to become a real boy by telling the truth and resisting temptation.

There's a lot to like about this fun, colorful morality tale. Puppets. Music. Boys turning into donkeys! *Heee-aww*. It's a classic. But if you listen closely, you'll also hear a few things that may sound a little off, including the famous song lyric "Always let your conscience be your guide."

Think about that. What is a conscience, anyway? Among other things, it has been described as the "inner policeman" who tells us what's right and wrong. But all of us have a moral code that is a bit different depending on where we've grown up and the things we've been taught. And let's face it, since we're sinful by nature (see Romans 8:5) it's awfully risky to trust in anything coming from inside us . . . including our conscience.

On a similar note, you may also hear a pop singer or a character in a movie tell you to follow your heart. Jeremiah 17:9 warns that the heart is deceitful and wicked. How can we know if it's telling us the truth?

Even though a message sung by a cute cricket or a charming Disney princess may sound good, we need a more reliable guide than our conscience or our heart. Fortunately, we have one: the Bible. God's Word is eternal, which means his truths don't change over time. They don't get squishy from one situation to the next. And the same rules apply to everyone. So when you have a big decision to make, give a little whistle, and always let Scripture be your guide.

DADDY-*Daughter Time*

Can you think of a movie or song that tells you to follow your heart? What could go wrong if someone always lived by that advice? Despite a wayward song lyric, Jiminy Cricket does play a very important role in Pinocchio's life; he's a friend who holds him accountable for his behavior. We all need that, and the Holy Spirit is that friend for us. To whom are you accountable?

WHAT'S THE WORD?

The human heart is the most deceitful of all things, and desperately wicked. Who really knows how bad it is? JEREMIAH 17:9

TEA FOR TWO

WHEN was the last time you enjoyed a steaming cup of tea? Making one couldn't be easier. You simply boil water, toss in a tea bag, and let it steep. *Mmmm.* But did you ever stop to consider who came up with the idea of soaking a little bag of leaves in a cup? Like many inventions, it was a happy accident.

At the dawn of the twentieth century, Thomas Sullivan was a tea and coffee merchant who, as was customary, sent out samples in tins to prospective clients. One day he thought of a way to save money by using small, hand-sewn silk muslin sacks instead of tins. Some folks weren't sure what to do with this new package, so they threw the whole bag into hot water. Impressed with the results, they requested more, praising Sullivan for his new, no-mess method of fixing tea. Voilà, the first tea bags were born.

Today, tea comes in dozens of flavors. Mint. Darjeeling. Raspberry. Earl Grey. Licorice. Cinnamon. The list goes on and on. Tea bags may look the same on the outside, but they're as different as chamomile and English Breakfast on the inside. Did you know that Christians actually have something in common with tea bags? It's this: despite our outward similarities, we don't really know what we're made of until we're in hot water.

Can you recall facing a "hot water" moment recently? We all have them. Some big. Some small. And the world is watching to see how we respond. Peter knew that when he wrote, "When your faith remains strong through many trials, it will bring you much praise and glory and honor on the day when Jesus Christ is revealed to the whole world" (1 Peter 1:7). Amid tense situations, we get a chance to honor God and show others what we're made of. It's one thing to bear the label "Christian"; it's another to live like one when the heat is on.

DADDY-*Daughter Time*

Take time to share a snack of tea and cookies with a twist. Each of you choose the other's tea bag from a box of assorted flavors. Remove any labels and see if you can identify the flavor. As you sip, discuss times you've found yourself in hot water. How did you respond? What situations make it challenging to live like a Christian? Encourage each other by recalling a time when you saw evidence of faith under pressure.

WHAT'S THE WORD?

When your faith remains strong through many trials, it will bring you much praise and glory and honor on the day when Jesus Christ is revealed to the whole world.
1 PETER 1:7

OOPS! CROSSED THE LINE

THE athletes' breath lingered in the crisp morning air. With each synchronized thrust, all ten dug their oars into frigid water, sending slender boats gliding across the lake's glassy surface. Moving as one, the Belarus national rowing team trained with great precision, relieved to be training at all. You see, the reservoirs back home were still frozen, so the independent republic of Pridnestrovie invited the squad to prep for the 2007 world championships on the Kuchurgan Liman, a saltwater lake it shares with Ukraine.

For the Belarusians, getting permission to tear across the Kuchurgan Liman in late March must have made them feel like teenagers who'd just been handed the keys to the family car. *"Buckle up and be safe!"* But whoever turned them loose on the lake neglected to share a rather important bit of information: "If you accidentally paddle into Ukrainian waters, expect its coast guard to arrest you, fine you, confiscate your boat, and throw you in jail." Which is exactly what happened.

Wouldn't it have been helpful for the Belarusians to know the boundaries—and the consequences—before they got in over their heads? Maybe someone did tell them. But if so, like teens impatiently jingling the car keys, maybe they rolled their eyes and said, "Yeah, yeah, we know" or "That's not fair! Susie gets to cross the international border!" You see where this is going, don't you?

The best parents define boundaries, curfews, and other guidelines in their children's lives. They do it because they don't want to see their kids get hurt. Plus, God commands parents to repeat his rules at home, on the road, at night, and in the morning (see Deuteronomy 6:6-7). Parents don't want to be killjoys. They establish rules for the same reason God does—love. So the next time you're tempted to roll your eyes at your heavenly Father's warnings, just remember that he loves you and that he knows what will happen if you cross that line.

DADDY-*Daughter Time*

Can you recall a time when you felt a rule was unfair, only to realize later that it was there for your protection? What happened? Describe some of the boundaries your family has established. Read the Ten Commandments in Deuteronomy 5. Now consider how each rule is intended for your benefit and how breaking God's law could prove costly.

WHAT'S THE WORD?

You must commit yourselves wholeheartedly to these commands that I am giving you today. Repeat them again and again to your children. Talk about them when you are at home and when you are on the road, when you are going to bed and when you are getting up. DEUTERONOMY 6:6-7

THIS IS YOUR
BRAIN ON MUSIC

ON this date in 1983, the bestselling album ever, Michael Jackson's *Thriller*, hit number one, where it stayed for thirty-seven weeks. Have you ever gotten a song stuck in your head? All it takes is a few bars for some tunes—and their lyrics—to loop in there for hours. That's not always a bad thing. Catchy hooks can help children study the alphabet, learn books of the Bible, or remember the days of the week. And a lingering praise chorus can turn our attention to Jesus when we least expect it. Indeed, music gives words staying power.

However, there's another side to music's Velcro-like ability to stick. For example, have you ever been haunted by a commercial jingle, an annoying TV theme song, or an off-color chorus to a racy pop hit? You didn't set out to commit it to memory, but it's hanging around just the same. So what's behind music's hold on us?

While working at emergency rooms in New York, Dr. Richard Pellegrino often rescued drug addicts with Naloxone, a drug that binds opium receptors in the brain and short-circuits the high. Those same receptors also bind natural endorphins, which play a crucial role in how we experience music. Further experiments with Naloxone have shown that music significantly changes how we process and retain information!

In an article published in *Billboard* magazine, Dr. Pellegrino warned of "music's immense power, and the responsibility that musicians and producers have to use that power wisely." He concluded, "Take it from a brain guy: In twenty-five years of working with the brain, I still cannot affect a person's state of mind the way that one simple song can." Wow!

Of course, you don't need to look far to see that the music industry doesn't always act responsibly. So it's up to us to choose tunes wisely. To guard our hearts and minds. To make sure lyrics promote God's truth rather than, as Colossians 2:8 says, the "empty philosophies and high-sounding nonsense" of the world around us. How does your favorite music measure up?

DADDY-*Daughter Time*

Why do you prefer certain musical styles over others? Which artists do you enjoy most and why? While in the car this week, take turns listening to and discussing each other's favorite CDs. Be as specific as you can about what makes that music meaningful to you.

WHAT'S THE WORD?

Don't let anyone capture you with empty philosophies and high-sounding nonsense that come from human thinking and from the spiritual powers of this world, rather than from Christ. COLOSSIANS 2:8

HUNGRY FOR POWER

EXPLOSIVE power. The Greeks had a word for such impressive energy and miraculous force: *dunamis*. That's where we get our word *dynamite*. Take a moment to think of three things, either natural or man-made, known for their explosive power. What were the first examples you came up with? A divided atom? An Olympic sprinter? A rocket, dragster, or bolt of lightning? How about this one: a kernel of popcorn.

Don't let its size fool you. Under the right conditions, there's a lot of power packed into that little grain. The main reason is its nonporous hull. Since traces of water inside can't escape as the kernel heats up, pressure builds after the moisture reaches its boiling point of 212 degrees Fahrenheit. When the interior of the kernel hits 350 degrees and 135 pounds of pressure per square inch, watch out—it's gonna blow! Once people saw what popcorn could do, even those who didn't understand the source of its explosive power wanted a taste.

In chapter 8 of the book of Acts, a man named Simon was also hungry for power he didn't understand. But in a bad way. This sorcerer had been wowing all of Samaria with magic. Then one day he got a taste of truly dynamic power when Jesus' apostles came to town. He watched as they laid hands on newly baptized believers and prayed for them to receive the Holy Spirit. It blew Simon away. He selfishly wanted that ability, too, and even offered to pay for it (see Acts 8:18). Peter rebuked him, saying, "You have no part or share in this ministry, because your heart is not right before God" (v. 21, NIV).

The world is full of Simons who get a glimpse of God's supernatural power and want to tap into it for selfish purposes. Even Christians should be careful of craving power, asking ourselves why we're praying for some miracle or mighty work. Is it to see God's will done? To see him get the glory? If so, stand back. You may feel as insignificant as a popcorn kernel, but under the right conditions you have God's power within you to do amazing things.

DADDY-*Daughter Time*

Has all this talk of popcorn made you hungry? Visit popcorn.org, and select a recipe to whip up for your family. Eat it together, and celebrate the Lord's power in the spirit of Psalm 21:13. What examples of his power have impressed you in the pages of Scripture? How have you seen God do dynamic things in your life?

WHAT'S THE WORD?

When Simon saw that the Spirit was given when the apostles laid their hands on people, he offered them money to buy this power.   ACTS 8:18

SIMON SAYS WHAT? February 28

IT didn't take long for TV's *American Idol* to become a national obsession. The undiscovered vocal talent. The chance for viewers to impact the outcome. And, of course, Simon Cowell. The caustic Brit's brutal honesty left a mark on pop culture . . . and on people. Take Mandisa Hundley. Early in season five, this gifted Christian blew away the judges with her audition, only to have Simon make cruel jokes about her weight after she'd left the room.

Mandisa didn't learn about the remarks until the show aired—at a viewing party in her honor. "I swallowed hard and tried to smile," she wrote in her book *Idoleyes*. "I'd gone from my life's highest moment to one of its lowest, and had to do it under the watchful eyes of my closest friends who saw my hurt and tried to encourage me. They even prayed with me that I'd be able to forgive Simon, and that somehow Jesus would be glorified."

A week later, those prayers were answered on national television. During a face-to-face encounter with the judges, Mandisa gently told Simon how much his comments had stung, adding, "The good thing about forgiveness is that you don't need someone to apologize in order to forgive them. So, Simon, I want you to know I have forgiven you, because if Jesus could forgive me for all the things I've done wrong, I can certainly extend the same grace to you."

Simon was humbled. They shared a hug. And Mandisa went on to finish among *Idol*'s Top 10 that season before landing a record deal and becoming a successful gospel singer. And you know what? She also realized that Simon had a point. Mandisa used that experience as motivation to live a healthier lifestyle.

Of course, not every insult hurled in our direction is worth taking to heart. Paul encourages us in Colossians 3:13 to "make allowance for each other's faults, and forgive anyone who offends you. Remember, the Lord forgave you, so you must forgive others."

DADDY-*Daughter Time*

What do you think of Mandisa's response to Simon? How might you have handled that situation? Refusing to forgive those who've hurt us can eat away at us like a cancer. How can holding a grudge hurt someone emotionally, physically, and spiritually? Do you need to forgive someone? Talk about that together. Then pray for the strength to, like Mandisa, follow our Savior's example in Luke 23:32-34.

WHAT'S THE WORD?

Make allowance for each other's faults, and forgive anyone who offends you. Remember, the Lord forgave you, so you must forgive others. COLOSSIANS 3:13

WALK IN THE PARK

IF you've ever visited Yellowstone National Park, you know it's like stepping onto another planet. Hot springs give off strange gases and create beautiful colors. Geysers—the most famous being Old Faithful—spout water hundreds of feet into the air. Mudpots bubble up acidic water. Steam vents hiss and roar as water boils through cracks in the earth's crust. Then, of course, there's the amazing wildlife, raging rivers, and beautiful mountains. Yellowstone is truly a crown jewel in God's creation. And on this day in 1872, President Ulysses S. Grant signed a bill that established Yellowstone as the first national park.

In those days travel was difficult, and few knew the beauty of Yellowstone that's nestled in parts of Wyoming, Montana, and Idaho. In 1871 an expedition led by Ferdinand Vandeveer Hayden explored the region. Thomas Moran sketched and painted landscapes of the area, while photographer William Henry Jackson captured some striking images. At the end of their journey, Hayden traveled to Washington, DC, and turned in a five-hundred-page report to Congress. Soon after, Congress approved a bill to protect the natural wonders of Yellowstone. Grant signed it into law—making Yellowstone the first national park not only in the United States, but also the world.

As Christ followers it's our duty to protect God's creation as well. The Bible is clear that God made the earth and everything in it (see Nehemiah 9:6). And he commands us to protect and care for his creation. That may mean picking up trash in a nearby park or obeying signs in wilderness areas that say, "Keep on the Trail." Maybe your family will begin a recycling effort in your neighborhood. Show your appreciation for God's creation by doing your part to treat all of it like a national park.

DADDY-*Daughter Time*

There are nearly sixty national parks in the United States, and it's never too early to plan a visit. You can also check out hundreds of national monuments or historic sites. Go to nps.gov and click on "Find a Park" to locate one close to you. Maybe you can plan a family vacation with a stop at one of the many national parks. As you decide where to visit, pray together to thank God for life and his beautiful creation.

WHAT'S THE WORD?

You alone are the LORD. You made the heavens, even the highest heavens, and all their starry host, the earth and all that is on it, the seas and all that is in them. You give life to everything, and the multitudes of heaven worship you. NEHEMIAH 9:6 (NIV)

IN THE SPOTLIGHT

ARE you a Mac or a PC?

Some people love working on Apple Macintosh computers. Others like PCs, personal computers. The choice really comes down to preference. Macs look cool but usually cost more. PCs may have more functions and memory. But there's one thing Mac users love: the Spotlight feature that looks like a little magnifying glass in the upper right corner of the screen. By clicking on the Spotlight icon, you can find nearly anything on your computer.

But it wasn't always that way. In the early 2000s, finding a specific file on your computer felt a lot like searching for a needle in a 100-gigabyte haystack. Apple CEO and founder Steve Jobs said, "It is easier to find something from among a billion web pages with Google than it is to find something on your hard disk." Jobs solved this problem by introducing a system-wide search capability called Spotlight on Macintosh operating systems in 2005. Let's say you wanted to find that paper you wrote for school about how videos of kittens are way cuter than videos of puppies. You could type in "surprised kitty," and automatically Spotlight would search for those words in every file and e-mail on your computer!

As impressive as the Spotlight search may be, it's nothing compared to God's ability to see into the innermost parts of our hearts. The Lord knows our every thought. King David said, "The LORD searches every heart and understands the intention of every thought" (1 Chronicles 28:9, HCSB). That's just as true in today's technical age as it was when David first said it to his son Solomon thousands of years ago. We can't tuck away any mean thought that God doesn't know about. We can't hide prideful desires from our Creator.

God's ultimate spotlight brings everything to the surface. Because we can't hide anything from him, we need to make the decision to give over our entire hearts to him—even the deepest, most secret parts.

DADDY-*Daughter Time*

If you have a Mac, use the Spotlight function to search for different things. See how it can find the smallest detail of information anywhere on your computer. (If you have a PC with a similar function, do that instead.) Talk about what it feels like to know that God searches our hearts even more intimately.

Are you trying to hide anything from God? It's impossible to do. Pray and ask God to forgive you for anything you've tried to keep from him. Then commit to not hiding anything in the future.

WHAT'S THE WORD?

The LORD searches every heart and understands the intention of every thought.
1 CHRONICLES 28:9 (HCSB)

ROLE OF A LIFETIME

HAVE you ever been part of a play? The costumes. The lights. The excitement of performing. It can be a lot of fun. But it's also a lot of work.

To do well in a play, it's important to learn the script. A script tells the actors exactly what they have to do to be successful. It contains all the lines for the actors to say. It gives stage directions so actors know where to enter a scene and what emotion to portray. If a script isn't very good, it doesn't matter how good the acting is. The play is going to be a flop. Glitzy costumes and awesome sets won't help either.

As Christians we have the world's best script—the Bible. Although the Bible doesn't tell you exactly what to say, it does tell you how to act. God's Word gives you his commands and explains how to treat other people. God doesn't demand that you memorize the whole Bible like you memorize a script. (Although that's not a bad idea, some of the details in the final chapters in the book of Numbers can get sort of dry.) All of the Bible is important, and some verses should be memorized in the scripts of our lives. Micah 6:8 is one of those. It says, "The LORD has told you what is good, and this is what he requires of you: to do what is right, to love mercy, and to walk humbly with your God."

Isn't that cool? God, as our director, tells us exactly what's required to live for him.

DADDY-*Daughter Time*

Memorize Micah 6:8 together. Keep practicing until you perfectly remember this important verse from the Bible. To help you, get a couple of pieces of paper and pens. Divide the paper into three sections. Label the sections:

> Do what is right.
> Love mercy.
> Walk humbly.

Write down ways that you can live out God's command in each area. When you live out God's script, you're sure to be a star.

WHAT'S THE WORD?

The LORD has told you what is good, and this is what he requires of you: to do what is right, to love mercy, and to walk humbly with your God.   MICAH 6:8

CHURCH CHAT

IF you're happy and you know it, go to church. Okay, that's not how the song goes. (You can clap your hands now if you want.) But studies have found that kids who go to church are happier. Researchers at Mississippi State University recently discovered that kids in religious families were better behaved and happier than other children. The study also showed that children whose parents regularly attended church had greater self-control, social skills, and ability to learn.

Wow! It makes sense that church would help you grow closer to God and better understand his Word. But who knew it could make you smarter, friendlier, and more joyful? Add faster and stronger, and church almost sounds like superhero school.

Maybe church *is* like superhero school. After all, you do learn about the greatest hero of all time: Jesus Christ. As we follow Jesus, he builds our character and helps us to be more self-sacrificing and honorable. Jesus may be the ultimate hero, but when girls are asked to name their heroes, the number-one answer is their dads.

The Bible is in agreement. God wants dads to be the heroes of their families. Dads have an important role. They often work to provide for the needs of their families. They're also the protectors. Plus, they can bring a lot of fun. God's Word adds that a dad must teach his children about God. Psalm 78:5 says, "[God] established a testimony in Jacob and set up a law in Israel, which He commanded our fathers to teach to their children" (HCSB). God actually commands fathers to pass along his laws and his story to their children.

DADDY-*Daughter Time*

Fathers, what are some ways that you teach your children about God? Going to church is probably a big part of that. But what else can your family do to grow closer to God?

Talk together about the best part of going to church. Is it the friends? The teaching? The worship? Next time you're in church as a family, make sure to thank your pastor (or pastors) for all they do.

WHAT'S THE WORD?

[God] established a testimony in Jacob and set up a law in Israel, which He commanded our fathers to teach to their children. PSALM 78:5 (HCSB)

EXTREME SKIER

BROOK Sexton loves tearing up the slopes outside Alta, Utah. Known for its deep powder and challenging terrain, Alta features some of the best skiing in the United States. Brook blends in well with the rest of downhill enthusiasts. But on closer inspection, you'd see Brook's orange vest isn't a fashion accessory; it's a reminder of her limitations. Brook's skiing isn't limited, but her sight is. You see, Brook was born blind. She tried skiing at age ten and fell in love with the sport. Now she's able to zip down extreme black-diamond runs.

To navigate the difficult trails, Brook wears a special earpiece. Steve Paige follows about fifty feet behind her and gives her directions. He says his commands have to be short and specific, such as "turn right," "slight left," or "watch out—mogul." As far as Brook is concerned, she has to put total trust in her guide to keep her from hitting an obstacle or another skier. She carefully listens to Steve's constant instructions to stay safe.

"I can't see where the trail is, but I can feel where it is and tell which way is downhill," Brook told a Fox TV station in Utah. "It can be scary; you have to trust your guide."

The same thing is true in your Christian walk—you have to trust your guide. Just before Jesus was arrested and crucified, he called the disciples together and said that he had much more to teach, but it would be more than they could understand. However, Jesus would send the Holy Spirit, and "when the Spirit of truth comes, he will guide you into all truth" (John 16:13). The Holy Spirit is equal but distinct from the heavenly Father and Jesus the Son. The three of them make up the Holy Trinity. It's the Spirit's job to guide, comfort, and teach us. It's our job to listen to the Holy Spirit and follow his directions.

DADDY-*Daughter Time*

The concept of the Trinity is difficult to understand. Some Bible scholars like to explain it in terms of water. Water can take on three forms: ice, water, and steam. But it's all H_2O. Similarly, God is Spirit, Son, and Father. Talk together about God's triune nature. Even if you don't totally understand it, that's okay. God is so vast and amazing, it'd be impossible for us to understand everything about him. For a quick activity, walk from your bedroom to the kitchen with your eyes closed. Rely totally on the instruction of the other person to get there safely.

WHAT'S THE WORD?

When the Spirit of truth comes, he will guide you into all truth.   JOHN 16:13

BE A DO-GOODER

ISN'T the English language fun? You can see a letter *C* while sailing on the sea. Or how would you like to draw a two, too? There are even these weird words called contranyms that can mean the opposite of themselves.

For example, you can *clip* something together or *clip* it off. *Dusting* can mean to remove dust (when cleaning the house) or to apply dust (when looking for fingerprints). An object can move *fast* and hold *fast*, which are quite different. The same is true with *bolt*. You can *bolt* something down so it doesn't move or *bolt* when you quickly run away from a situation. *Off* is often a funny word. You can turn *off* your alarm clock to make things quiet, or your alarm can go *off* to make things loud.

Then there's the word *bad*. For years *bad* was bad. But in the late twentieth century, *bad* suddenly became good. When someone said, "That's *bad*," she meant "That's cool." It's too bad that *bad* turned good, because that's pretty confusing.

Language is a reflection of society. As society slips further away from God's laws, our words can get even more crass and confusing. In this age of tolerance, holding on to biblical standards can be looked at as bad. But God doesn't want you to be confused. By his standards, *bad* is always bad.

In the book of Romans, the apostle Paul wrote, "Hate what is wrong. Hold tightly to what is good" (12:9). God wants us to act according to what's right. His standard is the only one that matters.

By believing in the truth of God's Word, Christians are sometimes viewed as closed-minded "haters." At times it can feel like loosening our standards and ignoring parts of the Bible would make life easier. But that would be wrong. Instead we should strive to do what is good.

DADDY-*Daughter Time*

Are there any areas of your life where wrong attitudes or actions have seeped in? Do you always hold tightly to what is good in the movies you watch, the music you listen to, the websites you visit, the words you speak, and the relationships you keep? Commit to living a good life, even when it may cause bad things to happen to you.

Now get a piece of paper and see if you can come up with any other contranyms.

WHAT'S THE WORD?

Don't just pretend to love others. Really love them. Hate what is wrong. Hold tightly to what is good. ROMANS 12:9

GUILTY AS SIN

MARK enjoyed helping his daughter memorize her Bible verses for Sunday school every week. As Amanda said this week's verse, Mark carefully followed along in the Bible.

"'For whoever keeps the entire law, yet fails in one point, is guilty of breaking it all.' James 2:10," Amanda said.

"That's perfect," Mark said. "You'll definitely get points for that one on Sunday."

Then Amanda asked something that caught Mark off guard. "Am I guilty, Dad?"

"Are you guilty of what?" Mark said.

"Am I guilty of breaking the law?"

Thinking quickly, Mark answered, "Do you always obey our house rules? Do you share and not fight with your brother and friends?"

Mark's precious ten-year-old scrunched up her face in thought. Then she answered, a little teary eyed, "No."

"So you *are* guilty," Mark said, hugging her. "But you can be forgiven. If you have Jesus in your heart, you're not guilty anymore."

Have you ever thought about that verse? Once Amanda understood James 2:10, it hit her that nobody's good enough to earn his or her way to heaven. Everybody's made a mistake. And making one mistake means we're guilty of breaking the whole law.

As scary as that sounds, there's no need to worry when Jesus is on our side. The Bible says Jesus speaks to the Father in our defense when we sin (see 1 John 2:1). Can you picture that? We're down here on earth doing something stupid, and Jesus is in front of his Father, saying, "My sacrifice is enough. That little one is forgiven." Now that's an awesome God.

DADDY-*Daughter Time*

Take a few moments to get serious with God. On other days, you'll be encouraged to go on bike rides or do fun activities. Today, just be still together and think about your gift of salvation. Jesus died so you could be God's children. Instead of being guilty of breaking the whole law, God sees you as blameless. We deserve condemnation, but we find forgiveness.

Set a timer for three minutes. Bow your heads and pray together, specifically thanking Jesus for his grace and mercy. Admit that you can't keep his law perfectly. And thank him that you don't have to because his sacrifice wipes away your guilt.

WHAT'S THE WORD?

Whoever keeps the entire law, yet fails in one point, is guilty of breaking it all.
JAMES 2:10 (HCSB)

TORNADOES. Floods. Earthquakes. Tsunamis. It seems every few months a natural disaster makes headlines. What do you do when you hear about a cataclysmic event? Charles Wesley wrote songs.

When an earthquake hit London, England, on February 8, 1750, Wesley wrote a series of hymns. His words encouraged the British people to repent of their sins and acknowledge God. He also affirmed God's power to protect his people. Ironically, a month later when Wesley was teaching people his new songs, a second earthquake hit London. One of the hymns, which he called "Psalm 46," says,

> *God, the omnipresent God, Our strength and refuge stands*
> *Ready to support our load, And bear us in his hands:*
> *Readiest when we need him most, When to him distressed we cry,*
> *All who on his mercy trust, Shall find deliverance nigh.*

Although the language doesn't sound like modern English, Wesley's powerful words remind us that God is everywhere and able to hold us in his hands. When we need him, he's ready. Wesley spent much of his life writing words to draw people closer to God. During his career, he published the words to more than six thousand hymns and wrote the words to at least two thousand more songs. Some of his most famous hymns include "Christ the Lord Is Risen Today," "O for a Thousand Tongues to Sing," and "Hark! The Herald Angels Sing."

The next time you hear about something bad happening in the world, think about your response. Maybe you feel sorry for the people involved. Perhaps you pray for the victims or your family members in the area. Or maybe you become scared. All of those are natural reactions. Prayer is powerful, and God wants you to pray for those in need. But he doesn't want you to be afraid. Psalm 46:2 says that, because God is our refuge, "we will not fear when earthquakes come and the mountains crumble into the sea."

DADDY-*Daughter Time*

What is your favorite hymn? Some churches rarely sing these classic songs of the faith. If you don't know many hymns, go to popularhymns.com. You'll find clips of a hundred of the most popular hymns. Just click on a song and you can see all the lyrics. Read the lyrics to several songs, such as "Amazing Grace," "Victory in Jesus," or "I Surrender All." As you read, thank God for helping you in times of trouble.

WHAT'S THE WORD?

God is our refuge and strength, always ready to help in times of trouble. So we will not fear when earthquakes come and the mountains crumble into the sea. PSALM 46:1-2

IT'S A BARBIE WORLD

BARBIE is the most popular fashion doll ever! Millions upon millions of these dolls have sold in the last fifty years. And on this day in 1959, Barbie was born. Mattel toys cofounder Ruth Handler created the doll after watching her daughter Barbara play with paper dolls. Ruth named the new toy "Barbie," after her daughter. Then she introduced the doll at the 1959 American Toy Fair. Barbie was a hit from the beginning.

Even today, Barbie remains popular. Mattel says 90 percent of girls between the ages of three and ten own a Barbie doll. More than five hundred Facebook groups have been created to honor her. Older women seem to like the doll even more than young girls do. One woman in Germany claims to have the world's largest Barbie collection with over six thousand dolls. She hopes to eventually own more than ten thousand Barbies. Over the years, Barbie has had 108 careers (including Olympic-medal winner, engineer, model, and four-time presidential candidate) and fifty different pets.

More recently, Barbie has come under attack. Critics say the doll creates an unrealistic body image for girls. One fashion model posed to show how many cosmetic surgery procedures she'd need to look more like Barbie—she stopped counting at ten. Another woman actually had over fifty surgeries in an attempt to look like Barbie. That's sad.

The truth is, God doesn't want you to look like Barbie. He wants you to look like . . . well, you. Genesis 1:27 reminds us that "God created man in His own image; He created him in the image of God; He created them male and female" (HCSB). Think about that: you are created in the image of God. The Creator's image is reflected in the diversity and differences of people's appearance. Look around. God doesn't make cookie-cutter creations. He makes each person unique with different hair color, nose length, body size, eye shape, and lip fullness. So instead of looking in the mirror and desiring to look like Barbie or a famous model, be content with how you look . . . because you're beautiful.

DADDY-*Daughter Time*

Believe it or not, dads can struggle with their image too. Not everybody can look like a bodybuilder or a professional athlete. Go stand in front of a mirror. Take turns looking at yourself and saying, "I like me just as I am, because God created me this way." At first you may feel silly, but as those words leave your mouth, know that you're speaking the truth.

WHAT'S THE WORD?

God created man in His own image; He created him in the image of God; He created them male and female. GENESIS 1:27 (HSCB)

GET THE MESSAGE?

CAN you identify who said the following famous words?

a) "Come, Watson, come! The game is afoot."
b) "There can be no question, my dear Watson, of the value of exercise before breakfast."
c) "I am a brain, Watson. The rest of me is mere appendix."
d) "Mr. Watson, come here. I want to see you."

The first three quotes were spoken by fictional detective Sherlock Holmes to his loyal friend Dr. Watson in Sir Arthur Conan Doyle's popular books. The last quote comes from the inventor of the telephone—Alexander Graham Bell.

Bell and Thomas Watson worked to improve the telegraph machine, which was the main mode of long-distance communication from the late 1830s to the mid-1870s. But its dots and dashes had to be interpreted and were a pretty clunky way to communicate. Then on March 10, 1876, Bell was experimenting with "talking with electricity" when he uttered the famous words "Mr. Watson, come here. I want to see you." He spoke those words during a successful experiment to his assistant, who was sitting in the next room.

Today, it's hard to imagine communicating without a phone. And technology has advanced even further with cell phones and the ability to talk over the Internet. With the ease of communication, it's simple to let others know what you're thinking. And that can be a problem, because we don't always have the kindest thoughts. James 3:2 says, "We all make many mistakes. For if we could control our tongues, we would be perfect and could also control ourselves in every other way." James is basically saying it's impossible to control what we say, so being perfect is impossible.

Everybody makes mistakes with their speech and wishes they could take back their words. Before your tongue gets you in trouble, try to think about the effect your words are going to have and the legacy they might leave. Alexander Graham Bell will always be remembered for saying, "Mr. Watson, come here. I want to see you," which is a lot better than being known for uttering, "Yo, Watson. Get your lazy self out here!"

DADDY-*Daughter Time*

Can you think of some words you'd like to take back? We all can. If you haven't yet apologized for some unkind words, make a point to ask forgiveness of that person soon. Instead of regretting what you say in the future, try to make your words worth remembering. Controlling your words can be anything but, as Sherlock Holmes would say, "elementary, my dear Watson."

WHAT'S THE WORD?

We all make many mistakes. For if we could control our tongues, we would be perfect and could also control ourselves in every other way. JAMES 3:2

SWEET TREAT

WHAT'S the best part about Kit Kat bars and Popsicles? *They're both sweet and delicious.* Yes. But maybe the coolest thing is that they're easy to share. According to the official Popsicle website, the classic Twin Popsicle ice pop was introduced during the Great Depression in the 1930s so two children could share a treat for just a nickel.

The invention of the Popsicle—like many other inventions—happened by accident. In 1905, eleven-year-old Frank Epperson left a mixture of powdered soda, water, and a stirring stick in a cup on his porch. Overnight, temperatures dropped and the mixture froze. In the morning, Frank found the frozen pop and called it an "Epsicle." The treats were a hit with his friends at school. Eighteen years later, Frank changed the name to Popsicle, because by that time Frank's children were always asking him for one of "Pop's 'sicles."

On this day in 1986, Popsicle announced plans to stop selling the traditional two-stick frozen snack for a one-stick model. Do you think the demise of the two-stick Popsicle is a sign of the times? Maybe kids today are less willing to share, so they want solo pops. That would be kind of sad. In the early church, followers of Jesus shared everything. Acts 2:44-45 says, "All the believers met together in one place and shared everything they had. They sold their property and possessions and shared the money with those in need."

That's amazing to think about. Early Christians shared *everything*. Can you imagine what it'd be like to sell what you have to help fellow believers and those in need? God may not be calling you to sell all your stuff, but he does want you to share. Earthly possessions are temporary. They lose value and fall apart. When you share what you have, you make somebody else feel better as you pass along the gifts God gave to you. God doesn't want us to hoard our stuff. Share generously with others and see what happens.

DADDY-*Daughter Time*

Make your own frozen treat together. You'll need your favorite fruit juice, paper cups, straws, and plastic wrap. Just pour the juice into the cup and cover it with plastic wrap. Push the straw through the plastic wrap and place the cup in the freezer. In a few hours, you can enjoy your treats together and talk about the benefits of sharing.

WHAT'S THE WORD?

All the believers met together in one place and shared everything they had. They sold their property and possessions and shared the money with those in need. ACTS 2:44-45

MORE THAN JUST COOKIES *March 12*

WHAT'S the first thing that comes to mind when you think about the Girl Scouts? Is it Thin Mints or really cool sashes covered with awards? Today, the Girl Scouts may be best known for their cookies. But that's not what Juliette Gordon Low had in mind when she founded the organization on March 12, 1912. Juliette wanted the Girl Scouts to be a place where girls could develop physically, mentally, and spiritually. She hoped girls would get outside and experience camping, hiking, and basic first aid. Eighteen girls gathered at her home in Savannah, Georgia, for the first meeting. Now there are more than 3.7 million Girl Scouts worldwide, and at least 50 million girls have gone through the program.

While Juliette lived a privileged life in Georgia, she also had her share of struggles. Growing up, Juliette enjoyed writing poems, acting in plays, swimming, and rowing. Chronic ear infections plagued Juliette, and she lost most of the hearing in one ear during her late teens. She married at twenty-six, but at her wedding a piece of rice lodged in her good ear as she and her husband left the church (traditionally, wedding guests threw rice at the newlyweds for good luck). The rice punctured her eardrum and her ear became infected, resulting in a total loss of hearing. When her husband died in 1905, Juliette looked for ways to best use her life. In 1911, she met Sir Robert Baden-Powell, the founder of the Boy Scouts. A year later she founded the Girl Scouts, and the rest is history. Her organization has helped girls for more than one hundred years.

The Bible tells us God created us to do good works (see Ephesians 2:10). He gives us special skills and abilities that we can use for his glory. As you look at Juliette's life, she was always giving back. She didn't let her near deafness stop her from impacting millions of lives.

DADDY-*Daughter Time*

What good works has God prepared you to do? Are you outgoing? Do you play an instrument? Maybe you could visit a retirement center to cheer somebody up. Do you enjoy animals? Maybe you could volunteer at an animal shelter to care for the dogs. God has given you unique talents that you can use for him. Your dad might be able to help you identify some. If you have any cookies in the house, enjoy some milk and cookies as you discuss how you can use your abilities for God.

WHAT'S THE WORD?

We are His creation, created in Christ Jesus for good works, which God prepared ahead of time so that we should walk in them. EPHESIANS 2:10 (HCSB)

DOG YEARS AND HUMAN YEARS

March 13

TYPICALLY when we talk about the ages of dogs, we often use the term "dog years." While not entirely accurate, you can calculate the actual "age" of your dog by multiplying every "dog year" by seven "human years." Dogs just age faster and don't live as long as humans. (But it's a good thing they live longer than fruit flies, whose average life span is thirty days.) When you think about it that way, little Pusuke accomplished something remarkable. The Shiba mix from Japan, who was the world record holder as the oldest dog on earth, passed away at the age of twenty-six in December 2011. The comparable human age was calculated to be between 118 and 185 years old.

That's amazing, for either a dog or a human. The story was more remarkable because Pusuke survived being hit by a car only three years earlier.

Sometimes we see things in this world that seem unbelievable. People live to ages once unimaginable. They survive traumatic situations. Some people who were once thought to be long lost—perhaps dead—are found again. But these things are not really inexplicable. These circumstances, as amazing as they can be, are reminders that there's a God who can do what seems impossible.

Take the example of Abraham and his wife Sarah. In Genesis 18, when Abraham was ninety-nine years old and Sarah was ninety years old, God told Abraham that in another year Sarah would have a son.

Sarah's reaction was understandable: she laughed. She thought they were too old to have a baby. She forgot, or didn't believe, that God had promised them years earlier that they would have a son . . . and more descendants than the stars in the sky.

One year later, exactly when God said it would happen, Abraham and Sarah became the parents of Isaac (see Genesis 21:1-2). When we read God's promises, we should always remember one thing: he will do anything holy and righteous, even the impossible, to keep his word. The reminders of his extraordinary abilities are all around us!

DADDY-*Daughter Time*

Do a quick search together of some "incredible but true" stories of heroism, survival, or lost and found. Make special note of how many times people use the words *miracle* or *unbelievable*.

Give God praise together for the amazing, "impossible" things he does. And keep your eyes and ears open. The next time something amazing happens, just remind each other: "That's not unbelievable; that's just God!"

WHAT'S THE WORD?

The LORD kept his word and did for Sarah exactly what he had promised.
GENESIS 21:1

A HEAD ABOVE THE REST

WHAT'S the size of a grapefruit, feels like warm butter, and uses about 30 percent of your body's energy to run properly? It's your brain! Your brain is an amazing supercomputer with an estimated one quadrillion connections. That's about as many connections—1,000,000,000,000,000—as there are grains of sand in the world! And your brain loves to learn—God made it that way.

Scientists say that some of your brainpower is determined by your parents. You sort of get what they have. But a majority of your brainpower is determined by you. That means if you study hard, feed your brain healthy foods (like nuts, fish, fruit, and green vegetables), drink lots of water, try new things, and keep reading and learning, then you can be smarter than your parents. (Just don't tell your dad. . . . Oops! He probably read that, huh?) Your brain is like a muscle; if you feed it and give it a workout, it will get stronger.

Want to know something else cool about your brain? When you're a follower of Jesus, you can have the mind of Christ. In other words, your brain will be able to understand God's truths and know his thoughts in a way that other people can't. First Corinthians says God's Spirit can teach us spiritual truths. To people who don't know God, having a goal to serve others can seem foolish. But we understand that God's teachings are the best way to live, because "we have the mind of Christ" (1 Corinthians 2:16).

As this school year continues, don't get tired of learning. It's easy to develop a case of spring fever and want to take a break. But keep reading, keep trying, and keep following God . . . your brain will thank you for it.

DADDY-*Daughter Time*

Give your brains a workout. Go to a computer and search for "Eugene's sudoku." It should take you to Focus on the Family's *Clubhouse* website page with a list of sudoku puzzles. Print out a couple of copies of the same puzzle. Fold under the answer key at the bottom of the page (no peeking!). Then get a couple of pencils and race to see who finishes first. Remember the rules of sudoku: you must complete the grid so that each row, column, and three-by-three box contains every digit from one to nine. That means you can't have any repeated numbers in a line or box. When you're done, drink a glass of water and thank God for your amazing brains.

WHAT'S THE WORD?

"Who can know the LORD's thoughts? Who knows enough to teach him?" But we understand these things, for we have the mind of Christ. 1 CORINTHIANS 2:16

STAY CONNECTED

KIDS' thumbs get more exercise today than at any other time in history. How do we know? Just by looking at the number of text messages being sent.

It's estimated that more than 2.5 billion text messages are sent every day in the United States. The average teenager sends and receives nearly 3,500 texts each month. With cell phones it's possible to stay connected with family and friends all the time. Have you ever wished you could talk to your best friend, update your Facebook page, and text your mom—all while you're riding your bike? Okay, that would be dangerous. But the truth is, we want to be able to communicate with who we want, for as long as we want, from wherever we want, at any time that we want.

The first cell phones showed up in the early 1970s. They were as big as a brick and weighed as much as one too. Only the rich could afford them, because they cost thousands of dollars. Today, phones are fairly cheap, and nearly five billion are being used around the world.

Cell phones come in handy when we want to talk with family or friends. But we've had the ability to communicate with God "wirelessly" for thousands of years. The Bible tells us to "pray in the Spirit at all times and on every occasion. Stay alert and be persistent in your prayers for all believers everywhere" (Ephesians 6:18).

As the world becomes more interconnected, we shouldn't take for granted our all-access pass to the Creator of the universe. God gives us unlimited minutes and perfect Wi-Fi reception to talk with him anytime and about anything that concerns us. God wants us to look around and constantly pray to him. And as we see God answer our prayers, he becomes even more real in our lives.

DADDY-*Daughter Time*

Wireless technology is relatively new. If you don't believe it, just ask your dad what he had to do when he wanted to call home from the movies. Cell phones give us a glimpse of how easy it is to pray to God. We can do it from anywhere and at any time, and he never drops our call.

Take advantage of God's invitation to pray "at all times and on every occasion." Start for five minutes a day and strive for a continuous conversation. Commit to communicating more with the people in your life . . . and your heavenly Father.

WHAT'S THE WORD?

Pray in the Spirit at all times and on every occasion. Stay alert and be persistent in your prayers for all believers everywhere. EPHESIANS 6:18

ARE YOU POSITIVE?

WHAT do you think when you see a glass on the table filled up about halfway with milk?

If you think, *Wow, that glass is half full,* then you're an optimist.

If you think, *Oh, that glass is half empty,* then you're a pessimist.

If you think, *Hey, my brother forgot to clear the kitchen table again!* then you're going to be a good mom. Just kidding. But seriously, how you view the world and the people around you says a lot about who you are.

Research shows that how positively you see other people is a direct reflection of how satisfied you are with your own life. When a person describes others positively, she tends to be more enthusiastic, happy, and kindhearted. On the other hand, those who perceive others negatively are more likely to be narcissistic (focused on themselves) and depressed. In other words, when you view people negatively, you may be judging *yourself* more than the person you're talking about.

Jesus talked about judging others several times in the Bible. Basically, he said the same thing every time: Don't do it. In Matthew 7:3, Jesus says, "Why worry about a speck in your friend's eye when you have a log in your own?" Sometimes we can get so focused on the people around us that we don't evaluate our own lives. It's easy to see when a fellow student is peeking at answers from another person's test. It's harder to notice when we do the same thing by copying a friend's homework assignment that we forgot to do the previous night. By working on our own thoughts and actions, we can better live for Christ and show his love to others. And in the end, that effort is going to make us very positive people.

DADDY-*Daughter Time*

Do you struggle with negative thoughts? It's easy to fall into a negativity trap every now and then. But researchers have proven that optimistic people out-perform pessimists in all areas of life. So try to look on the bright side!

Get some paper and pens. Write down a few things that bring about negative thoughts. Now wad up that paper and throw it in the trash. When you focus on God and the good things he gives you, it's easier to be positive. Pray and ask God to help you be positive and make a beneficial impact on the people around you.

WHAT'S THE WORD?

Why worry about a speck in your friend's eye when you have a log in your own?
MATTHEW 7:3

March 17   # TRUE SUCCESS

IF you were going to call your life a success twenty years from now, what would it look like? Would you be living in a big house? Drive a fancy car? Be married to a cute guy? Have a couple of little kids of your own? Be the first female president of the United States? All of those things certainly seem to reflect success.

Having a heart after God may not immediately jump to mind. It certainly doesn't rank too high on the world's success meter. But to God there's nothing more important. When you know God's commands and follow his ways, you'll be a success. First Kings 2:3 confirms that fact: "Observe the requirements of the LORD your God, and follow all his ways. Keep the decrees, commands, regulations, and laws written in the Law of Moses so that you will be successful in all you do and wherever you go."

That's a pretty big promise. Do you think it's true? Since God never lies—in fact, he can't lie—you know that you can trust it. So to be a success, you must know God more closely and focus more on following him. Earthly success fades and is forgotten. True success is found only by serving God and seeking his will for your life.

DADDY-*Daughter Time*

Write down as many of God's commands as you can think of together:

_____
_____
_____
_____
_____
_____

What do you notice about the things in your list? Do you see any patterns or similarities?

God wants us to put him first, act unselfishly, show love, help the less fortunate, think of others, respect authority, and watch what we say. When we do those things with a heart for serving him and telling the world his Good News, we'll always be a success.

WHAT'S THE WORD?

Observe the requirements of the LORD your God, and follow all his ways. Keep the decrees, commands, regulations, and laws written in the Law of Moses so that you will be successful in all you do and wherever you go.   1 KINGS 2:3

MORE THAN WORDS

IT was Amy's third trip to the principal's office this month, all for the same offense. Now detention. Frankly, she didn't understand the fuss. Nobody in her old school seemed to care if she used bad language. But at this new Christian school, even mild profanities were a big deal. Crumpling the detention slip, Amy thought, *Why can't my teachers see that they're just words?*

"I've heard people argue that words are just noises we make," explains Alex McFarland, who speaks and writes for teens to stand up for their faith. "They're sounds. They don't really mean anything. But such a position is contradictory. To deny the power of language, one must debate with . . . words!"

Clearly, words do have a specific meaning and hold great power. It's sad to think how frequently we hear off-color expressions in school, online, in entertainment, and on the job. All of it adds up, making it easy to assume that profanity is just a normal part of everyday conversation. It's not, of course. But even if it were, Christians are called to a higher standard. God's Word warns us to control our tongues (see James 1:26) and to keep "unwholesome talk" from spilling past our lips (see Ephesians 4:29, NIV). More to the point, Colossians 3:8 urges followers of Christ to overcome bad habits, including "dirty language."

The English language is vibrant and rich, full of diversity and subtlety. With such a colorful palette at our disposal, it seems silly to settle for words that could blacken our hearts, offend others—including God—and cause people to lose respect for us. God wants us to experience freedom in all areas of life. So we shouldn't forget that when we open our mouths, we're not just expressing ourselves, but we're also representing Jesus.

DADDY-*Daughter Time*

What boundaries has your family established in the area of language? Do people you respect tend to think more or less of someone who uses profanity? In 1 Corinthians 15:33, the apostle Paul warns that "bad company corrupts good character." Have you ever found yourself tempted to use inappropriate language after hearing others do it, either in person or in entertainment? If so, what does that say about the need to make sure the voices speaking into your life are saying the right things? Do you feel God leading you to make any changes?

WHAT'S THE WORD?

You used to do these things when your life was still part of this world. But now is the time to get rid of anger, rage, malicious behavior, slander, and dirty language.
COLOSSIANS 3:7-8

OUTREACH TO OUTCASTS

WHEN you think of Hawaii, you probably picture beautiful, sandy beaches and warm temperatures, surfing, lying in the sun, and eating coconuts. But Hawaii wasn't always the fun vacation spot that it is today, especially on the island of Molokai.

Around 150 years ago, Chinese workers brought the disease leprosy to Hawaii. You might have read about leprosy in the Bible. Jesus healed many lepers when he walked the earth. But during the mid-1800s, there were no cures for this disease (there are now) that attacks the skin, nerves, and muscles. Because the disease could be spread by contact, the Hawaiians took those who had leprosy and put them on Kalaupapa—a remote part of Molokai that's surrounded on three sides by the Pacific Ocean and on the fourth side by two-thousand-foot-high cliffs. Basically, it was a prison that held the lepers until they died.

Half a world away in Belgium, Joseph de Veuster felt called to missionary work. On March 19, 1864, he arrived in Hawaii. Known as Father Damien, Joseph loved being a missionary to the Hawaiian people. But once he learned about the lepers and their horrible living conditions, he felt compelled by God to help.

Father Damien brought hope to Molokai. He worked with the lepers to build houses, schools, and churches. He studied treatment options. He taught them about Jesus. He even bandaged their skin. And when the necessity arose, he dug their graves and built their coffins. Although Father Damien died of leprosy at the age of forty-nine in 1889, he is still remembered for his Christian service in all the Hawaiian Islands.

One of Father Damien's favorite words was *participation*. He looked for needs, rallied help, and met the needs. Where do you see opportunities to serve the people around you? Who are the outcasts? Look for ways to follow Jesus' example with your service. Matthew 20:28 says, "Even the Son of Man came not to be served but to serve others and to give his life as a ransom for many."

DADDY-*Daughter Time*

You don't have to travel to a remote Hawaiian island to make a difference for Jesus. The opportunities could be right in your neighborhood. Do you have an elderly neighbor who could use help with housework or would be cheered up with a plate of cookies?

Talk it over and then try to do one act of service this week. Write down what you want to do: _____
_____.

WHAT'S THE WORD?

Even the Son of Man came not to be served but to serve others and to give his life as a ransom for many. MATTHEW 20:28

CHANGING A KING'S HEART   *March 20*

HAVE you ever known someone who would make up his or her mind about something and not change it no matter what you said? That can be pretty frustrating, especially when you are convinced that person is wrong about something important. And it can really hurt if he or she has authority over you and treats you unfairly.

It happened often in the Bible. Pharaoh didn't want to free the Israelites from slavery. King Ahab wanted to kill God's messenger, Elijah. King Nebuchadnezzar built an idol and forced people to worship him, under penalty of death. How do you handle times when you are convinced the person in authority over you is wrong or being unfair? One option is to appeal respectfully to your authority, hoping to make your case. Another is to appeal to God.

You see, God can change the hearts of people, if he knows it's best. There's no limit to the type of people whose hearts God can turn. A pharaoh, a king, a teacher, a parent . . . anyone.

There's a great example in the book of Ezra. For years, the Jews were ruled by foreign kings who went back and forth on whether or not they could return to Jerusalem and rebuild the Temple after being scattered around the world. The rebuilding started and stopped until the reign of King Darius of Persia. God's prophets explained to one of the king's governors that the promises of past kings had not yet been kept. Darius searched the records to see for himself. Sure enough, it was true. So Darius ordered that the rebuilding be finished. For seven days, the Israelites celebrated "because the LORD had filled them with joy by changing the attitude of the king of Assyria" (Ezra 6:22, NIV). The next king, Artaxerxes, continued to support the Jews' return home! Ezra went on to praise God for influencing the king's heart, and God was honored above all.

DADDY-*Daughter Time*

Talk about how you and your dad handle disagreements. Does your family have a way for its members to ask for a different decision with respect and love? Think about some ways to discuss disagreements while still showing love and respect to one another. Are there people in your life whose hearts you'd like God to change: a teacher, a bully, a friend, a grandparent? Make a habit of praying for the Lord to change their hearts in a way that would glorify him.

WHAT'S THE WORD?

Praise be to the LORD . . . who has put it into the king's heart to bring honor to the house of the LORD . . . and who has extended his good favor to me before the king.
EZRA 7:27-28 (NIV)

GOOD ADVICE

DO you know what Christopher Columbus, Amerigo Vespucci, Meriwether Lewis, and Ferdinand Magellan had in common?

They were explorers. Yes.

They were men. Correct again.

But they all also probably spent a lot of time wandering around being lost. Columbus is famous for discovering America, but he was really looking for a shorter way to sail to Asia. He got "lost" and found a whole continent. Getting off track helped Columbus, but things usually don't turn out that well for most guys. Have you ever driven around with your dad when he's obviously lost? What did he do?

Chances are he did *not* ask for directions. According to a study by a British insurance company, male drivers travel 276 unnecessary miles each year because they refuse to ask for directions when they're lost. The wasted time and extra gas add up to more than $3,000 thrown away per year. That's pretty pricey. It'd be smart if dads stopped to ask for directions or checked their smartphones to find out where they were. (To cut him some slack, Columbus never could've done this in the middle of the Atlantic Ocean.)

King Solomon was considered the wisest man of his time. In Proverbs 15:22 (HCSB) he wrote, "Plans fail when there is no counsel, but with many advisers they succeed." Just like it's a good idea to ask for directions, it's a good idea for you to listen to advice. Your dad and mom have a lot more life experience than you do. Often they've lived through a similar situation that you're going through and can give you solid advice. A youth pastor, older sibling, or grandparent can be a source of good counsel as well. By getting and following sound, biblical counsel, you'll save a lot of wasted time and energy in the long run.

DADDY-*Daughter Time*

Go to a Chinese restaurant together. At the end of your meal, read the notes in your cookies to each other. Did you receive any good advice? Probably not.

Fathers, can you remember a time that you should've listened to some advice and didn't? What were the consequences? On the flip side, what's the best advice you ever received? Share that advice with your daughter. Daughters, reassure your dad that you'll always try to listen to him.

WHAT'S THE WORD?

Plans fail when there is no counsel, but with many advisers they succeed.
PROVERBS 15:22 (HCSB)

WORLD'S STRONGEST WOMAN

ANETA Florczyk is strong.

How strong? you ask. Well, in 2008 she broke her own world record by using her hands to roll five metal frying pans into round burrito-like shapes in one minute. Later that same year, she set another world record by lifting twelve adult men over her head (one at a time) in two minutes. And her feats of strength don't end there.

Born in a tiny Polish hamlet near Malbork, Aneta started training in powerlifting when she was sixteen. She quickly started winning competitions and joined the Polish national weight-lifting team in 1999. In 2000, she competed in the Junior World Championships and also won second place in the European Championships against much older competitors.

But Aneta truly started to gain fame when she began competing in the World's Strongest Woman competitions, where athletes perform various acts of strength, including flipping over 450-pound tires, lifting 225-pound logs, and picking up 150-pound barbells in each hand and walking farther than the length of a football field. Aneta won her first World's Strongest Woman title in 2003 in Zambia. And she went on to claim world championships in 2005, 2006, and 2008. Proving that she had grace in addition to power, Aneta competed in the Polish version of *Dancing on Ice* in 2008. She ice skated against other stars to ten different songs and placed third on the popular TV show.

Anyone who can bend frying pans into burritos is obviously strong. Aneta worked out for hours in the gym to build her immense strength. As believers in Jesus Christ, we have special access to the greatest power source in the universe— God himself. In 1 Chronicles 16:11, King David instructs believers to "search for the LORD and for his strength." David knew that only the Lord can provide supernatural strength to get us through the difficult times in life. So take David's advice and "continually seek him."

DADDY-*Daughter Time*

Go outside and try to lift your car together. Just kidding. Instead you can have a push-up competition. Daughters are allowed to do push-ups from their knees, while dads must perform traditional push-ups with only their toes and hands touching the ground. Who can do the most? Dads, can you do a push-up with your daughter sitting on your back? Don't hurt yourself.

After competing in your feat of strength, pray to God and thank him for being your source of power.

WHAT'S THE WORD?

Search for the LORD and for his strength; continually seek him.　　1 CHRONICLES 16:11

FORGIVE LIKE GOD

IT'S easy to feel good about ourselves when we extend a little forgiveness. Our younger brother accidentally pulls the arm off one of our favorite dolls and we cut him some slack. A friend sits with somebody else at lunch, and we smile and say, "That's okay." Our dog chews up one of our shoes, and we pet him on the head.

But our efforts to show compassion look lame compared to what the almighty God demonstrates toward us. In the Old Testament, God's people turned their backs on him, married people they were told not to, worshiped false gods, and committed countless wicked acts. While God judged the Israelites for their sins, he remained ready to forgive if the people came back to him. In Joel 2:13, the prophet says, "Return to the LORD your God, for he is merciful and compassionate, slow to get angry and filled with unfailing love. He is eager to relent and not punish."

Our culture, even our churches, tends to judge people and write them off. Sometimes we don't extend grace. We believe that some people can't change. Our God is different. He remains gracious and loving—even when we ignore him or break his laws. God always forgives when we turn our hearts toward him and return to following his ways. We deserve destruction, but we receive Jesus. What an awesome God we serve!

DADDY-*Daughter Time*

Forgiveness can be tricky. Sometimes we think we've forgiven somebody, but seeing that person creates a gnawing feeling in our stomachs. It's hard to be like God: merciful, compassionate, and loving.

Get a couple of pieces of paper and pencils. Talk about times in your life when it was difficult to forgive. Does talking about it bring up those old feelings? It's natural to get emotional when we feel wronged. But God wants us to totally forgive, just like he totally forgives us.

Write down the name of a person you need to forgive. Neatly fold the paper. Now tear it into tiny little pieces. It's over! Choose to totally forgive and think the best about that person. That's what God does for you.

Pray together and thank God that once we pray to ask for forgiveness, he not only forgives but also removes our sins from us as far as the east is from the west.

WHAT'S THE WORD?

"Don't tear your clothing in your grief, but tear your hearts instead." Return to the LORD your God, for he is merciful and compassionate, slow to get angry and filled with unfailing love. He is eager to relent and not punish. JOEL 2:13

SARAH AND THE CHOCOLATE FACTORY

SARAH Johnson had never seen a homeless person. So during a family vacation to Southern California in 2009, the ten-year-old was shocked to see people sleeping on the street and holding signs that said, "Need Food." Sarah didn't know what it was like to go hungry. Her life was filled with sweet things—literally. She lived with her parents in central Pennsylvania, where her dad worked in the chocolate industry. For the rest of the vacation, Sarah had a hard time eating at restaurants because all she could think about was the people without food. During most meals, Sarah asked for her food to be wrapped up so she could give it to somebody on the street.

When Sarah returned home, she wanted to do more. So with her dad's help, she built a chocolate house. No, not a candy house made of chocolate. She turned her family's house into a gourmet chocolate factory. Using her dad's business connections, she ordered forty pounds of cacao beans from Ecuador, Brazil, Venezuela, and the Dominican Republic. Then she roasted the beans, ground up the yummy nibs of the bean, and slowly mixed in sugar and cocoa butter. Making the chocolate wasn't easy, but she wanted it to be special because the money would go to help special people. Once the chocolate hardened, Sarah wrapped it in colorful foil to represent what country it came from. Then she set up an online auction where people could buy her chocolate. All the money went to Water Street Mission in Lancaster, Pennsylvania. When the auction was over, Sarah had raised $7,000 to help homeless people. And she had learned a couple of things . . . how to make chocolate and how to make a difference!

DADDY-*Daughter Time*

God wants us to make a difference for him. The money Sarah donated may have changed a life forever. In the Bible, Jesus said, "I tell you the truth, when you did it to one of the least of these my brothers and sisters, you were doing it to me!" (Matthew 25:40). In other words, when you help someone who's sick or give somebody clothes or something to eat or drink, you're directly serving the King.

During this Easter season, look for ways you can help King Jesus by serving the less fortunate in your area. You don't have to make chocolate, but think of something sweet that you can do.

WHAT'S THE WORD?

The King will say, "I tell you the truth, when you did it to one of the least of these my brothers and sisters, you were doing it to me!" MATTHEW 25:40

HEAR THAT?

WHAT'S the best way to communicate? If you said "talking," that's a good answer. But there's a whole lot involved in good communication. Talking is important. To communicate well, you need to be able to express yourself in an understandable way. Talking too fast or not loudly enough can limit people from understanding you. But experts say nonverbal communication speaks louder than words. Those nonverbal cues include body language, facial expressions, eye contact, inflection, and tone of voice. Do you sound irritated or happy? Are you rolling your eyes? Are your arms crossed? Do you maintain eye contact, or do you seem distracted?

The other key to communication is the opposite of talking—it's being silent and listening. Sometimes it's hard not to interrupt, especially if you're in an argument or if you get excited and want to say something. But staying quiet and focusing on what's being said will help you understand better and respond more effectively. That's why it says in the Bible, "The one who gives an answer before he listens—this is foolishness and disgrace for him" (Proverbs 18:13, HCSB). Always try to listen before you speak; otherwise you could sound foolish, like Macy:

Victoria: I'm having a terrible day.

Macy: Wasn't that math assignment hard last night? Miss Jenkins is so unfair.

Victoria: Yeah, but history. *Ugh.* I can't remember all those dates.

Macy (still thinking about math): Yeah, math homework should be outlawed.

Victoria: Did you even hear what I said?

Macy (still not listening): Why do we even have to do math? I'm not going to be a scientist.

Victoria: Hello, Macy. We're talking about my history crisis here.

Macy (still in her own little world): What'd you get for problem six?

Victoria: Ugh.

DADDY-*Daughter Time*

While Victoria and Macy's conversation may be a little exaggerated, listening is key to any good relationship. It'll also help you do better in school. Practice your listening skills together. Have a conversation about your day. Daughters, you talk first. Dads, listen carefully and then repeat back to your daughter what she said, starting with "What I hear you saying is . . . (you don't like math class, or whatever)." Speak in little bits, so it's easy to remember and repeat back. When the daughter is done, it's Dad's turn to talk about his day. When you actively listen, you help create great communication.

WHAT'S THE WORD?

The one who gives an answer before he listens—this is foolishness and disgrace for him.
PROVERBS 18:13 (HCSB)

NOT SO PRETTY

NOBODY knows exactly what Jesus Christ looked like when he walked the earth. Paintings, movies, and animated videos usually show God's Son as an attractive man with a tall, athletic build, a thin nose, and somewhat blondish hair.

Biblical experts often have a very different view. They say Jesus was a square-shouldered, stocky, olive-skinned guy who stood just over five feet tall. He didn't stand out in a crowd. He wasn't the best athlete. Kids may have made fun of him for the way he looked.

The prophet Isaiah wrote that the Messiah wouldn't be beautiful. "There was nothing beautiful or majestic about his appearance, nothing to attract us to him" (Isaiah 53:2).

Jesus didn't draw people to himself with his looks. He didn't have a team of makeup people to make him look beautiful and dress him in all the right clothes. People followed Jesus because of his love, compassion, and the truthful words he spoke.

Whenever you feel plain and unimportant, remember that Jesus' outward appearance wasn't anything special. He had more important things to do than worry about other people's opinions of the way he looked. He was busy doing God's will. He put his relationship with God above everything else and cared most about what God thought of him. If other kids put you down, know that Jesus probably got the same treatment. Jesus wasn't the strongest, fastest, or best looking. He looked ordinary. But Jesus *did* the extraordinary, and his life changed the world.

DADDY-*Daughter Time*

Jesus may not have been much to look at, but his teachings and actions affected the history of the world. Get out a piece of paper and pencil, and write down different words that describe Jesus. Maybe you'll write *kind* or *wise*.

When you're done with your list, talk a little about each word. Then look at your list as a whole. How would you like to be described that way by the people who know you? It's probably a lot better than being thought of as "cute" or "handsome."

WHAT'S THE WORD?

There was nothing beautiful or majestic about his appearance, nothing to attract us to him. ISAIAH 53:2

DEAR DIARY

A lot of girls keep a diary. Boys do it too (they just call it a journal). A diary is a great place to write down your innermost thoughts and feelings. Your diary can help you express yourself in a way that you can't in other, less private situations. Keeping a diary can also help you remember big events in your life and keep you grounded when tough times come.

If you don't have a diary, experts say the best way to start one is to buy a diary that fits your personality. What's your favorite color? Do you like metallic or pastel colors, horses or flowers? Once you find the perfect diary, write down some information about yourself, such as your age, the school you attend, your best friend, and favorite hobbies. Then write in your diary like you'd talk with a friend. It's really pretty simple. Some people even write down what they're praying and then record God's answers. Years later, they go back and see how God worked in their lives.

Throughout history, diaries have provided insights into people's lives and the time in which they lived. There's just something powerful about the written word. God knows that, which is why he told Habakkuk, "Write my answer plainly on tablets, so that a runner can carry the correct message to others" (2:2). When you write something down, it has permanence. The message is clear and correct. Memories can fade and feelings change, but writing lasts.

If you haven't done it before, write down the things most important to you. What do you believe about God? What do you see him calling you to do? What are you passionate about? Do you have any weaknesses that require you to lean more on the Lord? What can you do better than anyone else? What are your favorite things about your family? Take a few minutes to think about those questions, and write down the answers. And save your diaries . . . because when you're older, you'll be glad to have your dear diary.

DADDY-*Daughter Time*

Why do you think it was so important to God for Habakkuk to write down what he said? Talk about why it's important to follow God's instructions.

Then go grab a couple of pieces of paper or your diary. Write down the answers to the questions in today's devotional. You can discuss your answers and even make up a few questions of your own. Save these papers someplace safe so you can go back and look at them later.

WHAT'S THE WORD?

The LORD said to me, "Write my answer plainly on tablets, so that a runner can carry the correct message to others." HABAKKUK 2:2

GOD BLESS YOU

NA Zdorovie. Salud. Gesundheit. A sneeze can elicit a number of responses, including "God bless you." But have you ever wondered where that expression came from? Although no one's certain, some believe it originated in AD 590 under Pope Gregory I when an outbreak of bubonic plague found its way to Rome. Sneezing was considered an early symptom, so it's thought that "God bless you" became a short prayer spoken over Mr. or Mrs. Achoo so they wouldn't get sick or infect others!

Other theories have existed too. Some folks worried that an individual's soul could be thrown from the body during a sneeze. Others felt sure the act was a defense mechanism for getting rid of an evil spirit. In either case, it wouldn't hurt to invoke God's blessing, right? Hence, a phrase was born. Fortunately, you don't have to unleash a massive sneeze to obtain God's blessing. The Bible points out a number of activities sure to gain the Lord's favor. Here are a few key ones:

- Obedience: James 1:25 explains that, if you study and observe God's perfect law, "God will bless you for doing it." Similarly, there's also a reward for obeying your parents (see Ephesians 6:1-3).
- Faithful Service: Jesus uses a parable in Matthew 25:14-30 to illustrate how much God values our wise investments on his behalf and our good stewardship of the time and resources entrusted to us. The master praises the servant and says, "Let's celebrate together!" (25:21, 23).
- Generous Giving: The apostle Paul reminds us in 2 Corinthians 9:6-8 that, like a farmer, we will reap the amount we sow. The payoff comes in verse 8, where Paul says, "And God will generously provide all you need. Then you will always have everything you need and plenty left over to share with others."

Don't wait for someone to acknowledge a sneeze. Look for opportunities to invoke God's many blessings—and be a blessing to others—by obeying, serving, and giving as generously as our heavenly Father does. He loves you and can't wait to demonstrate it.

DADDY-*Daughter Time*

Take a moment to count your blessings together. Have you ever received one that seemed to be a by-product of obedience or faithfulness on your part?

Learn more about what really happens when you sneeze. If you search online for "anatomy of a sneeze," you'll find an illustrated analysis courtesy of the *Washington Post*. Want to learn about a cough? That's there too!

WHAT'S THE WORD?

If you look carefully into the perfect law that sets you free, and if you do what it says and don't forget what you heard, then God will bless you for doing it. JAMES 1:25

"STICKS and stones may break my bones, but mean words crush my spirit." Okay, the popular saying ends with "but words will never hurt me." If you're honest with yourself, however, you'll probably agree that negative words can have a crushing effect.

How would it make you feel if your best friend walked up and said something mean about your new outfit? Or how about if your dad called you lazy for not cleaning your room? What if your brother called you selfish for eating the last doughnut? You'd feel bad, right? The truth is, words have a lot of power, and God knows it. Proverbs 16:24 says, "Kind words are like honey—sweet to the soul and healthy for the body." Isn't that cool to compare words to honey? Solomon could have written that "kind words are like honey—sticky on the fingers and tasty on corn bread." But he specifically said they're "sweet to the soul and healthy for the body."

Honey is refreshing and sweet. And scientists have discovered that honey is packed with antiseptic, antioxidant, and cleansing properties. Some people claim honey can help with acne, bad breath, colds, arthritis, and hair loss. Kind words may not be able to cure a stomachache (another claim made by honey lovers), but they can make another person feel better. Experts say it takes about ten kind statements to counteract one negative statement. Would you agree?

It's natural for us to focus on the negative. Somebody says something mean about us, and that's all we can think about. And once we start dwelling on the negative, it's easy to let negative things slip out of our mouths. When you're about to let an unkind word roll off your tongue, remember this verse. Do you want your words to make people feel sweet or to make them feel sick? It's not always easy to control our words, but it is possible.

DADDY-*Daughter Time*

Watch the movie *Charlotte's Web* together sometime this week. Do the words that Charlotte spins in her web build up Wilbur or tear him down? What's the overall effect of her words and those of the other barnyard animals? What can you learn about words from this fictitious barn spider?

Go through the other questions about this movie in the *Charlotte's Web* section of appendix A, Father-Daughter Movie Nights. When you're finished, say at least one kind thing to each member of your family.

WHAT'S THE WORD?

Kind words are like honey—sweet to the soul and healthy for the body.
PROVERBS 16:24

FRIEND OF GOD

THINK about your best friend. What do you picture? Do you have any special memories? It's great to have a friend. Someone to hang out with and talk with. Somebody who's always got your back.

Now think about God. What comes to mind? You might think of power, or Savior, or Lord, or teacher. *Friend* probably wasn't the first thing to enter your head. But *you* are a friend of God. You are a friend of the most powerful being in the universe. Let that sink in. It's the truth. If you know Jesus as Savior, God calls you friend. Our relationship with God is what makes Christianity different from other world religions. From the beginning of recorded history, God was close to his people. In Deuteronomy 4:7 Moses says, "What great nation has a god as near to them as the LORD our God is near to us whenever we call on him?" The answer: none.

No other people can say they're as close to their god as we are to the one true God. Earlier in the Bible, Moses, the writer of Exodus, describes how he interacted with God. Exodus 33:11 says, "Inside the Tent of Meeting, the LORD would speak to Moses face to face, as one speaks to a friend." Okay, we're not all Moses. (First, because we wouldn't all look good with a beard. *Ha!*) But God wants us to live out our faith, just like that hero of the Bible did. And as God guided his people in Moses' time, he guides us today by his Spirit and through the Bible. We don't need to go into a "Tent of Meeting" to talk with God. We can pray to him anytime we want . . . just like a good friend.

DADDY-*Daughter Time*

Do you treat God like a distant, powerful force, or a close, personal friend? What are some ways you can treat God more like a friend?

Talk together about the qualities of a good friend. You probably want a friend who's loyal, caring, unselfish, and truthful. Add some more things to this list: _____.

Does God fit all those characteristics?

Now talk about how you build a deep friendship. You might spend time together, talk on the phone, text each other, and do things that you both enjoy. You can do those things with God by praying, reading his Word, and keeping a journal. But instead of building up a friendship, a lot of Christians neglect their relationship with God by not spending much time with him. Try to learn something new about your Friend this week.

WHAT'S THE WORD?

Inside the Tent of Meeting, the LORD would speak to Moses face to face, as one speaks to a friend. EXODUS 33:11

CAPE CRUSADER

FREEZING rain bashed against her forty-foot sailboat. Wind swirled outside her cabin window. But in the midst of the storm, sixteen-year-old Abby Sunderland smiled. On this day in 2010, Abby became the youngest person ever to sail around Cape Horn without any help. But that was only one of the goals for this young adventurer from Thousand Oaks, California. She had left the United States more than two months earlier, trying to become the youngest person to sail around the world alone, nonstop, and without assistance.

Abby had hoped to connect with her dad after accomplishing this feat. He had flown to the tip of South America to see his daughter make history. Cape Horn is known as the Mount Everest of sailing—it's wrought with dangers that include huge waves and hurricane-force winds. Abby passed about fifty miles south of Cape Horn. Her dad planned to sail out and take a photo of her, but the weather conditions were too dangerous.

A few weeks later Abby's dream of sailing around the world unassisted came to an end when mechanical problems on her boat forced her to pull into Cape Town, South Africa. Abby had been by herself for a hundred days and didn't realize how much she missed being with people. But once the repair was made, she returned to sea. About two months later a rogue wave capsized Abby's boat and broke the mast—stranding her about two thousand miles away from Australia in the middle of the Indian Ocean. Abby didn't panic. She trusted the Lord and leaned on the truth of her favorite Bible verse: "If I ride the wings of the morning, if I dwell by the farthest oceans, even there your hand will guide me, and your strength will support me" (Psalm 139:9-10). Abby set off her emergency distress beacon and waited to be saved. In just a day, God helped guide rescuers to Abby's boat and brought her back to safety.

DADDY-*Daughter Time*

Abby first started dreaming of sailing around the world when she was thirteen. A few years later some of those dreams became a reality. What are your dreams? Abby dreamed big, trusted God, and had an amazing adventure. God has an equally awesome adventure planned for your life. As you make decisions in the future, tell God that you're going to trust his hand to guide you. Then rely on his strength for support.

WHAT'S THE WORD?

If I ride the wings of the morning, if I dwell by the farthest oceans, even there your hand will guide me, and your strength will support me.   PSALM 139:9-10

NO FOOL TODAY!

IT'S April Fools' Day today, or as they say in Scotland, it's Hunting the Gowk, which means "hunting for an easy target to prank." Nobody's exactly sure why or when this day of trickery began. Some historians say it started in France more than 425 years ago. Others believe this wacky day sprouted up in numerous cultures as people celebrated the beginning of spring.

Did someone try to trick you today? Maybe you tried to play a prank on somebody else. April Fools' jokes can be funny, but they can also sting, so keep your tricks fun. No one likes to feel like a fool.

In the late 1940s, a young missionary-minded college student named Jim Elliot penned some powerful words in his journal: "He is no fool who gives what he cannot keep to gain that which he cannot lose." Do you see what he was getting at? Jim based his decisions according to the conviction that his life (which "he cannot keep") was less important than missions work that could save souls for eternity (results that "he cannot lose"). A couple of years later, Jim died while sharing the Good News of Jesus Christ with an isolated tribe in Ecuador. Jim's words went on to inspire generations of Christians to serve God.

The apostle Paul, in Philippians 3:8, expresses something very similar about earthly things being less important than eternal matters. He says, "Everything else is worthless when compared with the infinite value of knowing Christ Jesus my Lord." Think about that. *Everything else, besides Jesus, is worthless.*

Paul had been a fool once. He thought keeping rules and punishing Christians were the most important things in life. But when he met Jesus Christ and learned that Jesus wants a relationship (not just a rule follower), Paul's life was changed forever. He was no fool that day . . . or any other day after that.

DADDY-*Daughter Time*

Share some of your favorite, and not so favorite, April Fools' experiences. Ask your dad to describe some from his childhood. For a fun prank, stuff a family member's shoes with cotton balls. When he or she goes to put them on, the shoes will feel too small.

As you think about Jim's and Paul's words, do you share their conviction? Prayerfully consider how you might sacrifice some of your "treasures" to help others learn about Jesus.

WHAT'S THE WORD?

Yes, everything else is worthless when compared with the infinite value of knowing Christ Jesus my Lord. For his sake I have discarded everything else, counting it all as garbage, so that I could gain Christ. PHILIPPIANS 3:8

ANGER. RESCUE.
RINSE. REPEAT.

SOME people are like a shampoo bottle. If you squeeze them, bubbles come out. Just kidding. But you know these people. They never learn to change their behavior. It seems like all they do is wet hair, lather, rinse, and repeat. According to the Bible, this may be particularly true of people who get angry easily.

Every action has consequences. While Jesus' sacrifice paid the ultimate price for our sins, an earthly consequence often exists for the bad decisions we make. Some people try to avoid the consequences by blaming others or shirking responsibility. We may even try to help our friends remove the pain of their poor choices, because we think it's a kind thing to do. But Proverbs 19:19 has a warning for us: rescuing a person with a bad temper won't teach him or her anything. Just like when you shampoo, the effects of the "cleanup" don't last long, and you'll end up doing it again.

If you have a hot-tempered friend, then you know she usually doesn't think very rationally. She probably jumps to a conclusion and gets angry. When a quick-to-get-angry person doesn't have to pay a penalty, she's more likely to keep doing the same thing over and over again. On the other hand, if that person has to live with the consequences of her rage, she may be less likely to repeat her angry actions.

Later in Proverbs 22:24-25, we read that a hot-tempered person will only have a negative impact on us. These verses give us a good warning in choosing our friends and managing our relationships. We would do well to take this counsel to heart. Angry people must suffer consequences, and we should not interfere with what God wants to do in their lives. Who knows, maybe God wants your friend to experience his type of "character conditioner," so your friend's life—like conditioned hair—can be more smooth.

DADDY-*Daughter Time*

Discuss why you think the Bible is so specific about the consequences for easily angered people. Who are some people you know who seem to get angry far too quickly? Do you see people in their lives who try to protect them from consequences?

If there are ongoing anger issues in your family, pray together about them. Ask God for wisdom and peace.

WHAT'S THE WORD?

Hot-tempered people must pay the penalty. If you rescue them once, you will have to do it again.　PROVERBS 19:19

BAD HAIR DAY

CAN you think of someone whose hair is more famous than he or she is? Dads and moms probably remember Farrah Fawcett's flowing blonde hair in the 1970s. And Justin Bieber's locks made him an icon in the first decade of the twenty-first century.

Styles, colors, and straightness of hair can vary. So can the number of hairs on your head. An average human has between 100,000 and 200,000 strands of hair. (Sorry, dads, if your pate is less replete with hair.) And most people's hair grows around six inches each year. According to one scientific study, straight hair tangles more easily than curly hair, though it's not clear why. Isn't hair fascinating?

Your hair is probably really important to you, but to Samson it meant everything. As a Nazirite, he vowed to never cut his hair. Samson's long hair (groomed in seven stylish braids) was a sign that he had been dedicated to God's service. God gave him amazing strength because of his obedience. Samson killed men with the jawbone of a donkey and carried away massive city gates. But then he carelessly told a woman about the source of his strength. She betrayed Samson to his enemies, they cut his hair, and he temporarily lost his power.

You can find another bad hair story in 2 Samuel 18. Absalom, King David's rebellious son, got his long hair tangled in some branches. He was killed as he hung by his flowing locks. But one of the most amazing biblical facts about hair is that God knows *exactly* how many strands you have (see Luke 12:7). God is not an impersonal God who doesn't have time for us. He knows us down to the number of hairs on our heads. Whether we have long, tangled, short, or bouncy hair, God knows us intimately. Remember that next time you pick up a brush!

DADDY-*Daughter Time*

Have a fun discussion with your dad about hair. If your dad has old photos, look at some of his hairstyles. How did you used to wear your hair? Talk about how hair affects your view of others and your opinion of yourself.

Assuming you won't have time to count the number of hairs on your head, share with each other a fact about yourself that not everyone would know. This knowledge will remind you how special it is to be known by someone who loves you very much.

WHAT'S THE WORD?

What is the price of five sparrows—two copper coins? Yet God does not forget a single one of them. And the very hairs on your head are all numbered. So don't be afraid; you are more valuable to God than a whole flock of sparrows. LUKE 12:6-7

A PROMISED LAND

RARELY does a nation mourn the death of one man. But on this day in 1968, a voice that had led the United States to deal with racial inequality and discrimination was silenced in Memphis, Tennessee. The murder of Dr. Martin Luther King Jr. disturbed and grieved the nation. He died a violent death even though he used nonviolence and the powerful truth of God's Word to stir the people's conscience.

Dr. King constantly received death threats. He understood the risks of his work. The night before his unexpected death, his last speech expressed the undying hope he had for the future—even though he knew he might not live to see his hope become a reality:

> Like anybody, I would like to live—a long life; longevity has its place. But I'm not concerned about that now. I just want to do God's will. And He's allowed me to go up to the mountain. And I've looked over. And I've seen the Promised Land. I may not get there with you. . . . I'm not worried about anything. I'm not fearing any man. Mine eyes have seen the glory of the coming of the Lord.

Like Moses at the end of his life, Dr. King put his trust in God's will. Moses had led his people to the edge of the Promised Land, but God didn't allow him to enter it (see Deuteronomy 34:4-5). Instead of fighting against God, Moses accepted God's timing and trusted the Lord's will.

DADDY-*Daughter Time*

Dr. King's last speech reminds us to trust God, not man, for our dreams and our futures. Are there things that you hope to see happen in your lifetime? People you hope to see saved in Jesus? Relationships you hope to see healed or restored? Talk together about your hopes and dreams for your family, church, or country.

WHAT'S THE WORD?

Moses went up to Mount Nebo from the plains of Moab and climbed Pisgah Peak, which is across from Jericho. And the LORD showed him the whole land, from Gilead as far as Dan. . . . Then the LORD said to Moses, "This is the land I promised on oath to Abraham, Isaac, and Jacob when I said, 'I will give it to your descendants.' I have now allowed you to see it with your own eyes, but you will not enter the land."
DEUTERONOMY 34:1, 4

NO ONE RIGHTEOUS

A recent study found that if you put two quantities of food in front of an infant, the child almost always picks the larger quantity. Interesting, huh? Maybe it means babies can count, and we just don't know it. Maybe they're always hungry. Or perhaps this study showed that we're all born selfish.

Some people think that humankind is basically good. They want that to be true, because it would mean that as a people we could rise above injustice and sin and build a better world on our own. But here's reality: humanity is sinful from the inside out. We don't have to teach sin to children, because it comes naturally. We're innately selfish and sinful.

Paul explains this basic truth well in Romans 3 when he writes, "No one is righteous—not even one. No one is truly wise; no one is seeking God" (vv. 10-11). He goes on to say that "everyone has sinned; we all fall short of God's glorious standard" (v. 23). Why is this so important to understand? If we ignore this truth, we will try to find solutions to our problems within ourselves. And we'll forget that we need God's help as we fall flat in our own efforts to do right.

Humanity often tries to make the world better by itself. But as history shows over and over again, trying to do good things without God leads to death, corruption, and misery. We need to be aware of our sin so we can see our need for a Savior.

The next time you hear someone say that humankind is basically good, remember this truth. No one is righteous. Not even the sweet older couple in the front of the church on Sunday mornings or the little baby in the nursery. They may look perfect, but everyone needs Jesus.

DADDY-*Daughter Time*

Ask each other what you would do for a day if you had no consequences. Be truthful. What do your answers show you about your heart?

Find someone you respect who is much older, perhaps a grandparent or an older person in your church. Ask that person the same question. Then ask if he or she still struggles with sinning like he or she did at the age you are now. The answer may surprise you!

WHAT'S THE WORD?

As the Scriptures say, "No one is righteous—not even one. No one is truly wise; no one is seeking God." ROMANS 3:10-11

GUARD YOUR HEART

CAN you think of a more vital organ than your heart? While some organs aren't totally necessary to your survival (hello, appendix), the heart is a must-have helper. It pumps blood throughout the body to keep you alive. You probably knew that, but did you know there's a special wrap around your heart that stands guard over it? It's called the pericardium.

The outside of the pericardium protects the heart from the movement of other organs around it. This amazing sac also acts as a barrier to protect the heart from infections. On the inside, the pericardium contains a lubricant that surrounds the heart to reduce friction (and wear) on the muscle during its many thousands of contractions in your lifetime. This wrapping also limits how much your heart can expand, which protects it from overfilling with blood and bursting.

Think of the pericardium when you read this verse from Proverbs 4:23: "Guard your heart above all else, for it determines the course of your life." To guard your heart, you must protect it from the inside and from the outside—just like the pericardium. Our hearts are drawn to the things that we treasure (see Matthew 6:21). So we need to be cautious about what we set our minds on. When we allow something into our hearts that isn't godly, it's like the pericardium letting in an infection. But we must also guard our hearts from the inside. Emotions can course through us. If we allow our hearts to overflow with emotions, we can find ourselves feeling like our hearts might burst.

Just like we have to sometimes visit a doctor for a checkup on our hearts, we need to seek help from people who care about us to help us with our spiritual hearts. Don't be afraid to take advantage of wise family members and friends who can help you protect this precious source of life.

DADDY-*Daughter Time*

What parts of your heart and emotions feel vulnerable sometimes? Describe to your dad a time when you might have felt like your heart, figuratively speaking, might burst. What are some emotions or situations that you might need help with?

Talk about how you two can help each other to guard your hearts. Add this as a prayer request for your time together. Ask God to help you guard your heart, to keep your affections on good things, and to be open to help from others when you realize that your emotions may cloud your judgment.

WHAT'S THE WORD?

Guard your heart above all else, for it determines the course of your life.
PROVERBS 4:23

RUN LIKE THE WIND . . .
AND DON'T LOOK BACK!

WHY did Demosthenes cross the road? To get away from danger.

That's not a joke (which is probably why you didn't laugh). According to legend, the famous Greek orator, Demosthenes, served as an infantryman at the bloody Battle of Chaeronea. When his side was about to be overwhelmed, he fled the battle. Answering critics who accused him of cowardice for leaving a scene where thousands of fellow soldiers died, Demosthenes reportedly replied, "The man who runs away may fight again."

While debate continues in military circles as to the validity of Demosthenes's thinking for actual wartime, according to God's Word this is the perfect approach to take when a situation looks as if it may become dangerous to your soul. In the book of Amos, God pleads with his people to turn away from their idols and turn back to him. In his appeal, God warns them: "Do what is good and run from evil so that you may live!" (Amos 5:14). The Israelites didn't have to think too hard to remember an example from their past where running away was the right idea. In Genesis 39, Joseph, one of Jacob's sons, served as the top servant for Potiphar, the captain of Pharaoh's guard. Potiphar's wife, who should have been faithful to her husband, found Joseph attractive and made unwanted advances toward him. Joseph refused her affection, reminding her that he was trusted to care for all Potiphar had, including her. To accept her affection would be to sin against Potiphar and God. She continued to pressure him until Joseph finally ran away.

Although this wise flight from evil saved Joseph from sinning, he wound up in prison (but that's another story). The inescapable lesson for us is that escaping sin may require us to run away from it—not stand up to it. When we run away, we live to stand for what's right another day.

DADDY-*Daughter Time*

Does running away from evil seem like cowardice, courage, wisdom, or foolishness? Why? What are some situations that you two can think of where God's warning to run from evil would apply? Have you ever had to do that? Make a list of tempting or dangerous situations that you will promise to each other to run from.

WHAT'S THE WORD?

Do what is good and run from evil so that you may live! Then the LORD God of Heaven's Armies will be your helper, just as you have claimed. Hate evil and love what is good. AMOS 5:14-15

LIFE IN THE BLOOD

HAVE you ever cut your finger? What's the first thing you did? Some people pop their finger in their mouth to keep the wound clean. Others put pressure on the cut to stop the bleeding. There are also people who calmly watch their finger bleed, marveling at how blood works.

When you think about it, blood is pretty remarkable. Girls have around ten pints of blood in their bodies—that's as much liquid as thirteen cans of soda. Dads have about thirty-two ounces more. Blood serves a variety of roles in our bodies. It carries oxygen and nutrients to cells and carries away carbon dioxide and other wastes. God designed your body to constantly create red blood cells. But your blood also contains disease-fighting white blood cells and platelets that help your blood clot. Blood isn't just an oozy, gooey fluid. It's a living part of your body.

Before scientists discovered how blood worked or understood how it keeps us alive, God explained the importance of blood to the Israelites. In Leviticus 17:11, God said, "The life of the body is in its blood." He wanted them to understand the connection between blood and life because they needed to understand how blood was part of their relationship with him. In the Old Testament, God required a blood sacrifice for the payment of sins. And people had to continually make sacrifices.

But here's the amazing thing: when Jesus died on the cross, he spilled his blood as a payment for everybody's sins—once and for all. When we ask Jesus for forgiveness and put our trust in him, his blood sacrifice purifies us in God's eyes. Jesus could've called on legions of angels to save him. Instead he suffered a painful death, willingly giving his life and his blood, so we could have a relationship with God. Jesus understood the power of blood. By knowing him, we can too.

DADDY-*Daughter Time*

The next time someone in your family has a wound that needs a bandage, remember this verse. To help you, write it down and tape it to a box of bandages. As you thank the Lord for healing your cuts, scrapes, and wounds, also thank him for his death on the cross. Because of his blood, we can be pure before God.

WHAT'S THE WORD?

The life of the body is in its blood. . . . It is the blood, given in exchange for a life, that makes purification possible. LEVITICUS 17:11

DON'T LET THE
SUN GO DOWN

AS a young man prepared for his wedding, his grandfather walked into the room. The man's grandparents had a long—though sometimes admittedly rocky—marriage, but they had grown in their love even through the hard times. The young man asked him for his best piece of marriage advice. His grandfather replied without hesitation: "Never go to bed angry; always make up before you say good-night so you don't have to wake up worrying about it the next morning."

Have you ever been so upset at a friend that you didn't want to see or talk to her for a while? If you have, then you know that gnawing feeling that rolls around in your stomach until things are right. *Tick. Tock. Tick. Tock. Tick. Tock.* When a relationship is hurting, it's important to take care of the hurt as soon as possible. Don't think, *Oh, I'll just talk to him or her tomorrow.* Every day that goes by without fixing the problem adds to the pain, the hurt, and the misunderstanding.

The apostle Paul warns people about letting anger control them. In Ephesians 4:26-27, he says, "Don't let the sun go down while you are still angry, for anger gives a foothold to the devil." Paul's advice is simple: take care of it. Today. Tonight. But not tomorrow. The longer you're angry at someone, the more time Satan can make the problem bigger than it ever had to be.

The biggest obstacle to overcoming anger can be our pride. It's easy to convince ourselves that we have a right to be angry, that the other person should make the first move, or that tomorrow would be a better time to do something about it. We are never promised *tomorrow.* If we have today, let's do what we need to fix our broken relationships, to right what's wrong, and to get right with each other.

DADDY-*Daughter Time*

Cut up an apple with your dad. Eat all of it, except for one piece. Leave it on the counter overnight. What does it look like in the morning? If it's okay with your mom, leave the fruit out two or three more nights. Does it get better or worse? The heat of our anger is like the heat of the room on the fruit . . . it speeds up the rotting process.

Discuss how this applies to the verses in Ephesians. Commit together to not let the sun go down when you're angry with another person.

WHAT'S THE WORD?

"Don't sin by letting anger control you." Don't let the sun go down while you are still angry, for anger gives a foothold to the devil. EPHESIANS 4:26-27

WOULDN'T it be fun to freeze time? Some moments in life are so fun and so full of joy that it'd be nice to slow everything down and enjoy them even longer. But as the saying goes, "Time flies when you're having fun." So often your favorite moments can be over before you know it.

On the other hand, sometimes it feels like time has stopped. When you're bored or when hard times come, it can feel like the day . . . is never . . . going . . . to end. Weather might make a day feel longer too. According to some scientists, bad weather can add or take away microseconds from the length of a day. They say the earth's spinning speed can be affected by the weather or by other forces such as earthquakes or tsunamis. Of course, the total effect of these powerful forces only makes a difference of a few millionths of a second. When you add up all the little variations in speed over twelve months, they might add up to just *one second*.

God can do something way more impressive. As Joshua led an army to defend an ally from the attacks of five Amorite kings, God assured Joshua that he would have victory. During the battle, his enemies became confused. Joshua asked God to hold the sun and moon still until the battle was won. And God answered Joshua's prayer. The sun and moon froze in place for about a day.

That's way more than a few microseconds! As powerful as nature can seem, remember that creation is never more powerful than the Creator. If God's massive creation obeys the Creator, shouldn't we do the same?

DADDY-*Daughter Time*

Reminisce together about a day in your past that you wish could've lasted longer. What special memories made that day worth extra time? Ask your dad about a day that was special to him when he was about your age.

While we don't have the power to slow down time or make days longer, we can be aware that time goes quickly and never comes back. Enjoy some old family movies or photos, and thank God for the time that he has given you today with your dad.

WHAT'S THE WORD?

On the day the LORD gave the Amorites over to Israel, Joshua said to the LORD in the presence of Israel: "O sun, stand still over Gibeon, O moon, over the Valley of Aijalon." So the sun stood still, and the moon stopped, till the nation avenged itself on its enemies. . . . The sun stopped in the middle of the sky and delayed going down about a full day. JOSHUA 10:12-13 (NIV)

A SPECIAL PRAYER
OF BLESSING

HAS anyone ever said a prayer of blessing for you? It can be a powerful and moving experience to be blessed in prayer by someone who loves you. Many times in the Bible a person would declare a blessing on someone with a brief prayer. Often it was fathers blessing their children—usually at an important time in the family's life or history.

The Bible records some of the greatest, most meaningful blessings ever given. For example, when Jesus was baptized by his cousin, John the Baptist, God spoke a blessing out of the sky, saying, "This is my dearly loved Son, who brings me great joy" (Matthew 3:17). Talk about affirmation! In another blessing, Jacob blessed his grandsons Ephraim and Manasseh shortly before his death. He put his hands on his grandsons and said, "May the God before whom my grandfather Abraham and my father, Isaac, walked . . . may he bless these boys. May they preserve my name and the names of Abraham and Isaac. And may their descendants multiply greatly throughout the earth" (Genesis 48:15-16). Can you imagine the impact on these young men? They were reminded of their heritage, the faithfulness of God to their family, and the hope of God's promises yet to come!

The Bible records powerful blessings and, what's more, God even commands his priests to bless his people. In Numbers 6:22-26, the Lord told Moses to have Aaron and his sons speak this special blessing of protection over his people: "May the LORD bless you and protect you. May the LORD smile on you and be gracious to you. May the LORD show you his favor and give you his peace" (vv. 24-26). It's a simple but powerful blessing we can share with each other, too.

DADDY-*Daughter Time*

Dads, for the next week pray this prayer for your daughter every night. If you can't be home, call your daughter to give her this blessing. Daughters, you can bless your dad with this prayer before he goes to work in the mornings.

After doing this for a while, talk about how this blessing affected each of you. Try writing your own prayer of blessing for each other that you can keep with you at all times.

WHAT'S THE WORD?

The LORD said to Moses, "Tell Aaron and his sons to bless the people of Israel with this special blessing: 'May the LORD bless you and protect you. May the LORD smile on you and be gracious to you. May the LORD show you his favor and give you his peace.'" NUMBERS 6:22-26

April 12   # TASTE AND SEE

IN Disney's Pixar movie *Ratatouille*, Remy tries to show to his brother, Emile, the joys of eating with the unique flavors of cheese and grapes.

> Remy: Close your eyes. Now take a bite of . . . [Emile swallows the first bite of cheese whole.] No, no, no! Don't just hork it down! . . . Chew it slowly; only think about the taste. . . . See? . . . Creamy, salty, sweet—an oaky nuttiness. . . . Now taste this. [Remy hands him a grape.] . . . Whole different thing, right? Sweet, crisp, slight tang on the finish. . . . Now—try them together! [Emile enjoys the combined taste, realizing differences from the individual tastes.] . . . Now imagine every great taste in the world being combined into infinite combinations—tastes that no one has tried yet—discoveries to be made!

God blessed us with five senses—touch, sight, hearing, smell, and taste—so we can enjoy his creation. But our ability to taste may be the most personal. When two different people look at a lake, they both see a lake. But put the same meal in front of them and they will differ in how they eat and what they eat based partly on their sense of taste.

David once wrote, "Taste and see that the LORD is good" (Psalm 34:8). Tasting something new gives us bigger perspectives, sometimes surprising us. Ever notice how small children are afraid to try a new food because of how it *looks* to them? But when they taste it, a sense of joy and awe can spread on their faces (unless they don't like it, which usually results in them spitting it out).

To taste and see God's goodness is to do more than just think about him. We should be experiencing his goodness in our lives. When we slow down and "taste" God, we'll find that he's never bitter. He only adds richness, goodness, and sweetness to life.

DADDY-*Daughter Time*

Go to the grocery store and buy two foods that you've never tasted before. You might try a new fruit, a type of cheese, a piece of chocolate, or a different kind of potato chip. Go home and try them. Describe the tastes to each other. Now combine them into one bite, and describe that new taste and how unique it is.

Are there some parts of God's Word and his character that you've never tasted? Maybe you can combine "flavors." Discuss two of your favorite verses and consider how the truths of those verses together give you a unique way of knowing God better.

WHAT'S THE WORD?

Taste and see that the LORD is good. Oh, the joys of those who take refuge in him!
PSALM 34:8

A HUMBLED KING

HAS a work of art, a song, or a movie caused you to have an emotional or physical response? A tender scene in a movie can make us cry. But there's one song that's guaranteed to make us stand to our feet.

On this day in 1742, George Frideric Handel's *Messiah* premiered in Dublin, Ireland, in honor of Easter. Less than a year later, this musical work of art was first performed in London before an audience that included King George II. According to lore, when the majestic tones of the "Hallelujah Chorus" began, King George II stood to honor the King of kings. Naturally, everyone in the hall followed his example. Thus began a tradition that remains to this day: all concertgoers stand for the duration of this majestic choral piece that repeats "Hallelujah, for the Lord God omnipotent reigneth."

King George II wasn't the only person to have a physical reaction to *Messiah*. As Handel was composing this piece, friends walked into the room and found him weeping. When asked what was wrong, Handel explained that he was overcome by the awesome majesty of God, saying, "I did think I saw all heaven before me and the great God himself."

Handel wrote this masterpiece in just twenty-four days, and it's caused people to take a stand for God ever since. You can honor God by standing for the "Hallelujah Chorus" (which is usually played around Christmas now), but God desires for you to stand up for him in your everyday words and actions. Revelation 19:6 describes a scene that will happen when the Lord returns. At that time a great crowd will stand and shout, "Praise the LORD! For the Lord our God, the Almighty, reigns." Don't wait to take a stand for God. It might not always be easy, but if you do, maybe you'll cause others to stand with you . . . like King George II.

DADDY-*Daughter Time*

Talk with your dad about a time when you or he had to stand alone. Someday, everyone will honor the Lord as King of kings. Until then, resolve together to look for ways to stand up for him and tell people how wonderful he is— whether you have to do it alone or not.

WHAT'S THE WORD?

From the throne came a voice that said, "Praise our God, all his servants, all who fear him, from the least to the greatest." Then I heard again what sounded like the shout of a vast crowd or the roar of mighty ocean waves or the crash of loud thunder: "Praise the LORD! For the Lord our God, the Almighty, reigns." REVELATION 19:5-6

April 14

YOU'VE probably seen a lot of images of orphans living in other countries. But did you know that 100,000 children in the United States are considered legal orphans? They live in the foster-care system and hope to one day have a family to call their own. That sounds like a lot of children—and it is. But there are over 300,000 churches in the United States. If members from just a third of those churches followed the teaching of James 1:27, then every orphan in the United States might have a home. That verse says, "Pure and genuine religion in the sight of God the Father means caring for orphans and widows in their distress."

Being without a family can be a distressing and lonely life. But God is a God of community. He doesn't want people to stay lonely. His desire is that Christians would care for those who need it most: orphans and widows. Maybe that's why King David once said that "God places the lonely in families" (Psalm 68:6).

When we put our trust in what Jesus did through his death and resurrection, God actually adopts us into his family. In Ephesians, we read that "God decided in advance to adopt us into his own family by bringing us to himself through Jesus Christ" (Ephesians 1:5). The verse also points out that it gives God "great pleasure" to adopt us into his family. God loves to see families open their homes to the lonely. Is it easy? No. Important? Clearly, yes.

DADDY-*Daughter Time*

Do you know any families who hope to adopt a child or be foster parents? Make a list of them and pray together for their families. Adjusting to adoption, while a beautiful act of love, is not always easy, and those families need our prayers.

Consider how your family might encourage and support families who are trying to adopt. Perhaps you could help raise money for the adoption costs or simply develop a network of friends and family who would join you in praying regularly for these adopting families. See how many people you can encourage to help "place the lonely in families."

WHAT'S THE WORD?

Father to the fatherless, defender of widows—this is God, whose dwelling is holy. God places the lonely in families. PSALM 68:5-6

NOT TOO IMPORTANT
TO HELP

TRADITIONALLY in the United States, today is "Tax Day." Every April 15, income taxes come due. So it's natural that there's one thing on most adults' minds today: money. *How much do I have? How much did I make? How much did I give away to charities? How much tax do I owe?*

For some people, money is on their minds all the time. When they think about their assets, they're really answering the question: *How important am I?* They define themselves by their wealth. If they have a lot of money, they feel important. Less wealth damages their self-image.

Fortunately, that's not how God sees us. To him, everyone is important. Jesus died to give everyone in the world an opportunity to live eternally with him.

Today is also the anniversary of a tragedy that has inspired books, movies, and oceanic expeditions. On this day in 1912, the "unsinkable" luxury ship RMS *Titanic* sank on its initial voyage from England to New York. With only twenty lifeboats to serve over 2,200 passengers, the ship's crew continuously cried out, "Women and children first!" Just over seven hundred people survived.

Tales of heroism and self-sacrifice following the *Titanic's* strike of an iceberg have become legendary. Ida Straus was given the chance to board a lifeboat. She and her husband, Isidor, owned the famous Macy's department store in New York City. Because of their wealth, many people considered them to be very important. But Isidor didn't put himself above anybody else. He refused to board a lifeboat as long as women and children were still on board the ship. He encouraged his wife to escape, but she said, "We have lived together for many years; where you go, I go." They were last seen together sitting on the boat deck until a wave engulfed them.

No amount of money could make Isidor and Ida feel more important than anyone else, nor less dedicated to each other. Similarly, God tells us to remember that we are never too important to help someone in need (see Galatians 6:3). As Christians, one of our greatest callings is to help those around us.

DADDY-*Daughter Time*

Make a list of things, besides money, that make people feel important. Talk about how important those things *really* are to a person's value.

Imagine if you and your dad had been on the RMS *Titanic*. Would you have had the courage to give up a seat on a lifeboat to save someone's life?

WHAT'S THE WORD?

If you think you are too important to help someone, you are only fooling yourself. You are not that important. GALATIANS 6:3

TO FORGIVE FOR GOOD

HAS a friend ever said she forgives you for something you did but then acted like she was still holding a grudge? It makes you wonder if she ever really forgave you in the first place. The deeper the hurt, the harder it is to truly forgive.

Joseph's older brothers thought this might be true in their case, because they had hurt their brother in the worst way. They sold him into slavery and lied to their father by pretending that Joseph had been killed. In Genesis 45, Joseph, now an Egyptian ruler, revealed himself to his stunned brothers who had come to Egypt years later for help. Joseph quickly added that he forgave them, because God had used their actions to send him to Egypt and save the lives of many people during a famine.

But in Genesis 50, after their father had died, the brothers were once again afraid of their brother. They figured that Joseph would now have his revenge, so they told him that their father had instructed them to beg Joseph for forgiveness for their sins. Joseph broke down and wept. He grieved that his brothers were still afraid about something he'd forgiven them for long ago. He assured them, again, that they had nothing to fear from him and that he would continue to take care of them and their families.

Joseph treated his brothers the way God treats us. In Psalm 103:12, David writes that when God forgives, he sends our sins "as far from us as the east is from the west." And in Isaiah 43:25, God says that he "will blot out your sins for my own sake and will never think of them again." When we forgive, we should forgive like God—and Joseph—forgiving for good and not holding a grudge. Thank God, we do not need to worry about him bringing up old sins against us. We will never hear him say, "Well, I forgave you, but I just can't get over it. . . . You'll have to pay for that again." Forgiven for good is forgiven forever.

DADDY-*Daughter Time*

If either of you has ever had someone hold a grudge against you, discuss what that feels like. What does that do to your relationship with that person? Do you avoid him or her or still hang out together?

Consider whether or not you have grudgingly "forgiven" someone but haven't let go of the hurt. Ask God together to help you forgive like he does.

WHAT'S THE WORD?

I [God]—yes, I alone—will blot out your sins for my own sake and will never think of them again. ISAIAH 43:25

NO VICTIMLESS CRIMES

April 17

THE cookies looked delicious. Mom had baked a fresh batch of chocolate chip cookies the night before, and they were almost overflowing from the cookie jar. Joanna really wanted one. She hadn't had time to eat all her lunch at school, and dinner was still a couple of hours away. *It's not going to hurt anyone,* Joanna thought. *I'll still eat a good dinner, and nobody's going to miss one cookie.*

In Joanna's mind, it was a "victimless crime." Nobody would get hurt, so it really wasn't wrong . . . well, except for the fact that Mom had said to stay out of the cookie jar.

A lot of Christians think like Joanna. They believe if their sins don't hurt anybody but themselves, then they're no big deal. Besides, they're forgiven, so these little sins only make God's grace more evident. The apostle Paul had a strong answer for this kind of thinking. He said, "Since we have died to sin, how can we continue to live in it? . . . Do not let sin control the way you live; do not give in to sinful desires" (Romans 6:2, 12).

All sins—even little ones that nobody finds out about—affect God and our relationship with him. In Isaiah 53, the prophet explains that there are no victimless crimes. Any sin against God's laws must be paid. And this prophecy about Jesus says all our sins are laid on him. Jesus, God's only Son, died for our sins. Every time we disobey or act selfishly a consequence is created. Are you glad you have a Savior who was willing to pay the price for every single one of your "crimes"?

DADDY-*Daughter Time*

Think about things that are wrong to do but don't seem to hurt anyone else. Make a list of those things and talk about why you think no one gets hurt.

Now next to each one, write the word *Jesus*. Remember that he is the one who paid with his life for each and every sin we commit. Ask the Lord to help you remember that for every sin there is a penalty. Thank him for paying that penalty for you, and ask him to help you avoid sinful desires.

WHAT'S THE WORD?

Do not let sin control the way you live; do not give in to sinful desires.   ROMANS 6:12

LOOKING THE PART

"YOU gotta look the part! Dress for the job you want, not the job you have." This advice has been repeated for years in schools and businesses. If you want to succeed, you have to *look* like you're already a success. If you want to be popular, you have to wear all the right clothes. Is that really true? Maybe we should be asking the question, is that right?

Proverbs 13:7 says, "Some who are poor pretend to be rich; others who are rich pretend to be poor." At first that can seem like a strange verse—some people are obsessed with making a good impression, while the others show humility. Or maybe the rich person here is just being thrifty.

Sam Walton started the giant discount stores Walmart and Sam's Club. When he died in 1992, he was one of the richest men in the world, worth over $23 billion. But he lived a humble life. He flew coach instead of first class. He wore the same clothes that were sold in his stores. And he always drove an old 1979 pickup truck. At a museum in Arkansas honoring his life, a sign displays the answer Sam gave when asked why he drove an old truck: "I just don't believe a big showy lifestyle is appropriate. . . . What am I supposed to haul my dogs around in, a Rolls-Royce?"

Perhaps that verse in Proverbs means God doesn't want us "putting on airs." Instead of trying to look like we have more than we do, God wants us to be humble, to be ourselves, and to follow his will for our lives. Jesus, the Son of God, was with the heavenly Father when the universe was created. He lived in the splendor of heaven. Yet he came to earth to live the simple life of a carpenter's son, teaching and healing and loving a lost humanity. He was wealthier than anyone could ever imagine, but he never made anyone feel like they couldn't come to him. Maybe that's what God wants us to show the world through our humility as well.

DADDY-*Daughter Time*

Have you ever noticed people who are obsessed with how wealthy they are or how wealthy they look? Discuss how those people tend to make others around them feel.

If you were to have one million dollars tomorrow, what would you buy? Consider how your answers show you what's most important in your own heart. Ask God to give you the courage to live humbly and to be yourself.

WHAT'S THE WORD?

Some who are poor pretend to be rich; others who are rich pretend to be poor.
PROVERBS 13:7

HANNAH'S PROMISE

"O LORD of Heaven's Armies, if you will look upon my sorrow and answer my prayer and give me a son, then I will give him back to you."

Wow! That's quite a promise. But that's exactly what Hannah said to God in 1 Samuel 1:11. Hannah was a woman with a deep desire to be a mommy. But after years of marriage to Elkanah, she was childless. Others teased her cruelly year after year, especially during special visits to the Tabernacle. Instead of being understanding, Elkanah simply marveled at Hannah's sadness. He even told her that she shouldn't be downhearted because, although she had no children, she had him. Elkanah clearly loved Hannah, but he seemed to really struggle to know how to comfort her aching heart.

During a trip to the Tabernacle, Hannah pleaded with the Lord for a child. Eli, the priest, saw her praying. After Eli realized Hannah was pouring her heart out to the Lord, he blessed her with the promise that God would answer her prayer. And God did.

Hannah had a boy. She named him Samuel. Her greatest hope had come true. Instead of being tempted to go back on her promise to God, Hannah kept her word. When Samuel was a few years old, Hannah returned to Eli and dedicated her son to God's work in the Tabernacle (see 1 Samuel 1:26-28). Though it may have been hard, she did not hesitate.

Every year at the time of sacrifices, Hannah brought a new coat for Samuel. But she never tried to take him back. Eli again blessed Hannah with a new promise that she would have more children. She ended up having three more sons and two daughters.

DADDY-*Daughter Time*

What promises have you made that were hard to keep? Did you keep them? Discuss how hard it would be to make Hannah's promise. Talk about how Hannah's promise, and her willingness to go through with it, was like what God did for us. After all, he gave his only Son, Jesus, so we might have eternal life!

When you pray, don't be afraid to ask God for your truest heart desire. He always answers.

WHAT'S THE WORD?

"Sir, do you remember me?" Hannah asked. "I am the woman who stood here several years ago praying to the LORD. I asked the LORD to give me this boy, and he has granted my request. Now I am giving him to the LORD, and he will belong to the LORD his whole life." And they worshiped the LORD there. 1 SAMUEL 1:26-28

WHEN DAD GETS HOME

AMANDA knew she should've been working on her history homework. But the new website was much more fun. Secret worlds. Exciting relationships. Complex challenges. All her friends already had characters, and the website said it was free. Well, she did have to enter in her parents' credit-card number. But it wouldn't be charged. Everything seemed to be going well . . . until the credit-card bill came.

"What's this?" Dad said, walking into Amanda's room. He pointed at line after line of charges from a website.

"But . . . but it was supposed to be free," Amanda said, starting to cry.

"What was free?" Dad said. "There are hundreds of dollars of charges. How did you get our credit-card number?"

"I went into Mom's purse," Amanda said. "I'm so, so sorry."

"Oh, you'll be sorry," Dad said. "You won't be seeing an allowance for a long, long time. And you're grounded."

Amanda's predicament demonstrates not only the fear we have of being disciplined, but also the shame we feel when we're caught sinning. Even when we fool ourselves into thinking our actions aren't that bad, we instantly recognize sin when we are caught in it.

The Bible tells us that someday the Lord Jesus will come back to earth. The apostle John urges Christians to live in good fellowship with God so they won't be ashamed when Jesus returns (see 1 John 2:28). God wants us to live without fear, without shame, and ready to welcome Christ's return with courage!

DADDY-*Daughter Time*

Surprises can be fun. Have you ever had a surprise birthday party? Or maybe you've visited family and surprised them because they didn't know you were coming? Talk about what's fun, and sometimes not fun, about these surprises.

Imagine that Jesus came back tonight. Talk about what you would want him to find you doing. Discuss some of the choices you made today. Did your actions reflect your faith in Christ? Pray together that the Lord will help you remember that Jesus can come at any time as you choose how to live each and every day.

WHAT'S THE WORD?

Dear children, remain in fellowship with Christ so that when he returns, you will be full of courage and not shrink back from him in shame. 1 JOHN 2:28

LIPSTICK AND RINGS FOR PIGS

April 21

YOU can't put lipstick on a pig. Actually, you can, but you just get a silly-looking swine. Have you ever heard the saying about putting lipstick on a pig? It means you can try to dress up something that's bad to make it seem okay, but you won't be able to fool anyone. It still stinks.

The expression has been used about untrustworthy politicians attempting to get elected, crumbling buildings that should be demolished instead of redecorated, and clunker cars that should be scrapped rather than fixed up. It's kind of a cool expression, especially because it originated in the Bible. The wise King Solomon writes, "A beautiful woman who lacks discretion is like a gold ring in a pig's snout" (Proverbs 11:22). The idea is the same: a beautiful woman who doesn't act like a lady cannot hide her foolishness. That doesn't mean she won't try.

Actually, we're all in a similar boat. Because we are sinful people, we constantly try to make ourselves look better. We make excuses for missing homework, hide wrongdoings, and try to put ourselves in the best possible light. Instead of trying to apply lipstick on a pig, we should work harder to show discretion. Being discreet also means having modesty about our bodies. We need to make wise decisions and be in control of our actions.

Some TV shows and movies make it look fun to be unrestrained, wild, and free. But look a little closer behind the glamour and you'll often find a pig with lipstick and gold rings. And it's going to stink.

DADDY-*Daughter Time*

Take out some markers or crayons and see who can draw the best pig. Decorate your pigs with lipstick and gold rings. Do you still see a pig? Talk about how people's choices affect their true beauty.

Then look up the meaning of the word *discreet* in a dictionary or online. Make a list of people in your life who show discretion. Are those the same people you can count on for advice, go to in times of trouble, or join with in celebration? Remember where true beauty comes from . . . and stay away from pigs.

WHAT'S THE WORD?

A beautiful woman who lacks discretion is like a gold ring in a pig's snout.
PROVERBS 11:22

PROTECTION OR WORSHIP?

"IT'S not easy being green." Kermit the Frog may have said that years ago, but today everybody wants to be green. From energy-efficient cars to recycled clothing, green is in. This trend is often traced back to this day in 1970. That's when US Senator Gaylord Nelson started the very first Earth Day.

Earth Day began as a way for people concerned about the environment to organize, teach, and protest. It brought together millions of citizens who were worried about air and water pollution, traffic, wildlife, and plant health. At first glance, this looks like a great idea. Caring for the earth is wise. God created it to provide everything we need to survive: air, water, shelter, food, etc. The first chapter of the Bible even commands that we take care of this world. God told Adam to tend and watch over Eden. Then after Adam and Eve saw each other, God said, "Fill the earth and govern it" (Genesis 1:28). That was no small task!

But just as God tells us in the Bible to be good stewards of his planet, he also warns against worshiping creation. In the book of Romans, we read that humanity has "worshiped and served the things God created instead of the Creator himself" (1:25). And that's where problems can spring up with something even as well intentioned as Earth Day. Some people who believe in going green act like people are the earth's biggest problem, instead of God's greatest creation. Sure, humans have caused some environmental issues, but we've also learned about the consequences of past actions and come up with solutions. As caretakers of God's creation, we should strive to improve the environment while also being productive in life.

Caring for the earth is fantastic and pleases God. But we must be cautious not to substitute our love for God and respect for human life with a worshipful love of the Earth.

DADDY-*Daughter Time*

Talk together about what parts of the environment mean the most to your family. How do you see God's handiwork in creation? One way is to notice the order in creation and how everything works together in harmony. Help the planet and make it more beautiful by planting flowers or buying a houseplant. When you care for God's creation, it pleases him.

Read the chapters of Job 38–39 together. Consider what God's questions to Job tell us about God's concern and care for creation.

WHAT'S THE WORD?

God blessed [the human beings] and said, "Be fruitful and multiply. Fill the earth and govern it. Reign over the fish in the sea, the birds in the sky, and all the animals that scurry along the ground." GENESIS 1:28

FICKLE TASTES

IT'S the real thing. It adds life. It opens happiness. Do you know what *it* is? Well, if you believe the ad slogans, then you'll say it's Coca-Cola. The formula for Coke was invented in 1886. Six years later, the Coca-Cola Company launched and enjoyed decades of success with its original—and very secret—soda syrup formula.

But on this date in 1985, the company released a brand-new version of Coke with an all-new formula. The company had secretly tested the new formula all around the United States. Taste test after taste test confirmed people preferred the new formula over original Coke . . . and even over their biggest rival, Pepsi. So when new Coke hit the market, it was an overnight success, right?

Wrong. After three months of angry reactions from customers, "Coca-Cola Classic" brought the old formula back to the public. When people didn't know the name of the soda in the cup, they loved the new Coke formula. But in the end, the better taste didn't matter. Customers longed for what they knew best.

It seems not much has changed in thousands of years. The Israelites prayed to be free from slavery in Egypt. God dramatically saved them and promised them a better home. You'd think everybody would be excited about God's plan. Not really. The complaining started early. First, they needed more water. Then the food was bland. Fear of other nations crept in. Pretty soon the people decided they'd be better off back in Egypt . . . in slavery (see Numbers 14:2-4).

God's people must have forgotten what life in Egypt tasted like. They must have ignored that God's Promised Land would flow with milk and honey—being far sweeter than they could imagine. People are fickle. They change their minds quickly, forget priorities, and complain easily. Just ask Moses and Aaron or the people who run the Coca-Cola Company.

DADDY-*Daughter Time*

Discuss whether or not you think it's easy to trust God and wait for his best. Pray to God that your tastes won't change and you'll always thirst for him.

Just for fun, do your own blind taste test. Pick out two or three similar flavored drinks (root beer, iced tea, cola). Have a family member secretly pour them in glasses and see which one you like best. Did your picks surprise you?

WHAT'S THE WORD?

Their voices rose in a great chorus of protest against Moses and Aaron. "If only we had died in Egypt, or even here in the wilderness!" they complained. . . . "Wouldn't it be better for us to return to Egypt?" Then they plotted among themselves, "Let's choose a new leader and go back to Egypt!" NUMBERS 14:2-4

April 24

WHAT do our siblings, our parents, our friends, and our family members have in common? *They're all human.* Correct. They might also share other traits. But one thing's for certain: sooner or later, because all humans are sinful, they will disappoint or hurt you. *Wow, what a downer,* you might be thinking. *Is there any good news?*

Yes. Because we know people will hurt us, we don't have to let that ruin the relationship. It's easy to get caught up in an emotional situation. Tempers flare, tears flow, hurtful words are exchanged. God created our emotions, but he doesn't want us to be ruled by them. When we focus on a present problem, we can neglect to see the future. And in the future, we're all going to need our friends and family. Proverbs 17:17 reminds us that "a friend is always loyal, and a brother is born to help in time of need." King Solomon understood that we need our friends and family throughout our lives. That's why we need to protect our relationships with them, even when they let us down.

Dads have a special responsibility to help daughters protect those relationships. That's why they often get in the middle of disagreements between siblings and other family members to offer comfort and advice. Sometimes it's easier for dads to have a forward-looking view of how important those relationships will be in the future.

So protect and appreciate your relationships. Keeping relationships healthy today is important to your tomorrow.

DADDY-*Daughter Time*

Talk to some adults, including your dad, about how important their childhood friends and siblings are to them. Do they regret things from the past that caused them to lose a friend or be distant from family?

Make a list of the friends and family that mean the most to you today. Ask God and your dad to help you protect those relationships and build them up so that they can help you in the future and so you can be there to help them, too.

WHAT'S THE WORD?

A friend is always loyal, and a brother is born to help in time of need.
PROVERBS 17:17

THE BEST THINGS TO SAY

ROMANS 12:15 instructs Christians to "be happy with those who are happy, and weep with those who weep." For many of us, it's far easier to be happy when others are rejoicing than to share in someone's sorrow. One of the reasons is that it's difficult to know what to say to someone who's sad. Want to know a secret? Sometimes it's best to say nothing at all.

Consider the story of Job. God gave Satan permission to test Job's loyalty by allowing him to suffer. After losing animals, workers, and all his children, Job was struck with painful sores all over his body. He was in great pain. Three friends came to visit Job and comfort him. For seven days and nights, they simply sat with Job and said nothing. They saw how great his suffering was and didn't know what to say (see Job 2:11-13). That's a helpful example for us as we try to comfort those close to us.

We don't have to say all the right words. Just like in a movie theater, silence can be golden. Just being with someone shows that person that you love him or her no matter what. So don't shy away from a friend who's sad. You might know someone who lost a grandparent, had a pet die, or has parents going through a divorce. It's during those times that people need friends most of all. God might give you exactly the right thing to say. But even if you say nothing at all, be there for your friends and "weep with those who weep."

DADDY-*Daughter Time*

Can you remember a time when you were so sad that you didn't want to talk? Just a hug from a family member or friend can mean so much as you sense the other person's love for you. If you can think of a time that a hug helped, let that person know.

Then look together for an opportunity to "be there" for someone who's going through a rough time. Plan to take some food or flowers to that person, and let the hurting individual be himself or herself while you are there, assuring him or her of your love.

WHAT'S THE WORD?

When three of Job's friends heard of the tragedy he had suffered, they got together and traveled from their homes to comfort and console him. . . . When they saw Job from a distance, they scarcely recognized him. . . . Then they sat on the ground with him for seven days and nights. No one said a word to Job, for they saw that his suffering was too great for words. JOB 2:11-13

A FASHIONABLE WAY TO HELP

WHAT to wear? For some girls, it's the most difficult decision they'll make all day. But Allyson Ahlstrom knew other girls who really didn't have much to wear, and sometimes their clothing options caused them to be teased. The fourteen-year-old didn't just see the problem; she did something about it. In 2010 she started a project called Threads for Teens that benefits underprivileged girls in her city. Allyson didn't want to do a clothing drive to get hand-me-downs. She wanted these teenagers to have the latest fashions.

Allyson started by sending out more than four hundred letters and e-mails to clothing manufacturers to ask for donations. Soon donations overwhelmed Allyson's home. She talked to the city about her idea and was given a store—rent free—for her project. All the display racks and fixtures were donated by a local department store. In less than a year, Allyson's idea had become reality. Most of the girls who come to Threads for Teens are referred there by social workers. Many of these teenagers live in group homes or foster care. Others come from homeless situations. Each girl is allowed to choose two head-to-toe outfits—for free! Allyson stocks jeans, dresses, jewelry, purses, shoes, shirts, even prom attire. Due to their situations in life, some girls walk into Threads for Teens feeling worthless, but they all walk out feeling like a million bucks.

The Bible talks a lot about helping the needy. Some of those verses inspired Allyson to start her project. In Leviticus 23:22, God's people are told to not harvest the grain from the edges of their fields. "Leave it for the poor and the foreigners living among you," God says. Basically, God is telling his people to leave a little of their surplus to bless the needy among them.

DADDY-*Daughter Time*

Do you have any surpluses in your life? You might not have a lot of money, but you might have some time to help. You don't need to create a cool store like Allyson (although Allyson's dream is to have Threads for Teens stores in all fifty states). Maybe you could gather canned goods from your neighbors to donate to a food bank. Perhaps your family could do a yard sale and give the money to help the homeless. No matter how big or small your contribution might be, God can use you to help others.

WHAT'S THE WORD?

When you harvest the crops of your land, do not harvest the grain along the edges of your fields, and do not pick up what the harvesters drop. Leave it for the poor and the foreigners living among you. I am the LORD your God. LEVITICUS 23:22

DEPENDING AND WAITING ON GOD

"JUST wait." It sounds so easy. But if you've ever been excited about an upcoming event, then you know waiting takes a lot of effort. As the pages of the Bible unfold, one of the themes that pops up over and over again is the difficulty people have with trusting in God's promises and waiting patiently for his timing.

- Abraham had trouble waiting for a son when God had already promised he'd have more descendants than the stars in the sky.
- The Israelites had trouble waiting for the Promised Land.
- King Saul had trouble waiting for God's prophet and blessing before battle.

When we look back on these stories, they can almost make us laugh to ourselves. *Why can't they just trust God?* we wonder. *It's plain to see that he can do what he said he would!*

In Luke 2, there's a fantastic example of two people who truly trusted that God would be true to his word. When Jesus was presented as a newborn in the Temple, a righteous man named Simeon was led by God's Spirit to be there. God had told Simeon that he would not die before seeing the Messiah. When Simeon saw Jesus, he rejoiced that the prophecy had come true, and he blessed Jesus. Then Anna, a widow who had dedicated her life to worship and prayer in the Temple, saw what happened with Simeon and joined him in rejoicing that the Messiah had finally come. She talked about Jesus to everyone—telling them the long-awaited Messiah had come.

Early on in God's Word, we're told that he is faithfully loving and merciful. Lamentations 3:25-26 says, "The LORD is good to those who depend on him, to those who search for him. So it is good to wait quietly for salvation from the LORD."

That sounds easy (and a little obvious), but sometimes waiting is hard.

DADDY-*Daughter Time*

Trusting your dad is similar to trusting God. Talk with him about how he feels when he knows you trust him, and how hard it is for him when he knows you doubt him.

Memorize the verses below. Remind each other of these truths when you struggle to have patience with God and each other.

WHAT'S THE WORD?

The LORD is good to those who depend on him, to those who search for him. So it is good to wait quietly for salvation from the LORD. LAMENTATIONS 3:25-26

April 28 **"YOU'RE THE DIAMOND . . ."**

"AM I beautiful, Daddy?"

Daughters have asked this question of their fathers for ages. The desire to be beautiful is in the heart of every little girl. Naturally, the first man in her life, her dad, has the privilege of helping her see and appreciate the beauty God has given her.

The Bible has a lot to say about beauty: it can be diminished by our actions; it can be distracting when it becomes too important; it comes from both the inside and the outside; inner beauty is more important.

Becca constantly asked her daddy about her beauty. After a while, her dad noticed that her questions seemed to be about what made her beautiful, not *if* she was beautiful.

"Does this dress make me pretty?"

"Do you think this hairstyle makes me pretty?"

"Do you like my necklace? Does it make me pretty?"

Eventually it dawned on him that she thought her beauty came from things. So one day he sat down with Becca and pulled out her mother's engagement ring.

"Do you see this ring?" he said. "The band of gold is pretty, right?"

Becca agreed.

"What about the diamond? Is it beautiful and valuable?"

She agreed again.

"If you took this diamond and put it on any other ring, what would it do to that ring?"

"It would make the ring even more beautiful!" she said.

"That's right. Honey, you need to know that you are the diamond, not the ring. You *are* beauty. Your smile and personality make what you wear and how you style your hair more beautiful, not the other way around. You are the jewel. Don't confuse the two. Be yourself, and you will make everything around you more beautiful."

DADDY-*Daughter Time*

How does it make you feel when your dad says you're beautiful? Describe to him how important it is to hear those words from him.

Make a list of what you think enhances how your dad looks, while he makes a list of the things that bring out your beauty. Now make lists for each other of the things that make the other attractive because of who they are and what they do. Share your lists with each other. And remind each other often, "You're the diamond, not the ring!" God looks at us like jewels (see Isaiah 49:18), so we should look at each other in the same way.

WHAT'S THE WORD?

"Look around you and see, for all your children will come back to you. As surely as I live," says the LORD, "they will be like jewels or bridal ornaments for you to display."
ISAIAH 49:18

RIGHT ON TIME! *April 29*

DID you ever wonder why Jesus was born two thousand years ago instead of much earlier? Or much later? Why did God pick that year to send Jesus to save humanity? Timing is everything. Often it seems our lives are ruled by time. We have schedules for everything. Classes start and stop at particular times. Jobs require workers to show up and leave at set times.

Timing is also important to comedy. People find jokes funny not just because of what's said but how a joke is told. If a comedian waits just long enough before giving a punch line, the audience has a chance to think about the humor, guess the end, and enjoy the delivery of the joke more than the joke itself. Time can also seem random. Things happen that change our lives in an instant. Then there's that whole "falling back" and "springing forward" that we do with our clocks every year.

But God is never random with his timing. While we wait and wonder what will happen next in life, God precisely manages time. Knowing that the Master of the universe controls all the timing in our lives should give us great comfort. God even tells us that when we don't give up doing what's right, "at just the right time we will reap a harvest of blessing" (Galatians 6:9). And in his master plan of timing, God chose the very precise moment—the very best time—to send Jesus to earth to die for us so that we could escape our sin and live forever (see Galatians 4:4-5). We may not understand why God chose that timing or why he chooses the timing he does with our lives. But we can always be confident that his timing is best.

DADDY-*Daughter Time*

Dads, can you recall a time when God provided something at just the right moment? Discuss what that did for your faith and whether or not it was hard to be patient.

Talk about how hard it must have been for the Jews to wait for the Messiah. How will today's devotional thought help you wait on the Lord?

WHAT'S THE WORD?
When the right time came, God sent his Son, born of a woman, subject to the law. God sent him to buy freedom for us who were slaves to the law, so that he could adopt us as his very own children. GALATIANS 4:4-5

STOP BEING A BABY

BABIES have quite a life. All they have to do is cry, and people come running to meet their every need. *Are you hungry? Do you want to play? Are you bored?* Babies don't even have to get up to go to the bathroom. Okay, that's kind of gross. But a lot about a baby's life can look pretty appealing—lounge around in pajamas, smile every now and then, and you're the star of the family.

But think about what would happen if you were stuck being a baby. How frustrating would that be? You wouldn't be able to express yourself, read, do art, play sports, or learn to drive a car. The Bible compares Christians who don't grow in their faith to babies. Hebrews 5:12 says, "You have been believers so long now that you ought to be teaching others. Instead, you need someone to teach you again the basic things about God's word. You are like babies who need milk and cannot eat solid food." If you're stuck drinking milk, you're never going to grow strong. Progressing to solid food is part of growing up. Plus, babies don't know right from wrong when it comes to what they eat. Stickers? *Yes, please.* Paper? *I'll have seconds.* Books? *The pictures look scrumptious!*

No wonder parents feed babies milk, formula, and mushy baby food for so long. Babies just don't know yet what's good and bad. The same is true for us. As we grow in our understanding of God and his Word, we'll be hungry for better, healthier knowledge—like food for our souls. Then we'll know how to live wiser, happier, and more productive lives.

DADDY-*Daughter Time*

Just for fun, try taste testing jars of baby food while wearing a blindfold. See if you and your dad can guess the flavors without looking. Is that the kind of food you'd want to go back to eating?

Look together at the list of teachings in Hebrews 6:1-3. Pick a teaching that you and your dad could explore. Check out what some online commentaries and teachers have to say about that subject. Always strive to grow in your faith, and leave the baby stuff behind.

WHAT'S THE WORD?

You have been believers so long now that you ought to be teaching others. Instead, you need someone to teach you again the basic things about God's word. You are like babies who need milk and cannot eat solid food. For someone who lives on milk is still an infant and doesn't know how to do what is right. Solid food is for those who are mature, who through training have the skill to recognize the difference between right and wrong. HEBREWS 5:12-14

PUT YOUR BEST
FACE FORWARD

DO you enjoy potatoes? A spud can put a smile on a person's face in plenty of ways. Chips. Fries. A side of hash browns with breakfast. But on this date in 1952, kids got extra excited about potatoes because a brand-new toy allowed them to play with their food without getting in trouble. Did you know the original Mr. Potato Head was simply a box full of hands, feet, facial features, and accessories that children would stick into a real potato?

By 1964, federal regulations forced Hasbro to make those interchangeable parts safer. As a result, they were no longer sharp enough to penetrate a regular spud, so the company developed a hollow plastic body. Mr. Potato Head has changed some over the years. Even so, the basic concept remains the same: starting from scratch, develop a character and shape its personality by giving it the eyes, ears, hands, and feet that reflect the type of tater you want it to become.

Have you ever stopped to think that maybe God wants to do the same thing with us? The problem is, we get in the way and insert inferior parts. He wants us to have eyes full of compassion, but we insist on wearing our "angry eyes." The Lord prefers lips that worship him and speak encouragement, yet our "loud mouths" complain all the time. Are your hands raised in a fist, or are they open and outstretched, offering help to other potatoes who cross your path?

Revelation 4:11 reminds us to honor the one who designed us. God's worthy of glory—and our cooperation. Maybe you could pray something like this: "Lord, I'm just a humble spud. A common tater. But in your hands, I can be really special. Give me your eyes. Your ears. A mouth that says only what you want it to say. Bless me with feet that will walk the path you've prepared for me, and hands committed to doing your work. Amen."

DADDY-*Daughter Time*

Tell your dad/daughter which of his/her "interchangeable parts" you've seen honoring God. Consider which of your own the Holy Spirit has been prompting you to upgrade. If you own a Mr. Potato Head toy, play with it together. Or if you'd rather go old school and get really creative, craft body parts out of cardboard, wire, etc., and attach them to a real potato!

WHAT'S THE WORD?

You are worthy, O Lord our God, to receive glory and honor and power. For you created all things, and they exist because you created what you pleased. REVELATION 4:11

THIS PRIZE IS NO GIMMICK

WHAT'S the coolest prize you've ever found at the bottom of a cereal box? How about a deed to some real estate? That's what Quaker Oats offered kids in 1955 on its popular radio show *Challenge of the Yukon*. Quaker purchased just over nineteen acres of worthless land in the Klondike, a region romanticized during the gold rush. And every box of puffed rice and wheat contained a deed for one square inch of that parcel.

Owning even a square inch of Canadian soil was enough to have children dreaming of mining, farming, raising sled dogs, and building log cabins in the great white north. None of which happened, of course. Beyond the fact that each deed was thirty-five times larger than the plot it represented, the certificates had no legal value, since they were never registered individually. A decade later, Quaker allowed all of the land to be repossessed rather than pay $37.20 in property taxes. It had served its purpose. Quaker sold twenty-one million boxes of breakfast cereal in a matter of weeks and walked away with the lion's share of the market.

Sadly, some people think of heaven like that square inch of land in the Klondike. It feels distant. They see little value in it. And even those who want to believe what Scripture says wonder if it's all just an illusion that will disappoint them in the end. But God's not into gimmicks. His promises are true, including what awaits Christians after death (see Philippians 3:20-21; Hebrews 11:13-16; Revelation 21:1–22:6). When Jesus tells us what we stand to inherit (see Matthew 25:34; John 14:1-3), the promise comes from the one who has been there and validated our "deed" with his sacrificial deed on the cross.

A city of pure gold . . . and Jesus is there. Now that's a gold rush!

DADDY-*Daughter Time*

Talk about heaven. See what the Bible has to say. What do you look forward to? Do you feel any anxiety about it? Just for fun, visit a supermarket and stroll the cereal aisle. See who can find the box with the best prize inside (you decide if mail-in offers count). Also, notice that healthy cereals are on the top shelves, whereas sugary brands with cartoon characters are lower for kids to find.

WHAT'S THE WORD?

Don't let your hearts be troubled. Trust in God, and trust also in me. There is more than enough room in my Father's home. If this were not so, would I have told you that I am going to prepare a place for you? JOHN 14:1-2

HARDER THAN
IT HAS TO BE

"I'VE got a million things to do," Natalie said, stress punctuating each syllable, "but this is one job I can cross off my list!" Nobody could doubt Natalie's hard work. Of course, why she felt the need to alphabetize all of the preschool's picture books is anyone's guess. In a few minutes, a squadron of four-year-olds with jelly on their fingers would return from snack break to yank them off the shelves again.

Do you know people who make life harder for themselves than it has to be? You know the type. They carry a twenty-pound backpack from one class to another instead of just taking the books they need. They spend an hour laboring over an e-mail rather than investing ten minutes in a phone call. We all have our reasons for overcomplicating things. But that said, Sultan Baybars remains a mystery.

According to *Ripley's Believe It or Not!*, Baybars was an Egyptian who lived from 1223 to 1277. He swam back and forth across the Nile River every day for seventeen years. Impressive. But that's not the strange part. For some reason he did it while wearing a suit of armor and dragging a thirty-eight-pound weight.

Believe it or not, we can also bear unnecessary weight or anxiety in our walk with Jesus Christ. Note that Jesus did not say, "Come to me, all of you who are weary and carry heavy burdens, and exchange them for other heavy burdens." No way! He said in Matthew 11:28 that if we take our burdens to him, he'll give us rest. The Lord tells us to take his yoke upon us and let our souls relax, "for my yoke is easy to bear, and the burden I give you is light" (Matthew 11:30).

So the next time you're feeling overwhelmed in life, figure out where that's coming from . . . and resist the temptation to swim the Nile in armor.

DADDY-*Daughter Time*

Do you know people who overburden themselves like they're swimming in armor? How can you help to ease their burden? Are you experiencing "rest" in your relationship with Jesus? If not, it may be that you're too hard on yourself, or perhaps someone else is making your faith feel like a duty. Parents can even do that to their children without realizing it. Together, identify unnecessary stresses or burdens in your day-to-day lives, and pray for rest.

WHAT'S THE WORD?

Jesus said, "Come to me, all of you who are weary and carry heavy burdens, and I will give you rest." MATTHEW 11:28

WHAT GOES UP . . .

"WHERE there's smoke, there's fire."

"Out of sight, out of mind."

"No pain, no gain."

Phrases like these become clichés because we use them a lot. And that's because they're true . . . usually. The next time someone tries to tell you, "What goes up must come down," just say, "Hold your horses!" On this date in 1984, professional baseball player Dave Kingman hit a towering pop fly that never came down. More on that shortly. First, let's consider a few ways God has challenged natural laws and familiar clichés:

- You may have heard it said, "There's nothing new under the sun." How about shadows moving backward? The sun reversed course as a sign to King Hezekiah (see 2 Kings 20:9-11). God performed a similar miracle when he halted the earth's rotation for Joshua's army, allowing for an extra twelve hours of midday sun (see Joshua 10:12-13).
- "It's time to sink or swim" is a fairly common expression. However, Jesus modeled a third option when he walked to his disciples on the Sea of Galilee (see Mark 6:49-52). Likewise, God spared the Israelites a watery fate by parting the Red Sea so they could escape Pharaoh's army on dry ground (see Exodus 14:21-22).
- When people say that something came "straight from the horse's mouth," they're not actually referring to a talking animal. But after God let Balaam's donkey speak perfect Hebrew, Balaam could have used that expression literally (see Numbers 22:26-31).

From floating ax heads (see 2 Kings 6:1-7) to flaming bushes that don't burn up (see Exodus 3), physical laws can have exceptions when the God who established them steps in. Not that Dave's pop fly qualifies as a miracle. That was more of a fluke. During a game inside Minnesota's Metrodome, the Oakland A's slugger hit a ball so high and hard that it lodged inside one of the roof's drainage holes and never came out. Kingman was awarded a ground-rule double. Better yet, he has the distinction of being the only batter to hit a ball that still hasn't landed.

DADDY-*Daughter Time*

Have fun with science. Light several small candles. Pour one-third cup of vinegar into a small pitcher, then add a quarter cup of baking soda. Wait about fifteen seconds for the mixture to settle before tipping the pitcher slightly an inch or two above each flame. The liquid stays in, the flames go out!

WHAT'S THE WORD?

Then Moses raised his hand over the sea, and the LORD opened up a path through the water with a strong east wind. The wind blew all that night, turning the seabed into dry land . . . with walls of water on each side! EXODUS 14:21-22

A RISK WORTH TAKING

SOME people gamble with their lives. More than merely dangerous behavior (like forgetting Mother's Day—always the second Sunday in May), serious thrill-seekers literally stare down death to pursue their passions, convinced that the rewards are worth the risks:

- Japanese puffer fish, called *fugu*, is a very expensive, highly toxic delicacy. If it isn't cleaned just right, a diner's night on the town could end in paralysis and death. In fact, since the poison required to kill an adult could fit on the head of a pin, special laws govern which chefs can prepare fugu (licensing takes up to seven years) and how to dispose of the remains. Still, some folks can't get enough of it.
- There's a hole in the ground near Mexico City that's deep enough to hold the Empire State Building. More than 100,000 swallows live inside, earning it the name Cave of the Swallows. Daredevils leap into its mouth and free-fall at one hundred miles per hour before parachuting the rest of the way . . . if they succeed. Chutes can be shredded by the cave's jagged walls or collapse when birds get tangled in the lines. Yet people keep jumping.
- Another example of someone staring death in the face without flinching occurred just outside a town called Lystra. A man was pummeled with rocks, dragged to the outskirts, and left for dead. As soon as he regained consciousness, he headed back into town to preach to the very people who tried to kill him. That man was Paul (see Acts 14:8-20). He didn't risk his life for a meal. He didn't do it for the adrenaline rush. He did it to rescue strangers from an eternity separated from God.

When Paul embraced the Christian life, it wasn't a halfhearted hug. And while people these days will jeopardize life and limb for all sorts of things, Paul's passion for lost souls convinced him that the people of Lystra were worth the risk (see Philippians 1:21).

DADDY-*Daughter Time*

Would you be tempted to eat fugu or parachute into the Cave of the Swallows? Why or why not? Who or what would you risk your life for? Talk about Paul's bold decision, and ponder several unanswered questions from Acts 14:20: What took place when the believers gathered? How did Barnabas feel? What occurred when Paul marched back into Lystra and spent the night there?

WHAT'S THE WORD?

Some Jews arrived from Antioch and Iconium and won the crowds to their side. They stoned Paul and dragged him out of town, thinking he was dead. But as the believers gathered around him, he got up and went back into the town. ACTS 14:19-20

YOU COMPLETE ME

WITH only three days until the big yard sale, Lori was running out of time. Her father had asked her to go through her clothes closet, as well as the toys in her window seat, in search of things she didn't need anymore. As she got started, the first item to go was a long, snaking plastic tunnel that had been part of her hamster's home. Well, *home* may not be the best word. It was more of a weekend rental. That's how long it took Lori to tire of caring for her new pet, which she gave to a neighbor before she could settle on a name.

"I won't be needing this anymore," she said, gathering up the pieces, some of which still had stray cedar shavings clinging to the inside. As the teen retrieved a curved piece of plastic from beneath her bed, a shiny black case caught her eye.

"Hey, there's my old clarinet!" she exclaimed. Lori had started taking music lessons the week she turned eight. She quit at eight and a half. In fact, as she kept rummaging through her belongings, she noticed a trend. There was the scouting uniform that never met a merit badge. Ice skates she'd worn twice. Meanwhile, the jewelry-making kit she couldn't live without sat covered in a layer of dust, all of its sequins, baubles, and beads still in their preassigned plastic trays.

Does this sound familiar? It's easy to get excited about a new project or activity, only to get bored or distracted and leave it unfinished. Some people make a habit of it. But there's a lot to be said for praying about which commitments we take on, then seeing them through to completion. The next time you're tempted to call it quits, let Philippians 1:6 inspire you to stay the course. That verse is a wonderful reminder that God himself has an important project in the works—you—and refuses to give up until it's done!

DADDY-*Daughter Time*

How does it feel to know that God is working on you and refuses to quit until you've reached completion? Do you have a hard time sticking with things until they're finished? Why? Why is it important to finish what we start? How does this relate to marriage and family life? What half-completed task needs your attention right now? Maybe it's something the two of you could accomplish together.

WHAT'S THE WORD?

I am certain that God, who began the good work within you, will continue his work until it is finally finished on the day when Christ Jesus returns. PHILIPPIANS 1:6

RAIN, RAIN GO AWAY

DOES rain make you happy or sad? If you said sad, you have plenty of company. A lot of people get bummed out by it. Maybe that's because rain cancels baseball games and fireworks displays. It sends picnickers scrambling for cover and messes up perfectly styled hair. But our disdain for rain may have as much to do with what it has come to symbolize. We're conditioned to think of rain as a metaphor for trials.

In cartoons, it's the little black cloud that settles over an already troubled soul, creating a personal downpour four feet wide. In poetry or song lyrics, rain serves as shorthand for the blues; just as talk of sunshine represents happiness, showers usually spell trouble. And most of the time when characters in movies are getting rained on, things aren't going smoothly. Have you ever seen someone on the big screen encounter a rainstorm (thunder and lightning optional), a car not working, and a creepy old house? Nothing good comes from that trifecta!

Therefore, it's natural to assume that, in the second half of Matthew 5:45, Jesus is referring to trials when he says that God sends rain on both the just and the unjust. In other words, just because you're living for God, don't be surprised when hard times come. We all share the weather. When it's bad, it's bad for everyone. But odds are, the Lord meant just the opposite. To people living off the land, rain was a huge blessing.

In 1 Kings 17:1, the prophet Elijah tells Israel's evil King Ahab not to expect rain or even dew for several years. It was a punishment from God. Because where there's drought, there's famine. And where there's famine, people die. You can imagine the rejoicing when, at the end of chapter 18, the rains finally returned. So the next time rain gives you the blues or makes driving a hassle, imagine crops flourishing and farmers smiling. I think of those raindrops as God's gift of fresh drinking water to someone in need. As Romans 12:15 says, "Be happy with those who are happy." Just stay away from creepy old houses.

DADDY-*Daughter Time*

What do you like about rain? Share your favorite rainy-day memories. Then take two minutes to see how many song lyrics you can think of that use rain as a metaphor for hardship. Time yourselves. Then take two more minutes to list songs that speak of it as a blessing.

WHAT'S THE WORD?

Your Father in heaven . . . gives his sunlight to both the evil and the good, and he sends rain on the just and the unjust alike. MATTHEW 5:45

TAKEN FOR A RIDE

IF you were one of the thousands of passengers aboard New York City's A train at 3:58 p.m. on this date in 1993, Keron Thomas took you for a ride. In fact, he manned the controls for the next three and a half hours, making eighty-five stops in Manhattan, Brooklyn, and Queens. The thing is, Keron didn't work for the transit authority. He had never driven a subway train before. And he was only sixteen years old.

Fortunately, no one was hurt (he even kept the train on schedule). Still, for posing as a motorman, Keron was charged with reckless endangerment, forgery, and criminal impersonation. "C'mon, give the kid a break," someone might argue, "he really loves trains." True enough. His mother told the *New York Times* he was obsessed with trains. But without a license and proper credentials, by law you're not allowed to engineer a subway train. Period.

"Yeah, but he's a nice kid who often talked to actual motormen about their work. And he spent hours studying subway manuals in hopes of taking the civil service test. He even showed up that day carrying regulation equipment: a brake handle, a safety vest, and a reverser key. Isn't that good enough?" They're all good things, true, but the law's the law.

Sadly, people also approach their future this way. They figure if they're nice enough, hang out with spiritual people, or read the right books, they deserve a place in heaven. Some even carry "regulation equipment": a Bible, a piece of religious jewelry, a bumper sticker that says "America Needs a Faith Lift." But much like a teenager thinking that a little knowledge and good intentions give him the right to drive off with a subway train, we're breaking God's law if we don't possess a license granted by the proper authority. Jesus is that authority. Only by trusting in his sacrificial death and resurrection can we spend eternity in heaven. Jesus said it himself: "God so loved the world that he gave his one and only Son, that whoever believes in him shall not perish but have eternal life" (John 3:16, NIV). Anyone who says otherwise is an impostor trying to take you for a ride.

DADDY-*Daughter Time*

What do you think of Keron Thomas's attempt to fulfill his dream? Why are laws—natural and spiritual—necessary? Do you know anyone expecting to slip into heaven without Jesus? It may be time to give that person a gentle wake-up call.

WHAT'S THE WORD?

God so loved the world that he gave his one and only Son, that whoever believes in him shall not perish but have eternal life.   JOHN 3:16 (NIV)

THE NATURE OF TECHNOLOGY

HAVE you ever been frustrated by a glare on your TV screen, computer monitor, or cell phone? Well, scientists developing nanotechnology have come up with a solution by studying one of God's remarkably designed creatures. The eye of a moth contains hundreds of thousands of tiny bumps. Each is smaller than wavelengths of incoming light, so the moth's eyes don't reflect at night. This helps it avoid predators. Applying that principle to plastics could revolutionize screens of all kinds, not to mention windows, eyeglasses, and more. Here are some other ways nature has inspired technology:

- The bumps (or tubercles) on the flippers of humpback whales provide more lift, less resistance, and greater efficiency than a smooth surface when moving through air and water. This discovery could improve everything from wind turbines to airplane wings.
- Ever wonder how we got Velcro? An engineer picking burrs out of his clothing examined one under a microscope and found tiny barbs that caused the burr to latch on. More recently, analyzing the feet of geckos has allowed scientists to create a reversible adhesive. Now it's sticky—now it's not!
- Advanced swimsuits modeled after sharkskin have sparked controversy in competitive circles for their ability to increase speed and reduce drag in the water. The first was introduced at the 2000 Sydney Olympics, where 83 percent of all swimming medals were won by athletes wearing the "shark suit."

These are just a few things we've gleaned from God's creativity. But even more than changing our world through technology, the Lord wants to change us and how we relate to him. That's why he reveals himself in nature, so that people will marvel at creation and turn to the Creator (see Romans 1:20). Nonglare TV screens are great, but seeing God more clearly is even better.

DADDY-*Daughter Time*

What have you learned from observing God's creation? Want to observe moths in a more natural setting than watching them head-butt a lightbulb? Paint a tree trunk with a mixture of brown sugar, water, and yeast, and cover your flashlight with red cellophane. (Smashing rotten watermelon on a tree also works.) Since moths can't see red light, you can watch them together at night when they come to feed.

WHAT'S THE WORD?

Ever since the world was created, people have seen the earth and sky. Through everything God made, they can clearly see his invisible qualities—his eternal power and divine nature. So they have no excuse for not knowing God. ROMANS 1:20

UNDER THE INFLUENCE

"IT was just one little drink!" Bella protested, but she could tell from her sister's rigid posture and stern expression that she wasn't buying it. To be honest, she didn't know how much alcohol she'd consumed at the party. It started with a hard lemonade, maybe two. Then her friends kept bringing her this funny-tasting punch that made things worse.

"Touch your nose, Bella," Katie said. It took Bella a few seconds to orient herself. Katie tracked her sister's finger and waited for . . . contact. "That's your forehead. I can't believe you!"

"You're not gonna tell Mom and Dad, are you?" she begged.

"No," Katie replied, her soused sis flashing a relieved smile that would vanish seconds later, "because *you* are."

Too many teens like Bella don't realize the serious consequences of consuming alcohol. Those who do often figure they'll beat the odds. After all, being young and healthy makes it easier to absorb the toxins and bounce back, right? Actually, adolescence is the worst time to drink, because alcohol kills brain cells that are still growing and developing. It also impairs judgment. That's especially dangerous for young drivers. Bad things can happen when a person's head isn't clear. Furthermore, since most alcoholics began drinking at a young age, it's possible that starting the habit early contributes to addiction.

Christians have yet another reason to avoid getting drunk: God forbids it. In Ephesians 5:18 the apostle Paul warns, "Don't be drunk with wine, because that will ruin your life. Instead, be filled with the Holy Spirit." If we claim Christ, God should have full control of our lives. The Bible tells us to love the Lord with all of our hearts, minds, and strength. We can't do that if we're under the influence of something else.

DADDY-*Daughter Time*

Put yourself in Katie's situation. Did she handle it well? What might you have done differently? Are you clear about the rules in your home concerning alcohol use? Have you observed peers making bad choices? What happened? Dad, if you have life experience in this area, take a moment to share as honestly as possible. Read Proverbs 23:29-35 together for Solomon's wisdom concerning strong drink.

WHAT'S THE WORD?

Don't gaze at the wine, seeing how red it is, how it sparkles in the cup, how smoothly it goes down. For in the end it bites like a poisonous snake; it stings like a viper. You will see hallucinations, and you will say crazy things. PROVERBS 23:31-33

THE POWER OF STORY

THE end credits started to roll just as Clara reached the bottom of her popcorn bucket. Brushing away a little tear, she said, "That was one of those happy-sad movies, wasn't it, Dad? Dad?"

Her macho father hastily tried to compose himself before the houselights could come up. "Huh? Oh, yeah," he managed. "It's amazing—*sniff*—how much they can make you care about a bunch of toys, isn't it?"

Like Clara and her dad, maybe you've been moved by a well-told story. It could be epic in detail, like a novel, or as short as a three-minute country song. Have you ever wondered why stories have such an impact on us? It's probably because God hard wired us to connect with them. That's why Jesus often used parables to drive home important truths when teaching his disciples (see Mark 4:33-34).

For example, in Matthew 7:24-27 the Lord could have said, "The world is unstable. Follow me." Short and to the point. On to the next lesson, right? But he didn't do that. Instead, Jesus spun a tale of two gents planning extreme home makeovers: a wise man who built his house on the rock and a foolish man who built on sand. The storms came and wiped out the foolish man's house, but the one on the solid foundation stood firm—just like people who place their trust in the Savior. Pretty cool, huh? In a few short lines, Jesus established the scene, created characters, introduced conflict, and provided a happy ending (at least for the wise builder), all for the purpose of conveying a bigger truth.

Since God designed us to connect with stories, it's important that we choose ours carefully. The books we read. The movies we watch. Even the three-minute songs we listen to. Each has its own way of looking at the world, which may or may not reflect God's truth. Meanwhile, some of the best tales of good and evil, romance, and redemption are essentially parables for the greatest story ever told: the gospel.

DADDY-*Daughter Time*

Write down five of your favorite stories and why they mean so much to you (don't forget songs). Discuss your lists together. Has a story ever inspired you to change something about yourself or to behave heroically? Plan a date to watch one of the father-daughter movies listed in the back of this book.

WHAT'S THE WORD?

Jesus used many similar stories and illustrations to teach the people as much as they could understand. In fact, in his public ministry he never taught without using parables; but afterward, when he was alone with his disciples, he explained everything to them. MARK 4:33-34

MIRROR, MIRROR

WHEN you rolled out of bed this morning, chances are you didn't give thanks for Baron Justus von Liebig, who was born on this date in 1803. But maybe you should have. Because, if you're like most people, you took a minute to fix your hair or straighten your tie with the help of a mirror.

Of course, people had been gazing at their reflections for centuries before Justus came along. In water. In shiny objects. However, this renowned German chemist took things to a whole new level. It all started when he was a boy fascinated by the pharmaceuticals, dyes, and salts sold by his merchant father. Despite being labeled "hopelessly useless" by his schoolmaster, Justus earned a PhD by the age of nineteen, was teaching college at twenty-one, and through lots of trial and error, made numerous discoveries—including artificial fertilizer. Yet one of his most helpful inventions came from the notion of coating a glass surface with reflective, metallic silver.

Have you ever seen your image in a mirror and noticed something embarrassing or out of place? A stain on your clothes? Windswept hair? A chocolate-milk mustache? You dealt with it right away, didn't you? It would be silly not to. According to James 1:22-25, we should have a similar response when we gaze into the Bible and notice that our lives aren't reflecting God's truth. Once we see that something is out of place, it's up to us to make it right by adjusting an attitude or changing a behavior as soon as possible. Otherwise, we can get distracted and forget what the Lord just showed us. More than just embarrassing, not dealing with our issues could cause real problems.

DADDY-*Daughter Time*

Some people spend lots of time in front of the mirror trying to get the outside looking just right. How much attention to our appearance is too much (see Proverbs 31:30)? Why is it more important to focus on the inside? Have you ever felt the need to make a change in your life, large or small, after reading Scripture? Did you do it? If not, were you embarrassed to have someone else point out your "chocolate-milk mustache"?

WHAT'S THE WORD?

But don't just listen to God's word. You must do what it says. Otherwise, you are only fooling yourselves. For if you listen to the word and don't obey, it is like glancing at your face in a mirror. You see yourself, walk away, and forget what you look like.
JAMES 1:22-24

LEARNING FROM
JEPHTHAH'S VOW

A lot of Bible stories have happy endings. Jephthah's isn't one of them. In fact, it may be one of the saddest father-daughter tales recorded in Scripture. But it's an important history lesson, because by learning from other people's mistakes, we can avoid similar heartbreak in our own lives.

Jephthah was a godly warrior forced to leave home by hateful brothers. That had to hurt. But when Israel needed a key victory against their oppressors, guess who they begged to command the troops? Yep, Jep. They said if he won, he'd be top dog in all of Gilead. He took the job, no doubt wanting to prove his worth, advance his career, and show the men in his family they were wrong to mistreat him. And who could blame him?

So how does Jephthah's daughter factor into all of this? As he and his men prepared to engage the enemy, Jephthah told God that, in exchange for victory over the Ammonites, he would sacrifice the first thing to come out of his house to greet him when he arrived home. A goat? A sheep? That's probably what he was thinking. Much to his dismay, it turned out to be his only child, his beloved daughter. It's all right there in Judges 11.

Jephthah became so focused on succeeding at his job that he overlooked something even more important—his child. A lot of men do that today. They would never consciously sacrifice their families on the altar of career, but for any number of reasons they get so caught up in work that they lose perspective. Fortunately, dads can learn from Jephthah's mistake by realizing that a truly great legacy starts with being a hero at home. And here's the cool part: daughters can help by making Dad feel even more valued and appreciated around the house than he feels through work!

DADDY-*Daughter Time*

Talk about Jephthah's vow. Was it necessary to bargain with God? Although the Lord commands men to provide for their families (see 1 Timothy 5:8), and he created them to derive satisfaction from their careers, just about every father at some point has let the demands of work overshadow his role as a dad. If you've felt that tug-of-war in your home, humbly discuss and pray about it together. Are there practical ways you can strike a better balance?

WHAT'S THE WORD?

When Jephthah returned home to Mizpah, his daughter came out to meet him, playing on a tambourine and dancing for joy. She was his one and only child; he had no other sons or daughters.   JUDGES 11:34

JUMPING THE SHARK

ARE you familiar with the expression "jumping the shark"? This fishy phrase was inspired by an episode of the TV sitcom *Happy Days*, in which a tough greaser in a leather jacket—a classic 1950s icon of cool—sped on water skis toward a penned-up shark. As he hit the ramp, a formerly down-to-earth show devoted to sock hops and poodle skirts changed forever. Ratings spiked. Respect plummeted.

Today, we say that an ongoing creative effort has jumped the shark when, after showing signs of decline, it resorts to an absurd stunt just to boost ratings or revive interest. It's a defining moment that reeks of desperation. Instead of quitting while it was ahead, the series or brand lingers to the point that it winds up sacrificing what made it popular in the first place.

A biblical example is King Hezekiah. A godly ruler of Judah, the ailing king learned through the prophet Isaiah that he was going to die and that he should get his affairs in order. In desperation, Hezekiah wept and prayed. So the Lord said he could live another fifteen years (see Isaiah 38:5). Like a TV show about to be canceled, Hezekiah suddenly got renewed for another season! But the king's character began to decline. He grew prideful. He forgot that God was the source of his blessings. Then he really jumped the shark in an ill-conceived attempt to boost his ratings with the powerful, godless nation of Babylon.

One day, some Babylonian messengers visited Hezekiah. Eager to impress his guests, the king proudly showed them all of his treasures (see 2 Kings 20:12-13). That would be like you opening your wallet to strangers and giving them a guided tour of your most valuable possessions. Bold move. Bad move. Hezekiah's pride in worldly wealth offended God, who said that one day Babylon would carry off every bit of it—including his sons (vv. 16-18). That absurd stunt by a lingering king proved he had lost what had earned him God's favor in the first place.

DADDY-*Daughter Time*

Do you think Hezekiah would've been better off leaving this life when the Lord first intended? Why or why not? What does this say about trusting God's timing? Discuss why extra days are only valuable if we use them wisely. Watch the cheesy TV moment that inspired an idiom; check out the YouTube video "Fonzie Jumps the Shark."

WHAT'S THE WORD?

Go back to Hezekiah and tell him, "This is what the LORD, the God of your ancestor David, says: I have heard your prayer and seen your tears. I will add fifteen years to your life." ISAIAH 38:5

ONE DAY AT A TIME

IN the spring of 1941, the Nazis controlled Western Europe. Americans, still fatigued from economic depression, braced for war. Grim times. Even Yankees slugger Joe DiMaggio couldn't seem to shake off an early-season slump. That is until May 15, when he earned a hit against the Chicago White Sox. He got one the next day too. And the next. Soon, a beleaguered nation began to cheer daily for Joltin' Joe's amazing hitting streak to continue. At fifty-six games, it remains one of the greatest achievements in sports—a record many believe will never be broken.

"As [the streak] surpassed the two-month mark, even people who didn't follow baseball got caught up in the frenzy, wondering how long he could keep it going," author Les Krantz wrote in his book *Reel Baseball*. "Radio stations interrupted whatever program was on the air when the bulletins crossed the wire about DiMaggio getting another hit."

DiMaggio's feat inspired a country in need of a heroic model of consistency and perseverance. But performing well over time—in any endeavor—doesn't just happen. It takes hard work and determination. We need to develop good habits and a sense of purpose that will get us through dry days and trying times. For example, DiMaggio was asked why he hustled so hard on every play. He replied, "Because there's always some kid who may be seeing me for the first time. I owe him my best."

Who deserves your best? One obvious answer is God, but it may also be a member of your family, a friend, a neighbor, a colleague at work, or someone in your church. Are you ready to step up to the plate? What good habits will help you be the person God wants you to be? In 1 Corinthians 15:58, the apostle Paul reminds us to "be strong and immovable. Always work enthusiastically for the Lord, for you know that nothing you do for the Lord is ever useless." When you consistently work for the Lord, you may end up with an impressive streak of your own.

DADDY-*Daughter Time*

Is there a particular behavior you wish you could turn into a habit? What's stopping you? Talk about healthy spiritual disciplines that all Christians should make a regular part of their lives. How are you doing in those areas?

DiMaggio's hitting streak became a pop-culture phenomenon that spawned the novelty song "Joltin' Joe DiMaggio" by Les Brown and His Band of Renown. Take a minute to listen to it together online.

WHAT'S THE WORD?

My dear brothers and sisters, be strong and immovable. Always work enthusiastically for the Lord, for you know that nothing you do for the Lord is ever useless.
1 CORINTHIANS 15:58

A PREVIOUS ENGAGEMENT

WITH business a little slow, Connie stepped from behind the counter and began wiping down tables with a rag. That's when she heard the door jingle. "Hey, kiddo," Kathy said as she walked in. "Sorry to bother you at work, but I heard you wanted to talk. Everything okay?"

Connie grinned, motioning her friend into the privacy of a nearby booth. "He sent me another message today, Kathy. It was soooo sweet. I don't know for sure, but I think he may be planning to propose to me." Her enthusiasm contained a trace of anxiety as she measured her friend's reaction.

"Well . . ." Kathy began cautiously.

"I'll admit," Connie interrupted, "it's a little scary to think about, especially since he hasn't been in town in, like, forever. And I can't honestly say I've prayed about it yet. But so many of my online friends think we're a perfect couple!"

"Really?" Kathy replied. "How well do those people know you?"

"Um, not as well as you do. And I totally respect your opinion. Which is why I was hoping you might change your mind about me and Mitch."

Deciding who to marry is one of the most important decisions you'll ever make. And since romantic feelings can cloud a person's judgment, it's always wise to consider the opinions of those who know you well and want the best for you.

You'll find a good example of this in Genesis 24. That's where Abraham sends his most trusted servant on a quest to find the right wife for his son, Isaac. As head of their household, this particular servant knew Isaac well. And Abraham believed that this man would seek God and choose wisely, which he did. Rebekah was a beautiful, sensitive girl from a good background. And she had a servant's heart.

You might say you're not looking for a spouse right now. Well, the same truth applies to other decisions, large or small, that can impact our lives or the lives of others. God wants us to consider his opinion first and foremost and seek out mature Christian counsel. As Proverbs 19:20 (NIV) says, "Listen to advice and accept instruction, and in the end you will be wise."

DADDY-*Daughter Time*

Imagine yourself sitting in the booth with Connie and Kathy. What advice might you offer? What questions would you ask? What qualities do you think are most important when choosing a mate? Read 2 Corinthians 6:14-15 (NIV). Discuss what it means to be "equally yoked" and why this matters to God.

WHAT'S THE WORD?

Go instead to my homeland, to my relatives, and find a wife there for my son Isaac.
GENESIS 24:4

WHAT AN INCREDIBLE SMELL YOU'VE DISCOVERED

IF you hear the words *fragrance department*, what comes to mind? Girls may recall a favorite scent or carefree hours floating from one counter to another, sampling perfume on their wrists. For a dad, it's more like navigating the Death Star trench in *Star Wars*. He enters the aisle and stares down the exit. Can he make it through unscathed? Saleswomen appear on his right and left like gun turrets, each armed with a bottle of something smelly and expensive, ready to fire. A Chanel rep drops in on him from behind, setting her sights. *Stabilize rear deflectors. Stay on target.* His pace quickens. *Oh no, I'm hit!*

Most guys would rather not get perfumed by a strange woman. But one man didn't mind so much. During Passover, Jesus was hanging out at a home in the town of Bethany when a woman walked in with a jar full of a very pricey perfume and proceeded to pour it on his head. He didn't even try to jump out of the way! Others at the table scolded her and complained that it was a waste of money. But not the Lord.

"Leave her alone," Jesus said. "Why criticize her for doing such a good thing to me? You will always have the poor among you, and you can help them whenever you want to. But you will not always have me. She has done what she could and has anointed my body for burial ahead of time. I tell you the truth, wherever the Good News is preached throughout the world, this woman's deed will be remembered and discussed" (Mark 14:6-9).

Wow, talk about validation. Here it was Passover, and this humble woman seemed to be the only one aware of what they were really celebrating. Jesus was the promised Passover lamb about to be sacrificed for the sin of the world. In this case, the drive-by perfuming was an act of worship. Want to know something else? The apostle Paul wrote in 2 Corinthians 2:14 that we're a blessing to others every time we pour out the "sweet perfume" of the gospel and tell people about Jesus. Have you sprayed anyone lately?

DADDY-*Daughter Time*

How do you feel about perfumes and colognes? Why do you think Paul called the gospel of salvation a sweet perfume to a lost world? The movie *Star Wars* debuted in May 1977, changing summer blockbusters forever. See if you can name the five top-grossing movies of all time. Then look online to see if you're right.

WHAT'S THE WORD?

[God] uses us to spread the knowledge of Christ everywhere, like a sweet perfume.
2 CORINTHIANS 2:14

IF someone asked you which of Jesus' apostles was a little too, shall we say, "self-focused" at times, who would come to mind? Judas perhaps? After all, he betrayed the Lord for thirty pieces of silver. Then there were the sons of Zebedee, whose mother asked Jesus for VIP seating for them in the Kingdom. Or how about Peter? He sure was bold, but when asked after Christ's arrest if he had walked with him, Peter denied it three times to save his skin.

Indeed, many of those early disciples got distracted by thinking about themselves when they should have been focusing on the bigger picture. But not the author of the Gospel of John, right? He's the quiet one who rested his head on Jesus' chest. He didn't even refer to himself in the first person, but simply as "the one whom Jesus loved." We think of John as observant, dutiful, and generally low-key. But boys will be boys.

It's actually kind of funny. In John 20 this mild-mannered fellow describes Easter morning. Hallelujah! Jesus has risen! It's all about the Savior, and John is fixated on prophecy fulfilled. Okay, not quite. No sooner does he mention racing toward the empty tomb than he makes it a point to say, speaking of himself, "The other disciple outran Peter and reached the tomb first" (v. 4). In the New International Version, he adds in verse 6, "Then Simon Peter, who was *behind* him, arrived." And for good measure, the author once again refers to himself as "the disciple who had reached the tomb first" (20:8, emphasis added).

Here, John is in the process of reporting the most important moment in history. The tomb is empty. Christ has gained victory over death! Yet John seems a bit preoccupied with his own victory, eager for the record to show that he beat Peter in a footrace. We're probably guilty of the same thing now and then as we serve God in a competitive, image-conscious society. But as a rule, we're always better off bragging about what God has done, rather than what we have done.

DADDY-*Daughter Time*

Take a moment to brag on God, naming the things he has done for you and in you. How do people today tend to draw attention to their own accomplishments, large or small? Is that healthy? Why or why not? Read Matthew 5:14-16 and discuss what can be a fine line between pursuing personal glory and seeking to glorify God.

WHAT'S THE WORD?

Peter and the other disciple started out for the tomb. They were both running, but the other disciple outran Peter and reached the tomb first.   JOHN 20:3-4

WORLD'S GREATEST LION TAMER

THERE'S nothing like a day at the circus. Not only is it a fun excuse to eat lots of popcorn and cotton candy, but you also get to watch acrobatic elephants, fire-juggling trapeze artists, and a dozen clowns who spill out of a tiny car. But the star attraction has to be the big cats. Ever since Ringling Bros. Circus debuted on this date in 1884, animal trainers with a chair in one hand and a whip in the other have stared down ferocious felines, risking life and limb to prove their dominion over these mighty beasts.

So who is the greatest lion tamer ever? Gunther Gebel-Williams was pretty amazing. He began training wild animals as a teenager and, during a storied career with Ringling Bros., entertained an estimated 200 million people. Another impressive act was Siegfried & Roy, a popular duo known for working with rare white cats in Las Vegas. Could they be the greatest of all time? Not by a long shot. That title belongs to an angel.

In Daniel 6, King Darius allowed himself to be duped into decreeing that his subjects couldn't pray to anyone but him. It was a ploy the king's officials concocted to trap Daniel, because they knew this faithful young man would keep kneeling to the God of Israel. Well, their plan worked . . . sort of. These royal schemers caught Daniel in the act, and Darius had no choice but to throw his otherwise loyal servant into a den of hungry lions.

If you've heard this story before, you know that no harm came to Daniel because God sent his angel to shut the lions' mouths (see Daniel 6:22). The best part is that after getting a front-row seat for this lion-taming feat, Darius sent a message to his kingdom stating that everyone should tremble before Daniel's God, "for he is the living God, and he will endure forever. His kingdom will never be destroyed, and his rule will never end" (Daniel 6:26). Indeed, God is still on the throne. And seeing him work in our lives remains the greatest show on earth.

DADDY-*Daughter Time*

If you could join the circus, what act would you perform? Read all of Daniel 6 together and see what else grabs your attention. Then visit ringling.com for a peek under the big top and to see if the circus will be making a stop in your area anytime soon.

WHAT'S THE WORD?

When [the king] got there, he called out in anguish, "Daniel, servant of the living God! Was your God, whom you serve so faithfully, able to rescue you from the lions?"
DANIEL 6:20

A SEAT OF HONOR

DO you care where you sit at the dinner table? On any given night, your favorite spot may be the one closest to the menu item you like best. But certain meals are special. Thanksgiving dinner, for example. In many homes, the host or senior member of the family will sit at the head of the dining-room table. It's a place of honor (as opposed to being exiled to the kitchen, where kids shout out the *SpongeBob* theme song and hide broccoli in their napkins).

Throughout the Bible, people used mealtime to show respect to others. In fact, that's what happens in 1 Samuel 9 the first time we meet Saul. He's not Israel's king yet. He's just a normal guy from that nation's smallest tribe. One day his dad sends him hunting for lost donkeys. After searching awhile with no success, Saul and his servant decide to visit a local prophet for advice on where they should look next. That prophet is Samuel. Samuel shocks Saul by telling him to stick around for a feast prepared in his honor with thirty guests already in place. He ushers the men into the dining hall, seats them at the head of the table, and tells the cook to bring them choice meat set aside in advance. That sounds like a surprise someone might get on a reality TV show, doesn't it?

Now, if you jump ahead to 2 Samuel 9, Saul's reign is finished and most of his household is gone. Out of respect and generosity, King David wants to honor a member of Saul's family. David has learned of a crippled grandson named Mephibosheth and, among other things, promises him, "You will always eat at my table" (9:7, NIV). Which he did. The Bible doesn't tell us exactly where he sat. But it just might have been closest to whatever menu item he liked best.

DADDY-*Daughter Time*

Share the coolest thing anyone has ever done to make you feel special. How have you gone out of your way to honor someone else? Imagine how Saul and his servant felt when they were given the best seats at a special meal. Together, plan a home-cooked meal for your family. Go all out. Set the table with good dishes, fancy napkins, candles, or other creative touches. Reserve seats of honor for each guest, giving the very best places to those least accustomed to royal treatment.

WHAT'S THE WORD?

Samuel brought Saul and his servant into the hall and placed them at the head of the table, honoring them above the thirty special guests.   1 SAMUEL 9:22

JESUS WEPT

A preschooler cries hysterically after skinning her knee. Her father frantically races outside to find her with only minor injuries. At first he's relieved, then he starts crying when he sees that she has used a black magic marker to color all the facial hair on his prized collection of early-seventies G.I. Joe dolls.

People cry for all sorts of reasons. We cry when we're hurt, when we're sad, and sometimes even when we're happy. That's why Grandma's eyes leak when you meet her at the airport, not just when you say good-bye. Meanwhile, some movies are so touching they can make the toughest he-man on the planet blubber like a baby (though if you catch him, he'll insist he's just sweating through his eyes). It's okay. It's natural.

Jesus cried too. After being summoned to the village of Bethany to heal a friend, he waited for Lazarus to "fall asleep" before hitting the road. It was all part of the Lord's plan. When he and his disciples arrived, the man's sisters were mourning both the passing of Lazarus and the apparent lateness of the Lord. In response, "Jesus wept" (John 11:35).

What brought our Savior to tears? Surely not the death of Lazarus, since Jesus purposely delayed his journey so as to resurrect him. He knew his friend would be up and about in no time. So we can rule that out. He may have been showing empathy, sharing the grief of others. There's also a strong argument that he was mourning the people's lack of faith in his power over death. Or perhaps some combination of those emotions streamed down his cheeks. Regardless, we know that Jesus does understand the pain of his beloved. Including you.

Hebrews 4:15 alludes to Christ's ability to sympathize with your struggles. Although fully God, he was also fully man, experiencing rejection, exhaustion, injustice, pain, hatred, temptation, and loneliness. Furthermore, Jesus was misunderstood, and he felt pressure from crowds always wanting something from him. And he wept. More than just a comfort, his example should inspire us to be sensitive to the hurting people God puts in our path.

DADDY-*Daughter Time*

Read John 11:1-44 together and pay special attention to Mary's and Martha's exchanges with the Lord. Why do you think Jesus wept? When was the last time you cried, and why? Can you think of a song or film moment that never fails to activate your tear ducts? Could someone in your life use empathy right now? How can Romans 12:15 remind you to be sensitive to what others are feeling?

WHAT'S THE WORD?

Be happy with those who are happy, and weep with those who weep.   ROMANS 12:15

NORMALLY, the smell of dinner would've relaxed Alyssa. But as she sat at the kitchen table crafting a text message, no amount of garlic or oregano could take her mind off the sarcastic comment she'd made to a girl at school. A remark she couldn't take back. Alyssa's parents exchanged sad, knowing glances as Mom grabbed some plates and Dad shifted saucepans. "Hon, why don't you just call her?"

"It's dinnertime, Dad. Besides, she won't pick up once she sees it's me."

Her mother sat down beside her. "Alyssa, you said you apologized as soon as you realized you'd hurt her feelings. That can't undo what happened, but you did the right thing. Now it's up to her to forgive you."

Alyssa's mind kept returning to the words of James 3:2-8, which compare the tongue to a spark capable of engulfing an entire forest, and to a rudder of a ship—small but powerful. Such a little thing, yet so hard to control. Evil. That's what the Bible calls it. She wished for an instant that God had never given her a tongue, then changed her mind as shrimp scampi and garlic bread arrived at the table.

"We've all done it," her father said gently. "Once those words come out, it's like squeezing toothpaste out of a tube. As much as you might want to, you can't put it back in." He reached for the grated cheese, musing, "And who would know better than Dr. Washington Sheffield, the Connecticut dentist who invented the collapsible metal toothpaste tube on May 22, 1892? Ya know, before that, toothpaste was sold in little ceramic pots." Aware that he was conversationally adrift, he noticed the women staring at him.

Alyssa leaned over and kissed him on the head. "Daddy, you're such a nerd." For a second, he pretended to be stung by her words. "Oh no," she said. "I did it again!" They all laughed so hard, they almost forgot to say grace.

DADDY-*Daughter Time*

Have you ever caused trouble by saying something careless? Have you been hurt by a thoughtless remark or joke? Why is forgiveness so important? Next time you're at the store, buy a cheap tube of toothpaste for each member of your family. Set a timer for ten minutes. Each of you squeeze the toothpaste onto a plate. See who has the most success at getting the toothpaste back into the tube.

WHAT'S THE WORD?

People can tame all kinds of animals, birds, reptiles, and fish, but no one can tame the tongue. It is restless and evil, full of deadly poison.   JAMES 3:7-8

WELL, DUH! . . . RIGHT?

HAVE you noticed that some questions seem so easy that you feel a little silly answering them? For example, which country makes Panama hats? How long did the Hundred Years' War last? What was the first name of King George VI? And what material is used to make a camel-hair brush? Insultingly easy, right? You knew immediately that the correct answers are Ecuador, 116 years, Albert, and squirrel fur. Huh?

Don't feel bad. Sometimes the "obvious" answer isn't as clear cut as we might think. That had to be what ran through the mind of one individual in Scripture who enters and exits so quickly that we don't get a name or gender.

As Jesus teaches the crowds and corrects the Pharisees in Matthew 12, there's a break in the action. The Lord's family has shown up. But they're too far away to get his attention, so they relay a message. In verse 47, someone tells Jesus, "Your mother and your brothers are outside, and they want to speak to you." Message delivered. But wait—a pop quiz from the Master! Jesus asks, "Who is my mother? Who are my brothers?" (v. 48).

In a split second, this poor soul had to wonder if Jesus was kidding around, or perhaps the heat of the day had taken its toll. The initial response may have been, "Um, the woman who gave birth to you and the boys who always whined that you were Mom's favorite." Or, if the messenger happened to be a friend of the family, the obvious answer could have been Mary, James, Joseph, Simon, and Judas (see Matthew 13:55).

Fortunately for this innocent bystander, he/she said nothing during that split second. Because in this case, the obvious answer would have been just as wrong as assuming that purple finches are purple. Jesus went on to satisfy his own question by pointing to his disciples and saying, "Look, these are my mother and brothers. Anyone who does the will of my Father in heaven is my brother and sister and mother!" (Matthew 12:49-50). You can bet nobody saw that coming! (Incidentally, purple finches are actually a raspberry or crimson color.)

DADDY-*Daughter Time*

What did Jesus mean when he extended his family to include anyone who serves God? It's easy to assume that we know certain things about our own family members. Finish this sentence: "Something you only think you know about me is _____." Then take a moment to clear up a misconception or two.

WHAT'S THE WORD?

Anyone who does the will of my Father in heaven is my brother and sister and mother!
MATTHEW 12:50

WAS IT WORTH IT?

IT may have seemed like a good idea at the time, but a photo op with a polar bear nearly cost a twenty-nine-year-old tourist her life. In 1994, Kathryn Warburton scaled two guardrails at the Alaska Zoo for a closer look at Binky. The bear quickly reached through the bars and clamped massive jaws around her thigh. She narrowly escaped. Since then, millions of people the world over have viewed Kathryn's painful lapse in judgment online. A steep price to pay for a snapshot.

Another rash, life-changing decision was made by a fellow named Esau. Remember him? He was Isaac's hairy heir, plucked from the womb mere seconds ahead of his twin brother, Jacob (giving Esau all the rights of a firstborn son). Well, this skilled hunter arrived home from the wilderness one day incredibly hungry. An irresistible aroma greeted him. His brother had a hearty stew simmering.

"I'm starved! Give me some of that stew!" Esau insisted.

"All right," Jacob replied, "but trade me your rights as the firstborn son."

How do you think Esau reacted? "No way! That's a rip-off! What kind of idiot do you think I am? I'm telling Mom!" Frankly, that response would have been better than the one he came up with. With his flesh screaming, "Feed me," Esau ignored the consequences and chose the stew. He valued instant gratification above his inheritance and his father's blessing. Before long, the hunter's belly was empty again, while his heart was full of regret.

We can be just as foolish when we allow ourselves to get swept up in the moment. We chase short-term satisfaction, perhaps sacrificing something far more valuable just to feed a temporary appetite. Often those choices can't be undone. So, what's your "polar bear photo" or "bowl of stew"? Are you ever tempted to give in to impulses that could sabotage the great plans God has for you? If so, invite Jesus to be the Lord of your desires. When we are weak, he is strong!

DADDY-*Daughter Time*

Was Jacob's stew really so amazing, or had Esau already devalued his birthright before getting a chance to trade it away? How does this relate to areas of your life? Pray for a long-term vision for the things God wants you to value most. Then you won't be as likely to put them at risk for momentary pleasures.

WHAT'S THE WORD?

"Look, I'm dying of starvation!" said Esau. "What good is my birthright to me now?"
. . . Then Jacob gave Esau some bread and lentil stew. Esau ate the meal, then got up and left. He showed contempt for his rights as the firstborn. GENESIS 25:32, 34

THE CLIMB

ALMOST *there*. Snow crunched beneath Erik's boots. He felt his heart quicken. Partly he felt exhausted, but even more so he felt the thrill of being so close to the summit. He'd recently cleared fifty feet of vertical rock. Just before that, he was hiking a ridge barely a meter wide with a 9,000-foot drop on one side and a 12,000-foot drop on the other. But he made it. On May 25, 2001, Erik Weihenmayer found himself standing atop Mount Everest, the tallest mountain on Earth, though he couldn't fully appreciate the view. You see, Erik is blind.

Just over seven years later, Erik became the first blind person to climb the Seven Summits—the highest peaks on every continent—when he summited the Carstensz Pyramid in Indonesia. How could he accomplish such a feat? For one thing, he's a great listener. His ears remain sensitive to things other climbers might miss, from potentially dangerous winds to different sounds made by the ice. He also surrounds himself with people who wouldn't steer him wrong. On his website, Erik explains, "I wouldn't have been able to achieve these things without an internal vision, without some creativity and persistence, and without the ability to build a great team of friends around me."

Life is a climb. Some days are more treacherous than others. And we all have blind spots that force us to rely more heavily on what we hear than on what we see. Isn't it comforting to know that we have a Shepherd who wants to lead us? In John 10:4-5, Jesus says his sheep follow him because they know the sound of his voice, yet they will flee from strangers. Studying God's Word makes us more familiar with his voice. As for the "strangers" Jesus mentions, those voices come from the world (see 1 John 2:15-17), our flesh (see Romans 7:18-25), and the enemy (see 1 Peter 5:8). Those things would love to throw us off course. All the more reason to choose our friends carefully, so we can keep each other focused as we trek toward the summit together.

DADDY-*Daughter Time*

How well do you recognize the Lord's voice? Discuss that, as well as practical ways you can make it easier to hear God. Are your traveling companions for the climb helps or hindrances?

To live this out, try being a trustworthy voice for each other. One of you puts on a blindfold while the other sets up obstacles in a good-size room. Take turns talking each other through the maze to a destination where a tasty prize awaits.

WHAT'S THE WORD?

After [the shepherd] has gathered his own flock, he walks ahead of them, and they follow him because they know his voice. JOHN 10:4

GOD'S MODIFIED MASTERPIECE

WHEN he started tinkering at the age of ten, George Vlosich III never dreamed he would be the professional artist he is today. It was just a hobby. A way to pass time on long car trips. Yet now his masterpieces hang in galleries all over the world. Each work of art takes between seventy and eighty hours to complete, and pieces have sold for more than $10,000. He's not a painter, sculptor, or photographer. Rather, George has mastered the Etch A Sketch.

Ever since the first Etch A Sketch rolled off the assembly line in 1960, the toy has entertained millions of people . . . and frustrated millions of others. Have you ever tried to create a curved or diagonal line by turning those two white knobs at the same time? Easier said than done. And there's no eraser on those things. The only way to fix a slipup is to shake the screen, which erases everything. As George explains, "The image is one continuous line, so if I make a mistake, I'm forced to start over."

Ugh! Just one mistake ruins the entire creation! Can you believe it? Well, of course you can. Because the same thing happened in the Garden of Eden.

As Genesis 3 tells us, sin entered the world when Adam and Eve disobeyed God by eating the forbidden fruit. Not only did that one mistake get them evicted from the Garden, but suddenly humankind had a sin sickness alienating us from our Creator. So our holy God had a decision to make. Would he grab his celestial Etch A Sketch, shake vigorously, and start over? He could have, but he didn't. Rather, the Lord chose to love us despite our ugly flaw, so much so that he modified his masterpiece, and Jesus entered the picture (see Romans 5:17).

Next time you play with an Etch A Sketch, take a moment to thank God for shaking up human history without starting from scratch.

DADDY-*Daughter Time*

On his website, George Vlosich says, "I've always acknowledged that art is a God-given talent." What gifts do you have in this area? If you own an Etch A Sketch, play with it together. Challenge each other to draw different things. Then learn more about George and see some of his creations at gvetchedintime.com.

WHAT'S THE WORD?

The sin of this one man, Adam, caused death to rule over many. But even greater is God's wonderful grace and his gift of righteousness, for all who receive it will live in triumph over sin and death through this one man, Jesus Christ. ROMANS 5:17

WHAT BAIT
ARE YOU USING?

THE waders. The rod and reel. That goofy hat with lures stuck in the brim. Debbie could always tell when her father was preparing for the first day of trout season. He loved to fish. She loved the opening day ritual of rising before dawn and stopping for doughnuts and hot cocoa on the way to the lake, which they would be doing the next day. As Dad sat on the front porch fiddling with his tackle box, Debbie stepped outside to see if her friend's mom was there to take her to the movies.

"Hey, Punkin, not too late tonight, okay?" her dad said. "Early morning tomorrow. I think this year we're gonna catch our limit."

He glanced up from a jar of salmon eggs just long enough to notice that his daughter was wearing short shorts, a tank top, and too much mascara. "Whoa, hold on a minute. You're not going out like that."

"But, Dad, the other girls—"

"Debbie," he interrupted, "you have to realize the signals you're sending when you look this way. I know you want to honor God and get the right kind of attention from—"

"Boys," Debbie said.

"Yeah, right . . . them," he said. "Trust me, boys are a lot like fish: the kind you attract depends on the bait you use. You really need to be more modest and less made up. It's partly for your own safety; you don't want to draw sharks. But also, as a godly young lady you need to think about how young men are wired so that you don't create a temptation."

"Are we still talking about fish?" Debbie asked playfully, realizing deep inside that her father was right. She turned to go inside. "If Ava shows up, tell her I'm changing."

"Well, don't change too much, Punkin," he replied. "I love you just the way you are."

DADDY-*Daughter Time*

Based on 1 Timothy 2:9-10, do you think Debbie's dad overreacted? Why or why not? When was the last time you experienced conflict over makeup or the clothes you wore? Do you have "house rules" about them? Clearly established boundaries (and consequences) should help keep disagreements from becoming battles. Agree on some limits together.

If you enjoy a certain outdoor activity—fishing, hiking, biking, camping, boating—plan a day trip together, just the two of you.

WHAT'S THE WORD?

I want women to be modest in their appearance. . . . For women who claim to be devoted to God should make themselves attractive by the good things they do.
1 TIMOTHY 2:9-10

AH, the potato chip! Classic. Ridged. Kettle cooked. You can't beat a bowlful salted to perfection and seasoned with cheddar cheese, sour cream, or hickory-smoked goodness. Mmmm! As popular as they are at Memorial Day barbecues in America, fans all over the world enjoy potato chips in flavors ranging from prawn cocktail (England) and tofu in a spicy pork sauce (Japan) to roast lamb and mint (New Zealand). Strange, huh?

But not nearly as strange as the story behind how this salty snack food was created.

In the summer of 1853, a fussy customer at a New York resort sent back his thick-cut French-fried potatoes several times for being too thick. That's when chef George Crum purposely tried to make a petty prank. He sliced the spuds superthin and fried them to a crisp, hoping to irritate the guest with potatoes impossible to eat with a fork. Crum's plot backfired. The man loved them, and people have loved potato chips ever since.

In this case, a frustrated man set out to cause trouble, but it worked to everyone's benefit—kinda like what happened to Joseph's brothers in the Old Testament.

In Genesis 37, Joseph's brothers resented Dad's favoritism and little Joe's grandiose dreams, so they sold him into slavery and faked his death. But the Lord had other plans. In the years that followed, God orchestrated events so that Joseph became Pharaoh's right-hand man—a position of high honor. The dreamer guided Egypt through a severe famine, and guess who came looking for food one day? That's right—his brothers! Funny thing is, they didn't recognize him. Joseph eventually revealed his identity and assured them that all was forgiven. In Genesis 50:20, Joseph said to his brothers, "You intended to harm me, but God intended it all for good. He brought me to this position so I could save the lives of many people."

DADDY-*Daughter Time*

Have you ever been bullied or harassed or gossiped about? How did that feel? According to Psalm 37:7, how should we respond when people are scheming against us? If you're not familiar with the entire story of Joseph, take time to read it together in Genesis 37–50. Then go to the store together and pick out your favorite flavor of chips. Pop them open and pray that the same God who saw Joseph through his trials will make something glorious out of yours, too.

WHAT'S THE WORD?

You intended to harm me, but God intended it all for good. He brought me to this position so I could save the lives of many people. GENESIS 50:20

A GOOD GOAL

NORTHWESTERN University lacrosse standout Shannon Smith didn't like to see her teammates sad. So when the Wildcats faced Maryland for the second straight year in the 2011 NCAA Division I women's lacrosse final, the junior did everything she could to make her teammates happy. And it worked. The previous year Northwestern had led 6–0 before the Terrapins stormed back to win the game 13–11.

But on this day in 2011, Shannon scored half of Northwestern's eight goals to help the Wildcats to an 8–7 victory over Maryland. Shannon's four tallies—including the game winner that came with 4:36 left in the contest—gave her an amazing eighty-six goals for the season. The junior attacker was named the tournament's Most Valuable Player, but after the game all she wanted to talk about was her team. "Ever since last season, I've told myself that I never want to see the hurt in my teammates' eyes again," Shannon said to reporters. "So I was going to do everything it took to win this national championship." Her efforts helped Northwestern win its sixth championship in seven years.

Shannon's four goals in the championship game were noteworthy, but the reason she wanted to score was even more impressive. She didn't want her teammates to be sad. There are situations in life when you're going to be sad: a pet dies, someone says something mean to you, you lose a big game, you don't get the part in the play that you wanted. At those times, it's nice to have a friend—or teammate—who can cheer you up. And there's no better friend than Jesus. Psalm 147:3 (NIV) says the Lord "heals the brokenhearted and binds up their wounds." When you're brokenhearted, Jesus is there. He's the perfect team captain who can comfort you when you lose and celebrate with you when you win.

DADDY-*Daughter Time*

Shannon's dad played a big part in her success on the lacrosse field. When she was in elementary school, he signed her up for a lacrosse camp. Shannon kept going to that same camp and improving every year. Northwestern's coach ran that camp, so that's where Shannon went to school. Her dad had bought 150 tickets so family and friends could cheer her on as the Wildcats won the championship.

What's your favorite sport? It may or may not be lacrosse. Whatever it is, take some time to play it together. Dads, you'll probably enjoy tossing around a softball, shooting some hoops, bumping a volleyball, or going on a short run. As you exercise together, thank God that he's always there to comfort you.

WHAT'S THE WORD?

He heals the brokenhearted and binds up their wounds. PSALM 147:3 (NIV)

KEEPIN' IT REAL

MAYBE there's been a time that you have been driving as a family, only to have these seven words fill the air: "Don't make me pull this car over!" Kids hate to hear 'em. Parents hate to say 'em. But sometimes the behavior in the backseat demands attention. Which brings to mind a situation that occurred in the New Testament between the apostle Paul and the still-immature church at Corinth.

You've probably heard the expression "keepin' it real." It means being true and authentic, avoiding hypocrisy. The apostle Paul was all about keepin' it real. In fact, as he concluded his second letter to the Corinthians, he said he was very concerned about the people there and what he would discover when he visited them for a third time: "I am afraid that when I come I won't like what I find, and you won't like my response. I am afraid that I will find quarreling, jealousy, anger, selfishness, slander, gossip, arrogance, and disorderly behavior" (2 Corinthians 12:20).

Paul wondered if their faith was real. He worried that people claiming to follow Jesus were sinning up a storm and not really living like Christians. And as the one in authority over them, he warned them that he was prepared to get tough. When Paul wrote 2 Corinthians 13:10, it was his way of saying, "Don't make me pull this church over!"

No one enjoys being disciplined, be it at home, at work, at school, or on the athletic field. Getting scolded hurts. It can be embarrassing. And yet we all need to be held accountable for living responsibly and following the rules, both for our own good and for the benefit of others. It was true of the early church, and it's still true today.

DADDY-*Daughter Time*

Has an authority figure's discipline ever left a lasting impression on you? What happened? Behaving like a Christian at church or youth group is relatively easy. Most folks there love Jesus and follow a similar code of conduct. But which settings or people in your life make it a challenge to live as a Christian? Why? Pray for each other as you seek to emulate Christ daily in every area of your lives.

WHAT'S THE WORD?

I am writing this to you before I come, hoping that I won't need to deal severely with you when I do come. For I want to use the authority the Lord has given me to strengthen you, not to tear you down. 2 CORINTHIANS 13:10

I WILL NOT BE MOVED

SOME people take a stand for what they believe in. Others take a seat. In an attempt to defend the honor of his favorite baseball team, Cleveland grocer Charley Lupica scaled a sixty-foot flagpole on this date in 1949 and settled onto a four-foot-square platform. He vowed to stay there until his beloved Indians recaptured first place. It was a long, hot summer. On the plus side, restaurants donated food. However, he missed the birth of his fourth child. After 117 days, the Indians had fallen out of contention, and Charley finally climbed down from his perch on September 25.

No doubt Charley had his share of supporters, mainly fellow Indians fans. Go, Tribe! Hang in there, Charley! Yet others mocked him, convinced he was loopy. In fact, kids threw firecrackers at him on the Fourth of July. So, do you think Charley was a hero or a fool? Your answer probably depends on whether you feel he suffered for a worthy cause.

As a Christian, you may know what it's like to take a stand. But instead of defending your favorite sports team, you've had to defend your faith. Or maybe you refused to go along with the crowd when your friends urged you to do something dishonest or inappropriate. Resisting peer pressure and living for Jesus is hard at any age. But Ephesians 6:14 gives you some good advice on how to do it: "Stand your ground, putting on the belt of truth and the body armor of God's righteousness."

Three young men in the Old Testament—Shadrach, Meshach, and Abednego—took an unpopular stand. They wouldn't bow down to King Nebuchadnezzar's ninety-foot gold statue of himself. You can bet people all over Babylon called the boys stubborn, difficult, and foolish. Yet despite the gossip and the threat of a fiery fate, they refused to worship anyone but God. Now that's a stand. You can read about how the Lord honored their steadfast faith in Daniel 3. He'll honor yours, too!

DADDY-*Daughter Time*

Think of a time when you stood up for what was right, even though it would have been easier to back down. What did you feel so strongly about? Did people respect you? Were there consequences?

In the late 1940s, sports fans waved felt pennants emblazoned with their team's name and logo. Design and create a pennant together that shows where your loyalties lie. You can browse online for ideas.

WHAT'S THE WORD?

Stand your ground, putting on the belt of truth and the body armor of God's righteousness. EPHESIANS 6:14

FAIR PLAY

OLIVIA knew she shouldn't take the last piece of her brother's birthday cake. It was his favorite: triple chocolate with a layer of chocolate mousse and chocolate frosting on top. That was *her* favorite too.

He had two pieces yesterday, and I only had one, Olivia thought. *Plus, he said he's going to try to be nicer to me. This would be nice . . . very nice.*

Olivia glanced around the kitchen. Her brother was nowhere to be seen.

Typical, she thought. *He's always doing things with his friends and doesn't have any time for me.*

The more she thought about it, the madder she became and the better the cake looked.

"I deserve this cake for everything I put up with from him," Olivia said as she slid the luscious cake onto a plate.

Have you ever been like Olivia? You know what the right thing is but convince yourself it's okay to do the opposite. It's easy to make the wrong thing look right if it gets us something we want.

We do the same thing with friends. If a kid is rich, we might try to be her friend so she'll give us something. If somebody is popular, we might hang out with her so we can be popular too. Instead of looking at what we can get from somebody, we should make decisions about who to hang out with based on who they are.

God calls us to act differently from people who don't know him. He says the right thing is the right thing *all* the time. Colossians 4:1 puts it this way: "Masters, be just and fair to your slaves. Remember that you also have a Master—in heaven." God commands masters to treat their slaves fairly, so we should treat our family members even more so. Plus, this verse reminds us that God is always watching our actions from heaven.

DADDY-*Daughter Time*

Sometimes it can feel like the Bible has a lot of rules that hinder us from doing what we want. But when you follow God's rules, you'll discover how much is added to your life—things like joy, peace, and blessings.

Share with each other a time in your lives when you were tempted to do the wrong thing but then made the right decision. What happened? Maybe you can also think of a time when you chose poorly and suffered the consequences of your actions.

Oh yeah, and *always* let your brother have the last piece of his birthday cake . . . unless he says you can have it.

WHAT'S THE WORD?

Masters, be just and fair to your slaves. Remember that you also have a Master—in heaven. COLOSSIANS 4:1

WET AND WILD

WHY did the Christian Student Fellowship group at the University of Kentucky organize the world's largest water balloon fight in 2011? The reason is obvious—it was fun! How else would you describe nearly 9,000 people throwing more than 175,000 water balloons at each other? That's one big water war. But organizers had an even bigger reason to create this wet and wild event at the Johnson Center Field. They wanted University of Kentucky students to know about their God-centered group. "We're a Christian ministry on campus, and we're here for students," one organizer said.

As you go through life as a Christian, you'll discover things are more fun and you're more effective in your faith when you receive support from other believers. When you're in a group of encouraging Christ followers, you can "spur one another on toward love and good deeds" (Hebrews 10:24, NIV). The leaders at Christian Student Fellowship want to do exactly what their name says—be a place of fellowship for Christian college kids. They organize 150 different events during the school year, put together small-group Bible studies, do outreach into the college community, serve the homeless in the area, and take part in many other activities. Do the students grow deeper in their faith? Yes. Do they have fun together? Oh yeah.

Some people picture Christians as dour-faced party poopers. But life with Jesus is anything but blah. God wants you to have fun and draw others to him. And putting on the world's largest water balloon fight accomplished both of those things.

DADDY-*Daughter Time*

Watch the official video of this event by searching for "CSF World's Largest Water Balloon Fight 2011" on the Internet. Think of how many people and how many hours it took to fill all those balloons and to plan the event. Then think about how quickly 175,141 balloons were thrown into the air. It looks like fun, doesn't it?

Have some fun together by filling up a balloon with water. Then go outside and stand back-to-back. Take one giant step forward and turn around to face each other. Toss the balloon back and forth without letting it break. Every time you catch it, take another step backward. See how far apart you can get before the balloon breaks. Try it again with another balloon. Thank God for fellow Christians who encourage you to show love and do nice things for those around you.

WHAT'S THE WORD?

Let us consider how we may spur one another on toward love and good deeds.
HEBREWS 10:24 (NIV)

June 3

WHEN you picture a pirate, what sort of image comes to mind? Is it a scruffy sailor sporting a sword and an eye patch, with a parrot on his shoulder? How about a professional baseball player from Pittsburgh? Or maybe some sixth grader you know who downloads music illegally from the Internet? All of those would qualify. But chances are, it was the first one.

Now imagine yourself standing on the deck of a creaky old vessel flying the Jolly Roger. Hear the wind beat against the sails as the ship slices through rolling waves. Smell the salt air. The buccaneers aboard argue as they struggle to decipher a frayed piece of cloth bearing a big black *X*. Why? Because X marks the spot . . . for treasure! Pearls. Rubies. Gold doubloons. Family photos.

What? Okay, granted, most rum-swilling plunderers wouldn't consider a chest full of family photos "riches," but a very famous Hollywood pirate does. Perhaps best known for his role as Captain Jack Sparrow in the *Pirates of the Caribbean* movies, actor Johnny Depp is talented, wealthy, and famous. Yet he considers the privilege of becoming a father among his greatest treasures.

In an interview with *Newsweek* magazine, Depp said, "When I became a dad for the first time, it was like a veil being lifted. . . . Suddenly there was clarity. I wasn't angry anymore. It was the first purely selfless moment that I had ever experienced. And it was liberating. In that moment, it's like you become something else. The real you is revealed."

It's easy to think of treasure as material loot. But it could be just about anything. Your treasure is whatever has captured your heart, which says a lot about your values and priorities. That's why Jesus told his disciples to invest in things of lasting value, not possessions that could decay or be stolen (see Matthew 6:19-21). So, are your treasures pirate proof?

DADDY-*Daughter Time*
What's your greatest passion? Is there a difference between a prized possession and the kind of treasure Jesus is referring to in Matthew 6? For what would you be willing to give up that special possession? (Here's a hint: that is your treasure!) For countless dads, fathering a little girl has been a life-changing blessing. Take time to tell your daughter how she has changed your life.

WHAT'S THE WORD?
Wherever your treasure is, there the desires of your heart will also be.   MATTHEW 6:21

FULL OF HOT AIR

JOSEPH and Jacques Montgolfier thought they'd discovered a new type of gas. (Stop laughing! It's true, and it didn't come from eating beans.) The French brothers invented the first balloon and believed it could fly because of Montgolfier gas (hey, they discovered it, so they could name it whatever they wanted). It turned out their balloon flew because it was filled with hot air, and air rises when it's heated. In the Montgolfiers' case, the air rose very, very high.

On June 4, 1783, the Montgolfier brothers flew a hot-air balloon over 6,562 feet into the sky over Annonay, France. Joseph and Jacques were paper makers who experimented with fabric-lined paper to make the first hot-air balloon, which they called a *Montgolfiere*. Even before the US Constitution was written, the Montgolfiers flew the first balloon. Shortly after this day, they sent up a balloon with passengers—a sheep, a duck, and a rooster. On October 15, 1783, the first people got to fly in a hot-air balloon.

Have you ever heard the saying "full of hot air"? It means a person is puffed up and thinks a lot of himself or herself. The Montgolfiers' balloon was full of hot air, but hopefully the brothers' egos were not. The Bible warns against being full of yourself. In the Old Testament, the Edomites thought a lot of themselves. They built their homes in the mountains and thought they could withstand any attack. The Edomites even pillaged nearby people groups. But in the book of Obadiah, the Lord says through his prophet, "Even if you soar as high as eagles and build your nest among the stars, I will bring you crashing down" (v. 4). The moral to that verse is don't be full of hot air.

DADDY-*Daughter Time*

Do you know people who seem full of themselves? Pride can be a dangerous thing. If you know a prideful person (maybe it's a mean girl or a bully), trust that God will bring him or her down. That's what he did to the Edomites.

Pray together and ask God to help you always remain humble . . . even if you get to fly in a hot-air balloon.

WHAT'S THE WORD?

You have been deceived by your own pride because you live in a rock fortress and make your home high in the mountains. "Who can ever reach us way up here?" you ask boastfully. But even if you soar as high as eagles and build your nest among the stars, I will bring you crashing down. OBADIAH 1:3-4

IN THE LORD'S ARMY

ARE you in the Lord's army? If you said, "Yes, sir," then you probably know the popular children's song and could be ready to enlist in The Salvation Army.

In the mid-1800s, William Booth felt God calling him to preach the gospel to the poorest of England's poor. William walked the streets, telling the homeless and hungry about Jesus Christ. By 1867, ten others had joined William in his efforts. Within the next seven years, more than one thousand volunteers and forty-two evangelists had come alongside to help William in his organization called The Christian Mission. But it was around this time in 1878 that William's ministry got its more famous name. William was reading a document that said, "The Christian Mission is a volunteer army." Then it hit him: it was an army—The Salvation Army. For more than 130 years, The Salvation Army has helped people and introduced them to Jesus Christ. Today, The Salvation Army assists children and families around the world who suffer from hunger and poverty or are victims of natural disasters.

Isn't it amazing that God used one man to spread the message of his love around the world? God did the same thing in Bible times through the apostle Paul. After Jesus died and ascended back into heaven, Paul went on three journeys to tell everybody about God's truth and forgiveness. In 1 Corinthians 9:22, Paul wrote, "When I am with those who are weak, I share their weakness, for I want to bring the weak to Christ. Yes, I try to find common ground with everyone, doing everything I can to save some." Paul knew everybody wouldn't accept Christ as Lord, but he did everything he could to make sure the world knew about his Savior.

DADDY-*Daughter Time*

Are you doing everything you can to tell people around you about Jesus Christ? That's one of your big responsibilities as a follower of Jesus. Talk together about activities you could do to spread the gospel. Maybe you could volunteer at a nearby homeless mission. Perhaps you could invite your friends to a vacation Bible school or volunteer to help out at VBS this summer. You don't have to try to save the world, but follow Paul's example and do everything you can to save some.

WHAT'S THE WORD?

When I am with those who are weak, I share their weakness, for I want to bring the weak to Christ. Yes, I try to find common ground with everyone, doing everything I can to save some. 1 CORINTHIANS 9:22

HELMET OF SALVATION

CAN you imagine playing softball without a helmet? That wouldn't be smart. A helmet is specifically designed to protect your head. And since your brain controls your body and forms your thoughts, it's important to guard it. According to the United States Consumer Product Safety Commission (CPSC), there are over 350,000 sports-related head injuries treated at hospital emergency rooms every year. The actual number of head injuries is probably higher, because the CPSC numbers don't include less severe injuries that are treated at doctors' offices or immediate-care centers or are self-treated. For kids fourteen and younger, the top-five sports that cause head injuries are

1. cycling;
2. football;
3. baseball/softball;
4. basketball; and
5. water sports (diving, surfing, waterskiing, etc.).

Helmets save thousands of lives every year. But one helmet has saved millions of people for thousands of years: it's the helmet of salvation.

You've probably talked about the armor of God in church or colored in a little armor-wearing soldier in Sunday school when you were younger. But as a refresher, Ephesians 6:17 says, "Put on salvation as your helmet." All of God's armor has a purpose, but the helmet may be the most important piece. Think about it. There's the belt of truth, breastplate of righteousness, shoes of peace, shield of faith, helmet of salvation, and sword of the Spirit (see Ephesians 6:14-17).

Just like in sports, a helmet protects our heads—the part of the body most responsible for keeping us alive. God gives us the helmet of salvation to save us from an eternity separated from him. By putting on the helmet, we're protected against Satan's schemes and can have supreme hope for our future in heaven. Plus, we can be confident that God's helmet will help us fend off the curveballs—and fastballs—that life throws our way.

DADDY-*Daughter Time*

Have you prayed to God for his helmet of salvation? If you've never asked God for his protection and to be on his team, you can do it now. Just pray something like this:

Jesus, I've disobeyed your rules. I believe you took the punishment for my mistakes on the cross and rose again from the dead so I could be forgiven. Thank you! I accept your gift of salvation and ask you to be the Lord of my life. Amen.

If you just prayed that prayer, tell your family, your pastor, everyone! They'll want to celebrate with you!

WHAT'S THE WORD?

Put on salvation as your helmet, and take the sword of the Spirit, which is the word of God. EPHESIANS 6:17

MONEY MATTERS

MONEY doesn't grow on trees. You've probably heard that before. Money does come from hard work. In 2 Thessalonians 3:10, Paul reminded the people of Thessalonica that "we gave you this command: 'Those unwilling to work will not get to eat.'" At first that may sound harsh. But the truth is, a person earns a wage and the ability to purchase food through effort.

The Bible talks a lot about money. On more than two hundred occasions, money is specifically mentioned or addressed in a parable. Obviously, God views this as an important topic, so we should do the same. Many financial experts say the best way for children to learn about money is through earning an allowance. Have you ever noticed it's easier to spend other people's money than your own? When you receive a gift card from a family member, it's easy to go through the whole thing during one trip to the department store. But when you earn a dollar, you might agonize for twenty minutes, deciding on just the right candy bar. And it better be on sale!

The sooner you learn the relationship between work and money the better. An allowance is earned, not simply given. Your allowance should be tied to chores and other extra duties around the house. Keeping your room clean may be expected for being part of the family. But a parent may want to pay you an allowance for vacuuming the living room or pulling weeds. Every family has different standards, so it's good to talk about them.

And as you start earning money, make sure to remember that all money is God's. Honor him by giving some back for his work.

DADDY-*Daughter Time*

Learning money-management skills is important in the life of a Christian. God provides for our needs, and he expects us to make good decisions with the money he gives us. Little things can make a big difference in our personal finances. Investment advisers say pennies here and there can add up to thousands of dollars in the long run. Adults who regularly buy coffee or eat lunch at restaurants may be missing out on big bucks. Over the course of thirty-five years, these little expenditures can add up to more than $100,000. If these same monies were invested at just 3 percent interest for thirty-five years, they would equal nearly $250,000!

If your daughter doesn't already have a bank account, go together to open one. Many banks have great programs to help teach kids about money.

WHAT'S THE WORD?

Even while we were with you, we gave you this command: "Those unwilling to work will not get to eat." 2 THESSALONIANS 3:10

IMITATE ME

HAVE you ever been around a mimic, someone who copies every move or sound you make? If your little brother mimics you, it can get annoying . . . fast. But it can be fun to watch a professional mimic, or impressionist, who re-creates all kinds of characters, famous people, and noises.

Children become mimics at an early age. God created us this way so we could learn from the world around us. We develop language skills as babies in part from hearing sounds and words over and over again. Then we try our best to reproduce them. Babies also learn facial expressions from watching their parents and older siblings. As children grow, some of them continue to hone their abilities to imitate. They learn accents, change their tone and rate of speaking, and do a great job sounding like somebody else.

The best impressionists try to use the same words as the person they imitate. They learn the mannerisms, figure out emotions, and copy personalities. In our walk with God, we need to be mimics. In fact, God commands us to imitate him and his Son, Jesus Christ. Ephesians 5:1-2 says, "Imitate God, therefore, in everything you do, because you are his dear children. Live a life filled with love, following the example of Christ." What words did Jesus say? How did he speak and interact with people? How did he react when people needed help?

The more we imitate God, the more Christlike we become. And as our words and actions reflect Christ, people will begin to see him in us and want to know more. When we mimic Jesus, it's never annoying.

DADDY-*Daughter Time*

Take turns doing impressions, or imitations, of people you both know. See if you can guess who the other is attempting to imitate (try not to be mean in your imitations). Mix things up by mimicking famous people as well as family and friends.

Daughters, tell your dad what aspects of his character and personality you resemble already and which ones you most admire and want to imitate. Dads, tell your daughters what you see in them that reminds you of God's character.

WHAT'S THE WORD?

Imitate God, therefore, in everything you do, because you are his dear children. Live a life filled with love, following the example of Christ. He loved us and offered himself as a sacrifice for us, a pleasing aroma to God. EPHESIANS 5:1-2

WHAT A RIDE!

ARIANNA couldn't believe it . . . the race had already started. Arianna and her dad had been competing in mountain-bike races for a couple of years. Due to a misunderstanding, the pair had shown up at the wrong place to begin a race in Michigan. Once Arianna's dad learned where the real starting line was, they jumped back in the car and drove as fast as they could. But by the time they got to the actual race, all the other competitors had begun. Instead of giving up, Arianna snapped on her helmet, tightly fastened her shoes, and ran her bike to the starting line. She leaped on her blue-and-green mountain bike and tore down the trail. It didn't matter that everybody else had a six-minute head start, Arianna wanted to race.

The Michigan mountainside was a blur as Arianna pumped her legs toward the finish line. If her dad had taught her anything about mountain-bike racing, it was always to work hard and never give up. That advice helped the ten-year-old whenever she wrecked on her bike, which inevitably happened two or three times per race. After several minutes, Arianna started to see some of the other competitors, which made her ride even faster to catch up. Nearly forty minutes into the race, the eight-mile competition was almost over. Arianna had passed so many other riders that she couldn't keep track of them all. Only one racer was ahead of her. Within a half mile of the finish line, Arianna flew past the last of her competition to take first in the Under-12 division.

"Always try your best, even when it's challenging," Arianna said after the race. "God will be with you to help you through it. Just keep going."

DADDY-*Daughter Time*

That's good advice, and so is this: "Do you not know that in a race all the runners run, but only one gets the prize? Run in such a way as to get the prize" (1 Corinthians 9:24, NIV). By trying your best and not giving up, you'll be running to get the prize.

As a fun activity, plan a father-daughter bike ride. You can ride around your neighborhood or find a bike trail. Remember to be safe, and always wear a helmet. As you're riding, tell God that you want to run for him in such a way as to get the prize.

WHAT'S THE WORD?

Do you not know that in a race all the runners run, but only one gets the prize? Run in such a way as to get the prize. 1 CORINTHIANS 9:24 (NIV)

PROTECT YOURSELF

SUMMER vacation. What could be better? The sun. The amusement park rides. The fun photos. How cool is it to snap an especially cute shot and post it to your Facebook account with the caption "Wish you were here"? Maybe you do wish other family members and friends could join you on vacation. But before you share your summer experiences on the web, make sure you're back home first.

Why? Because it's wise. Home-security experts recommend not posting photos on Facebook while you're still on vacation, because many burglaries are committed by someone you know or by someone connected to someone you know. Families need to do everything possible to keep their homes safe. And sometimes it's the little things—like waiting to post photos—that make a big difference.

While it's important to take simple steps to safeguard our homes, it's even more important for us to safeguard our lives. The Bible says one of the best ways we can protect ourselves is to pursue wisdom. "Don't turn your back on wisdom, for she will protect you. Love her, and she will guard you" (Proverbs 4:6).

By making wise decisions, we guard our hearts. Maybe that means not watching a video on YouTube or turning off a popular song with questionable lyrics. Perhaps it means not going to a party where you know kids are doing things that go against your family's values. Love wisdom by digging into God's Word and understanding his laws. The Bible is full of wisdom that's just as true today as it was when Jesus walked the earth two thousand years ago. Don't turn your back on wisdom. Pursue it. It'll make you safer and stronger in the long run.

DADDY-*Daughter Time*

Take a few minutes to look up these verses about wisdom. Write down a nugget of truth that you want to remember to help you be wise:

Job 28:28 _____

Proverbs 19:20 _____

1 Corinthians 1:30 _____

James 1:5 _____

What are some ways that wisdom can guard you?

WHAT'S THE WORD?

Don't turn your back on wisdom, for she will protect you. Love her, and she will guard you.   PROVERBS 4:6

HORSING AROUND

IS there anything more awesome than watching a horse gallop? Some horses can run more than forty miles per hour. The speed and gracefulness of horse racing make it one of the oldest sports in the world. And no races are more prestigious than horse racing's Triple Crown. Beginning with the Kentucky Derby during the first Saturday in May, the fastest horses go on to compete in the Preakness Stakes (third Saturday in May) and the Belmont Stakes in New York. The races only take a couple of minutes each as the horses run for about a mile and a half. In the history of the sport, only eleven horses have won all three races. The first horse to do it was Sir Barton, who won the Belmont on this day in 1919.

Since then Gallant Fox, Omaha, War Admiral, Whirlaway, Count Fleet, Assault, Citation, Secretariat, Seattle Slew, and Affirmed have claimed the Triple Crown. Affirmed's victory was the most recent in 1978. Experts say winning the Triple Crown is so difficult because these three races are run within five weeks. The tracks are different, the distances change, and the conditions can vary—from mud to loose dirt. Any horse strong and fast enough to win the Triple Crown will be remembered in history.

Horses play a big role in the Bible. Nearly 150 verses mention horses, and one of the coolest is Revelation 19:11, which says, "I saw heaven opened, and a white horse was standing there. Its rider was named Faithful and True." As awesome as it is to see a horse run, it's even more awesome to imagine Jesus riding to victory on a white horse.

DADDY-*Daughter Time*

Read more about how John describes Jesus coming back to earth in Revelation 19:11-16. What are your favorite parts about those verses? Write some down:

_____

_____

_____

If your schedules allow, plan to go look at horses or go horseback riding. You may be able to visit a horse at a petting zoo or county fair. As you ride or look at these amazing animals, picture Jesus on his white horse. Praise the Lord that one day he'll ride to victory.

WHAT'S THE WORD?

I saw heaven opened, and a white horse was standing there. Its rider was named Faithful and True. REVELATION 19:11

CACHE THE WAVE

DURING the spring of 2000, Dave Ulmer wandered into the Oregon woods and hid a plastic container of little toys. This would be a boring story if nobody found the cache, or hiding place for little treasures. But Dave hoped people would find it, so he posted the cache's coordinates online. A day later it was apparent Dave's original stash had been found because a person had signed the logbook, left a trinket of his own, and taken a toy for himself. Within the week, additional caches popped up in California, Kansas, and Illinois. Almost instantly, the hobby of geocaching was created. Today, geocaching is one of the hottest high-tech hobbies. Nearly 1.6 million active geocaches exist around the world with more than five million people participating in the activity.

The funny thing is that Dave didn't try to start a popular hobby. He just wanted to celebrate the fact that average citizens could use Global Positioning System (GPS) satellite navigation. Before May 1, 2000, GPS could be used only by the government and military. Although Dave didn't mean to, he tapped into a basic human drive—we love to search for things. Think about how excited you'd be to find a treasure map marked with a giant *X*. God designed us to have a desire to search so we could find him. He says in Jeremiah 29:13, "If you look for me wholeheartedly, you will find me." Now that's cool!

By using God's GPS, the Bible, we can know where we are in our relationship with him and how to grow even closer to him. With a little effort, we can discover God's hidden treasures, which are way better than any trinkets found in a buried coffee can.

DADDY-*Daughter Time*

Geocaches can be found in more than one hundred countries across all seven continents—even Antarctica. Chances are there are some hidden near your home. If you own a GPS device, go to geocaching.com to find the coordinates for an adventure. Then go on a treasure hunt together.

If you don't own a GPS unit, try geocaching's less-techy "cousin" called letterboxing. All you need is a notebook and a rubber stamp. Instead of coordinates, letterboxing involves solving clues to find the hidden treasure. And instead of a box full of trinkets, letterboxes contain a journal and a rubber stamp. Go to letterboxing.org to find more information and hidden sites near your home.

As you search, remember to seek God with your whole heart. Be passionate about finding and following him.

WHAT'S THE WORD?

If you look for me wholeheartedly, you will find me.   JEREMIAH 29:13

CARRY ME

EYES looking up. Arms stretched high. Even if babies can't say the words *carry me*, it's obvious what they want. As dads, it's fun to remember the times when our little girls asked us to carry them. While human dads easily carry their daughters in their arms, fathers in the animal kingdom have some different techniques.

Daddy swans carry their children on their backs. The baby swans climb between their wings to get out of the water and go for a ride. Penguin daddies carry their babies on their feet. The little chicks sit on their fathers' feet and hide under a fold of skin to stay warm and safe. Marmoset monkey daddies can pick up their babies in their arms. Then the babies cling to their backs. They take the young babies to their mothers when they're hungry. Sea horse daddies carry their young in a little pocket. Siamese fighting fish help their babies by carrying them in their mouths. If a young fish is struggling to swim, the dad grabs it in its mouth and spits it at the surface of the water so it can try again.

Aren't you glad your dad doesn't carry you in his mouth? That would be gross. It's much nicer when your dad wraps his arms around you to hold and protect you. In the Bible, Moses compared God's protection to that of a father's. God guided and protected his people for forty years in the desert. Before the Israelites crossed the Jordan River into the Promised Land, Moses told the people, "You saw in the wilderness how the LORD your God carried you as a man carries his son all along the way you traveled until you reached this place" (Deuteronomy 1:31, HCSB). God is always there when his people hold up their arms and say, "Carry me."

DADDY-*Daughter Time*

Father's Day is right around the corner. This special day is celebrated around the world, but in the United States it's always the third Sunday in June. Ask your dad how he'd like to be celebrated this year. Or you can come up with a fun surprise.

Dads, relive some fun memories by giving your daughter a piggyback ride around the room or around the house. As you carry your daughter, each of you should think about how God's strong arms are always available to carry us.

WHAT'S THE WORD?

You saw in the wilderness how the LORD your God carried you as a man carries his son all along the way you traveled until you reached this place.
DEUTERONOMY 1:31 (HCSB)

LET YOUR BANNER WAVE

THINK fast: what is Betsy Ross famous for in American history? If you thought, *Hey, I think she sewed the first flag of the United States,* then you're correct.

Betsy and her husband, John, ran an upholstery business in Philadelphia during the late 1770s. When her husband died in the Revolutionary War in 1776, Betsy took over the shop by herself. In addition to fixing furniture, Betsy did other sewing as well. She knew George Washington and his wife, because the Washingtons sat near Betsy at Christ Church in Philadelphia. When the young nation needed a flag, Washington knew who to ask. According to the story, Washington, Robert Morris, and George Ross (Betsy's uncle through marriage) came to Betsy's shop and described how they pictured the flag. Betsy got right to work. Then on this day in 1777, John Adams introduced a resolution before Congress that stated "the flag of the thirteen United States shall be thirteen stripes, alternate red and white; that the union be thirteen stars, white on a blue field, representing a new constellation."

The new flag symbolized freedom. It stood for a new beginning. Seeing the flag gave American soldiers a sense of dignity and purpose as they fought for independence. It took until 1783 for the war to officially come to an end. Since that time, the original flag has gone through a number of changes—mainly the addition of thirty-seven more stars to symbolize additional states. And in 1916, President Woodrow Wilson issued a proclamation that Flag Day would be celebrated on June 14 every year to honor the Stars and Stripes.

DADDY-*Daughter Time*

If you live in the United States, put out your flag to honor your country on this day. Pray and thank God for the lives of all the people who fought for your freedom. At the same time, remember where true freedom comes from. In John 8:36, Jesus says, "If the Son sets you free, you are truly free." Praise God for the freedom that's found only in him.

As a fun activity, create a flag for your family together. You can use scraps of fabric or markers and paper. Decide what colors fit your family best. What design do you want on it? When you're finished, display your flag for your family and explain what all the colors and symbols represent.

WHAT'S THE WORD?

If the Son sets you free, you are truly free.   JOHN 8:36

June 15

WHAT'S the best part of going to the movies? For many people, the answer would be watching the movie trailers before the featured attraction. *Bam. Pow. Boom!* Movie trailers make every film look exciting.

Creating cool movie trailers is big business. Hollywood spends tons of money marketing its summer blockbusters. If a movie costs $100 million to make, distributors will generally spend half that amount—or $50 million—to promote it and create a buzz on opening weekend. When a movie doesn't do well its first few days in theaters, it can be gone and forgotten in days. A good portion of a movie's success comes down to having an exciting trailer.

Some trailers have been rumored to cost more than $4 million. But it's not unusual for over half a million dollars to be spent on a single movie trailer. Production companies are paid those big bucks to choose the right music and pick the right scenes so after just a couple of minutes we think, *Wow, I want to see that.*

As Christians, we should live our lives like a movie trailer. After people spend a few minutes with us, they should say, "I want to see the rest of the show." And the real show is Jesus Christ. Our words and actions should attract people to our Lord, not turn them off. Second Corinthians 5:20 says, "We are Christ's ambassadors; God is making his appeal through us. We speak for Christ when we plead, 'Come back to God!'" As Christ's ambassadors, we must appeal to people and help draw them into the theater to see God's movie. Unlike many Hollywood features that disappoint once you see the actual show, Jesus never does. With God, the real "movie" is far better than the trailer. God's movie surpasses anything we could imagine. Once people meet the real Jesus, many of them understand what's been missing in their lives. But it's our job to live like a trailer and say, "Come back to God!"

DADDY-*Daughter Time*

What's your favorite movie? God's story is *waaay* more exciting. And the best part is that you can live his movie with him! Does your life draw people to God's main attraction? Think of things you can do that will make people want to meet Jesus. Movies can disappoint, but Jesus is the feel-good hit of a lifetime.

WHAT'S THE WORD?

We are Christ's ambassadors; God is making his appeal through us. We speak for Christ when we plead, "Come back to God!" 2 CORINTHIANS 5:20

STEP IT UP

WHY did the chicken cross the road?

To get a little exercise. Okay, that's not how the joke goes. But it's no joke that a lot of kids exercise less today than they did in the 1980s. Schools have dramatically cut physical education classes and time at recess. Hours spent in front of a computer are way up. (Only around 48,000 personal computers were sold in 1977, compared to 125 million that were made in 2001.) Experts say kids should exercise at least an hour a day, but a lot of children aren't that active. So what can you do to get more exercise?

Well, you could become Amish. Because this group of people doesn't use many modern conveniences—such as cars, computers, and TVs—they end up doing a lot more activities. A study by the University of Tennessee found that Amish men are six times more active than other Americans. Amish men walked an average of 18,425 steps a day, while the average American takes about 3,000 steps. Of course, becoming Amish isn't easy, and the majority live in Pennsylvania, Ohio, or Indiana.

Another option to boost activity is joining a sports team. Sports can provide fun, friendship, and competition. Hundreds of thousands of girls will play some kind of sport this summer—with soccer and softball being the most popular. But you don't have to sweat buckets to become healthy. Simply walking six thousand or more steps a day can result in huge benefits. Taking more than ten thousand steps is even better. Asking for a pedometer to count your steps could be a fun way to see how you're doing.

The key to exercise is to get moving. The apostle Paul said, "I discipline my body like an athlete, training it to do what it should" (1 Corinthians 9:27). Discipline yourself by committing to an evening walk with your family. You could also get a friend to agree to ride bikes a couple of times a week. Or maybe you could join a sports team. When you stay active, you'll be healthier . . . and happier.

DADDY-*Daughter Time*

Discuss different ways you could exercise together. Do you like to walk, kick a soccer ball, throw a Frisbee, or ride bikes? Plan to go outside and get ten minutes of exercise at least three times this week. Being active benefits your mind, body, and spirit. So think like Nike—and just do it.

WHAT'S THE WORD?

I discipline my body like an athlete, training it to do what it should.
1 CORINTHIANS 9:27

LIP SERVICE

BOYS and girls are different. You probably figured that out long ago. And nowhere is that more obvious than when comparing boys' and girls' mouths. Sure, girls wear more lip gloss, but there's an even bigger difference. Girls' mouths tend to move more.

Researchers say girls speak two to three times more words per day than boys. Some studies have found females say around twenty thousand words a day compared to around seven thousand words for males. The number of words is just one difference. Girls also talk faster—saying nearly twice as many words per minute than boys. Another difference? Well, boys are better at making gross sound effects than girls. (Although there's never been an official study to prove that.)

Talking is important. It's good to be able to share your thoughts and feelings. But there's another important part of communication: listening. And listening isn't easy. To be a good listener, you need to actively pay attention. Plus, you can't be thinking about how you want to respond when you're listening—which is a natural thing to do. You just need to focus on what is being said. In the book of Ezekiel, the Lord spoke to his prophet, saying, "Let all my words sink deep into your own heart first. Listen to them carefully for yourself" (3:10). In other words, God wanted Ezekiel to listen to him, totally understand what he was saying, and then go tell other people. That's good advice.

When you listen to somebody, you can learn what's important to them, what their likes and dislikes are, and what they truly believe. Just as we can have a conversation with a friend or family member, we can listen to God by reading his Word or listening for his prompting through the Holy Spirit. And once we understand what God is saying to us, we'll definitely have something to talk about.

DADDY-*Daughter Time*

Words are important. What you say and what you hear make a big difference in your life. In the next day or two, gather the whole family together to play the telephone game—that's when one person whispers a message into someone's ear and that message is passed down a line of people. At the end of the line, the final person says the message out loud to see if it was communicated correctly. Many times some of the words get mixed up in the translation, usually in a funny way.

See if your message makes it through clearly. After playing, talk about the importance of listening.

WHAT'S THE WORD?

Then [the Lord] added, "Son of man, let all my words sink deep into your own heart first. Listen to them carefully for yourself." EZEKIEL 3:10

BLAST OFF

GROWING up, Sally Ride hit powerful overheads on the tennis court. But when people looked to the sky on this day in 1983, they might have seen Sally zoom overhead on the space shuttle *Challenger*. What made this day extra special was the fact that Sally became the first American woman in space.

During her early years, Sally dreamed more of drop shots than blastoffs. She started playing tennis at ten and quickly earned a national ranking. After graduating from high school, she went after her tennis dreams but realized she wasn't good enough to make it as a professional player. Instead she put her energies into education. She earned two undergraduate degrees and a master's degree from Stanford University and then discovered NASA was looking for astronauts. More than eight thousand people applied. Sally was one of thirty-five to be accepted. She joined NASA in 1977, and six years later found herself in space. In 1984, Sally returned to the heavens in the *Challenger*. In all, Sally logged over 343 hours in space. She also earned numerous honors, including being inducted into the National Women's Hall of Fame and the Astronaut Hall of Fame.

With her two missions into space, Sally got a unique perspective on God's creation. She noticed that the stars didn't look bigger, but they were brighter. Going into space is a powerful experience for astronauts. James Irwin was an early space pioneer and the eighth person to walk on the moon. During one of his missions, he looked at the earth and said, "Seeing this has to change a man, has to make a man appreciate the creation of God and the love of God."

DADDY-*Daughter Time*

Make a rocket together. You'll need a 35-mm plastic film canister, paper, tape, scissors, water, and Alka-Seltzer. Make the rocket by cutting the paper and wrapping it into a cone shape. Tape it to the film canister with the lid facing down. Fill the canister about one-quarter full of water. Break the Alka-Seltzer into four pieces, drop them in, quickly put on the lid, and place the rocket on the ground. In a few seconds, it'll blast into the air!

You can also make a fun blast by dropping a Mentos candy into a twenty-ounce Diet Coke bottle. (Both of these things should be done outside.) As you do these activities, remember the words of the prophet Jeremiah: "O Sovereign LORD! You made the heavens and earth by your strong hand and powerful arm. Nothing is too hard for you!" (32:17).

WHAT'S THE WORD?

O Sovereign LORD! You made the heavens and earth by your strong hand and powerful arm. Nothing is too hard for you! JEREMIAH 32:17

GENTLEMEN, AND LADY, START YOUR ENGINES

YOU can find a lot of jokes about women drivers, but nobody laughed at Sara Christian behind the wheel. Sara competed in NASCAR's first race on June 19, 1949, at Charlotte Speedway, and she remains one of the most famous female drivers in racing history.

Born in Georgia in 1918, Sara married Frank Christian. The couple shared a passion for automobiles. In fact, Frank owned the number 71 Ford that Sara drove in that first NASCAR race. A month later the couple competed against each other at the Daytona Beach Road Course to become the first husband and wife to race in the same NASCAR event. The original NASCAR race was a "strictly stock" affair, which means the cars were basically like the ones sold to the public. Only the slightest modifications were allowed. Glenn Dunnaway learned that fact the hard way when he was disqualified at Charlotte after winning the race. (His back springs were altered.) Jim Roper won the first NASCAR race instead, with Sara placing thirteenth. Sara may have done better, but her car overheated during the two-hundred-lap contest.

Sara competed in six of the eight NASCAR races that first year and had her best finish (fifth) at the Heidelberg Raceway in Pittsburgh, Pennsylvania. She was named the United States Drivers Association Woman Driver of the Year in 1949. Years later, she was inducted into the Georgia Automobile Racing Hall of Fame.

During the first NASCAR race, Sara learned an important lesson: little things make a big difference. A lot of things can be done to stop a car from overheating. But her car overheated late in the race, and it affected her final placing. In Song of Solomon 2:15, the power of little things is explained this way: "Catch the foxes for us—the little foxes that ruin the vineyards—for our vineyards are in bloom" (HCSB). Little foxes can do big damage. God wants you to guard yourself from the seemingly little things—an occasional cuss word, a rare viewing of an inappropriate TV show, the biting remark about a friend—because those little things can ruin everything.

DADDY-*Daughter Time*

Can you identify any "little foxes" in your life? God doesn't expect you to be perfect, but he does expect you to look at your life and see what little tweaks need to be made to become more like him. When we let the little foxes hang around, they can eventually ruin our lives.

WHAT'S THE WORD?

Catch the foxes for us—the little foxes that ruin the vineyards—for our vineyards are in bloom. SONG OF SOLOMON 2:15 (HCSB)

BEARY, BEARY GOOD

IS there anything better than going to a summer carnival? Where else can you eat a deep-fried Snickers bar and get nauseated riding the Tilt-A-Whirl? What fun! But one thing stands above the rest: the carnival games with their awesome prizes.

"Daddy, Daddy, win me the gigantic blue bear," Sophia called, running toward the baseball toss.

Rick looked at the challenge. It seemed easy enough. Throw a baseball and try to knock over three metal bottles with one toss. Three pitches for five bucks seemed steep, but he'd played a little baseball in middle school, so how hard could it be? Rick found the answer—extremely hard. Every time he thought he'd thrown a perfect strike, one of the bottles remained standing. *Plunk.* Five dollars. *Plunk.* Five dollars. *Plunk.* Five more big ones.

"You can do it, Daddy," Sophia cheered before every throw.

Rick tried not to think about the money running through his fingers. Finally, after his twentieth throw (or was it the thirtieth?), Rick toppled all three bottles with one mighty pitch. He threw up his hands as if he'd just won the World Series, and his daughter jumped into his arms. The carnival worker handed over the prize. Sophia hugged the gigantic blue bear so tightly that its head nearly popped off.

Did you know that God looks at you like Sophie looked at that blue carnival bear? You are prized. You are valued. You are precious. He loves you and desires a relationship with you. First John 3:16 tells us, "We know what real love is because Jesus gave up his life for us." You cost a lot more than a forty-dollar carnival bear. More than two thousand years ago, God sent his greatest treasure, his Son, to earth so Jesus could die for your sins. God loved you—and made a huge sacrifice for you—before you knew him. No price was too big for God to pay to have a relationship with you.

DADDY-*Daughter Time*

Come up with your own carnival game. Maybe you could stack three paper cups and knock them over with a Ping-Pong ball. Perhaps you could set up a soda bottle and try to throw a bracelet over it. As you decide what game to play, talk about the huge sacrifice that God made for you. How does it feel to know that God prizes you so much that he'd send his Son to die for you? Pray and thank God for his amazing love.

WHAT'S THE WORD?

We know what real love is because Jesus gave up his life for us. So we also ought to give up our lives for our brothers and sisters.   1 JOHN 3:16

ORIGINAL SPORTS BABE

ARE you a tomboy? Would you rather climb a tree or swing a bat than play with dolls? Babe Didrikson was a tomboy. She never met a sport she didn't like . . . or wasn't really good at. Babe was good at basketball, track, golf, baseball, tennis, swimming, diving, boxing, volleyball, handball, bowling, skating, cycling. You name the sport, Babe could probably beat you at it.

After starring in basketball in high school, Babe qualified for five events at the 1932 Summer Olympics in Los Angeles, California. Rules limited her to competing in just three events. No problem. Babe won the javelin toss and set a world record in winning the eighty-meter hurdles. She also would've taken gold in the high jump, but a judge's ruling caused her to take the silver medal instead. Following the Olympics, Babe traveled the country with a basketball team called Babe Didrikson's All-Americans. She even pitched more than a few baseball games. In 1933, she turned her talents to golf. (Not to mention tennis, playing up to seventeen sets a day.) In 1948, Babe won her first US Women's Open (she ended up winning three). From 1933 to 1953, she won eighty-two tournaments, including an amazing seventeen in a row from 1946 to 1947.

As a teenager Babe told everybody her goal was to be "the greatest athlete who ever lived." She worked hard to achieve that goal. She'd practice for hours until she mastered the correct technique. Sportswriters said her work ethic made her the best, but Babe also worked smart. The Bible says in Ecclesiastes 10:10 (HCSB), "If the ax is dull, and one does not sharpen its edge, then one must exert more strength; however, the advantage of wisdom is that it brings success." Babe wouldn't "swing a dull ax blade." She sharpened her skills by being wise and looking for little ways to improve. And in the end, the Associated Press named her the Greatest Female Athlete of the first half of the twentieth century.

DADDY-*Daughter Time*

God wants you to be wise with how you work. Instead of trying harder, sometimes it's better to work smarter. Talk together about a problem you recently had to solve. It could be at work, at school, or on the athletic field. Did you overcome your problem through strength or brains or a combination of both? God gave us strong bodies to accomplish our goals, but don't forget that he gave us bright minds as well.

WHAT'S THE WORD?

If the ax is dull, and one does not sharpen its edge, then one must exert more strength; however, the advantage of wisdom is that it brings success.   ECCLESIASTES 10:10 (HCSB)

SAND MAN

DO you enjoy going to the beach? The waves, the sun, the sand. Growing up, Randy Hofman loved playing in the sand, whether he was at the beach or in a sandbox in his backyard. As an adult, Randy continued playing in the sand. In 1974, he moved from New York City to Ocean City, Maryland, to follow his dream of being an oil painter. As he walked down Ocean City's famous boardwalk, he saw a man creating images in the sand. But these weren't just any images; he was making sand sculptures of biblical scenes. Soon Randy started assisting in the sandy creations. And when the man moved away, Randy continued spreading the gospel through thousands of Christian sand sculptures. Samson, Moses, Noah, Jesus, you name it; if it's in the Bible, Randy has probably crafted it.

These aren't simple sand castles. Randy's details are stunning. You'd think he'd have intricate tools, but all he uses is a shovel, a plastic knife, and his hands. First, he digs up a wet pile of sand. He climbs to the highest point and starts creating. Some sculptures take him eighteen hours to complete. When he's finished, Randy sprays a mixture of water and Elmer's glue on the sand to help the sculpture stay together. Over the years, Randy has given away over one million tracts that explain God's amazing gift of salvation to people who stop to look at his sand-sational sculptures.

With all the sun, the beach is already a bright place. But that doesn't stop Randy from shining brightly for God. In Matthew 5:14, Jesus says, "You are the light of the world—like a city on a hilltop that cannot be hidden." You can shine for him wherever you are: at dance class, at school, at the park, at softball practice, or even at the beach. As you go about your life, don't be afraid to be a light for Jesus. Who knows, maybe he'll use you to shine into the lives of millions of people around the world.

DADDY-*Daughter Time*

If you live near a beach or are planning a family vacation, make time to play in the sand. If you have a sandbox, go outside and have a sand-castle-making contest. And be sure to check out Randy's amazing creations online. You can go to randyhofman.com to see photos. Or search for "Randy Hofman sand sculpture video" and click on the one set to "You Are My King (Amazing Love)." As you watch the images, pray together and ask God to use you as a light to draw people into a relationship with Jesus Christ.

WHAT'S THE WORD?

You are the light of the world—like a city on a hilltop that cannot be hidden.
MATTHEW 5:14

FEEL THE LOVE

SELFISHNESS comes easily. Showing love is hard. But God wants our words and actions to reflect his love. Answer these questions honestly to see how well you follow God's command to "love one another" (2 John 1:6).

True or False: Your best friend calls at the last minute to say she can't spend the night at your house. You've been looking forward to this all week, so you decide to find a new best friend.

True or False: Your youth pastor organizes a service project for Saturday morning. You think about going, but you decide to sleep in and watch the Disney Channel instead.

True or False: Your family takes a road trip. Hooray! But instead of letting you listen to your iPod, your mom plays a CD and wants everybody to sing along. You refuse to sing and stare out the window.

True or False: You want to call a friend, but your brother is talking to your uncle about an upcoming hunting trip. Instead of waiting patiently, you repeatedly tap him on the shoulder, hoping he'll get annoyed and hang up.

True or False: Mom says she's too busy to take you to the mall. You huff away and complain that you never get to do what you want.

How'd you do? It's not easy to show love all the time. If you answered true just once or twice, you can see how your selfish nature shines through now and then. Focusing on other people can be difficult at first. We naturally want to do things to help ourselves and that make our lives better. But when we purposefully try to show love to others, we ultimately show love to God—and that's our true purpose in life.

DADDY-*Daughter Time*

Talk about a time when you may have acted selfishly. How could you have turned around your actions and shown love to those around you instead? When you love others, you gain more friends and actually become happier. As you look ahead at your summer, commit yourself to following one of God's greatest commands: to love one another.

WHAT'S THE WORD?

I am writing to remind you, dear friends, that we should love one another. This is not a new commandment, but one we have had from the beginning. Love means doing what God has commanded us, and he has commanded us to love one another.   2 JOHN 1:5-6

MILK MAN

GOT milk?

French scientist Louis Pasteur did. But in the mid-1800s, his milk contained harmful bacteria. Sometimes children died after drinking cow's milk that was filled with dangerous microorganisms. Pasteur dedicated most of his life to fighting diseases. He discovered if milk was heated, the heat killed deadly bacteria and made milk safe for drinking. Milk is still "pasteurized" today.

Pasteur was more than just a milk man. Among other things, he developed the standard that doctors boil or heat their medical instruments before operating, formulated a vaccination for anthrax, and helped find a remedy for rabies. But if you travel to Pasteur's grave in Paris, France, you won't find the words "Master of the Microbe" written on his headstone. It doesn't say, "Ain't It Great to Inoculate." On his grave, it simply says, "Joseph Meister Lived."

Nine-year-old Joseph Meister and his mother showed up at Pasteur's lab during the summer of 1885. Joseph had been bitten by a mad dog. At that point in history, rabies was a certain death sentence. Pasteur had been working on a vaccine for rabies, but it hadn't been properly tested. Joseph's mother pleaded for Pasteur to give her son the shots. Pasteur knew it was Joseph's best chance at life, so he gave Joseph thirteen shots. And Joseph Meister lived.

Isn't it cool that Pasteur wanted to be remembered as a man who saved lives? You can be remembered that way too. The Bible says, "You are royal priests. . . . As a result, you can show others the goodness of God, for he called you out of the darkness into his wonderful light" (1 Peter 2:9). Pasteur had to test and experiment. His remedies weren't always effective, and sometimes people died. But Jesus Christ is a 100 percent effective remedy for sin. All you have to do is inject him into the world around you and let him do the work.

DADDY-*Daughter Time*

This may seem like a weird question to think about, but what do you want on your tombstone? Do you want it to say, "Drew others into the light"? How about "Loved God and loved people"? That'd be a lot better than "Made a lot of money, bought a lot of stuff, now buried with none of it."

Gather some paper and markers. Together, talk about what you'd like to be remembered for. Then draw colorful gravestones with those words on them.

WHAT'S THE WORD?

You are royal priests, a holy nation, God's very own possession. As a result, you can show others the goodness of God, for he called you out of the darkness into his wonderful light.
1 PETER 2:9

SHE AIN'T HEAVY, SHE'S MY OPPONENT

SOFTBALL isn't just for girls. According to USA Softball, an estimated nine million girls, boys, men, and women compete in the sport around the world. One of the most memorable softball games took place on a tiny field in 2008. It wasn't the frenzied action that made the fans stand up and cheer that afternoon. But the actions of the players remain etched in the memories of hundreds at the game and thousands who watched on the Internet.

In the second inning, Western Oregon University's right fielder Sara Tucholsky belted a three-run home run. Sara had never hit a home run during her four-year college career. She was so excited watching the ball that she missed first base with her foot. Realizing her mistake, she turned back and awkwardly twisted her knee, tearing some ligaments. Sara screamed in pain, crumpled to the ground, and crawled back to first base. According to the rules, teammates and coaches couldn't help Sara around the bases.

Her only home run was about to be wiped from the record books, but then Central Washington's Mallory Holtman stepped in. Mallory was the best player her college had ever seen. She called over teammate Liz Wallace, and the two of them picked up Sara. They carefully carried her around the bases, letting her touch each base with her good foot. By the time the trio reached home plate, nearly everyone in the stands was standing and crying. They couldn't believe an opposing player would help the other team score a run. Those runs proved to be the difference in the game as Western Oregon defeated Central Washington University 4–2.

The Bible tells us, "Don't forget to do good and to share with those in need. These are the sacrifices that please God" (Hebrews 13:16). Mallory saw Sara's need and stepped in to do the right thing. It might have cost her team the game, but nobody cared (not even her coach). Everybody knew they'd witnessed a great act of sportsmanship.

DADDY-*Daughter Time*

Go to a computer and search for "Sara Tucholsky—An Inspiring Softball Story." Watch this five-minute video together. What do you think the coach meant when she said Mallory had the "character to do the right thing at the right time"? As Christians we need to display that same character and do the right thing at the right time. Be aware of the needs of others, and then be willing to sacrifice to meet those needs.

WHAT'S THE WORD?

Don't forget to do good and to share with those in need. These are the sacrifices that please God. HEBREWS 13:16

CAMPFIRE STORIES

THE best part of camping out can be summed up in six letters: S-M-O-R-E-S. And to make s'mores, you must have one thing. Chocolate! Graham crackers and marshmallows are also key ingredients. But to make the s'more come together in one delicious bit of hot, yummy goo, you must have fire.

For a lot of kids, the campfire is the highlight of camping. The crackling wood, the smell of burning pine, the glowing embers. Besides making s'mores, there are a lot of great things you can do around the campfire. You can sing songs, look up at the stars, or tell scary stories. (Why is there always one about a guy with a hook?) Anyway, summer is the perfect time to get away and enjoy making a campfire. And as you lounge around those burning logs, think about how God is like a campfire. After all, a campfire provides safety, warmth, and pleasure—all things that God gives to us.

In the Bible, God is compared to or appears as fire or light more than one hundred times. Who can forget God speaking to Moses through the burning bush or leading the Israelites by a pillar of fire? The prophets Zechariah and Malachi write that God will use fire to refine us to make us more like him (see Zechariah 13:9; Malachi 3:2). And in Deuteronomy 4:24, Moses writes, "The LORD your God is a consuming fire, a jealous God" (HCSB).

God wants to consume us. He desires total devotion in every area of our lives. His fire burns in us—purifying us and strengthening us to stand strong for him. Like a campfire must be stoked with extra wood, we also must fuel our flame for the Lord through prayer, Bible reading, and Christian fellowship. Then we will glow brightly in his power.

DADDY-*Daughter Time*

According to the National Association of RV Parks and Campgrounds, thirty million Americans go camping every year. As a father and daughter, plan a family camping trip together. It could be at a nearby campground, in your backyard, or even in your family room. Make sure to get all the ingredients for s'mores. If you can't make a campfire, you can make s'mores in a microwave.

As you eat your treats, talk about how God demands to be in charge of every part of your lives. Commit yourselves to burn brightly for him.

WHAT'S THE WORD?

The LORD your God is a consuming fire, a jealous God.   DEUTERONOMY 4:24 (HCSB)

HAPPY BIRTHDAY TO HER

WHAT'S the most well-known song in the world? If you guessed "Happy Birthday to You," you're right. Made up of just six different notes and six different words, it's the song most often sung on the planet. While this song's popularity is unrivaled, "Happy Birthday to You" had a very humble beginning. Kindergarten teacher Mildred Hill wrote the simple melody in 1893, and her sister Patty wrote the words: "Good morning to you. Good morning to you. Good morning, dear children. Good morning to you." The song first appeared in the book *Song Stories for the Kindergarten* so teachers could sing it to their students. In 1912, the words "Happy birthday to you" replaced the original lyrics. Nobody knows who wrote the new words, but because the tune was Mildred's, she was given the copyright to the song in 1935. (Actually, Mildred's sister Jessica got the copyright, because Mildred died in 1916.) Due to other court cases, "Happy Birthday to You" is still protected by copyright law until 2030 and brings in around $2 million a year. Wow. Happy birthday to Mildred! Actually, Mildred was born on this day in 1859, so it is happy birthday to her.

Isn't it fun to celebrate a birthday? While it's good to celebrate the day you were born, you might also want to celebrate an equally important date: the day you were born again. Do you remember the exact date that you prayed to accept Jesus Christ as your Savior? If you don't, maybe your parents do. On the day you accepted Christ, you set off a huge party in heaven. In Luke 15, Jesus tells the story of the lost sheep. At the end he says, "There will be more rejoicing in heaven over one sinner who repents than over ninety-nine righteous persons who do not need to repent" (v. 7, NIV). Isn't it cool to think about a party in heaven? Maybe the angels even sang "Happy Birthday to You" on your spiritual birthday.

DADDY-*Daughter Time*

Tell each other about the day you prayed to ask Jesus to come into your life. What do you remember? If you know the exact day, write it on the calendar and plan to celebrate it this year. Your spiritual birthday is one of the most important days in your life because it marks the time that your eternity became secure. You're going to heaven! And that's a great reason to celebrate.

WHAT'S THE WORD?

There will be more rejoicing in heaven over one sinner who repents than over ninety-nine righteous persons who do not need to repent. LUKE 15:7 (NIV)

ROCKY MOUNTAIN RETREAT

DAWN and Courtney couldn't wait to go on the Rocky Mountain mother/daughter retreat. Well, at least Dawn really wanted to go. Now that Courtney was a teenager, she had started to pull away and not include her mom as much in her life. Dawn hated to say it, but their relationship was a lot like the mountains they'd be visiting—rocky.

But after a week of encouraging each other in rock climbing, studying the Bible, and talking about dreams, Dawn and Courtney started seeing each other in a fresh way. Dawn saw that Courtney wanted to make some of her own decisions and figure out her passions. And Courtney began to understand that her mom and dad wanted the best for her and still needed to be a big part of her life. On the final night, moms were asked to stand up and say some words to their daughters in front of the group. Dawn looked her daughter in the eyes and said, "Courtney." But that's the only word she could get out as she gripped her daughter in a hug and the two cried in each other's arms. Several minutes passed before Dawn got herself together and started again with, "You bring me great joy. . ."

In the Old Testament, God instructed the priests to bless the Israelites. Numerous cultures have ceremonies where parents bless their children. Sadly, many Christian families miss out on this important rite of passage. The story of Jesus' baptism appears in three of the Gospels. In each account, when Jesus rises out of the Jordan River, a voice comes from heaven saying, "You are my dearly loved Son, and you bring me great joy" (Mark 1:11). God spoke this blessing on his Son before Jesus' ministry even began. Prior to any of Jesus' miracles or teachings, God blessed him—not for anything he had done or was going to do—for simply who he is.

DADDY-*Daughter Time*

All children desire to hear their parents tell them "I love you" and to know their parents are proud of them for who they are—not for what they accomplish.

Fathers, tell your daughters about a time when your parents said they loved you in a meaningful way. How did that affect you? Does your daughter know you love her unconditionally? Make time to tell your daughter how much joy she brings to your life in front of your whole family.

WHAT'S THE WORD?

A voice from heaven said, "You are my dearly loved Son, and you bring me great joy."
MARK 1:11

MAKE A SPLASH

NOTHING feels better on a hot summer day than going to a swimming pool and jumping into the deep end. Can anybody say, "Cannonball"? Ask your dad about going to the pool as a kid. He probably couldn't wait to climb the high dive and plunge into the deep water. Many diving boards and high dives have been removed from pools lately. A lot of recently built pools don't even have a deep end. That's kind of sad.

We live in a shallow society. It's reflected in shallow swimming pools and shallow friendships. Many kids (and adults) remain content splashing at the surface of a relationship, instead of diving in. But friendship—just like a swimming pool—is best experienced by jumping into the deep end. Sure, it's a little scary, but the risk is worth it. Deep friends stay committed to each other. They're there for each other during good and hard times. They'll go the extra mile when things get tough. As it says in Matthew 5:41, "If anyone forces you to go one mile, go with him two" (HCSB). Jesus said those words concerning the Roman law that allowed soldiers to ask anybody to carry their backpacks for a mile. Instead of doing the minimum required by law, Jesus said to go farther.

When you go farther and put extra effort into a relationship, you create more than a friend. You get a lifelong sister who'll gladly go the extra mile with you.

DADDY-*Daughter Time*

William Penn may be most famous for founding the state of Pennsylvania. But he also championed democracy and religious freedom. (You didn't know you'd get a history lesson today, did you?) In the late 1600s, he wrote *Some Fruits of Solitude*, in which he commented on various aspects of life, including the qualities of a friend:

"A true Friend unbosoms freely, advises justly, assists readily, adventures boldly, takes all patiently, defends courageously, and continues a Friend unchangeably. These being the Qualities of a Friend, we are to find them before we chuse one. The Covetous, the Angry, the Proud, the Jealous, the Talkative, cannot but make ill Friends, as well as the False. In short, chuse a Friend as thou dost a Wife, till Death separate you."

What do you think about Penn's words (and how about the funny spellings)? Is it possible to find a friend like that? Talk about your different friends. Can you think of a friendship that you want to take to a deeper level? If so, go the extra mile to do that.

WHAT'S THE WORD?

If anyone forces you to go one mile, go with him two.   MATTHEW 5:41 (HCSB)

I'VE GOT THE JOY

WHAT spreads faster than a cold and is actually fun to catch? It's laughter. Pure laughter is contagious. It can spread around a room in an instant—turning grumpy faces into joyful ones. Don't believe it? Just walk into a room and start laughing. What happens? Okay, you may get some strange looks at first, but eventually everybody will start laughing too. That's because laughter is hard to ignore. Have you ever noticed how many times people look at each other when they're laughing in a group? It's as if they share the joke even more deeply by looking at each other and saying with their eyes, *Isn't that funny!*

Laughter not only spreads, it also breaks down walls. It's hard to stay mad when someone's laughing. The joy of laughter just can't easily be contained.

The joy that comes from the Lord has a similar, infectious quality. When we radiate the goodness of God, people notice. Maybe you've experienced a worship service where God's Spirit creates an atmosphere of joy. Sometimes when we serve God together, it fosters a special kind of joy that spreads among God's people. The apostle Paul experienced that. In Philippians 2:17-18, he says that service to God is like an offering and that he wants Christ followers "to share that joy. Yes, you should rejoice, and I will share your joy."

When we sacrifice our time, money, energy, and skills to serve others in Jesus' name, we create a type of irresistible joy. And like laughter . . . it's very catching!

DADDY-*Daughter Time*

Sometime at the dinner table or in a restaurant just start laughing together. If others ask what's so funny, don't tell them. Just laugh even harder. Notice everybody's reactions. To spread some genuine laughter, get a joke book and share some of your favorite jokes.

As a family decide to spread some real joy by doing a service project this summer. Maybe you can tell your church what you're doing and it will catch on. Remember that God can use you to spread the joy of service for him.

WHAT'S THE WORD?

I will rejoice even if I lose my life, pouring it out like a liquid offering to God, just like your faithful service is an offering to God. And I want all of you to share that joy. Yes, you should rejoice, and I will share your joy. PHILIPPIANS 2:17-18

"THE BOOK THAT STARTED THIS GREAT WAR"

July 1

THE Bible outsold every other book during the nineteenth century. But second on the list of bestsellers was *Uncle Tom's Cabin*. Written by Harriet Beecher Stowe, the novel attempted to show the harsh realities of slavery in America. It was shocking, infuriating, and eye opening to different parts of the United States. When the book first released in 1852, it divided a pre–Civil War America. The book strengthened support for abolitionists who wanted freedom for slaves, while hardening pro-slavery attitudes from those who supported slave owners.

According to legend, when President Abraham Lincoln greeted Harriet in 1862, he said, "So you are the little woman who wrote the book that started this great war." On this day in 1896, Harriet passed away. While her book has since been criticized for some racial stereotypes of African Americans, it was also credited with being a "vital antislavery tool." Why had a schoolteacher written such a novel? Harriet admitted that her goal was to speak up for the slaves who, at that time in the country's history, had no voice of their own. "I feel now that the time is come when even a woman or a child who can speak a word for freedom and humanity is bound to speak," she once said. "I hope every woman who can write will not be silent."

Harriet's courage to write the novel that stirred the nation could be traced right back to the book of Proverbs. In the last chapter of the book, King Lemuel writes that we should "speak up for those who cannot speak for themselves" (Proverbs 31:8). That's just what this lady from Brunswick, Maine, did. And her work influenced the course of freedom for many.

Speaking out for the oppressed and voiceless must be something that we all do.

DADDY-*Daughter Time*

With your dad, make a list of people who cannot speak out for themselves. How might you speak out for them in your school, your church, or your community? Do some research together on one of the groups of people on your list, and think of ways you can provide support and act on the biblical call to speak out. Add this topic to your prayer time together.

WHAT'S THE WORD?

Speak up for those who cannot speak for themselves; ensure justice for those being crushed. Yes, speak up for the poor and helpless, and see that they get justice.
PROVERBS 31:8-9

FAMILY IS MADE
FOR COMFORTING

EMMA couldn't be comforted. The pain was too deep and the loss to her family too fresh. Ten-year-old Olivia wanted to make her older sister feel better. The tears Emma cried seemed endless and added to the younger sister's heavy heart.

One day, Olivia had an idea. She'd make a card for her sad sister. Olivia wanted to show Emma that she loved her no matter what and that she understood and accepted her sister's grief. Olivia especially wanted Emma to understand how sad it made her to see her sister cry and how much she wished she could make everything better. Inside the card, Olivia drew a picture of her sister crying. She wrote these words: "Tears are made for crying, and family is made for comforting."

That card bonded these sisters in a very special way. Emma appreciated that her younger sister would care enough to let her cry and love her enough to want to help her through the sadness.

Emotions can be powerful. Most dads, by their personality, are not as emotional as their daughters. But even though they may not express their emotions similarly, dads often feel the pain as deeply and want to comfort their family. First John 3:18 tells us to show our love with our actions. That's what Olivia did. Family can be a great source of comfort. Our actions, more than mere words, show our love for each other with tender compassion. Plus, it's cool to remember that God is greater than our feelings, and he wants to comfort us as well.

DADDY-*Daughter Time*

Dads, admit it: sometimes we know something is wrong with our daughters but we don't know exactly what or why. Daughters, don't assume that your dad should be able to just figure it out. Talk together about a recent emotional struggle. Daughters, be willing to open up with your dad and answer his questions honestly. Dad, be willing to listen and better understand the situation. Pray together that you can open up and share each other's burdens better as a family.

WHAT'S THE WORD?

Dear children, let's not merely say that we love each other; let us show the truth by our actions. Our actions will show that we belong to the truth, so we will be confident when we stand before God. Even if we feel guilty, God is greater than our feelings, and he knows everything.   1 JOHN 3:18-20

MAKING PLANS WITH ROOM TO GROW

CHRISTIANS often struggle with a question that's core to their walk with Christ: How can I find and do God's will for my life?

Should I get up and do something? they wonder. *Or should I wait for God to do something to show me?* The answer to both of those questions is yes.

Many people in the Bible received specific directions, or callings, from God. But a number of other godly people simply lived their lives without God always directing them to "do this" or "go there." They followed what they knew to be right and wise, until God gave them different plans.

Noah's righteous heart gained him the lifesaving job of building an ark. Apparently righteousness was a rare characteristic for that era. Job was tested by Satan, specifically because he lived his life in a way that honored God and cared for others. Jonathan, a prince who could've become king, lived a brave life that honored God while he served David, his friend and the future king of Israel. What these people, and others like them, have in common is this: they were people of action who lived on purpose for God, but also allowed God to redirect them.

In Proverbs 16:9, Solomon wrote, "We can make our plans, but the LORD determines our steps." He understood that God doesn't want us to sit around and wait for a "burning bush" before doing anything for him. But if God decides to put a burning bush in front of us, he wants us to be prepared to change our plans and make room for his directions.

So the next time you're wondering if you should get up and "do" or wait for God to do something for you, remember that you can do both. Like Solomon later wrote in Proverbs 19:21, "You can make many plans, but the LORD's purpose will prevail."

DADDY-*Daughter Time*

Finding God's call and accomplishing his purpose for your life isn't always easy. Together pick a decision that you or your family is facing. On one side of a piece of paper, write down the questions you would like God to answer that would help you know exactly what he wants you to do. On the other side, write down some truths you already know from God's Word that would help you today. Pray together that the Lord will help you do what is right.

For a fun movie on responding to a calling, watch *Alice in Wonderland*. The questions in the Father-Daughter Movie Nights appendix can help start a great family discussion.

WHAT'S THE WORD?

You can make many plans, but the LORD's purpose will prevail.   PROVERBS 19:21

WHAT FREEDOM ISN'T

TODAY in the United States, we celebrate freedom and liberty. It's Independence Day. The Second Continental Congress of the thirteen American colonies actually approved declaring independence and separation from Great Britain on July 2. Two days later, the Declaration of Independence, the official document explaining that action, was approved and announced.

The declaration would start a war . . . and eventually a nation. The famous opening lines of the second section say, "We hold these truths to be self-evident, that all men are created equal, that they are endowed by their Creator with certain unalienable Rights, that among these are Life, Liberty and the pursuit of Happiness."

The word *liberty* inspires hope, freedom, and opportunity. But what does this freedom allow? There are many freedoms written in America's governing documents, including the Constitution and its first ten amendments, the Bill of Rights. But freedom for Americans does not mean a free-for-all. Does the freedom of speech allow you to yell "Fire!" in a crowded theater? No. That false alarm could get you arrested. You want to push someone walking down the street because you don't like how they look? That's not tolerated either.

Freedom doesn't give you permission to do anything you want. Freedom carries with it the responsibility to use that freedom well. This is no different for Christians. In Romans 14 and 1 Corinthians 10, Paul explains that although Jesus gives freedom from sin and death, not everything we do with that freedom is a good decision.

Actions have consequences. Actions can offend others, even behaviors that aren't necessarily wrong. We need to be willing to refrain from flexing our freedom, if those actions hurt somebody around us. We are called to live selflessly, not selfishly. Freedom frees us to live for others instead of living for ourselves.

DADDY-*Daughter Time*

Find a book or website that lists the Bill of Rights. Pick which two are your favorites and discuss why you like those freedoms. After reading Romans 14 and 1 Corinthians 10, discuss some things that your family believes a Christian is free to do but that might not be helpful. Discuss what you think God would want you to do with those freedoms based on these verses.

WHAT'S THE WORD?

You say, "I am allowed to do anything"—but not everything is good for you. You say, "I am allowed to do anything"—but not everything is beneficial. Don't be concerned for your own good but for the good of others.   1 CORINTHIANS 10:23-24

HAVE you ever been to a surprise party? The excitement of waiting for the guest of honor builds as the person opens the door. Squeals of laughter and delight can hardly be contained as the birthday girl steps into the room, and then . . . "Surprise!"

Shock. Laughter. Wide eyes and confusion. It's usually a big shock for the one being surprised. Maybe you've been the one who was surprised. Do you remember what was going through your mind? *What's happening? I did not see that coming! Who's here?*

Not all surprises are as fun as a surprise party. A friend does something mean that's totally out of character. A pet dies. A parent loses a job. Your family is forced to move. A tornado hits a small town. Those are surprises we could do without. It's never fun to be blindsided by bad news. As unpredictable as life can be, it's nice to know we serve a God who never gets surprised. He never wonders what just happened or what's going to happen next. Check out these verses:

- "How great is our Lord! His power is absolute! His understanding is beyond comprehension!" (Psalm 147:5)
- "You know what I am going to say even before I say it, LORD. You go before me and follow me. You place your hand of blessing on my head." (Psalm 139:4-5)
- "[God] looks throughout the whole earth and sees everything under the heavens." (Job 28:24)

In other words, when we are shocked, delighted, surprised, blown away, stunned, or otherwise speechless, God simply says, "I saw this coming; it is part of my plans. I know what comes next. I know where this is going and what I want you to do."

So even when we're confused, we can take comfort that God knows the future and that his plans always come to pass (see Isaiah 46:9-10).

DADDY-*Daughter Time*
Share with each other something that really surprised you, in either a good or bad way, in the last year. Discuss the emotions and thoughts that ran through your head when it happened. What does it mean to you to know that God cannot be shocked? How might that truth affect you when you are dealing with an unexpected event?

WHAT'S THE WORD?
Remember the things I have done in the past. For I alone am God! I am God, and there is none like me. Only I can tell you the future before it even happens. Everything I plan will come to pass, for I do whatever I wish. ISAIAH 46:9-10

BECOMING A REAL FRIEND

YOU might already know the story of Anne Frank, a Jewish girl who lived and died during World War II. Anne is remembered for her bravery and courage while hiding from the Nazis in Amsterdam, the Netherlands. It was on this day in 1942 that Anne's family went into hiding. The Secret Annex, what their hidden rooms were called, was located behind a bookshelf. For over two years, she stayed in these closed quarters. Of course, because of her diary, not much has remained secret about her life.

Anne's father, the only family member to survive the war, later recovered her diary and published it as a tribute to his dear little girl. By reading *The Diary of Anne Frank*, we learn about the horrors of war through the eyes of a young girl. Her honesty is obvious in everything she writes, including her difficulties in getting along with her older sister, Margot. Considering the small space and typical family dynamics, that's not a surprise. Margot was three years older than Anne. Their personalities were very different. Anne's diary showed that, over time, she learned to appreciate Margot's more quiet and gentle temperament, and Margot respected Anne more. Anne wrote that "Margot's much nicer. . . . She's not nearly so catty these days and is becoming a real friend. She no longer thinks of me as a little baby who doesn't count."

The friendship between these two sisters would be tested through hardships that most people could never even imagine. The two years they had together in hiding before being sent to the concentration camps laid a foundation for loyal love that was with them to the end.

Their kindness was rewarded as Anne and Margot turned what had been a difficult clash of personalities between sisters into a strong bond. Proverbs 11:17 reminds us that kindness is rewarded, while cruelty destroys relationships. Sometimes showing our friends and family a dose of kindness and respect helps us appreciate our differences and see the best in each other.

DADDY-*Daughter Time*

Talk about the different personalities in your friends and family. Where do differences make it easier to appreciate one another? Where do differences make it harder? Ask God to help you appreciate the unique qualities in your siblings, friends, and neighbors. Be determined to show kindness to those you clash with at times.

WHAT'S THE WORD?

A gracious woman gains respect, but ruthless men gain only wealth. Your kindness will reward you, but your cruelty will destroy you. PROVERBS 11:16-17

WELCOME TO THE FAMILY

WHAT state comes to mind when you hear the words *cold, big,* and *beautiful*? Here's more information. It's as wide as the lower forty-eight states combined, sometimes gets twenty-four straight hours of sunlight, contains three million lakes, and is home to more bears and bald eagles than any other state. You've probably guessed by now that we're talking about Alaska.

On this day in 1958, President Dwight D. Eisenhower signed into law the Alaska Statehood Act. After nearly a century of American control as either a military district or territory, Alaska was ready to become the forty-ninth member of the United States of America. The law made it possible for Alaska to become a state, but there were more steps involved. The process finished six months later when, on January 3, 1959, Alaska officially joined the United States.

Alaskans celebrated that day, but the festivities in Washington, DC, seemed tame. President Eisenhower signed documents proclaiming a new state and a new flag design with an added star. Then it was done. A new state hadn't been added to the union since Arizona joined in 1912, yet the party lacked spark. The *New York Times* reported, "History had been made with a minimum of ceremony and no pomp."

Big occasions are usually celebrated in big ways. When a sports team wins a championship, the city throws a parade. When a war ends, nations host massive parties and festivities. And when one person decides to accept Jesus as Savior, "there is joy in the presence of God's angels" (Luke 15:10).

Picture a celebration in heaven. What would it be like to join an angel party? God loves celebrating when someone turns from sin to him . . . and we should celebrate it too.

DADDY-*Daughter Time*

Read Luke 15. Notice the joy and celebration when someone comes to God. Do you know anyone who has recently put his or her faith in Christ? Think about ways to celebrate that decision to follow Jesus. A note or card, a little party, or a special journal notebook could be good ideas. Let the person know you rejoice with him or her . . . and with heaven!

WHAT'S THE WORD?

When she finds it, she will call in her friends and neighbors and say, "Rejoice with me because I have found my lost coin." In the same way, there is joy in the presence of God's angels when even one sinner repents. LUKE 15:9-10

DADDY, DADDY . . .

A preacher once shared a story of a Jewish child who needed his father's attention. The dad was busy visiting with someone, deep in intense discussion. The child eventually worked his way onto his father's lap, but still the dad's attention was fixed on the conversation. Finally, the child took his father's face in his little hands and cried, "Abba, Abba!" The conversation came to a stop. The dad lovingly turned his full attention on the child, smiled, and asked him what he needed.

Abba means "Daddy." It's the Hebrew word for the informal, intimate title that only a child can use with a father. A dad's heart melts when he hears his daughter cry out, "Daddy!" whether for help or for joy. Did you know that the Bible says we can call the almighty God by the name Abba? The creator of all things, the one who holds the universe in his hands, says we can call him Daddy. Galatians 4:6 explains, "Because we are his children, God has sent the Spirit of his Son into our hearts, prompting us to call out, 'Abba, Father.'"

Jesus himself called God Abba. Shortly before his crucifixion, Jesus prayed in the garden of Gethsemane and cried out, "Abba, Father," asking God to take away his suffering, while at the same time committing to follow the Father's will (Mark 14:36). In Romans 8:15-16, Paul writes that Christians can now also call God "Abba, Father" because God's Holy Spirit "joins with our spirit to affirm that we are God's children" (v. 16).

When we are saved, we are adopted into God's family. As his children, we are given the privilege to cry out, "Daddy! Daddy!" and can have confidence that he will come to love and comfort us.

DADDY-*Daughter Time*

Do you still call your father Daddy? Talk with him about how that makes him feel. Dads, explain the emotions it stirs in your heart when you hear your daughter cry out in pain. How do you feel when you hear "Daddy!" said with joy?

For the next few days, start your prayers out by saying, "Dear Abba, Father, Daddy," or simply begin with "Dear Daddy in Heaven." Discuss how that affects your view of God. How does it change the way you think about God and talk to him, knowing you can call him Daddy?

WHAT'S THE WORD?

Because we are his children, God has sent the Spirit of his Son into our hearts, prompting us to call out, "Abba, Father." GALATIANS 4:6

CAUTION: CONTENTS ARE HOT!

WE live in a litigious society. That's a fancy way of saying people like to look for an excuse to call a lawyer and sue somebody—really anybody—for every penny they can get. So companies have to protect themselves, which explains why real products have carried these warnings:

- "Caution: Hot beverages are hot!" —printed on a coffee cup
- "Wearing of this garment does not enable you to fly." —disclaimer on a child-sized Superman costume
- "May be harmful if swallowed." —warning on a shipment of hammers
- "Do not use as ear plugs." —caution on a package of Silly Putty
- "Not dishwasher safe." —label on a television remote control
- "Warning: May contain nuts." —statement on a package of peanuts
- "Do not use for drying pets." —warning in the manual for a microwave oven
- "Twist top off with hands. Throw top away. Do not put top in mouth." —label from a bottled beverage
- "Do not use while sleeping." —warning on a hair dryer
- "Caution: The contents of this bottle should not be fed to fish." —printed on dog shampoo

The people of Jesus' day had similar no-brainer instructions for their *lives* that had been passed down for generations. Don't murder. Don't commit adultery. Keep your oaths. Love your neighbor. An eye for an eye. These were all very obvious, time-honored cautions on the level of "Shin pads cannot protect any part of the body they do not cover"—another actual disclaimer. However, during his Sermon on the Mount in Matthew 5, Jesus expanded each of those warnings in unexpected ways.

For example, he said that simply resisting the temptation to kill someone isn't precaution enough; you must put an end to anger (see Matthew 5:21-26). Also, avoiding adultery means getting rid of impure thoughts as well as actions (see Matthew 5:27-28). And while loving neighbors is great, you have to love your enemies, too! (See Matthew 5:43-47.) Radical, huh?

DADDY-*Daughter Time*

How do you think people felt about Jesus' "updated instructions"? Discuss the need to set boundaries a healthy distance from dangerous lines we know we shouldn't cross. How does this apply to guy-girl relationships? To ethics at school or in the workplace? To the entertainment we consume? Together, come up with several general rules or laws that define appropriate behavior today but that Jesus might take a step further.

WHAT'S THE WORD?

You have heard the commandment that says, "You must not commit adultery." But I say, anyone who even looks at a woman with lust has already committed adultery with her in her heart. MATTHEW 5:27-28

REMEMBER WHO YOU ARE—AND BE HUMBLE

IN Disney's movie *The Lion King*, Simba ran from responsibility. He wrongly blamed himself for his father's death and shirked his true calling as the next king. There's a pivotal scene where Simba's father appears to him in a vision and says, "You are more than what you've become . . . remember who you are: You are my son, and the one true king."

It's a powerful moment. Simba has been in hiding, confused about his own identity and uncertain of his abilities. The same thing can happen to us as Christians. When we accept forgiveness and salvation through Jesus, we become adopted into God's family as sons and daughters. Yet we often doubt our abilities as God's children. With his Spirit living in us and through our own God-given talents, we can do amazing things for God's Kingdom. But we don't always feel like we have that ability or know how to live it out.

One thing we shouldn't do is become prideful (Get it? lions . . . pride). Sure, we're in God's family. Yes, we serve an awesome creator who sends his Spirit to indwell us. However, we're not mini-gods as some religions teach. And we can never become like God, although we should strive to have our character reflect his. The key to that is to remain humble.

Humility has the purposes of being a reminder that we'll always need God's love and help, and a testimony to show others what difference God makes in someone's life. First Peter 5:5-6 tells us that "'God opposes the proud but favors the humble.' So humble yourselves under the mighty power of God, and at the right time he will lift you up in honor."

As a cub, Simba was very prideful, and that got him in trouble. Once he humbled himself, sought instruction, and remembered who he was, he was able to take his rightful place as king. So remember who you are . . . and be humble. Someday God may lift you up as well.

DADDY-*Daughter Time*

Think about some people who are famous but show humility . . . sincere humility. What impression do they make on you and others? Do you know any people in your life who have done amazing things but have remained humble? Find out the source of their humility. Pray together that you will remember to be humbled by God—remembering who he is and who you are.

WHAT'S THE WORD?

"God opposes the proud but favors the humble." So humble yourselves under the mighty power of God, and at the right time he will lift you up in honor. 1 PETER 5:5-6

CULTIVATE CONFIDENCE

MONICA stared at the sign-up sheet for the musical. Auditions were tomorrow, and she really wanted to try out. Everybody said she had a great voice. But what if she didn't make it? Even worse, what if she made it and then totally messed up during a performance? She could embarrass herself . . . and her parents. *Yeah, I really don't feel like trying out,* Monica decided, walking away. *Maybe next year.*

What kept Monica from trying out? Fear certainly played a part. She kept coming up with the worst scenarios. But Monica's biggest stumbling block was confidence. Some Christians think confidence is like arrogance, so they believe they can't be confident and humble at the same time. However, the Bible is full of people who showed confidence in their calling and still remained humble. Their confidence allowed them to absorb the insults of others and step out to take risks.

Confidence helped Jesus stand silent before Pilate and others who lied about him. Confidence helped David confront the giant Goliath with just a few rocks. Confidence helped the apostles talk about Jesus even while they were being threatened by mobs of angry people. And confidence can make us bold, certain of the truth and our ability to stand up for it. The apostle John put it this way in 1 John 4:17: "As we live in God, our love grows more perfect. So we will not be afraid on the day of judgment, but we can face him with confidence because we live like Jesus here in this world." Even when we come face-to-face with God, we can be confident of our standing because of Jesus Christ.

So the next time tryouts roll around or you begin to be fearful, remember the confidence that comes from being a child of God. You don't have to be timid. You have the power of God living inside you. So remember who you are . . . and be confident.

DADDY-*Daughter Time*

Think of a time when you were comforted and made more confident by someone, maybe your father or another family member. Describe how that person said or did something that gave you courage. What helped the most?

If something is causing you to fear, pray together that God will specifically give you confidence to do the right thing.

WHAT'S THE WORD?

As we live in God, our love grows more perfect. So we will not be afraid on the day of judgment, but we can face him with confidence because we live like Jesus here in this world. 1 JOHN 4:17

GUILTY BUT UNPUNISHED?

DOESN'T it bother you when your younger brothers or sisters get away with something? If you're the oldest in your family, this can be especially frustrating. Behaviors that got you in trouble in the past seem to no longer receive a punishment. Or maybe you've seen it in school. One student is punished for her actions, while another—who does the same thing—gets away scot-free. That can be upsetting.

Even when it looks like someone doesn't get in trouble for what he or she has done wrong, God's Word tells us not to stew in anger about it. Punishing sin isn't our job; it's God's. David, who had a lot of wicked enemies who wanted to kill him, wrote, "Don't worry about the wicked or envy those who do wrong. For like grass, they soon fade away. Like spring flowers, they soon wither" (Psalm 37:1-2). Sometimes it appears as if bad people benefit from their actions. But that's never the case. Sure, some may gain earthly treasure, but eventually they'll all have to answer to God. God is patient, giving sinners time to repent and make things right. But he's also righteous and will not let sin go unpunished. The prophet Nahum reminded God's people of that fact: "The Lord is slow to get angry, but his power is great, and he never lets the guilty go unpunished" (Nahum 1:3).

God is consistent with sin. Every sin has a consequence. So even when it looks like some people have escaped punishment, you can be confident that the guilty will get what's coming to them. God is just. God is fair. We can rest in those facts when it looks like somebody is getting away with something . . . even when it's our little brother.

DADDY-*Daughter Time*

Isn't it frustrating when God shows mercy when you think somebody should be punished? That's why he's God and you're not. Have you ever heard of a criminal getting away with a crime? Although bad guys sometimes avoid the law, they can't avoid God's judgment. Do you have the courage to trust God to take care of those who do wrong? Pray and ask God to give you patience. At the same time, thank him for patiently loving you, in spite of all the times you mess up.

WHAT'S THE WORD?

The Lord is slow to get angry, but his power is great, and he never lets the guilty go unpunished. NAHUM 1:3

FOOLS WORSHIPING FUEL

WHAT would you think if you stopped at a gas station and your dad filled up the car, returned the nozzle, then bowed down in worship to the gas pump? That would be ridiculous and probably embarrassing. But God says people who worship idols do exactly that.

In Isaiah 44, God reminded his people that he is like no other god. Only he is all-powerful. Only he can create the things he creates. Only he can love his people with an unconditional love. For some reason, God's chosen people needed to be reminded of that again and again. They spent years going back and forth between worshiping other gods and worshiping the one true God. God explained to his people that only a fool would take wood, use some of it to make a fire, and use the other part to carve an idol (vv. 16-18).

Wood is fuel. It cannot create, it cannot think, it cannot love, and it cannot save. But it makes a great bonfire. And that's where a lot of idols ended up in the Bible.

In our lives, we might not have statues that we worship like the wood-carvers in Isaiah. Similarly, we're probably not going to be tempted to bow down to gas pumps. But we have to be on guard for other kinds of idols in our lives. An idol can be anything that we think about, dream about, or work for that takes a place above God in our hearts. We need to ask God to help us avoid putting our affections, and our trust, in anything other than him.

DADDY-*Daughter Time*

What are some things you've seen people make into idols? Fame? Popularity? Make a list together. If there is something on the list that you realize you've made more important than God, confess it to him and ask him to help you make that potential "idol" less important in your life.

WHAT'S THE WORD?

He burns part of the tree to roast his meat and to keep himself warm. . . . Then he takes what's left and makes his god: a carved idol! He falls down in front of it, worshiping and praying to it. . . . The person who made the idol never stops to reflect, "Why, it's just a block of wood! I burned half of it for heat and used it to bake my bread and roast my meat. How can the rest of it be a god? Should I bow down to worship a piece of wood?" The poor, deluded fool feeds on ashes. He trusts something that can't help him at all.
ISAIAH 44:16-17, 19-20

FREEDOM IN CHRIST

PHILLIS didn't know what was going on. She'd been pulled from her family, placed on a ship, and dragged into the middle of a strange town. Now a pale-skinned man was shouting in her face. Phillis was just seven years old. She was scared and confused. As the pale man raised his hand to hit her, Phillis winced. But the strike never came. Another man rushed from the crowd and placed some gold coins into the angry man's hand.

In 1761, Phillis went to live with John Wheatley; his wife, Susannah; and their children Mary and Nathaniel in Boston, Massachusetts. Formal schooling wasn't available for black children at that time, but Mary taught Phillis everything she knew. In less than two years, Phillis had an excellent understanding of English, not to mention Latin and Greek. Mary was amazed at Phillis's quick mind and excellent writing. Phillis started crafting beautiful poems before she turned ten. Her words often focused on the amazing salvation available to all through Jesus Christ.

Phillis was just fourteen when her first poem was published in the *Newport Mercury*, making her the first African American to publish poetry in America. She went on to write many more poems, including one for General George Washington. But her writings often came back to Christ. She once wrote,

> *How Jesus' blood for your redemption flows.*
> *See Him with hands outstretched upon the cross;*
> *Immense compassion in His bosom glows;*
> *He hears revilers, nor resents their scorn;*
> *What matchless mercy in the Son of God!*

Phillis's writings remind us that God died and rose again for all people. Titus 2:11 says, "The grace of God has been revealed, bringing salvation to all people." God doesn't love one people group or nationality more than any other. When Jesus came to earth, it was to be a sacrifice so everybody could know the mercy, forgiveness, and freedom found in God.

DADDY-*Daughter Time*

Phillis Wheatley is remembered for her amazing writing and accomplishments. Her poetry, even years after her death, helped free her people from slavery. Do you have a favorite historical character? What do you admire most about him or her? What can you learn from Phillis's life and the kindness that the Wheatleys showed her, especially Mary?

Take a few moments to thank God for people who stood up for him and his truth in the past. And praise him that he came to save all people.

WHAT'S THE WORD?

The grace of God has been revealed, bringing salvation to all people. TITUS 2:11

THE STORMS OF LIFE

HAVE you ever seen a willow tree during an intense storm? The tree has a natural, God-given ability to sway with a fierce wind. When powerful storms come, the willow tree bends without breaking.

Wouldn't it be nice if our lives had no storms? But the truth is, we will encounter storms. And when they hit, even with today's forecasting technologies, they can often catch us by surprise with their speed, strength, and duration. Some storms come and go quickly. Others seem to drag on for many, many days.

Willow trees have strong roots and pliable limbs, which help them make it through most storms. Buildings, on the other hand, are more rigid. They can't really sway with a storm. For a building to survive, a solid foundation is critical. Jesus talked about the importance of a firm foundation. In Matthew 7, he told a parable of two men who chose different foundations for their lives. Verses 24-27 tell us,

> Anyone who listens to my teaching and follows it is wise, like a person who builds a house on solid rock. Though the rain comes in torrents and the floodwaters rise and the winds beat against that house, it won't collapse because it is built on bedrock. But anyone who hears my teaching and doesn't obey it is foolish, like a person who builds a house on sand. When the rains and floods come and the winds beat against that house, it will collapse with a mighty crash.

Storms will come, even for Christians—especially for Christians. The Bible makes that very clear. We should not question whether the storms will come, but how we will weather them. Are you like the willow, with deep roots and a firm foundation? Or have you built a rigid house on a sandy foundation? God is truly the only one who can help us through the storms of life.

DADDY-*Daughter Time*

Discuss with your dad what makes up the foundation for people who don't believe in God. Why do you think followers of Jesus feel more safe and secure when difficulty and pain come storming into their lives? Get a paper and pencil and see if you can come up with five things Jesus taught that can provide comfort and hope when hard times hit.

WHAT'S THE WORD?

Anyone who listens to my teaching and follows it is wise, like a person who builds a house on solid rock. MATTHEW 7:24

BETTER THAN EVERYTHING IN THE WORLD

IN a 2010 study, Mexican media tycoon Carlos Slim Helu was deemed the wealthiest man in the world with an estimated worth of $53.5 billion. (Yes, that's billion with a *b*.) That put him just above Microsoft founder Bill Gates, who was worth $53 billion. Investor Warren Buffett came in third at $47 billion.

That's a lot of money. To get an idea of how much, think about this. If Carlos spent one million dollars every day, it'd take him nearly 150 years to go through all of his money.

As wealthy as these men in the study were, they couldn't compare to King Solomon. Many experts consider Solomon the richest man who ever lived. But Solomon also realized that wealth was meaningless. Anything he wanted, he could have: women, food, palaces. He accomplished great things, even completing God's Temple. He realized that even though there was brief pleasure in those things, they didn't matter. Things couldn't give his life real meaning and value.

The most powerful, wisest, wealthiest man in the world felt empty. Solomon wrote this: "Anything I wanted, I would take. I denied myself no pleasure. I even found great pleasure in hard work, a reward for all my labors. But as I looked at everything I had worked so hard to accomplish, it was all so meaningless—like chasing the wind. There was nothing really worthwhile anywhere" (Ecclesiastes 2:10-11).

It's too bad Solomon never knew the apostle Paul. In Galatians 2:20-21, Paul wrote, "I live in this earthly body by trusting in the Son of God, who loved me and gave himself for me. I do not treat the grace of God as meaningless." Money, possessions, accomplishments—none of those things compare to the meaning found in Jesus Christ. God's grace is powerful and meaningful, because it changes us from certain death in sin to glorious life forever.

DADDY-*Daughter Time*

Make a list of the favorite things you own. What are some things you wish you had? Would having those things make you more special than you already are in God's eyes?

Do you know anybody who's looking for meaning in things, instead of in Jesus? How can you help him or her find meaning in Jesus?

WHAT'S THE WORD?

My old self has been crucified with Christ. It is no longer I who live, but Christ lives in me. So I live in this earthly body by trusting in the Son of God, who loved me and gave himself for me. I do not treat the grace of God as meaningless. GALATIANS 2:20-21

July 17 — WHAT GOOD IS FLATTERY?

CARRIE the crow couldn't believe her eyes. A huge piece of cheese lay just off the trail. *Those picnickers must have dropped it,* she thought. She swooped down, picked up the cheese in her beak, and flew into a tree to eat it.

At that moment, Sammy the sly fox walked up. He saw the cheese and wanted it for himself.

"You're an especially beautiful crow," Sammy said. "There's no way your voice could be as beautiful as you are."

I do have a sweet voice, Carrie thought.

She opened her mouth to let out a caw, and the cheese fell from her mouth. Sammy quickly scampered under the tree, caught the cheese in his mouth, and sauntered off smiling slyly.

Do you think Sammy paid Carrie an honest compliment? Probably not. He just wanted the cheese and would say anything to get it.

Sometimes flattery can be confused for a compliment. That's because these two things can sound very similar. A compliment is when someone simply praises you. Flattery is when people praise us dishonestly because they want to manipulate us to do what they want. We need to understand the difference because flattery is rooted in dishonesty. Nothing good can come from dishonesty. In Psalm 5:9, David writes, "My enemies cannot speak a truthful word. Their deepest desire is to destroy others. Their talk is foul, like the stench from an open grave. Their tongues are filled with flattery."

Compliments inspire and encourage us. Flattery distracts. Flattery is about getting, not giving. Not only do we have to look out for those trying to flatter us, but we need to watch our own tongues. Do we give sincere, honest compliments? Or do we praise people to get something for ourselves, make ourselves feel better, or make them like us more? We need to make our praise sincere to others . . . and to God.

DADDY-Daughter Time

Dad, tell your daughter how you've learned to tell the difference between insincere flattery and sincere compliments. Talk honestly with each other about people in your lives who you're not sure if their praise is sincere or dishonest. If you have figured out that someone praised you insincerely, discuss how it made you feel about that person.

Are there people you have flattered for personal gain? Ask the Lord to help you have an honest heart and tongue.

WHAT'S THE WORD?

My enemies cannot speak a truthful word. Their deepest desire is to destroy others. Their talk is foul, like the stench from an open grave. Their tongues are filled with flattery.
PSALM 5:9

THE PERFECT MOMENT

FOURTEEN-YEAR-OLD Romanian gymnast Nadia Comaneci stared at the uneven bars. The announcers at the 1976 Summer Olympics said this could be a highlight of the games, because Nadia was so technically strong. The teenager sprinted at the bars, hit the springboard, and launched up to the high bar. She quickly settled into her routine, switching from bar to bar with ease. Thirty seconds later, she hit a perfect dismount and nailed the landing. The crowd in Montreal, Canada, erupted. The judges conferred, then posted their score: 1.00. For a moment people were confused, then they realized Nadia had scored a perfect ten! Nobody had scored a ten in the Olympics before, so scoreboards were not equipped to post a number that high.

After that first perfect score, which happened on this day in 1976, Nadia went on to earn perfect tens on six other routines. After earning those seven perfect scores, along with all of her other scores combined, she became the youngest Olympic gymnast to win an all-around gold medal and the first Romanian to take the all-around title.

A few years later, Nadia helped her country win its first team gold medal at the World Championships. She retired in the early 1980s as one of the most well-known, most admired, and most accomplished gymnasts of all time. After setting records, scoring perfect scores, and being admired by so many people, she was asked years later what she considered her best moment.

"My marriage to my husband, Bart Conner, in 1996 is my proudest personal moment," she said.

Nadia understood the power of love and family in her life. Fame, accomplishments, and records are great, but nothing compares to the sincere love of family.

King David expressed similar feelings when he said that God's faithful love was better than life itself (see Psalm 63:3). Love makes our relationship to God as our heavenly Father so special. And it's love that makes family mean so much that a world-renowned gymnast would call her marriage her proudest moment.

DADDY-*Daughter Time*

Have a somersault or cartwheel contest. Your family can judge who does the best. Maybe they can make signs and hold up the numbers.

Then talk together about the goals and dreams you have for yourselves. Are you ever tempted to think that these goals and dreams define your life? Now think about the relationships you have. Some may be broken or hurting. Ask God to help you appreciate the love of family and friends—no matter what may come in life.

WHAT'S THE WORD?

Your unfailing love is better than life itself; how I praise you! PSALM 63:3

July 19

MOST boys find humor in bodily noises. The same often isn't as true for girls. Belches, sneezes, the trick with the hand in the armpit, and, um, other strange sounds tend to fascinate and entertain boys. Years ago, a man was featured on a TV show because of his "talent" for saying the entire alphabet . . . in one belch. Many boys, and maybe a few girls, have tried to imitate him with varying degrees of success.

You may be thinking, *Gross!* And you'd be right. Loud and obnoxious belching is not particularly attractive. It doesn't usually make someone say, "Hey, he looks like a smart fella. I should get to know him!"

When we talk and interact with others, we can influence what they think about us—both positively and negatively. In Proverbs 15:1, Solomon writes that when someone is angry, a gentle response can cool down the situation. If, however, anger is met by more harsh words, things usually escalate. It can be hard to have a gentle response when someone else is angry. Many of us need God's help, because gentleness doesn't come easily. Solomon goes on to say that wise words make people want more knowledge. Wisdom makes people hungry for more. A fool, on the other hand, "belches out foolishness" (v. 2). It might make you laugh, but you don't necessarily want to hear more.

In both of these verses, Solomon reminds us that what we say and how we respond can either help a situation or make it worse.

DADDY-*Daughter Time*

Dads, have you ever been part of a belching contest? Belching can be gross as it expels hot air. Similarly, fools spout a lot of hot air too. Decide together how you'd like people to view you. Do you want to be wise or foolish? Easy question, right? It's not always simple to gently deflect angry words or attitudes. Pray together to ask God to help you stay calm when tempers flare.

WHAT'S THE WORD?

A gentle answer deflects anger, but harsh words make tempers flare. The tongue of the wise makes knowledge appealing, but the mouth of a fool belches out foolishness.
PROVERBS 15:1-2

NO LIFE IS A SURPRISE

A comedian once said, "Babies don't need a vacation, but I still see them at the beach. And that makes me mad. So I usually go over to the little baby and say, 'What are you doing here? You haven't worked a day in your life!'"

Babies stir up strong emotions. Although newborn babies come into this world averaging around seven pounds and eight ounces, they have a heavyweight impact on the people closest to them—parents, siblings, other family members, and friends. One author wrote, "A baby will make love stronger, days shorter, nights longer, bankroll smaller, home happier, clothes shabbier, the past forgotten, and the future worth living."

Sometimes babies are born with physical or mental problems. Some consider these little ones to be an "oops" in this world. But did you know that God does not look at any life as an "oops"? The apostle Peter called Jesus the "author of life" (Acts 3:15). God gave life to Adam and has been giving life to every person who has lived ever since.

King David once had a baby boy who did not live long. The baby had a deadly illness that claimed his life seven days after he was born. But David understood life. He knew death comes to everyone eventually because of sin. He believed only God creates life and cares about every single person that ever was. In Psalm 139, David acknowledges that even when he was growing in his mother, God watched him, knew him, and shaped him. Everything about him came from God's hand. In another psalm, David expresses hope that his life, made by God, would honor his creator (see Psalm 119) and give others a reason to "find in me a cause for joy" (v. 74). Life is something to celebrate!

So there are no such things as oops babies. No babies are unimportant, unknown, or unloved. God never makes mistakes, because no life is a surprise to the author of life.

DADDY-*Daughter Time*

Do you know a family who has a special needs baby? Maybe you have a friend or family member who thinks God made a mistake because of limitations in his or her life. Figure out how you might be an encouragement to these people. A lot of verses in God's Word explain how special they are. Celebrate with them that they are made by God.

WHAT'S THE WORD?

You made me; you created me. Now give me the sense to follow your commands. May all who fear you find in me a cause for joy, for I have put my hope in your word.
PSALM 119:73-74

CHOOSING HELPERS

THE fictional character Tom Sawyer is a mischievous, curly haired boy with a knack for finding adventure. But he is also a leader. In Mark Twain's classic book *The Adventures of Tom Sawyer*, we see that Tom has an unusual ability to inspire others. When Tom has to paint the fence as a punishment for skipping school, he convinces his friends that painting is a privilege—not a punishment. Pretty soon he's assembled a small crew who actually pay him to do his work.

Though Tom used his leadership skills to trick his friends, the truth is that leadership and authority are not always handled well in the real world, either. Some leaders do all the work, while others never do any work, expecting their assistants to do it all. And sometimes a foolish leader will simply give power to make important decisions to unwise or manipulative advisers. Such was the case with Queen Esther's husband, King Xerxes.

In the book of Esther, Xerxes had a wicked servant, Haman, who wanted to destroy the Jewish people. Haman was even trickier than Tom Sawyer, and he knew if he made the king believe the Jews were a threat, Xerxes might agree to kill them. Unfortunately, the king seemed disinterested about the decision (not knowing that his own beautiful and beloved Queen Esther was Jewish). So, since Haman offered to pay for this with his own money, the king carelessly gave the decision to Haman. Xerxes even let him use the royal signet ring, used for the king's personal signature, to make it official (see Esther 3:10-11).

In the end, the courage of Esther and her cousin Mordecai saved her people. Haman paid for his evil with his life. If only Xerxes had been more cautious with the power he gave to his helpers, the whole situation might have been avoided in the first place.

DADDY-*Daughter Time*

Daughters, have you ever been put in charge of something like a school project, a play, a team, or some children while babysitting? Talk about some of the directions you needed to give to others. What was hard?

Dads, talk about leadership positions you've had. How did you pick your helpers? Pray together for the leaders in your lives: bosses, church leaders, teachers, government officials. Ask God to help them choose their helpers wisely and use their authority for good.

WHAT'S THE WORD?

The king agreed, confirming his decision by removing his signet ring from his finger and giving it to Haman son of Hammedatha the Agagite, the enemy of the Jews. The king said, "The money and the people are both yours to do with as you see fit."
ESTHER 3:10-11

CHANGE IS HARD

SUMMER is a time for change. Statistics show that forty million US families move every year—most of them in the summer. Then there are changes at school. Even if you don't move, you still might be switching to a new school. There are changes in the weather, changes in our attitudes, changes in emotions, changes in our bodies, relationship changes. Whoever said "the only constant in life is change" knew what they were talking about.

Experts say change is a major cause of stress, which can lead to feeling overwhelmed. That's why it's nice to know that there are some things we can count on. We can have confidence in the love of family, and we can know that the sun will come up every morning and set every evening.

But sometimes we can't see the sun because of the changing weather (or if we live in Alaska). And family relationships can occasionally feel strained and distant. So is there anything in life that we can really count on to never, ever change?

Yes. Tucked in the first part of Hebrews 13 is a remarkable little verse that gives us hope and confidence that no matter what else swirls around us, there is one who never, ever changes: Jesus Christ. Hebrews 13:8 says, "Jesus Christ is the same yesterday, today, and forever."

Change is hard, but we have a Savior who is bigger than the changes. That means whether we are happy or sad, feel loved or hurt, fail miserably or succeed triumphantly, make the right choice or do the wrong thing, Jesus still lives, still saves, still loves, still rescues, and still has the power to do what we cannot do for ourselves. We can always count on Jesus . . . and that's never going to change.

DADDY-Daughter Time

What are some of the hardest changes that have happened in your life, or in your family, over the last year? Discuss how the changes you've gone through have impacted you. Have you asked God to help you through those changes? Spend some time thinking about changes coming down the road, and ask God to start preparing you for those challenges. Spend some time together, too, praising the Lord for being constant and unchanging.

WHAT'S THE WORD?

Jesus Christ is the same yesterday, today, and forever.   HEBREWS 13:8

TREATING PRECIOUS THINGS WELL

HOW do you treat your most prized possession? People go to great lengths to protect and care for their treasures. Maybe you've seen a classic-car owner who pampers and carefully waxes his car to keep it beautiful. Or perhaps you know a woman who only wears certain prized jewelry on special occasions. People use alarm systems, safes, and safe-deposit boxes to guard their valuables.

Jesus taught that what God makes holy, or sets apart for a purpose, should be protected too. That includes our bodies. For Christians, our bodies become temples for the Holy Spirit to live inside. Followers of Jesus understand that their bodies are not just their own personal possession, but they are also meant to honor God (see 1 Corinthians 6:18-20).

To those who don't know God, protecting their bodies seems like foolishness. The popular culture celebrates behaviors that harm the body, such as drug and alcohol use, tattooing, or piercing. Many fashions seem to flaunt the body instead of being modest and respectful. God wants us to enjoy the bodies he's given us, but those who carelessly use or "show off" their bodies take what should be treasured and treat it like trash.

Your body is holy. Don't waste your beauty on the world, when God intended it to be shared in a marriage relationship. When Jesus was teaching the people in Matthew 7:6, he said, "Don't waste what is holy on people who are unholy. Don't throw your pearls to pigs! They will trample the pearls, then turn and attack you." Jesus was mainly talking about holy teachings that the world often doesn't understand. But you could also take it to mean not to share the treasures God gives you—including your body—with those who would only abuse them. So be on guard, and treat everything God has given you as precious gifts.

DADDY-*Daughter Time*

Would you use a diamond ring to open a can of vegetables? Or would you grab an expensive power tool, cell phone, or computer to pound a nail into a piece of wood? Of course the answer is no. When we have something important to us, something designed for a purpose, we cringe at the thought that it could be misused. Talk with your dad about your body and your health. How is it special? How can you make choices that show your family and friends, and yourself, that you consider the gift of your body a treasure to protect?

WHAT'S THE WORD?

Don't waste what is holy on people who are unholy. Don't throw your pearls to pigs! They will trample the pearls, then turn and attack you. MATTHEW 7:6

PINE TAR AND FAIR PLAY

RULES are supposed to set a standard that makes things fair. But on this day in 1983, a rule in baseball just confused things and upset players on both teams. In the top of the ninth inning in a game between the Kansas City Royals and the New York Yankees, Royals third baseman George Brett hit a two-run home run that apparently gave his team a 4–3 lead. But once George crossed the plate, the New York manager asked the umpires to inspect the bat. Rules stated that players could use pine tar—a sticky substance—to help them grip the wooden bats. However, the pine tar could not extend more than eighteen inches up the bat.

The umpires judged that George had used too much pine tar. He was ruled out and the Yankees won. After seeing his run removed from the scoreboard, George freaked out. He rushed up to the umpires to argue the call. But it was too late . . . or was it? The Pine Tar Incident, as it became known, gained national attention. In less than a month, Major League Baseball ruled that the home run should count. The pine-tar rule was created to protect baseballs from getting dirtied between pitches—it didn't have any effect on George's home run. The game was restarted on August 18, and the Royals eventually won 5–4.

This infamous game highlights the importance of rules and standards. Can you imagine playing a game or living in a society that had no rules? One moment an action is illegal, then the next moment it's deemed fair. Fortunately, we serve a God who makes good rules and treats everybody with fairness. Proverbs 16:11 says, "The LORD demands accurate scales and balances; he sets the standards for fairness."

Whenever we enjoy sports with everybody playing by the rules, we can remember the one who first demanded honesty and fairness. After all, he's the one who wrote the rules for life!

DADDY-*Daughter Time*

What teams do you root for? Dig into your memory or research online for some controversial sports decisions. Notice how much passion is stirred up in fans and players during those situations. Now try inventing a game together that has no rules. Go outside and play it. Is it fun? Is it fair?

If you are involved in sports, discuss with your dad about how to use the rules to talk to others about God.

WHAT'S THE WORD?

The LORD demands accurate scales and balances; he sets the standards for fairness.
PROVERBS 16:11

July 25

DID this ever happen to you? You were coloring a beautiful picture, adding just the right amount of shading, when . . . *snap*! The crayon broke. You sorted through the smaller bits of broken crayon, trying to find the best piece. After removing the paper around the crayon and struggling to adjust your grip on the stubbier implement, you continued coloring.

After dealing with the frustration of broken crayons one too many times, Cassidy Goldstein needed an easier way to grip those smaller crayon bits. Remembering that her dad had given her mom flowers, the eleven-year-old scanned the trash for the small, clear plastic tubes used on the ends of the flower stems to keep them fresh. While the tubes weren't a perfect fit for holding the crayons, they worked pretty well. And a new invention, the "Crayon Holder," was born. A few years later, an official United States patent was issued for her idea. In July 2006, Cassidy was recognized as the Youth Inventor of the Year for her crayon holder.

Through their experiences, Cassidy and her dad learned that many significant inventions came from the minds of children. Inspired by those kids and their own journeys, Cassidy and her father created an organization, BKFK (By Kids For Kids). It encourages and publicizes the work of kids who use their resourceful, creative ideas for new inventions.

In Proverbs 12:27, Solomon writes, "Lazy people don't even cook the game they catch, but the diligent make use of everything they find." Cassidy's story demonstrates just how powerful a diligent, resourceful mind can be at any age. Instead of just giving up on her coloring, Cassidy found a new way to use something that was about to be discarded.

God has given us creative abilities like his own. Nature is filled with evidence of his incredible creativity. Being resourceful, using and reusing items in new ways, brings him glory and can really pay off for the diligent person. Hmmm, doesn't this make you want to go color?

DADDY-*Daughter Time*

Set up a temporary recycling bin in your house for plastics and/or glass. After a few days, pull out some of the items with your dad. Have a contest to see how many new useful (or goofy) ideas you can imagine in five minutes. Then think about a problem that needs a solution around your house. See if you and your dad can come up with a way to solve that problem with things you already have lying around. Have fun!

WHAT'S THE WORD?

Lazy people don't even cook the game they catch, but the diligent make use of everything they find. PROVERBS 12:27

JOY WHEN EVERYTHING'S GOING WRONG

HAS your life ever felt like a country song? You know how that joke goes: your best friend dumps you, your bike gets stolen, you kick your dog, a tree falls into your room, and nothing seems to be going right. Of course, when those things actually happen to you, they're not funny at all.

God's Word is full of situations where life became very difficult, even for those who loved him. Forced slavery, lack of food and water, wars, death, and betrayals—the Bible doesn't lack for tough times. But the cool part is that God didn't leave his people in misery. Time and time again, he showed up to save. God provided what they needed, reminded them who he was, and gave them reason to cheer.

Our circumstances in this world will never be free from difficulties. But even in the worst of times, God's joy can be found. The prophet Habakkuk sang a prayer for his people that makes this point. In a time of great suffering, God inspired Habakkuk to remind the people that God was still their source of joy and salvation. Though the plants and the land did not grow enough food, God was there. Though the animals died and the barns were empty, God had not forgotten them. Though disaster seemed just around the corner, God would save them as he always had (see Habakkuk 3:17-19).

When we experience times when everything seems to be going wrong, we can be sure of God's salvation and find joy and comfort in that. To have God's joy doesn't mean that we're always happy, but it does mean that we can be confident in his goodness . . . no matter what our circumstances.

DADDY-*Daughter Time*

Make a list of the worst disasters that have happened in the world over the last year. Add to the list some of the struggles you or your dad have faced with work in school or on the job. God does not want bad things to happen, and he is always there to help and to save. See if you can find some news stories from those disasters where God's people helped the troubled. Pray that the Lord will show you his joy and salvation in your circumstances too.

WHAT'S THE WORD?

Even though the fig trees have no blossoms, and there are no grapes on the vines; even though the olive crop fails, and the fields lie empty and barren; even though the flocks die in the fields, and the cattle barns are empty, yet I will rejoice in the LORD! I will be joyful in the God of my salvation! HABAKKUK 3:17-18

A late-night talk show host once joked that YouTube, Twitter, and Facebook would merge to create one super, time-wasting website called YouTwitFace. Facebook statistics show that over 40 percent of the world's population has an account. Twitter can't boast those kinds of numbers, but its membership grows daily.

The fact is, we live during a time when people can let the world know what they're thinking and why they're thinking it. While cultures around the world have spent centuries collecting knowledge to be taught from one generation to the next, today's technology enables people to be obsessed with the opinions of the present over the lessons of the past. And some of those opinions seem kind of shallow. Does it matter when a celebrity updates her Twitter account to let her followers know her favorite food, movie, restaurant, music, or public restroom?

At the same time, the digital age makes it possible to pass on information that would have required much more time, money, and travel just a couple of decades ago. Now you can even share the Good News of Jesus Christ with the click of a button! But sadly, most of what you find on the Internet are the opinions of the foolish and naive. These people speak their minds without the desire to learn or the curiosity to discover whether or not their opinions are fair and right. If they're confronted with a comment based on God's truth, they'll often respond, "That's your opinion, and I have a different one."

Foolish people only care about speaking opinions and not learning anything. That's the message of Proverbs 18:2. As we speak with our friends or follow people on the Internet, we should have the mind-set to try to understand. Often that understanding comes from the Bible or lessons learned from the past. Figuring out which opinions are smart, godly, and wise helps us express our opinions in a way that encourages understanding in others, too. And remember, just because someone has an opinion does not make it a good one.

DADDY-*Daughter Time*

Pretend you and your dad are planning your own website or blog about something you are passionate about. What would it feature, and how would you go about sharing what you know?

Think about the importance of helping people around the world understand who God is and what his Word says. Ask God to help you have a passion to improve understanding of him in this world through every tool imaginable.

WHAT'S THE WORD?

Fools have no interest in understanding; they only want to air their own opinions.
PROVERBS 18:2

GOD WANTS
CHEERFUL GIVING

IMAGINE opening two birthday gifts from two different friends. While you open the first gift, you notice the first gift giver looking at you excitedly. She can't wait to see your reaction! But when you grab the other gift, you notice the second gift giver seems agitated. She's totally disinterested, even rolling her eyes and crossing her arms. You learn later that the second person only got you a gift because she felt like she *had to*. Which gift would you appreciate more: the gift from the one who gave with great joy or the gift of the one who felt forced to give? Would the value of their gifts affect how much you appreciated them? Probably not. The attitude of the disgruntled gift giver would most likely cause you to have a poor opinion of her gift no matter what it was.

God has always encouraged his people to share what they have with him. These gifts and offerings remind us that anything we have comes from him. Some people share a lot with God, because they have an abundance. Others give less, because that's all they're capable of giving (although it's a lot for them—see Mark 12:42-44). How do you think God measures the value of a gift? Do you think he looks at the dollar amount?

No. Just like you'd judge the gifts by the attitudes of the giver, God measures the value of the gift by the heart with which it's given. The Bible says God loves a cheerful giver. He doesn't want people to give out of obligation. He wants them to be excited about giving to him, because then his work can be accomplished in this world. Deuteronomy 15:10 (HCSB) reminds God's people to "give to him, and don't have a stingy heart when you give."

So the next time you give something to God, check your heart. A glad-giver's heart makes the best gift to God.

DADDY-*Daughter Time*

Together look for someone or some organization that you feel God is leading you to help. Think separately about how much (or what) you'd like to give. You can give your time, money, or possessions. Share with each other what that gift might look like. Is one of you thinking way bigger or way smaller than the other? Ask yourself if you ever have a stingy heart when it comes to giving to God's work. Pray to God to help you always give cheerfully when you're giving to him.

WHAT'S THE WORD?

Give to him, and don't have a stingy heart when you give, and because of this the LORD your God will bless you in all your work and in everything you do.
DEUTERONOMY 15:10 (HCSB)

NO WORRIES

A 2011 study in Great Britain found that women worry more than men about losing their good looks. In general, the survey found that women had more anxiety than men. Does that sound right?

Everybody tends to worry. *Will I make the sports team? How will I find new friends at school? What will I be like when I grow up?* Some worries are natural, but the fact is, God doesn't want us to worry. Answer these questions honestly to test your worry woes:

1. True or False: You hear creaking noises in the night and immediately get afraid that *someone's in the house!*
2. True or False: You're supposed to get a shot before school starts, but you do everything to get out of it because you think it'll hurt too much or make you sick.
3. True or False: Everybody is taking turns reading from the Bible in your youth group. It's almost your turn, but all you can think about is messing up and people laughing at you.
4. True or False: Your older sister decides to make dinner for the family. After twenty minutes, you start to smell smoke. You scream and run out of the house because you're convinced it's on fire.

How many *trues* did you circle? If you circled three or four, worry might be making your mind blurry. It's hard to think straight or trust God when fear gets in the way. At times when you start to worry, remember what the apostle John wrote in 1 John 4:4: "You belong to God, my dear children. You have already won a victory over those people, because the Spirit who lives in you is greater than the spirit who lives in the world." When you know God personally, his Spirit lives in you. And the Holy Spirit is supremely powerful.

When you pursue God's will and seek his joy, you have nothing to worry about.

DADDY-*Daughter Time*

Talk about your worries with each other. Write down a few of those things. Share ideas with each other about how to overcome your fears. You can find great power in prayer. When you trust that God is in control and focus on his Spirit, your worries can seem pretty small. Go back and look at your list. Is there anything on it that God can't overcome? Always remember that the Spirit inside of you is greater than anything in the world.

WHAT'S THE WORD?

You belong to God, my dear children. You have already won a victory over those people, because the Spirit who lives in you is greater than the spirit who lives in the world.
1 JOHN 4:4

BETTER THAN WALKING
ON THE MOON

WHAT'S the most elite club at your school? The cheerleaders? The chess club? The basketball team? One of the most elite clubs in the world is reserved for men who have walked on the moon. Only twelve astronauts ever set foot on the lunar surface, and just six of those drove a car on it. On July 30, 1971, the Apollo 15 mission landed on the moon and astronauts David Scott and James Irwin did both. For almost nineteen hours over the next few days, Scott and Irwin climbed out of the lunar module four times for a variety of experiments, which included driving around the moon for the first time in the lunar rover.

Like many astronauts before him, Irwin was fascinated with the awesomeness of the experience. But his perspective was also shaped by his faith in God. Later, Irwin said, "Jesus walking on the Earth is more important than man walking on the moon."

And Irwin was right. Jesus came to the earth, lived, died, and rose again so every single person on the planet could be saved. No astronaut, no matter how celebrated and accomplished, could ever come close to that.

Three days after Jesus' resurrection, he met two disciples walking together in sorrow to the village of Emmaus. Jesus struck up a conversation with them about all the events that led to his death and the empty tomb. The report that Jesus was alive seemed too good to be true, and they just weren't sure they could trust it. Jesus explained how everything in the Scriptures pointed to his life, death, and resurrection. Later, as they ate together, they suddenly realized it was Jesus! "Didn't our hearts burn within us as he talked?" they asked themselves (Luke 24:32). They quickly went to the disciples and reported that Jesus was alive.

For these men, walking with Jesus was better than walking on the moon. And because Jesus invites all people to know him, salvation is also a way more inclusive "club."

DADDY-*Daughter Time*

Pretend you're walking on the moon. Don't be afraid to be silly. Move in slow motion, pretending that gravity isn't holding you down like it does on the earth. See who has the most convincing moonwalk.

Then consider the humility of an astronaut like James Irwin. Why do you think he thought that Jesus on the earth was bigger than himself on the moon? Don't be shy about inviting others to join with you in walking with Jesus.

WHAT'S THE WORD?

Suddenly, their eyes were opened, and they recognized him. And at that moment he disappeared! They said to each other, "Didn't our hearts burn within us as he talked with us on the road and explained the Scriptures to us?" LUKE 24:31-32

WHAT'S the best part of family reunions? The food can be great. Playing with all the cousins is cool too. But it's the stories people share that create lasting memories, especially when they're funny.

Remembering good times is a wonderful way to strengthen the bonds between family and friends. Those memories can help make a hard time in the present more bearable, remind you of the reasons you appreciate someone, or give you a better understanding of people based on events that shaped them in the past.

For thousands of years, the only way to pass down history was through stories. Systems for writing didn't develop until a couple thousand years before Jesus walked the earth. The printing press didn't come about until the mid-1400s. Historians believe China developed a type of press in 1041; however, Johannes Gutenberg made a press with wooden or metal removable letters so books could be more quickly created in 1440. Before all of this, there was only storytelling.

Families would gather around their grandparents to hear the history of who they were. Students would listen intently to teachers to learn the wisdom of the past. Reliving fond memories drew people closer together. Paul would often start or end his letters in the New Testament with a nod to the Christians he met at those churches. Paul began his letter to the church in Philippi by writing, "Every time I think of you, I give thanks to my God. Whenever I pray, I make my requests for all of you with joy" (Philippians 1:3-4).

The next time you get the opportunity to hear some family stories, devote all your attention to hearing every word. You might be encouraged and inspired, and you might learn a lot about the people you know and love.

DADDY-*Daughter Time*

Dads, can you come up with a few fun or funny memories of your early child-hood that your daughter hasn't heard before? Don't be discouraged if this takes a little time; sometimes memories don't kick up right away. But one memory might lead to more stories you can share.

Daughters, what are your favorite family stories? They could be about you, your siblings, or your parents. Notice how sharing these stories gives you a sense of belonging to your larger family story.

Think together of some joyful stories of distant family or friends. Take time today to pray for them, thanking God for them and for each other.

WHAT'S THE WORD?

Every time I think of you, I give thanks to my God. Whenever I pray, I make my requests for all of you with joy. PHILIPPIANS 1:3-4

DEAR DIARY

WOULD you let strangers page through your diary? In this age of viral vlogs and Facebook updates, some people are awfully transparent with their "private" thoughts. During World War II, however, one reflective teenager never could've imagined that her handwritten hopes and fears would be read all over the world for decades to come.

You might have read some of Anne Frank's story last month. In the diary she received for her thirteenth birthday, she wrote about friends, schoolwork, family, and playing Ping-Pong. But when the Nazi persecution of Jews in Amsterdam, the Netherlands, reached the point that Anne's family needed to go into hiding, her writing changed. She spent the next two years in a sealed-off room, journaling about the personality conflicts and cramped conditions she endured alongside seven other people. She also described the horrors of war. Still, Anne wrote, "It's a wonder I haven't abandoned all my ideals, they seem so absurd and impractical. Yet I cling to them because I still believe, in spite of everything, that people are truly good at heart."

Many people share Anne's courageous optimism in humanity's innate goodness. And sometimes our faith in others is rewarded. But the apostle Paul reminds us of our sinful nature (see Romans 3:10-12). No exceptions. From God's perspective, there's nothing good about our darkened hearts. Wow. That's not easy to hear, is it? Fortunately, Paul doesn't write this to depress us, but to encourage us. He uses this uncomfortable truth to reveal the depth of God's love and mercy (see Romans 5:6-11), noting that it would've been one thing for Jesus to lay down his life for upright people. It's even more impressive that he did it for sinners.

The great news is that we're not left to cling to our ideals, hoping in humanity's goodness. Rather, we can hold fast to the eternal truths of Scripture, because we know God is truly good at heart.

DADDY-*Daughter Time*

How might you have responded in Anne's situation? Learn more about her story, and read her final diary entry, which she penned on this date in 1944. This brave teen's focus may surprise you. Can you relate to any struggles she described? Have you ever thought of keeping a diary? If not, try journaling every day for a week. See how God uses your honesty to show you things about yourself . . . and about him.

WHAT'S THE WORD?

Most people would not be willing to die for an upright person, though someone might perhaps be willing to die for a person who is especially good. But God showed his great love for us by sending Christ to die for us while we were still sinners. ROMANS 5:7-8

PREPARE TO BOUNCE BACK

AS soon as Kelsey walked into the house, her father knew something was wrong. She headed straight for her room, muttering to herself, "My life is *over*. I can't believe I *did* that!"

Have you ever made a mistake that left you feeling foolish or defeated? Congratulations; you're human! Everybody makes mistakes. But it might encourage you to know that some really cool products started out as mistakes.

In the 1880s, Thomas Adams set out to turn resin from the Mexican sapodilla tree into a rubberlike, industrial substance. His experiments failed. But one day, after boiling the "chicle," he thought about popping some into his mouth. *Eureka!* Adams went into business, and in just a few years he found himself producing five tons of chewing gum every day.

About a decade later, a researcher trying to improve the vegetarian diet of sanitarium patients had another happy accident. Will Kellogg was boiling wheat in search of a digestible bread substitute, but left a pot standing too long. When he put the grains of wheat through the standard rolling process, each one came out as a thin flake. The patients loved it, and a cereal empire was born.

Then there's the lifesaving discovery by bacteriologist Alexander Fleming. In 1928, he was about to discard a failed experiment, but he paused long enough to look at his petri dish under a microscope. A mold had killed the deadly bacteria he was growing. What at first seemed like a disaster became one of modern medicine's greatest triumphs: the antibiotic penicillin.

Are you going through a tough time right now? Maybe like Kelsey, Thomas, Will, or Alexander, you've failed at something or made a big mistake. You're wondering if you'll ever bounce back. That can hurt. It may take a while to recover. And, frankly, things might never be the same. But God is in the redemption business. And Romans 8:28 promises that if you love him and have your heart set on following him, he'll bring something good out of your blunder.

DADDY-*Daughter Time*

What's the biggest mistake you ever made? Discuss how it felt at the time and how it looks now that some time has passed. Share something good that came out of it, even if it's simply something God showed you about yourself. Also, what's the best thing Kelsey's dad could have done when she came home upset?

WHAT'S THE WORD?

We know that God causes everything to work together for the good of those who love God and are called according to his purpose for them.   ROMANS 8:28

THE DAD WHO CAME DOWN

EVERY four years, the world's finest athletes gather to compete for national pride and Olympic glory. That's why British sprinter Derek Redmond flew to Spain for the Summer Games in Barcelona. Little did he know that he'd earn thunderous applause and global fame for finishing dead last.

On this day in 1992, the British record holder in the 400 meters settled into the blocks for a semifinal heat. The starter's pistol went off, and Redmond bolted around the track. But less than halfway through the race, he pulled up lame with a torn hamstring. The searing pain in the back of Derek's leg forced him to his knees. Undeterred, Derek stood up and started hobbling toward the finish line. The race was over, but he wasn't done. He limped for a while before hearing the familiar voice of his father, who had run out of the stands. Jim Redmond wrapped his arms around his courageous son. As tears streamed down Derek's face, the pair reached the finish line together.

"The biggest thing about it was that it was a dad who came to protect his son," Derek said years later. "Every parent can relate to that, to being there for their child. And there are a lot more parents out there than there are Olympians."

Words can't describe the importance of a father's love and support. When life's challenges seem too much to bear, a hug from Dad and the reassurance that you're not racing alone can make all the difference. Our heavenly Father is the same. Throughout the Bible, God reminds his children that he's always ready to help in times of trouble. He says in Isaiah 46:4, "I have made you and I will carry you; I will sustain you and I will rescue you" (NIV). He did this by sending Jesus to earth to die on a cross, and he will continue to be with you all the way to the finish line. Do you know what it's like to start a day in stride and end up hobbling? Well, you have *two* fathers waiting to wrap their arms around you.

DADDY-*Daughter Time*

Can you recall a moment when your dad came through in a way that confirmed his love and support? Share those memories with each other. Also consider times when God has supported, rescued, or comforted you.

Then join the sixty-five thousand fans who gave the Redmonds a standing ovation in Barcelona by watching their inspirational Olympic moment online.

WHAT'S THE WORD?

I have made you and I will carry you; I will sustain you and I will rescue you.
ISAIAH 46:4 (NIV)

BRINGING UP THE REAR

PEOPLE are afraid of all sorts of things, from germs to flying (not to mention germs you can pick up *while* flying). The National Institute of Mental Health says one in ten adults battle some kind of phobia, many of which have lengthy, clinical-sounding names. In fact, if you're freaked out by long words, you may suffer from hippopotomonstrosesquippedaliophobia. Really! (Whoever named that one had a twisted sense of humor, huh?) So, are you ready for a pop quiz? Name the common fears associated with claustrophobia, arachnophobia, acrophobia, and trypanophobia. If you said enclosed spaces, spiders, heights, and getting shots, then you really know your phobias! But have you ever heard of telesphobia? That's the fear of being last.

Frankly, no one enjoys being last: fewest votes in an election; final player chosen in gym class; last in line at a church potluck. (If you find yourself in that position, you could get stuck eating mystery casserole and Jell-O with vegetables in it. That's enough to send shivers up anyone's spine.) Some folks are downright paranoid about bringing up the rear. You may even find these people going out of their way to jockey for position at the front of the line, just to be safe. Take Jesus' disciples, for instance.

In Mark 9:33-37, Jesus asked the guys what they'd been arguing about on the road to Capernaum. They were too embarrassed to fess up, but Jesus already knew it was a debate over who was the greatest among them. The big dog. Disciple numero uno. So the Lord made it clear that greatness requires humility. "If anyone wants to be first," Jesus said, "he must be the very last, and the servant of all" (Mark 9:35, NIV).

If you're feeling a bit telesphobic right now, and the thought of being last to follow Christ makes you uncomfortable, how about placing third? Just greet each day with this motto: "God first. Others second. Me third." Jesus would probably be okay with that too.

DADDY-*Daughter Time*

What does *humility* mean to you? What are some practical ways you can put others ahead of yourself?

When you were a small child, you might have been afraid of the dark (nyctophobia), or thunder and lightning (astraphobia). But odds are, you've outgrown those fears. We're told in 2 Timothy 1:7 that God has not given us a spirit of fear. Do you have any fears or anxieties that you want God to help you outgrow? Pray about that together.

WHAT'S THE WORD?

Sitting down, Jesus called the Twelve and said, "If anyone wants to be first, he must be the very last, and the servant of all." MARK 9:35 (NIV)

NEW EACH MORNING

THE rising sun glistened on the surf. *Kaboom!* A large wave broke on the rocks, sending salty mist into the morning air. Smiling, Julie felt the spray on her face and drew a deep breath as she continued exploring tide pools teeming with activity. She loved southern Maine's winding shoreline. Its craggy rocks trapped all sorts of sea life when the waters receded. Crabs. Starfish. Periwinkles. Even though Julie had visited these pools at the same time yesterday, the ocean had crept in and backed out twice since then, refilling each rocky trough with new possibilities.

God's love is a lot like that. Lamentations 3:21-24 reminds us that his compassions never fail, and his mercies are new every morning. Rough going today? Ready for a reboot? No worries; tomorrow's another day. And just as the tide rolls in and out, depositing clean water and new residents into tide pools all around the world, you get to wake up each morning with a fresh start and a chance to see God work in exciting ways.

Did you know that Lamentations' message of hope arrives in the middle of one of the Bible's heavier books? If you've ever read it from the beginning, it's kind of a downer. That's because the Babylonians had destroyed Jerusalem in 587 BC, demolishing the Temple, killing a lot of priests, and making off with sacred vessels. Yet as the writer sifts through the emotional rubble and tries to make sense of Israel's crisis, he steps back from the pain long enough to consider who God is. He notes that the Lord is loving, faithful, and compassionate. That's cause for hope, no matter how dark things look or how badly we're hurting.

Indeed, when we know the character of our heavenly Father, we can have hope even when life pounds us like waves on the rocks. So keep looking for new blessings every morning. There's no telling what will roll in with the tide!

DADDY-*Daughter Time*

Have you ever awakened in the morning feeling overwhelmed by a trial, only to see God bless you unexpectedly? Share personal examples of his love, faithfulness, and compassion.

On a piece of paper, print your first names from top to bottom, one letter at a time. Then try to incorporate each letter in a word (written horizontally) that reflects an aspect of God's divine character. As you pray, thank him for who he is.

WHAT'S THE WORD?

Great is his faithfulness; his mercies begin afresh each morning. I say to myself, "The LORD is my inheritance; therefore, I will hope in him!" LAMENTATIONS 3:23-24

A LEGACY OF FAITH . . . AND RECIPES

DO you have a great grandmother? To be clear, that's not the mother of one of your grandparents who, technically, would be a "great-grandmother." Rather, do you have a really *great* grandmother? If so, what makes her special? Is it that she water-skis, bungee jumps, and hang glides even though she's well into her sixties? Does she run a company, write novels, or sing opera? Maybe she's an amazing cook or an expert Scrabble player.

While those are all impressive qualities, what sets some grandmothers apart as truly great is the spiritual legacy they pass down to future generations. The apostle Paul understood this. That's why, in a letter to young Timothy, he noted that the lad's "genuine faith" didn't happen by accident but could be traced back to his grandmother Lois, who believed in Jesus first (see 2 Timothy 1:5). Fortunately, many of us have grandmas like that today.

Shelby does. Her great grandmother is named Bery. Among her many activities, Bery remains extremely involved in her church, just as her parents did before her. She works with charities, teaches vacation Bible school, and spent thirty years running the church's food pantry—which may explain why Shelby serves meals and hands out toys at a homeless shelter in her community. Indeed, Bery's example and her commitment to pray for her grandchildren make her a modern-day Lois. And even though she showers gifts on Shelby whenever possible, her greatest gift will always be her love for Jesus Christ.

How about you? Is there a Lois in your life? Maybe you can think of a way to let her know the difference she has made. Have fun. Be creative. Just keep in mind that not all grandmas get the same thrill out of bungee jumping.

DADDY-*Daughter Time*

List five qualities that make your grandmother great. If that special lady has passed away, share your memories of her. If she's still with you, let her know how much you appreciate her. One way might be to create a poem, collage, or scrapbook representing her spiritual legacy and the people she's touched. You could also record an interview with her so that she can share tales of God's good deeds and "pass them on to your children and grandchildren" (Deuteronomy 4:9).

WHAT'S THE WORD?

I remember your genuine faith, for you share the faith that first filled your grandmother Lois and your mother, Eunice. And I know that same faith continues strong in you.
2 TIMOTHY 1:5

A CALL FOR COMPASSION August 7

THE shoe box was barely big enough. Amber held it in front of her at arm's length, walking home as briskly as she could without spilling water from the shallow dish she'd placed inside. "Everything's gonna be okay," she said, though she couldn't tell if she was reassuring herself or the wounded dove now in her care. "A bird with a bad wing wouldn't last long in these woods, but my father will know how to make you better."

A helpless animal has a way of bringing out our softer side, doesn't it? You immediately stop what you're doing and do what you can to help—even if that means grabbing a cardboard box, filling an eyedropper with sugar water, and making the frightened creature as comfortable as possible. But are you as nurturing with hurting *people*?

Jesus wants us to be. That's why he told the parable of the Good Samaritan. In the story, recorded in Luke 10:25-37, a Jewish man traveling alone runs into some robbers who strip him, beat him, and leave him for dead. Along comes a priest, who callously passes by. A little later, a temple assistant—called a Levite—rambles along. He, too, can't be bothered to help. Fortunately for the injured man, he receives mercy from a compassionate Samaritan.

Now keep in mind that Samaritans and Jews didn't get along. Sort of like sparkly vampires and werewolves with six-pack abs. Or New York Yankees and Boston Red Sox fans. So the fact that the Samaritan stops at all is pretty amazing. What's more, he doctors the injured man's wounds, takes him to an inn, and spends the night watching over him (see Luke 10:34). The next day, the Samaritan gives the innkeeper the equivalent of two days' wages and promises to pay more if necessary.

Jesus is more than just spinning a heartwarming tale; he wants us to follow the Samaritan's example. Are you up to the challenge?

DADDY-*Daughter Time*

Have you ever come across a wounded animal? How did that feel, and what did you do? Read about our call to compassion in Colossians 3:12. Do you find it easier to behave that way toward animals than with people? Why? Who has God placed in your life that may need a little extra kindness, gentleness, and patience? Pray for opportunities to love that person as Jesus does.

WHAT'S THE WORD?

Going over to him, the Samaritan soothed his wounds with olive oil and wine and bandaged them. Then he put the man on his own donkey and took him to an inn, where he took care of him. LUKE 10:34

August 8   # THE BEST TEACHER EVER

SCHOOL is just around the corner. In a few weeks, school shopping will give way to a new school year, new friends, and new teachers. A good teacher can make a huge difference in your education. Teachers inspire students to keep trying, to learn new things, to discover talents, and to enjoy the results of a job well done.

The Bible has many examples of good teachers, people who mentored the younger generation to make a huge impact on the world. The prophet Elijah helped Elisha become his successor for the people of Israel. Eli the priest helped Samuel learn the ways of service to God. Paul spent time teaching young Timothy how to lead other Christians with wisdom and grace. And Jesus, the best teacher of all, taught his disciples, and us, to better know him, the Scriptures, and the heavenly Father. In fact, Jesus is addressed as "teacher" more than any other title in the New Testament.

Even some popular modern stories have great teachers in them. In the original Star Wars trilogy, Luke Skywalker learns from both Obi-Wan Kenobi and Yoda. In the first *Karate Kid*, Daniel LaRusso has the help of Mr. Miyagi. In *The Fellowship of the Ring*, Frodo begins his quest with the help of the very wise Gandalf.

A great teacher helps us develop the wisdom we need in order to make good choices. The best teachers don't make decisions for us, but they help us understand the consequences of our choices and how they will impact our lives. God wants to be our greatest teacher. David writes in Psalm 25:5, "Lead me by your truth and teach me, for you are the God who saves me." When we understand how important God's truth is, we not only learn what is good and right, but we also receive hope for our lives.

DADDY-*Daughter Time*

Talk together about your favorite teachers. What characteristics made them your favorite? Have you shown your appreciation to them? If you haven't and still know how to contact them, send them a thank-you card or little gift to let them know how much they impacted your life.

Daughters, your parents can also be great teachers. Look to them when you have questions about life. Ask your dad how someone with wisdom and insight helped him understand how to make good choices when he was growing up.

WHAT'S THE WORD?

Show me the right path, O LORD; point out the road for me to follow. Lead me by your truth and teach me, for you are the God who saves me. All day long I put my hope in you. PSALM 25:4-5

ANOTHER REASON TO LOVE GIRAFFES

IF you were to rank the coolest animals on earth, giraffes would have to be pretty high on the list. Beauty. Grace. Unique design. What an amazing example of God's creativity! They're also living proof that animals could not have evolved the way many scientists claim they did—gradually, over billions of years, from a single organism.

Check this out: at eighteen feet, the bull giraffe is the tallest animal in the world. Its powerful heart has to pump blood all the way to its brain. That's a long way to go against gravity! But when this majestic creature leans down to drink, its heart is suddenly pumping along *with* gravity. That rush of blood to the head would kill the giraffe if not for a series of valves along the artery in its neck. They close in sequence, and just before the excess blood reaches the brain, it gets squeezed into a type of sponge. Pretty cool, huh? Wait, there's more!

Now suppose our long-necked friend at the watering hole gets startled by a predator. It jumps up to flee. Instead of passing out from a sudden loss of oxygen to the brain, those arterial valves reopen. The sponge gently squeezes its oxygenated blood into the brain, and another series of valves in the vein going *down* the neck closes. The giraffe is safe, stable, and ready to protect itself.

The question evolutionists have no answer for is this: How could such a complex system have evolved over time? If all of the parts weren't fully formed and functioning at the same time, the giraffe never could have lived. The truth is, giraffes didn't evolve as part of some cosmic accident. Rather, they were engineered by an intelligent creator. Genesis 1:25 says, "God made all sorts of wild animals, livestock, and small animals, each able to produce offspring of the same kind."

So the next time your science teacher or a Darwinist at work claims that all life evolved from some primordial soup, respectfully explain why you and the giraffe would disagree.

DADDY-*Daughter Time*

What are your favorite animals? How do you see God's workmanship reflected in them? Now that you know a little bit about how a giraffe's system works, observe one together at a zoo or online. You can also investigate how other creatures, such as the bombardier beetle, defy evolutionists' assumptions and point to intelligent design. Just Google it to learn more.

WHAT'S THE WORD?

God made all sorts of wild animals, livestock, and small animals, each able to produce offspring of the same kind. And God saw that it was good. GENESIS 1:25

August 10

EVERY artist is trying to say something. Every painting, song, poem, movie, or sculpture communicates a message from the one who made it. Even if an artist isn't trying to communicate something specific, a message still exists. Some artists say, "I'm leaving it up to the viewer to decide what the meaning of this artwork is." If you hear that, the artist might really be saying, "There's meaning, I just don't know what it is" or "I'm afraid to tell you what it is" or "I'm too lazy to decide and articulate what it is."

Sometimes when we engage in a piece of art we see meaning that was never intended to be there. Some people think that's a good thing. But for the artist who really wanted to express a specific theme, it can be frustrating when someone just doesn't get it.

When we create art—whether in school or for personal enjoyment—we should think about its meaning. Jesus used the art of storytelling to explain deep, spiritual concepts to people who needed to hear his truth. In Matthew 13:13, he said, "That is why I use these parables, for [those who are not listening] look, but they don't really see. They hear, but they don't really listen or understand." Through his use of stories, the people could better understand Jesus.

Art, like other forms of expression, is an opportunity to raise questions in people's minds and point them to God. Many great artists of the past were hired by the church and inspired by God to express biblical truths in their works. Even the Bible is a beautiful work of art. God used a variety of writers from different backgrounds to put together his wonderful story of love, betrayal, and redemption. The next time you don't understand something in the Bible, use the words from Psalm 119:27 to ask God for help, because there's a lot of meaning in his Word that God wants you to understand.

DADDY-*Daughter Time*

Go to an art gallery, museum, or local art exhibit at a church or coffee shop. This can be a great date for dads and daughters. (Find more fun dates in appendix B.) Talk about what you see, looking for clues in the art as to what the artist is trying to convey. You can also pick some other type of art: music, movies, poetry, books. Spend time with some creative works and see what you discover about the message and meaning of that art. Consider finding an artist both of you would enjoy researching and discussing.

WHAT'S THE WORD?

Help me understand the meaning of your commandments, and I will meditate on your wonderful deeds. PSALM 119:27

FASHION SENSE

HANGER in hand, Isabel bounced through the store, eager to show her friend a pretty, floral sundress she'd found on the back-to-school rack. She held it out to highlight the pattern. "Isn't this cute? It's just like the one Taylor Swift wore in her last video. Oh, wait, maybe I'm thinking of that actress on the *Teen Choice Awards*."

Examining the label, Blair wrinkled her nose in disapproval. "Can't be. I've never heard of the designer. But check out this vest by Gianni Kumlately. It's straight from Europe. What do you think?"

"I think it's *really* expensive," Isabel replied.

Blair knew Isabel was right, yet she would not be denied. "Sure, I'll have to babysit seven or eight times to afford it, but if that's what it takes to look fashionable, it's a price I'm willing to pay."

Do you know people like Blair or Isabel? They fret about their wardrobes. They stress over styles, brand names, and who's been seen wearing what. They spend way too much time and money trying to get a look that's going to make them feel better about themselves or win them points, socially—even if those fashions are sure to fall *out* of style almost as quickly as they fell in.

Jesus had a really healthy attitude toward outfits. He understood that we need clothes, but he told people not to worry about what they would wear. It's all just packaging. In the Lord's eyes, the lilies of the field are dressed more beautifully than the wealthiest king decked out in royal robes (see Matthew 6:28-29). That's because their natural beauty reflects God's glory. How about you? Do your attitude and character glorify the one who made you? There's nothing wrong with shopping smart and dressing well. But sometimes the best fashion sense is the sense not to be a slave to fashion. A warm smile and godly character never go out of style.

DADDY-*Daughter Time*

Have you ever felt the need to own a trendy piece of clothing? What happened, and where is it today? Search online together for "worst fashion trends ever." You'll laugh as you notice crazy looks that seemed like a good idea at the time and cost people a lot of money to follow the crowd. By the way, on this date in 1992, the largest shopping mall in the country, the Mall of America, opened in Bloomington, Minnesota.

WHAT'S THE WORD?

Why worry about your clothing? Look at the lilies of the field and how they grow. They don't work or make their clothing, yet Solomon in all his glory was not dressed as beautifully as they are. MATTHEW 6:28-29

WHEN NOT TO WEAR CAMOUFLAGE

DO you like bugs? Some of the most remarkable-looking insects in the world are really hard to find. Species of butterflies, katydids, and mantises can look like leaves, even *dead* leaves. God designed them this way for protection. Predators have a harder time noticing them because they blend in with their environment. Did you know that one of our Savior's best friends tried to do the same thing?

After Jesus' arrest, most of his disciples scattered, afraid that soldiers might come for them next. But not Peter. He followed at a distance, keeping tabs on the Lord. This led him to the home of the high priest, where he went into the courtyard to hang out with people around a fire. He tried to blend in—to camouflage his allegiance. But when a servant girl recognized him as a companion of Jesus, Peter's cover was blown. So he denied knowing Christ (see Luke 22:54-62).

Christians still do that sometimes. They want to follow Jesus, just not *too* closely, afraid it might cost them comfort, freedom, or social status. They do their best to blend in with their environment. It's a defense mechanism against predators. They try to look like the world, talk like the world, and act like the world. If anyone links them to Jesus, they might just deny it.

In John 15:19, Jesus tells his followers, "The world would love you as one of its own if you belonged to it, but you are no longer part of the world. I chose you to come out of the world, so it hates you." In other words, brace yourself for a bumpy ride. Living for Jesus won't always make you popular. Still, it's worth it. If you're ever tempted to blend in with the crowd, ask yourself, *Would I rather be mistaken for a dead leaf, or stand out for the living God?*

DADDY-*Daughter Time*

What does it mean when Jesus says we are "no longer part of the world"? Have you ever tried to be part of the world and hidden your faith, afraid to expose it to others? Why? Be encouraged by the rest of Peter's story, which shows that he grew to be a man of great conviction.

When you have time this week, explore nature together. Turn over rocks to find bugs and see what's living underneath. Also, search online for photos of "dead leaf insects."

WHAT'S THE WORD?

The world would love you as one of its own if you belonged to it, but you are no longer part of the world. I chose you to come out of the world, so it hates you.   JOHN 15:19

NOT-SO-SMOOTH CRIMINALS

MOST bad guys in movies and TV shows are evil geniuses. They confound police with elaborate plots, staying one step ahead of the law until the hero cracks their clever caper. However, a lot of real-life criminals aren't that bright. Take these guys, for example:

- A crook tried to disguise himself by putting a bag over his head, but he forgot that he was wearing his security-guard uniform . . . name tag included.
- Waiting to rob a convenience store, a man wanted to look natural passing the time, so he asked for a job application. It didn't take police long to apprehend the thief, who listed his real name and a relative's phone number on the form.
- Two men attempted to steal an ATM machine by chaining it to their truck's bumper, which got torn off when they hit the gas. Spooked by alarms, they fled, unaware that their rear license plate remained at the scene of the crime.
- A bank robber scrawled a stick-up note on the back of a personal check and made off with a bunch of cash, only to find several officers waiting for him when he arrived home.
- While robbing a corner store, a thief demanded a bottle of scotch from behind the counter. The clerk refused unless the crook could prove he was of legal drinking age. The crook handed over his driver's license to prove his age and forgot to take it back in his rush to escape.

In each case, these crooks were easy to identify. Authorities knew who they were and precisely where to find them. It's easy to think, What numskulls! Yet people are just as foolish to assume that they can pull one over on God, who knows everything. In Galatians 6:7-8, the apostle Paul warns that even when we think we're getting away with sin, it's just a matter of time before justice catches up with us. But if we live to please the Spirit, we won't have to worry about getting busted.

DADDY-*Daughter Time*

Rank the above thieves one to five for sheer dim-wittedness, then see how your lists compare. Why did you rank them as you did? Like Asaph in Psalm 73, does it bother you when sinful people seem to prosper? Can you think of an example?

WHAT'S THE WORD?

Don't be misled—you cannot mock the justice of God. You will always harvest what you plant. Those who live only to satisfy their own sinful nature will harvest decay and death from that sinful nature. But those who live to please the Spirit will harvest everlasting life from the Spirit. GALATIANS 6:7-8

A SCARY SCENARIO

THE phone rings. A sinister voice tells the babysitter that the bad guy is inside the house. . . .

I am so outta here! Sally thought, nearly upsetting the popcorn bowl as she leaped off the sofa. She raced to the bathroom and locked the door. Seconds later, someone jiggled the knob from the outside and rapped violently on the door.

"Sally, are you in there?" Susan yelled. "The girls are waiting. Don't chicken out. This is the best part of the movie!"

Sally didn't feel right about being exposed to an R-rated horror flick. The brutality. The language. Besides, she'd called ahead that afternoon to ask what film they'd be watching. Her host pulled a last-minute switch. But she'd already reassured her parents that any DVDs would be family friendly.

"I dunno, Sue," she said. "I mean, I'm not gonna tell you what to do at your sleepover, but we all told our parents we'd be watching that Disney movie about the dogs."

"You are such a Goody Two-shoes," Susan replied in disgust, slumping against the locked door. "Aren't you tired of kids' movies? We're in sixth grade now! A scary movie won't hurt you. Besides, if you don't come back and watch with us, everybody at school is gonna know you're a chicken."

That was low. The last thing Sally needed was for her classmates to think she spooked easily, making her an easy mark for every creepy kid with a rubber spider and a camera phone. Worse yet, she might never get invited to another slumber party! But on the other hand, what about her parents' trust? Or that voice inside that said filling her mind with trashy images was a bad idea?

What would God want me to do? Sally asked herself. She leaned back with a sigh, accidentally hitting the lever on the tank. *That flushing sound is my reputation going down the toilet,* she thought. *Now I just have to decide which reputation.*

DADDY-*Daughter Time*

If you were Sally, what would you do next? Why? Consider the wisdom of 1 Peter 3:14 that says if you suffer for doing the right thing, then God will reward you. In the end, whose opinion matters most? Talk about some of your family's rules for sleepovers and why they're important.

Then plan an end-of-summer slumber party of your own. Together, settle on the guest list, snacks, games, appropriate movie options, and other activities—including a special breakfast cooked by Dad!

WHAT'S THE WORD?

Even if you suffer for doing what is right, God will reward you for it. So don't worry or be afraid of their threats.   1 PETER 3:14

PEACE BE WITH YOU

WHAT does *peace* mean to you? A world without war? A day without conflict at home, stress at work, or harassment at school? Maybe it's a trek into a forest to enjoy the twitter of birds and a gently flowing stream. Or perhaps it's sitting quietly, seeking inner serenity or calmness. One thing's for certain: finding peace in our noisy, busy, sometimes hostile world can be as difficult as hunting for a black cat in a dark room—blindfolded!

That's right—blindfolded. You see, most people searching for lasting peace have trouble seeing it because worldly notions or symbols of peace get in the way. Take Woodstock, for example. A half-million idealistic young Americans rallied for peace, love, and social harmony at a historic outdoor rock-and-roll festival that began on this date in 1969. But that event is also remembered for rampant drug use, immodest behavior, and a spirit of rebellion that defined a generation. Is that real peace?

The Bible is a good place to start in your search for true peace. Did you know that the word *peace* appears nearly 450 times in Scripture? At one level, God warns us to avoid unnecessary strife by living at peace with others (see Romans 12:18; Hebrews 12:14). Jesus even refers to peacemakers as "sons of God" (Matthew 5:9, NIV). But beyond that, God wants us to experience a peace that's far more than just the absence of human conflict (see Philippians 4:7).

In John 14:27, Jesus told his disciples that he was leaving them the gift of *his* peace, which is unlike anything the world can offer. We have access to that peace too. It comes from understanding the Father's love and the security we have in Christ—not simply receiving peace *from* God, but being at peace *with* God. Will we still face trials? You bet. But take comfort in the words of the apostle Paul: "May God our Father and the Lord Jesus Christ give you grace and peace" (Philemon 1:3). Those are great passages to think about when you visit that relaxing stream deep in the forest.

DADDY-*Daughter Time*

What helps you feel peaceful? How is that different from being "at peace"? In the sixties, antiwar protesters placed flowers in the barrels of soldiers' guns. Speaking of flowers, have you ever tasted honeysuckle nectar? Track down a vine together, then gently pull the funnel-shaped flower out of its little green cup and pinch off the narrow end that was in the cup. *Mmmm . . .* sweet!

WHAT'S THE WORD?

May God our Father and the Lord Jesus Christ give you grace and peace.
PHILEMON 1:3

August 16

THROUGHOUT history, people have done pretty wacky things to please God. Take 1992, when cultists in the Philippines ran through the streets of Manila letting the air out of car and bus tires. Police arrested thirty-two people who believed flat tires led to salvation. Their leader, Alelio Bernaldez Pen, convinced them it was God's will. One cultist told authorities, "This is God's order to let out air. Air is from God. This is the solution to the crisis in our country."

If anything should be deflated, it's that theory. Have you ever wondered how some people manage to stray so far from the truth? It's primarily because they don't know who God is and what he expects, so they allow other forces to misdirect their sincere desire to please their creator.

The same can happen to us if we're not careful. Want to know God's will for your life in three words? There's nothing complicated or mysterious about it. Just "do what's right." That's it in a nutshell. We can know what's right by studying the Bible. Then, aided by the Holy Spirit living inside us, we do our best to live out the guidelines in Scripture. God reveals things to us in other ways, too, such as when we pray or receive wisdom from others. But always check the Bible for confirmation, because God will never tell us to do something that contradicts his Word.

Clearly, the most important things we can know are our sinfulness and the identity of the only one who can save us: Jesus. The "doing" part involves embracing him as our Savior and becoming new people. Then, according to Romans 12:2, "you will learn to know God's will for you, which is good and pleasing and perfect." And while there are some big decisions along the way—from career moves to choosing a spouse—following God's will usually comes down to the little choices you make every day that impact your world and shape your character.

DADDY-*Daughter Time*

Have you ever worried that one false move could derail you from God's plan? Talk about that. Rest assured his will for us is mostly about who we are becoming, since the Lord has granted us freedom to pursue dreams and apply our talents for his glory. Discuss your desires, gifts, and motivations. How do they fit within the biblical instructions given to every Christian?

WHAT'S THE WORD?

Don't copy the behavior and customs of this world, but let God transform you into a new person by changing the way you think. Then you will learn to know God's will for you, which is good and pleasing and perfect. ROMANS 12:2

READY, SET . . . STOP

HAVE you ever been excited about an upcoming event, only to have it postponed or canceled at the last minute? Rained-out ball games. Delayed vacations. Even spaceflights can get scrubbed just before liftoff. In the mid-1980s, the crew of one shuttle mission experienced that frustration *six* times. Here's what happened, and what the astronauts might have been thinking:

- December 18, 1985—Mission delayed twenty-four hours because it took too long to close the aft engine compartment. *Bummer. Okay, we'll try again tomorrow.*
- December 19—A rocket booster's hydraulic unit may have been rotating too fast. Launch canceled fourteen seconds pre-liftoff. It proved to be a false alarm. *We were soooo close! Well, better safe than sorry.*
- January 6, 1986—Launch called off at T minus thirty-one seconds when fourteen thousand pounds of liquid oxygen accidentally drained out of the shuttle's external fuel tank. *This is crazy. Still, blasting off with the tank half-empty would be crazier.*
- January 7—Bad weather at trans-Atlantic abort sites in Spain and Senegal forced NASA to pull the plug just nine minutes before go-time. *Seriously? Didn't anyone check the forecast?*
- January 9—Day's events scuttled when a liquid oxygen sensor broke off and lodged in the prevalve of a main engine. *Again with the liquid oxygen.*
- January 10—Heavy rain at launch site. *Lord, are you trying to tell us something?*

Imagine being one of those astronauts. Rough night's sleep. Prelaunch jitters. You're all ready to blast into orbit, look down upon Earth, and . . . not today. That had to be frustrating. However, someone monitoring the minutiae saw potential problems and cared more about the crew's safety than its schedule. Has God ever "scrubbed your launch"? You're primed for something big to happen, but his timing isn't your timing. If that occurs, be patient. Proverbs 16:9 says, "We can make our plans, but the LORD determines our steps." God loves you, sees every detail, and knows when all systems are go. Incidentally, that shuttle mission ended safely, but only after three aborted landings due to lousy weather!

DADDY-*Daughter Time*

How well do you handle last-minute delays or disappointments? Do you get frustrated or go with the flow? Apply Philippians 4:4-7 and Romans 8:28.

America's now-retired space-shuttle program experienced both triumph and tragedy. Go online to learn more about its missions, as well as the brave men and women who risked their lives to explore the cosmos.

WHAT'S THE WORD?

Commit your actions to the LORD, and your plans will succeed. . . . We can make our plans, but the LORD determines our steps. PROVERBS 16:3, 9

STOP THE PRESSES!

DOES your family subscribe to a local newspaper? With more and more people getting their news online these days, a number of daily and weekly papers have stopped the presses for good. That's a shame. There's nothing like throwing on a robe, strolling down the driveway, and retrieving the *Daily Boomerang*, the *Tombstone Epitaph*, the *Nome Nugget*, or the *Unterrified Democrat*. Aren't those great names? Here's another one that's a little odd: *Pravda*.

For many years, this was the official newspaper of the Soviet Communist Party. *Pravda* is the Russian word for *truth*, though at times readers had to wonder how much truth they were really getting. Launched by revolutionaries, the paper was eventually legalized but censored by the government. That country's leaders understood the power of the press and wanted to control the news. At least one editor turned out to be working undercover for the police. Could such journalism be trusted? Skepticism aside, oppressed workers in twentieth-century Russia snatched up *Pravda* daily, hungry for truth they hoped would set them free.

Jesus says in John 8:32 that the truth will set us free, but not the facts and figures found in your average newspaper. While it's true that being educated about things can make us wiser, the Lord wasn't talking about head knowledge in this case. Jesus was referring to himself. If we keep reading, we'll see in John 14:6 that truth has an identity. Christ says, "I am the way, the truth, and the life." That's liberating *and* revolutionary!

So when somebody tells you they're searching for truth, introduce them to the author of truth who set us free—in this life and the next—by dying on the cross. Jesus paid the sin debt we couldn't pay ourselves. Then he conquered death by rising from the grave, just as he said he would. Frankly, that's the kind of good news that should be grabbing headlines.

DADDY-*Daughter Time*

Discuss where you get your news and why you consider those sources reliable. How have your news-gathering habits changed over the years?

Freedom of the press is guaranteed by the US Constitution, but it also carries certain ethical responsibilities (for specifics, visit spj.org/ethicscode.asp). How is this also true of other freedoms you enjoy?

WHAT'S THE WORD?

Jesus said to the people who believed in him, "You are truly my disciples if you remain faithful to my teachings. And you will know the truth, and the truth will set you free."
JOHN 8:31-32

WINNING ISN'T EVERYTHING

LEGENDARY Green Bay Packers coach Vince Lombardi once said, "Winning isn't everything; it's the only thing." Would you agree? On a scale of one to ten, with ten being an unrelenting, trash-talking, take-no-prisoners passion for victory, how competitive are you? If you landed on the high end of the scale, you have a lot in common with Jackie.

Jackie hated to lose. Whether chasing a soccer ball, playing Wii, or trying to bankrupt her friends in Monopoly, she figured the only reason to play a game was to win it. Unfortunately, she also had a reputation for being a sore loser . . . especially on the softball field.

As a shortstop for the Mustangs, Jackie played hard. And well. But the team lost more often than it won, and by midseason her patience was wearing thin. That frustration came to a boil during a game against the crosstown rival Dragons, when she fielded a ground ball and flipped it to Grace at second base to get the lead runner.

"Safe!" the umpire yelled.

"You're kidding!" Jackie came unglued and walked toward the ump.

Grace quickly stepped into Jackie's path. "It's okay," Grace said, trying to settle Jackie down.

"Okay?" Jackie screamed incredulously. "He blew the call. She was out by a mile!" Then Jackie noticed a Bible verse scrawled on Grace's mitt: Proverbs 16:32. When they got back to the dugout, Jackie asked her about it.

"The beginning of that verse, 'Better to be patient than powerful,' helps when I'm hitting," Grace said with a laugh. Grace had to fight the urge to swing at the first pitch—even bad ones. "The rest keeps me cool under pressure. It says, 'Better to have self-control than to conquer a city,' or in our case, the Dragons. No one likes to lose, Jackie. But in the end, God cares more that we have victory over our emotions."

That made an impression on Jackie, who was never competitive again, right? No way! She still wanted to win as badly as ever. But now she had Proverbs 16:32 written on her glove, too, as a reminder that winning isn't the only thing.

DADDY-*Daughter Time*

Why is our society so obsessed with being number one? Is it wrong to be competitive? What would you consider a healthy, balanced view of competition?

Play a game together—or attend a sporting event—and listen to the people around you. How might *they* rate on a scale of one to ten?

WHAT'S THE WORD?

Better to be patient than powerful; better to have self-control than to conquer a city.
PROVERBS 16:32

IT'S A CAVE, MAN

WHERE'S the darkest place you've ever been? In a tent on a moonless night? In a closet during hide-and-seek? In the cellar, feeling your way around for a burned-out lightbulb? All of those places can be pretty black. But have you ever found yourself enshrouded in absolute darkness?

If your family visits the Black Hills of South Dakota, you can take an elevator three hundred feet beneath the earth's surface, deep into Jewel Cave. With more than 150 miles of mapped passageways, it's the second-longest cave in the world. At one point during the tour, your guide will turn off the lamps illuminating the calcite crystal walls, and for just a moment you'll be plunged into total darkness. No moon. No stars. Forget about waiting for your eyes to adjust. There's no light. Period. Experiencing the blackness of a cave gives us a better sense of the deep darkness mentioned in the Bible. One example is Matthew 6:22-23. Jesus compares our eyes to lamps that illuminate us—for better or worse. What we take in through our eyes impacts the rest of the body. Good eyes generate light. Those focusing on deceit or evil will yield darkness. Just a little darkness? No, more like Jewel Cave darkness. In Jesus' words, "If the light you think you have is actually darkness, how deep that darkness is!" (v. 23).

When God created the world, darkness covered everything. Aren't you glad he said, "Let there be light" (Genesis 1:3)? Later, when humankind fell into spiritual darkness, God turned on the light again. He sent Jesus, who says in John 8:12, "I am the light of the world. Whoever follows me will never walk in darkness, but will have the light of life" (NIV). So whenever you encounter darkness, remember to trust the light that never goes out.

DADDY-*Daughter Time*

With the help of biblegateway.com or another online concordance, search for Scriptures that mention darkness and light. Discuss what you find.

Then create an obstacle course in your yard or at a park. Take turns guiding each other—blindfolded—through a maze of simple tasks using only verbal cues. Why is it so crucial to have a trustworthy guide as we navigate darkness? How has God been that guide in your life?

WHAT'S THE WORD?

Your eye is a lamp that provides light for your body. When your eye is good, your whole body is filled with light. But when your eye is bad, your whole body is filled with darkness. And if the light you think you have is actually darkness, how deep that darkness is!
MATTHEW 6:22-23

ONLY ONE WAY
TO SOLVE IT

WHAT are your favorite kinds of puzzles? Word searches? Mazes? Connect the dots? Some of the trickiest brainteasers link the answers to each other so that, when all the boxes are filled, there can be only one possible solution . . . like crossword puzzles or sudoku. A single mistake and it falls apart. But as taxing as those mind games can be, it's satisfying when you finally discover that everything lines up just right!

Studying the Bible is a lot like doing an interlocking puzzle. We read Scripture to understand the God who created us and how he wants us to relate to him. We also learn how we should think and behave in certain situations and respond to other people. Then there's the matter of eternity. What's it like? Where will we spend it? Central to all of this is gaining an understanding of our sin nature and our need for a Savior. When linked together, the details all point to one possible solution: Jesus.

These days, it's not very popular to claim that Jesus is the only way to God, even though Jesus says so himself in John 14:6. People call it narrow minded. They argue that all roads lead to God and that all faiths are more or less the same. But that's like starting a crossword puzzle by saying, "Hmmm, one across. Well, I don't want to be narrow-minded. I can write down any nine-letter word. I'm sure it'll all work out in the end." Silly, right? Anyone serious about getting the puzzle right needs to consider the links and study the clues.

Lee Strobel and Josh McDowell did just that. Before becoming well-known defenders of the faith, both were skeptics committed to disproving the Bible. Each diligently worked the puzzle, intending to expose it as a fraud. Yet neither could deny how all of the answers fell perfectly into place. History. Prophecy. Physical evidence. The claims and miracles of Christ. In both cases, these men gave their lives to the Lord and, to this day, marvel as they scrutinize Scripture—a puzzle worth puzzling over!

DADDY-*Daughter Time*

What convinced you that the Bible is trustworthy and that Jesus is the answer? Do you have unanswered questions? Explore them together. See what changed the minds of hardened skeptics in Josh McDowell's book *Evidence That Demands a Verdict* and Lee Strobel's *The Case for Christ* (which has also been made into a powerful video).

WHAT'S THE WORD?

Jesus told him, "I am the way, the truth, and the life. No one can come to the Father except through me." JOHN 14:6

SWITCHING CAMPS

THE trigger felt good against Erin's finger. She crept stealthily through the campsite, avoiding dry twigs as she circled the tents, fully expecting the enemy to leap out at any moment. Then it happened.

"Hey, honey, don't shoot!" Erin lowered her mega-soaker water cannon and eyed her father suspiciously from across the picnic table. "Your brothers went rogue. I want to switch sides and join the girls' team." *Hmm.* Could he be trusted? Or was this just another trick to help the guys win the annual family-campout water war?

Sometimes it's hard to know what to believe when sworn enemies suddenly decide to change sides. Authorities in Texas faced that dilemma on this date in 1898 when Jim Miller, one of the deadliest professional killers in the West, joined the noble Texas Rangers. Would such a notorious outlaw really fight for justice? Apparently, not for long. Miller was adept at straddling both sides of the law and often managed to get away with murder. That is, until 1909 when a mob stormed Miller's jail cell and took the law into its own hands.

Fortunately for the early church, one foe-turned-friend never looked back, though you can understand why the saints were a little nervous at first. Saul of Tarsus was a killer, and he specialized in Christians. But one day, Saul had a life-changing encounter with Jesus on the road to Damascus. In no time at all, he was preaching fearlessly in the name of Christ. Still, some of the disciples remained skeptical. It's all there in Acts 9. Of course, Saul became the apostle Paul, a genuine hero of the faith who authored much of the New Testament. See what Paul wrote in 1 Timothy 1:12-13 about serving the Lord.

Have you ever doubted someone's salvation? Maybe you know that person's reputation and have a hard time believing he or she could change. Don't be so sure. If Jesus can redeem a guy like Saul, he can change anyone.

DADDY-*Daughter Time*

Like Erin's family, do you enjoy camping, engaging in water battles, or making s'mores over a fire? There's still time to do that this summer. No time to camp? No problem! Buy some water guns and have a family water fight.

WHAT'S THE WORD?

I thank Christ Jesus our Lord, who has given me strength to do his work. He considered me trustworthy and appointed me to serve him, even though I used to blaspheme the name of Christ. In my insolence, I persecuted his people. But God had mercy on me because I did it in ignorance and unbelief. 1 TIMOTHY 1:12-13

WHEN YOU CAN'T
HIT UNSEND

IN the third act of William Shakespeare's famous tragedy *Julius Caesar*, Mark Antony says, "The evil that men do lives after them; the good is oft interred with their bones." In other words, people tend to remember the bad things we do in life, while the good stuff gets buried with us. That's pretty pessimistic, especially for a guy who never had an indiscretion posted on YouTube.

We live in an unforgiving age, don't we? You may know people who have tweeted comments, uploaded videos, or shared photos on Facebook that they wish they could take back. But now those miscues are out there in cyberspace. Forever. And fair or not, they're making a statement. That's why it's so important to make every decision as if someone is watching, because these days, people probably are.

For thousands of years, God's people have known what it's like to live under constant surveillance. The Bible says the Lord observes our every move and knows each thought before we think it. Not because he's looking for embarrassing snapshots to show the angels ("Hey, Gabriel, come look at *this*"). Nor will he shame us to keep us in line. Quite the opposite. Under the "new covenant" described in Hebrews 8, God chooses not to remember our mistakes at all! Why? Because in addition to being omniscient, our heavenly Father is gracious and loving. Psalm 103:12-13 describes it this way: "He has removed our sins as far from us as the east is from the west. The LORD is like a father to his children, tender and compassionate to those who fear him."

Have you made significant mistakes? Whether those regrets are circulating online or just swirling in the privacy of your own conscience, you may find it hard to forgive yourself and move on. But God forgives you. Jesus took care of every sin at the Cross. So don't be burdened by past failures. If you've given your life to Christ, God sees you as righteous and ready to join him on the next leg of a lifelong adventure.

DADDY-*Daughter Time*

Have you ever wished you could hit Unsend on a decision? What happened? Regarding the unique risks we run in this digital age, talk about any anxieties you may feel, as well as safeguards that can protect you and your family. Also, share something God has shown you about his unconditional love and forgiveness.

WHAT'S THE WORD?

He has removed our sins as far from us as the east is from the west. The LORD is like a father to his children, tender and compassionate to those who fear him.
PSALM 103:12-13

THE LORD IS MY SHEPHERD

GETTING sheep to lie down is no easy task. Just ask Phillip Keller. In addition to growing up among shepherds in East Africa, he spent eight years immersed in the daily care of the critters Jesus compared us to. As you might imagine, when a herdsman like Phillip reads Psalm 23 (penned by David, who also had experience in this area) he sees things the rest of us might miss.

For example, the whole "lying down in green pastures" bit. You might think that any tired, lazy sheep would gladly plop down in a meadow on a hot summer afternoon. Not true! In his book *A Shepherd Looks at Psalm 23*, Keller points out four significant obstacles to a sheep being able to lie down:

- These timid creatures refuse to rest unless they are free from fear. And all it takes is one member of the group to show anxiety for the others to get skittish, even if they don't know the cause.
- Sheep will not lie down if they're hungry. You may have mental images of grazing flocks on lush countrysides, but most shepherds operate in dry, sun-scorched wastelands, as David did. Food is scarce. Sheep will roam until their bellies are full.
- They also can't relax if they're being pestered by flies or parasites. Rather, they shake their heads, stamp their feet, and run around, desperate for a break from those tiny tormentors.
- Sheep won't lie down if they're at odds with others in the flock. Did you know that jealousy, bullying, and other conflict (part of a social hierarchy called the "butting order") can cause restlessness, irritability, and even weight loss?

Of course, sheep have little choice but to rely on the shepherd to care for all of these needs. He fully understands them and wants his flock to be at peace. So why, when we face similar situations, do we try all sorts of solutions before turning to our shepherd, Jesus? Green pastures await if we trust the Lord!

DADDY-*Daughter Time*

How is each of the bulleted points similar to a challenge you've faced? Which makes resting most challenging for you? Read John 10 for Jesus' description of himself as the Good Shepherd, and ask him to meet your need.

If you live near a farm or petting zoo, visit sheep and talk with the person who cares for them. You may be surprised by how much you learn about them and about yourself.

WHAT'S THE WORD?

The LORD is my shepherd, I shall not be in want. He makes me lie down in green pastures, he leads me beside quiet waters. PSALM 23:1-2 (NIV)

DECLARING GOD'S GLORY

THE couple sat on a park bench beneath a full moon so bright they could've read by it. But Katrina didn't need a book to tickle her intellect. Every so often, the brainy young man holding her hand would burst forth with some scientific observation or obscure bit of lunar trivia.

"Isn't the moon beautiful, Eugene?" she asked.

"Ah yes, though also the source of an astronomical swindle, one might say." He adjusted his glasses. "Quite coincidentally, on this date in 1835 the *New York Sun* published its first article in a series earnestly describing life on the moon. Unicorns. Two-legged beavers. Its authors even reported furry, winged creatures resembling both men and bats. Preposterous as it may sound, for several weeks people believed what became known as the Great Moon Hoax."

A history buff herself, Katrina found Eugene's insights oddly charming. That's one reason they made such a great couple.

What thoughts go through your mind when you look at the night sky? Are you left in awe of God's creativity and power? A sense of awe inspired David to write Psalm 19, perhaps while tending his sheep with the moon as his night-light. Or do you gaze at the stars and imagine the Lord promising Abraham that his descendants would equal in number those twinkling lights (see Genesis 15:5)? Maybe, like the perpetrators of the Great Moon Hoax, you wonder if there's life somewhere out there and what it might look like.

The more we learn about the beauty and mechanics of our solar system, the more we can appreciate the amazing intelligence and wisdom required to set it and keep it in motion. Best of all, the Bible tells us repeatedly that the loving God who designed the heavens knows our names and cares for us as well.

DADDY-*Daughter Time*

From Photoshopped magazine photos to carefully edited reality shows, discuss some modern tricks the media plays on people these days. How do you think the public would respond to a Great Moon Hoax today? If you're curious about rumors you've heard, find out whether they're truth or urban legend at snopes.com. And while you're online together, search for stunning photos from space. Then take a walk under the stars and talk about . . . anything.

WHAT'S THE WORD?

The heavens proclaim the glory of God. The skies display his craftsmanship. Day after day they continue to speak; night after night they make him known. They speak without a sound or word; their voice is never heard. Yet their message has gone throughout the earth, and their words to all the world. PSALM 19:1-4

YARD-SALE PRICES

A trail of yellow yard-sale signs led Heather to the home of an elderly widow with a driveway full of antique treasures. Or old junk. It was kind of hard to tell the difference with some items. A discolored wicker picnic basket caught her eye. The woman wanted five dollars for it, which seemed like a lot for such a weathered relic. Rusty hinges. The weave was loose at one corner. It was cracked in a few places. A buck maybe . . .

"I remember why we bought that basket," a voice said. Noticing Heather's interest in it, the kindly woman proceeded to share how, in the summer of 1962, her husband had promised the children a special day in the country. Horseback riding. Swimming at the lake. A picnic lunch. They'd had the time of their lives. The woman grew wistful, fingering the lid on the old basket. "I found out later that his biggest client had threatened to take his business elsewhere simply because my husband refused to cancel our holiday for work. Joe didn't care. He loved us so. No sacrifice was too great if it meant keeping a promise."

Heather felt a little guilty for thinking ill of the basket at first. Knowing its history changed everything. Suddenly, five dollars seemed like a bargain. In fact, just as she was wondering how the woman could bear to part with it at any price, the lady smiled, removed the little pink sticker with her fingernail, and slipped the item back into her garage.

The people we encounter every day can be like that picnic basket. At first glance, we might be tempted to question their worth. They may be a bit battered or broken. But each has a story. And an important part of everyone's story is the truth that Jesus loved them enough to keep a promise and make a huge sacrifice on their behalf. That perspective changes everything—including our ability to love others. As it says in 1 John 4:19, "We love each other because he loved us first."

DADDY-*Daughter Time*

Do you own something that's worth a lot to you even though others might question its value? What is it? Why is it so precious? Is someone in your world a "basket" whose story needs to be heard? Maybe it's you. Do you ever find yourself questioning your own value? Know that God loved you and saw you as valuable even before you knew him.

WHAT'S THE WORD?
We love each other because he loved us first.　　1 JOHN 4:19

WATCHING THE WHEELS

THE supermarket door slides open. There they are, waiting for you, lined up one inside the other. Time to choose a shopping cart. You pick one and make sure it rides smoothly. You travel up and down the aisles together gathering produce, canned goods, snacks, and soda pop. Life is grand! But ninety pounds of groceries later, one of the wheels sticks. Now what? Do you push harder? Kick the ornery caster until it cooperates? Or do you transfer all of your items to another cart and abandon the broken one?

That last option can be mighty tempting—until you realize how much you've already invested in this basket, which you carefully selected only to have it let you down short of the checkout lane. *Ugh!*

Come to think of it, shopping carts are kind of like relationships. For example, maybe a loved one suddenly demands more time and emotional energy than he or she used to. Perhaps a friend did something to lose your respect, or a classmate or employee is making your life difficult. Sticky wheels.

What should we do in situations like these? We can start by realizing that Jesus knows what it's like to have a wheel go bad on a relationship. Look no further than Matthew 26:31-56. First, he told the disciples that they would disown him that very night. Then he took them to Gethsemane where, as he braced for the most stressful event in history, they couldn't even pray without falling asleep—twice! Immediately after that, Judas arrived and betrayed him.

Do you think it crossed Jesus' mind to switch carts at that point? Not likely. These faulty wheels didn't surprise the Lord. After all, he chose these guys in the first place. Can you imagine taking a defective shopping cart on purpose? The Lord does it all the time and commands you to do the same. "Just as I have loved you, you should love each other" (John 13:34). So when your relationships hit rough spots, focus on how much you've already put into them, and do your best to love as Jesus loves.

DADDY-*Daughter Time*

Some people assume that if they choose the right traveling companions, life's journey will remain smooth. Why is that unrealistic, even when selecting a spouse? Is one of your relationships a challenge right now? Are you tempted to switch carts? If appropriate, talk through that together. Ask God for a strategy that will help you push ahead.

WHAT'S THE WORD?

[Jesus said,] "I am giving you a new commandment: Love each other. Just as I have loved you, you should love each other. Your love for one another will prove to the world that you are my disciples." JOHN 13:34-35

I HAVE A DREAM

HOORAY for visionaries! Three cheers for dreamers! These world changers enrich society. They inspire us. They also make great movie heroes. Everyone loves a passionate, imaginative person filled with purpose and optimism, right? Well, not everyone.

When we think of biblical dreamers, one name always rises to the top of the list: Joseph. He had eleven brothers who despised him because he was Dad's favorite. Then those pesky visions kicked in. First, Joseph dreamed they were all out in the field tying bundles of grain, when his brothers' bundles bowed to his. Another dream featured the sun, moon, and eleven stars kneeling before him. In both cases, Joseph couldn't resist sharing all the details with his seething kin, which was sort of like pouring gasoline on a bonfire (see Genesis 37:5).

"Here comes the dreamer!" they said. "Come on, let's kill him and throw him into one of these cisterns. We can tell our father, 'A wild animal has eaten him.' Then we'll see what becomes of his dreams!" (Genesis 37:19-20). The brothers (who sold Joseph into slavery instead) hated hearing his grandiose dreams because they felt threatened by the possibility that the dreams might come true.

A modern example of this involves Martin Luther King Jr. You'll read about him a couple of other times this year. Well, on this date in 1963, he delivered his historic "I Have a Dream" speech to a gathering of more than 250,000 people in Washington, DC. It was a huge demonstration for civil rights and racial equality. King spoke of justice, brotherhood, freedom, and unity. Within two months of his landmark address, Congress passed a new civil rights bill. He also became *Time* magazine's Man of the Year, and was awarded the Nobel Peace Prize. Yet not everyone appreciated his message. Some felt threatened by it, much like Joseph's brothers. During his eleven-year crusade, King was arrested more than twenty times, assaulted, had his house bombed, and was eventually killed in 1968.

Indeed, even the noblest dreams will face challenges. But God wants you to dream big anyway, knowing that if he is the author of your dreams, no force on earth can keep them from coming true.

DADDY-*Daughter Time*

Talk about your own dreams. Then consider who might have felt threatened by the dreams to (1) invent a car that runs on salt water; (2) let cable subscribers pay for channels à la carte; (3) see Christianity flourish all over the world. Watch King's "I Have a Dream" speech together online, then talk about statements and images from that historic event.

WHAT'S THE WORD?

One night Joseph had a dream, and when he told his brothers about it, they hated him more than ever. GENESIS 37:5

ARE *you tired of classmates who stretch the truth to improve their image? Maybe you're sick of crafty coworkers inflating statistics or taking credit for things they didn't do. Then you need the* Exaggerator 3000! *This revolutionary device sets the record straight by sounding an alarm and issuing a Taser-like shock whenever someone tampers with truth to make themselves look better. Don't delay. Get yours today!*

Okay, there's not really an *Exaggerator 3000.* But wouldn't a gizmo like that be handy?

People aren't the only ones willing to tweak facts or alter embarrassing information if it will enhance their image. Countries do it too. On August 29, 1997, Japan's Supreme Court ruled that the Ministry of Education had acted illegally by pulling certain references from a high school history book. Apparently, the government didn't want Japanese students learning that their ancestors had performed deadly experiments on the Chinese during World War II. So they had tried to polish their national image by editing their history.

Of course, the greatest history book ever is God's Word. One case for the Bible's authenticity is that it doesn't ignore people's flaws and turn men of faith into stained-glass saints. We're told that Noah drank himself into a stupor. Abraham lied, and he fathered a child with his wife's maidservant. Moses killed a man in a fit of rage. John the Baptist questioned the Messiah's identity. The apostles deserted Jesus in his hour of need. Not the best publicity if someone were "inventing" a new religion. Nevertheless, God wasn't afraid to be honest in his Word. No embellished biographies. No enhanced images. We get it as it really happened, warts and all.

With that in mind, the next time you're tempted to tinker with facts or spruce up your image in order to impress someone, remember that God loves honesty. He's the author of truth. That's why Paul writes in Ephesians 4:25, "Each of you must put off falsehood and speak truthfully to his neighbor, for we are all members of one body" (NIV).

DADDY-*Daughter Time*

Do you ever feel the need to manage your image by hiding some things or exaggerating others? How so? How does it feel to know that even heroes of the faith weren't perfect? Together, read about God's unconditional love in Zephaniah 3:17, Romans 8:35-39, and Titus 3:4-7.

For a fun project, grab some paper and markers and make a design for the *Exaggerator 3000.* Be creative, then compare your drawings.

WHAT'S THE WORD?
Therefore each of you must put off falsehood and speak truthfully to his neighbor, for we are all members of one body. EPHESIANS 4:25 (NIV)

DEMAS THE DRIFTER

WHY do people sometimes quit an activity? One reason might be that it gets too difficult. Or perhaps it begins to cost them too much time or money. It could be that what looked promising at first simply fails to live up to expectations. Then again, a person may get lured away by the desire for something else. That last reason really sunk a guy named Demas.

The Bible tells us that Demas had been traveling with the apostle Paul, only to abandon the ministry and head to Thessalonica. In 2 Timothy 4:10, Paul reports that Demas deserted him because the man's heart was drawn to things of this world. His passions drifted, so he quit. Of course, people like Demas don't usually shift their loyalties all at once. Even Judas walked with Jesus for three years before betraying him. So how do hearts get lured away? And how can we keep it from happening to us?

Have you ever watched kids boogie boarding at the beach? They paddle into chest-deep water and catch a wave, riding back to the beach on their stomachs. It's loads of fun. But since shifting tides and currents usually pull you to the left or right whenever your feet leave the ocean floor, it's easy to be carried thirty or forty yards up the coast in a very short time without realizing it. That's why it helps to keep an eye on something on shore that doesn't move. A beach umbrella. A lifeguard stand. Your dad. By fixing your eyes on that stationary object, you realize when you've floated off a bit and can adjust right away.

For Christians, that rock-solid fixture should be Jesus. Hebrews 12:2 reminds us of that fact: "Let us fix our eyes on Jesus, the author and perfecter of our faith" (NIV). Don't get distracted by worldly things like Demas did. Be alert. Stay spiritually focused. If you keep your eyes on the Lord, you won't be as likely to drift away when pulled by the currents of this world.

DADDY-*Daughter Time*

How do you think Paul felt when Demas left him? Has anyone ever abandoned you in the middle of a job? Have you ever been guilty of doing it to someone else?

If you live near a beach, grab a couple of boogie boards and ride some waves together. Pick an object as your "constant" to focus on, and see how easy it is to drift when you look away, even for a few minutes.

WHAT'S THE WORD?

Let us fix our eyes on Jesus, the author and perfecter of our faith.   HEBREWS 12:2 (NIV)

GOING BALLISTIC

THE neighbors heard shots, but they didn't get a good look at the man who pulled the trigger. Now commotion erupts: flashing lights and yellow police tape. But justice could be found in a science lab. Once forensic scientists determine what gun was used and who owns it, authorities have all the evidence they need to solve the case. The process is called "ballistic fingerprinting." You see, every gun is unique. The inside of each barrel leaves a distinct set of stripes and scratches on the soft lead of a bullet. You can't see them with the naked eye, but for a trained ballistics expert, matching a slug to the weapon that fired it is as easy as nabbing a cat burglar based on a set of fingerprints.

Crime scene investigators and forensic scientists do a great job gathering evidence to identify a criminal. They might look at fingerprints, tool marks, fabric impressions, tire treads, hair, blood, gunshot residue, and other clues to track down who committed a crime. Many criminals try very hard not to leave any evidence. As followers of Jesus Christ, we should do the exact opposite.

God wants us to leave evidence that we are his children. Maybe that evidence shows in the kind things we do for other people or the decisions we make. Even better, perhaps people get clued in to our love for God because we tell them about Jesus. In Matthew 7, Jesus talks about gathering evidence to find out what kind of person you're dealing with. Jesus says that a good person produces good fruit, while a bad person produces bad fruit. "Just as you can identify a tree by its fruit, so you can identify people by their actions" (Matthew 7:20). What do your actions say about you? Are you leaving behind a lot of evidence that shows you follow Jesus?

DADDY-*Daughter Time*

There's no one exactly like you. Beyond fingerprints, how has God made you one of a kind? Are you using that uniqueness to glorify him? Think of some ways that you can leave behind evidence that you're a Christian. Write down a few ideas that you're doing now or want to do in the future. For a fun activity, get an ink pad and paper and compare your fingerprints. How are they similar, and how do they differ?

WHAT'S THE WORD?

Just as you can identify a tree by its fruit, so you can identify people by their actions.
MATTHEW 7:20

WHEN WILL MY LIFE BEGIN?

THE 2010 hit Disney movie *Tangled* retells the classic story of Rapunzel. In this modern update, Rapunzel is a smart, cheery, hardworking girl who has been trapped in a tower her entire life. In the midst of her daily routine, she sings a catchy song in which she wonders repeatedly, "When will my life begin?"

What she's really asking is, When will I be making my own decisions and having my own new adventures in life? That's a pretty common desire for girls growing past childhood. But if you really think about her question, the message of the song may be *Life* really *begins when I get to do what I want to do, when I want to do it.*

Really?

Okay, what do *you* want to do when you're old enough to try anything? Ask your grandma or mother what she wanted to do so badly as a kid that she couldn't wait until she was old enough. She might say that she wanted to stay up all night, or eat pizza for breakfast and ice cream for dinner.

But if you ask that same person if she would still do those same things today, you're likely to get a different answer. As people get older, they usually gain a better understanding of the consequences of their choices. And they get a sense of what's really most important.

Jesus always knew how to keep the most important things at the top of his life. His desire to be about his Father's business stayed the same from his childhood through adulthood. In John 6:28, some people asked Jesus what they should do to be an important part of his ministry. His answer was straight to the point: "This is the only work God wants from you: Believe in the one he has sent" (v. 29). Later in that same passage, Jesus added that he came down from heaven "to do the will of God who sent me, not to do my own will" (v. 38).

DADDY-*Daughter Time*

Talk about what you would like to do tonight or this weekend if you could do anything you wanted. Does your list have room for what God wants you to do? You might not find verses in the Bible that say things like "do not go to the sleepover" or "do practice your piano lessons." But there are a lot of great verses that tell us what pleases God.

If you have time, watch the movie *Tangled* and read through the questions in the Father-Daughter Movie Nights appendix.

WHAT'S THE WORD?

I have come down from heaven to do the will of God who sent me, not to do my own will. JOHN 6:38

WHAT WOULD JESUS ASK?   *September 2*

WITH the start of another school year, you're probably dealing with a lot of questions:

- What is the capital of Illinois?
- What is the square root of sixteen?
- What is the symbol for copper on the periodic table of elements?
- What is the noun in this sentence: "The angry cat meowed menacingly"?

Questions are a great way to pass along information and create communication. And nobody knew how to ask questions better than God's Son. The Gospels record more than one hundred questions that Jesus asked. Some of his questions were rhetorical, like when he said in Matthew 6:27, "Can all your worries add a single moment to your life?" (Uh, no.) Later, a religious leader asked Jesus, "Good Teacher, what should I do to inherit eternal life?" (Luke 18:18). Jesus quickly responded with a question of his own: "Why do you call me good? . . . Only God is truly good" (v. 19).

We can learn a lot from God's Son regarding the power of questions, especially when it comes to sharing our belief in Jesus. Instead of talking at people about our faith in Christ, we may be more effective by asking questions. Make sure your questions can't be answered with a simple yes or no. And try to ask open-ended questions that get your friends talking, so you can hear what they really believe.

Questions keep the communication flowing. Be ready to answer other people's questions as well. Sometimes your response might be, "I don't know. Let me find the answer and get back to you." Being forced to talk about what we believe strengthens our values as well. Following Jesus' example can be challenging. Asking questions is one small way that we can be like our Savior.

DADDY-*Daughter Time*

Questions can be key in communication between parents and children. Take several moments to ask each other a few questions to learn more about each other. Here are a few for starters:

- Who's your favorite superhero? Why?
- What's your favorite Bible story?
- What activity did you enjoy the most this week?

As you ask each other questions, try to have a conversation instead of making it feel like an interrogation. Then talk about ways you can use questions in your everyday life to be like Jesus. (By the way, Springfield is the capital of Illinois; the square root of sixteen is four; the symbol for copper is Cu; and *cat* is the noun.)

WHAT'S THE WORD?

"Why do you call me good?" Jesus asked him. "Only God is truly good."   LUKE 18:19

WHEN HAPPINESS HURTS

HAVE you ever sung the song "Happy All the Time"? The lyrics go, "I'm in-right, outright, upright, downright happy all the time. Since Jesus Christ came in and cleansed my heart from sin, I'm in-right, outright, upright, downright happy all the time."

It's a cute song and fun to sing, because *happy* is such a happy word. Just saying it can make you feel warm and fuzzy. Try it. Say "happy" ten times really fast. You're smiling now, aren't you?

It's natural to want to be happy. But happiness also has a dark side. Studies show that gang leaders, violent criminals, and bullies often feel happy about themselves. They get that feeling by having power over someone else.

God wants your happiness to come from a different place—a deep place where joy bubbles up even in the face of adversity. In the book of Matthew, Jesus tells his followers that people will mock and lie about them. But when you get put down for your belief in Jesus, he encourages you to "be happy about it! Be very glad! For a great reward awaits you in heaven" (Matthew 5:12).

Being happy when you're made fun of sounds impossible. But Jesus knew that true happiness isn't based on circumstances; it's built on joy that can only come from knowing him. Your life won't always be happy once you become a follower of Christ. You'll encounter difficult times. But when those tough times come, don't think that God has left you. He hasn't. And he never will. View the difficulties in your life as an opportunity to build godly character and find real happiness.

It's not possible to be "downright happy all the time" like the song says. But you can tap into the source of happiness every minute of every day no matter where you are. And that should make you want to sing, "I'm happy, happy, happy, happy, happy all the time."

DADDY-*Daughter Time*

Happiness isn't a bad thing, but God wants you to pursue character over happiness. Experts say that character comes from making sacrifices, facing challenges, and dealing with adversity. Share a couple of things with each other that make you happy. Maybe it's spending time together or watching a sunset on a summer night. Take a few minutes to ask God to help you focus on him and to be happy even when tough times come.

WHAT'S THE WORD?

God blesses you when people mock you and persecute you and lie about you and say all sorts of evil things against you because you are my followers. Be happy about it! Be very glad! For a great reward awaits you in heaven. MATTHEW 5:11-12

AMERICAN IDOL

QUICK, name all the *American Idol* winners.

Did you get them all? Probably not. You forgot the soulful sounds of Taylor Hicks, didn't you? Since the program began in 2002, it's become one of the most popular shows in the history of American television. And some of the show's winners have gone on to amazingly successful music careers—2005 winner Carrie Underwood jumps to mind.

But on this day in 2002, *American Idol* crowned its first champion as Kelly Clarkson won the title with more than eighteen million people watching on TV. Kelly had always loved music. She performed in several musicals in high school and sang at her school's talent show. After high school, she tried breaking into the music business but had little success until *Idol* came along.

Don't you love watching *American Idol*? Maybe not when the judges are mean or make fun of people. But it's cool to see contestants follow their dreams. And if *Idol* auditions are any indication, a lot of people dream of fame.

During the first season of the show around ten thousand people tried out. A lot of those folks may have had good motives, but others did it just to be in the spotlight. The Bible is clear: fame is fleeting. First Peter 1:24-25 says, "All flesh is like grass, and all its glory like a flower of the grass. The grass withers, and the flower falls, but the word of the Lord endures forever" (HCSB).

It's okay to have dreams. God has big plans for your life! But if your goal is fame, then your glory will fade fast. Put your dreams in the Word of God—then they'll last forever.

DADDY-*Daughter Time*

Do you have any dreams that are linked to a special talent you have? Dads, share your dreams from when you were a child. All of those dreams are great, but don't forget that our ultimate goal in life should be to honor and glorify God. Earthly fame is fleeting, but what you do for the Lord lasts for eternity.

Before ending this devotional time, think of a song you can sing together. If you have a karaoke machine at your house, get it out. You can also put on a favorite CD or something from your iPod. Have fun hamming it up with some fake microphones in your hands. (A hairbrush works great.) Thank God for the dreams he gives us and the life he blesses us with.

WHAT'S THE WORD?

All flesh is like grass, and all its glory like a flower of the grass. The grass withers, and the flower falls, but the word of the Lord endures forever. 1 PETER 1:24-25 (HCSB)

GOOD WORK

HUNDREDS of years before Jesus came to earth, a Greek slave named Aesop walked around telling stories to teach children important truths. We can still learn a lot from Aesop's Fables. Who can forget the story about the lion and . . . uh . . . that guy who pulled the thorn out of its foot? Or how about "The Buffoon and the Countryman"? Okay, those aren't some of his more popular stories. But you've probably heard about "The Boy Who Cried Wolf" or "The Tortoise and the Hare" (about a rabbit who challenges a turtle to a race, then gets overconfident and takes a nap, so the slow and steady turtle wins the contest).

One of Aesop's best-known fables talks about an ant and a grasshopper. The grasshopper loves to have fun. It spends the summer hopping around and singing. The ant, on the other hand, stays diligent in storing food for the winter. The only time the ant even speaks to the grasshopper is when it encourages its friend to "lay up food for the winter." Of course, the grasshopper ignores the advice and continues to mess around. In the end, the grasshopper ends up dying of starvation. That may sound harsh, but it teaches an important lesson. By slacking off instead of storing up food, the grasshopper suffers the consequences of its actions. The ant proves that diligence to complete a job pays off. The Bible talks directly about this principle in Proverbs 6:6, 8: "Take a lesson from the ants, you lazybones. Learn from their ways and become wise! . . . They labor hard all summer, gathering food for the winter."

God designed us to work. We have to work in school, work at home to help our families, and work to do well in sports or the arts. Working hard is a good thing. When you play instead of work, things go badly. Like it says in Proverbs 13:4, "Lazy people want much but get little, but those who work hard will prosper." As you look ahead at another school year, strive to be the kind of worker who energetically accomplishes her responsibilities.

DADDY-*Daughter Time*

Make up your own Aesop's Fable. First, decide what you want the moral to be. Maybe you could write about avoiding temptation. Perhaps you could call it "The Puppy and the Piece of Bacon." Get a piece of paper and write down your story. *Mmmmm,* bacon. That certainly sounds better than "The Rooster and the Pearl."

WHAT'S THE WORD?

Lazy people want much but get little, but those who work hard will prosper.
PROVERBS 13:4

FORGIVE AND FORGET

AN elephant never forgets. That's especially true if the question is, where'd I put my trunk? *Ha!* But it's also true when it comes to people who treat them badly. Research shows that elephants remember injuries and hold grudges against their abusers.

Aren't we the same way? When somebody is mean to us, we can remember it forever. Even when we think we have forgiven, old feelings can crop up when we see a person who has wronged us. Can you relate to any of these situations?

- Washing the dishes and cleaning your room sound way better than having a conversation with your ex–best friend.
- Every time you look at your little sister, you picture her taking your favorite bracelet and losing it (and that happened over a year ago).
- Your stomach bunches into a knot whenever you see that cousin who always teases you. But you feel immediately better when she goes away.

At the beginning of a new school year, it's natural for old feelings to come back—especially toward kids who have treated you badly. Instead of being stuck with a knotted-up stomach and raw emotions, trust that God has a better plan. He wants you to forgive.

In the book of Matthew, Peter asked Jesus a question about forgiveness. Peter knew that God wants people to forgive, so he said, "Lord, how often should I forgive someone who sins against me? Seven times?" (18:21). Wow, seven! To Peter, that probably sounded like a lot of times to show forgiveness. But Jesus replied, "No, not seven times, but seventy times seven!" (18:22).

Jesus didn't mean a literal 490 times. When the Lord said, "Seventy times seven," he was conveying that our forgiveness should be limitless, just like God offers us unlimited forgiveness when we pray to him and ask to be forgiven.

DADDY-*Daughter Time*

It's easy to say, "I forgive you." It's much harder to truly forgive. Is there a teacher, principal, or friend whom you need to forgive as the school year gets under way? When we fail to forgive, we hurt ourselves more than we hurt the person who wronged us. God wants us to live free from bitterness and grudges. Sometimes that means forgiving and forgetting.

Talk together about a situation in each of your lives that needs an extra measure of forgiveness. Then hold each other accountable to truly forgive and to move on with your lives.

WHAT'S THE WORD?

Peter came to him and asked, "Lord, how often should I forgive someone who sins against me? Seven times?" "No, not seven times," Jesus replied, "but seventy times seven!" MATTHEW 18:21-22

RESCUED FROM THE FLAMES

A badly burned, panic-stricken woman stumbles into the front yard. "Someone help my children!" she cries. Behind her, menacing flames dance up and down in the windows of her mobile home. Smoke rushes out the door. Then, in the blink of an eye, fifteen-year-old Terry Miller rushes in.

A gas explosion has engulfed the living room, stranding four-year-old Rachel Majewski in the kitchen. Terry hones in on her screams, snatches up the little girl, and carries her to safety before bolting inside again in search of Rachel's nine-month-old brother. The intense smoke drives Terry back into the yard empty-handed. Undaunted, the brave high school student draws a deep breath and enters the mobile home a third time, blinded by smoke and heat, entirely dependent on little Bradley's screams to guide him to the baby's crib.

No one was able to save the Majewskis' mobile home on this date in 2004. But Terry saved two children. All because he heard their cries.

When the heat is on, God hears our cries and comes to our rescue. The most dramatic example is when he sent his Son, Jesus Christ, to die on the cross for our sin and save us from the fires of hell. But the Bible tells of other miraculous rescues too. Hot ones. Remember when Shadrach, Meshach, and Abednego were thrown into a fiery furnace by King Nebuchadnezzar simply because they refused to bow down to a man-made idol (see Daniel 3)? Three guys were tossed into the flames, but everybody saw four walking around. Some experts believe it was God himself who delivered Shadrach, Meshach, and Abednego safe and sound.

Are you facing a fiery trial in your life? Cry out to the Lord. He'll hear you, just as it says in 2 Samuel 22:7. And whether he chooses to snatch you out of it immediately or join you in the midst of it, rest assured that God will come to the rescue.

DADDY-*Daughter Time*

If you're struggling with a difficult situation at work or school, discuss it together. Then ask God to intervene. If everything is going well, look for someone who needs a hero in his or her life. Maybe you have a neighbor who needs yard work done. Perhaps a family at church could use some help painting. God can use your efforts to make a big difference. We don't have to race into burning buildings to help our friends and neighbors. It's as easy as lending a hand.

WHAT'S THE WORD?

In my distress I cried out to the LORD; yes, I cried to my God for help. He heard me from his sanctuary; my cry reached his ears.   2 SAMUEL 22:7

LOOKING GOOD

DON'T you just love a day spent at the spa?

Not you, young ladies. We're talking to the dads. Over the last several years, men's interest in spa treatments has skyrocketed 700 percent. With manicures, pedicures, facials, massages, and haircuts, men now make up around 20 percent of day-spa clients.

A lot of dads wouldn't want to admit it, but we like to look good. Maybe we don't spend a bunch of money on makeup or a lot of time creating a hip hairstyle. But we care about our appearance. Why else would guys consistently spend billions of dollars on gym memberships and workout equipment?

There's nothing wrong with putting in effort to look good. Both dads and daughters want to appear cool, calm, and collected. But the problem arises when we put more time into primping our appearance than feeding our spirits. When Jesus walked the earth, he had a lot of interactions with the Pharisees. These religious leaders liked to appear as if they had it all together. They had a spiritual, better-than-you air about them. Jesus didn't like that. In Matthew 23:28, he told them, "Outwardly you look like righteous people, but inwardly your hearts are filled with hypocrisy and lawlessness."

That's definitely not the way we want to be described. When God looks at us, we want our good appearance to be a reflection of a heart fully devoted to him. We can't hide from God behind a cute outfit, smooth skin, and well-manicured nails. He looks right through us and sees our core. So instead of putting on a front, strive to be honest with yourself, others, and God. Put extra effort into the things that really matter: your relationships with God, family, and friends. With a little more time spent on your inner self, you'll even "look" better to those around you.

DADDY-*Daughter Time*

Does your mom have any facial-mask cream? If so, do family facials. Dads, make sure to participate too. Get out the camera and snap a few funny photos. Sometimes making yourself look good can seem a little silly.

As you wait for the mask to dry, talk about how outward appearances have little meaning in the scope of eternity. Come up with ideas as a family how you can put extra effort into reflecting Christ and worrying less about your reflection in the mirror.

WHAT'S THE WORD?

Outwardly you look like righteous people, but inwardly your hearts are filled with hypocrisy and lawlessness. MATTHEW 23:28

KNOWLEDGE IS POWER

TEACHERS don't like it. Students depend on it. TV shows make fun of it. And it keeps growing bigger every day. What is it?

Wikipedia, of course.

On this day in 2007, an article on the Spanish TV show *El Hormiguero* was posted. Nothing too special about that, except if you like funny ant puppets that talk about science. What made this post historic is that it was the two millionth article in English uploaded to Wikipedia.

Wikipedia launched in 2001. The word *wiki* comes from the Hawaiian language and means "quick." *Pedia* comes from the word *encyclopedia*. Entries in Wikipedia are written mostly by anonymous contributors who don't get paid. People of all ages, cultures, and backgrounds can add to or edit entries. That's probably what caused a character on a popular TV sitcom to say, "Wikipedia is the best thing ever. Anyone in the world can write anything they want about any subject. So you know you are getting the best possible information." Yeah, and maybe not.

Wikipedia is constantly changing. More than eighty thousand active contributors continue to add content. In 2011, Wikipedia had more than nineteen million articles, nearly four million of them in English.

Teachers don't like Wikipedia because the information can be so easily changed. Even Wikipedia says to be careful when using the website as a reference in a research paper. It warns you to always check links and find multiple sources.

Wikipedia isn't trying to be a single source of knowledge. Only God can claim that. Job 28:28 says, "The fear of the Lord is true wisdom; to forsake evil is real understanding." Searching Wikipedia won't make you smart. Only respecting and following God can give you wisdom. Turning your back on sinful choices gives you real understanding. And when you combine wisdom and understanding . . . now that will make you smart.

DADDY-*Daughter Time*

Every month more than four million people visit Wikipedia. Are you among them? Become one now by going to a computer and searching for something you know a lot about. See what Wikipedia says. Is it accurate? Did it leave something out?

The Internet is a wonderful tool to find information. It can also be a dangerous place filled with inappropriate material. Commit to each other to avoid evil when you're on the Internet.

WHAT'S THE WORD?

This is what [God] says to all humanity: "The fear of the Lord is true wisdom; to forsake evil is real understanding." JOB 28:28

SLAMMIN' TENNIS PLAYER *September 10*

STEFFI Graf may be the best women's tennis player in the history of the sport. From 1982 to 1999, Steffi won 107 tournaments—including twenty-two Grand Slam titles. The German juggernaut was ranked number one in the world for 377 weeks, 186 of them in a row! Her devastating forehand earned her the nickname "Fraulein Forehand" because she could hit winners from anywhere on the court with that stroke.

Steffi had many memorable moments, but 1988 was an especially good year as she won 96 percent of her matches. She claimed the gold medal in the Olympics, took first in the Australian Open, and notched victories in the French Open and at Wimbledon. Then on September 10, she won the US Open to give her tennis's Grand Slam. By winning all four major tennis events in one year, Steffi became the second youngest woman in history to earn a Grand Slam. In 1953, Maureen Connolly had become the first woman to earn a Grand Slam when she won the US Open just before her nineteenth birthday. Steffi was nineteen and three months old when she accomplished this rare feat.

Steffi will forever be remembered for her tennis abilities, but her family deserves some credit too. Her father introduced her to the sport when she was three, letting her swing a racket in the living room. At age four, she began playing the game on a real court. Her father coached her, and Steffi played in her first professional match at thirteen. Steffi worked hard at tennis and was rewarded for her efforts. The Bible says you should enjoy your successes when your hard work pays off. Ecclesiastes 3:13 puts it this way: "People should eat and drink and enjoy the fruits of their labor, for these are gifts from God."

As you go through this school year, be sure to work hard. But also make sure to relax and celebrate after your diligence pays off.

DADDY-*Daughter Time*

Blow up a balloon, draw a real or imaginary line in the room, and play a game of balloon tennis. You only get one hit when the balloon comes on your side of the "court." The point ends when the balloon hits the ground. If the balloon lands on Dad's side of the court, Daughter scores a point (and vice versa). Play to ten points and see who wins.

WHAT'S THE WORD?
People should eat and drink and enjoy the fruits of their labor, for these are gifts from God. ECCLESIASTES 3:13

A REAL AMERICAN HERO

PATRICIA Smith's mother is a hero.

Patricia was just two years old when terrorists flew airplanes into New York City's World Trade Center towers on September 11, 2001. Her mother, Moira Smith, a New York City police officer, died that day. Moira was at ground zero helping people escape the burning buildings. As she went back inside to rescue even more people, Officer Smith was killed when the south tower collapsed. Several months after the tragedy, Patricia accepted the New York Police Department Medal of Honor for her mother. Dressed in a red velvet dress with a green ribbon around her neck, little Patricia made a lasting impression at the ceremony at Carnegie Hall.

Years prior to Moira risking her life to save people on 9/11, she was a hero. During an interview on *Good Morning America* ten years after 9/11, Patricia told the story about when her mom was twelve years old and jumped into a swimming pool to rescue a little girl.

"Even before 9/11, she was a hero to somebody," Patricia said.

The Bible tells the story of a woman named Esther who was a hero to many people too. You'll actually read about her several times during the year. The book of Esther recounts the actions of this young queen who risked her life to save her people. Back then, a person could be killed for going before the king without an invitation. But Esther overcame her fear to let the king know about a terrible plot to kill her people. Just before Esther decided to risk her life, she had an important conversation with her cousin Mordecai, who said to her, "Who knows if perhaps you were made queen for just such a time as this?" (Esther 4:14).

Only God knows the plans he has for your life. Perhaps you'll be put into a place for "such a time as this." Queen Esther and Moira Smith will be remembered as heroes for the unselfish decisions they made. What will your decisions say about you?

DADDY-*Daughter Time*

Nearly three thousand people died in the 9/11 attacks. More than three thousand children lost parents that fateful day. Take a few minutes to remember the victims of 9/11. Pray for their families. Pray for the children who were affected by the loss. You can find lists of families on the Internet. Make it a point to remember those families in your prayers.

WHAT'S THE WORD?

If you keep quiet at a time like this, deliverance and relief for the Jews will arise from some other place, but you and your relatives will die. Who knows if perhaps you were made queen for just such a time as this? ESTHER 4:14

CAT ATTACK

CATHERINE Whitehill never liked the nickname "Cat." But she loved the sport of soccer, and it always seemed as if her teammates ended up calling her Cat.

In September 2003, Catherine was the youngest member on the US Women's National Team during the World Cup. But this young defender made the North Korea team feel as if it had just gone through a cat attack. The twenty-one-year-old scored two goals—her first ever in the World Cup—to help the United States advance to the quarterfinals. Catherine (then known as Cat Reddick) scored the first goal off a corner kick when the ball was headed to the far post and she knocked it in. Then she tallied on a nifty header in a crowd of players to make the final 3–0.

After the game, Catherine credited her teammates with setting her up for the goals and also acknowledged her Lord and Savior.

"I wouldn't be where I am today if it weren't for God," she said. "His plans are huge and so out of my control. My prayer before every game is, 'This is my sanctuary to worship you. Use me in a way to praise you on the field.' When you have a perspective like that, it makes playing so much fun."

Through 2011, Catherine played in 135 games for the US National Team and scored eleven goals.

Soccer requires eleven players working in unity to succeed. God's church is the same way. Everybody has a role to play and skills given to us by God. When we work together, we can reach our goals.

DADDY-*Daughter Time*

Catherine viewed soccer as a way to worship God. She knew her talents came from him and wanted to give him the glory. Paul says, "There are different kinds of gifts, but the same Spirit. . . . There are different kinds of working, but the same God works all of them in all men" (1 Corinthians 12:4, 6, NIV).

When we use our gifts and allow God to work through us, we can accomplish great things. As you use your gifts and hone them to make them stronger, remember Catherine's words and make the sporting field, classroom, stage, or concert hall a sanctuary to worship him.

WHAT'S THE WORD?

There are different kinds of gifts, but the same Spirit. There are different kinds of service, but the same Lord. There are different kinds of working, but the same God works all of them in all men. 1 CORINTHIANS 12:4-6 (NIV)

September 13

CAN you touch the tip of your nose with your tongue? Try it. While the longest human tongue was around four inches, most tongues are about two inches, which makes this a rare talent. As you try to touch your nose, take a close look at your tongue. It's sort of bumpy and strange. See how much you know about this amazing group of muscles.

> True or False: Those bumps on your tongue are taste buds.
> True or False: If your tongue is too dry, you can't taste much.
> True or False: Taste buds live as long as you do.
> True or False: Kids have a better sense of taste than adults.

Answers: The bumps on your tongue aren't taste buds; they're called papillae. Saliva helps your sense of taste, so it's true that a dry tongue has difficulty tasting. Taste buds live for around two weeks before being replaced. But as you age, fewer buds grow back. So it's true that children have a sharper sense of taste than adults. Don't believe it? Pour a glass of milk and let it sit in your refrigerator for a month (you may need Mom's permission for this experiment). Once it's good and spoiled, take turns drinking a sip. *Yuck!* Who thought it tasted worse?

Okay, that's not a good taste test. But the truth is if you don't control your tongue, you're going to end up with an even worse taste in your mouth. When you make a snarky comment, say something mean, lie, or let a profanity slip from your lips, you're doing more damage than would be caused by drinking spoiled milk. James 1:26 tells us if we don't control our tongues, then our "religion is worthless." Now those are some sour words.

DADDY-*Daughter Time*

Try this cool experiment: Cut up a raw apple and piece of potato. Dads, close your eyes and hold your nose. Daughters, place a piece of food in your dad's mouth. Can he tell if it's an apple or potato? Now close your eyes and hold your nose. Can you taste a difference? The truth is, your sense of smell helps your sense of taste. You can also try eating a piece of apple while smelling an onion. What do you taste? As you do these experiments, ask God to help your tongue speak sweet words—not sour.

WHAT'S THE WORD?

If you claim to be religious but don't control your tongue, you are fooling yourself, and your religion is worthless. JAMES 1:26

MEDIA MINDED

MEDIA is all around you: magazines, billboards, TV shows, movies, commercials, videos, and books. Because you're bombarded all the time, it's tough to live up to King David's standard of "I will refuse to look at anything vile and vulgar" (Psalm 101:3).

You might be watching Saturday morning shows or something on the Disney Channel when a commercial pops on that could only be described as vulgar. Or you may find yourself searching around on the Internet when a vile pop-up ad appears. Sometimes you can't control seeing inappropriate images. But some people don't even try to avoid harmful shows. During a two-year period in the mid-2000s, researchers at Dartmouth Medical School studied the movie-watching habits of families. After interviewing more than 2,600 parents and children, researchers found that 40 percent of nine-year-olds watched R-rated movies at least occasionally. A whopping 70 percent of twelve year-olds viewed films that contained adult content. That's sad.

In 1994, some people wanted to fight against the media. They didn't like the fact that the average child watched twenty thousand commercials a year but only talked with their parents for around thirty minutes per week. These people started National TV-Turnoff Week. During the third week of September (and again in April), families are encouraged to get away from screens (that includes TVs, computers, and movies). God sets high standards for our media choices. Strive to live by them.

DADDY-*Daughter Time*

Start planning now to take part in National TV-Turnoff Week. Gather the other members of your family and discuss why you want to avoid screens for seven straight days. You can also talk about the pros and cons of past media choices. Instead of watching TV or going to the movies, suggest doing some of these activities instead:

Cook dinner as a family
Make crafts
Go to a museum
Play board games
Look at stars through a telescope
Tell favorite family stories
Go fishing
Go on a bike ride

You can also come up with some of your own ideas. Enjoy your weeklong break from the media.

WHAT'S THE WORD?
I will refuse to look at anything vile and vulgar.   PSALM 101:3

UNLIKELY FRIENDS

TARRA and Bella are best friends. They love taking long walks to explore the beautiful Tennessee hillside. They eat together, play together, and even sleep near each other. Every time Bella sees her best friend, her tail wags and she barks in excitement. Oh yeah, Bella's a dog. A mixed-breed mutt to be exact. And Tarra is an elephant. More specifically, a 6,500-pound endangered Asian pachyderm.

The pair met at The Elephant Sanctuary in Hohenwald, Tennessee. Tarra arrived in 1995 after spending more than twenty years traveling the world entertaining people at circuses, amusement parks, and zoos. About ten years later, Bella just showed up on the sanctuary's land. Once the two found each other, they became inseparable. In 2007 when Bella hurt her back and couldn't walk or wag her tail, Tarra stayed faithfully near the office barn while Bella healed. Instead of wandering the sanctuary's 2,700 acres, Tarra stood staring at the offices. Several times during her recovery, workers carried Bella down to see Tarra. After a few weeks, Bella was well enough to again join her best friend in the wild.

Watching Tarra and Bella can teach us a lot about friendship and trust, especially when Bella rolls on her back and Tarra uses her foot to rub Bella's tummy. It'd be hard to imagine a more unusual pair of friends.

When Jesus walked the earth, he made some unlikely friends. Sure, he and the disciples were buds. They traveled together as Jesus taught them what it meant to live for God. But Jesus also hung out with people that society despised. Matthew 11:19 says Jesus was "a friend of tax collectors and other sinners!" He didn't show love to only the religious and popular people, because it was the sick and the sinful who really needed to know Jesus' life-changing message. Jesus wasn't afraid of what people would say about him; he always chose to do the right thing.

DADDY-*Daughter Time*

Think about people you know at school or church. Does someone pop to mind who needs a friend? If so, write that person's name here: _____.
What can you do to be a friend to that person?

A lot of times we hang out with people who are like us—and that's okay. We should have friends who share our interests. But at the same time, we shouldn't ignore people who are lonely or outcast. Sometimes we can learn a lot and make a big difference for God's Kingdom by making an unlikely friend.

WHAT'S THE WORD?

Matthew invited Jesus and his disciples to his home as dinner guests, along with many tax collectors and other disreputable sinners. MATTHEW 9:10

BEING THE BEST FOR GOD *September 16*

ALLIE wanted to be the best student her new school had ever seen. She jumped into her first day with enthusiasm. Teachers never had to ask Allie to do anything. She knew (at least she *thought* she knew) what it meant to be a good student. She showed up early for school, skipped lunch to do extra-credit assignments, read ahead in her textbooks, completed homework before it was assigned, and helped the teachers clean their classrooms and grade papers. She even came to school on weekends to pick up trash on the playground. Allie didn't have time to read the syllabus for a class or even look at the planning calendar to see what was actually due. She was too busy doing, achieving, and succeeding. But after a couple of months, Allie didn't feel like a success. She just felt tired and burned out.

Our relationship with Jesus Christ can be the same way. Once we pray to ask Jesus into our hearts, we're ready to change the world and tell all of our friends about God. The exuberance of being a new Christian is huge. We'll quit spreading rumors, stop making mean remarks, and start helping little old ladies cross the street—just to show God how much we love him. But the truth is, if we're too busy doing "God's work" that we don't read God's book, we might be wasting our energies on things God doesn't think are important. And after a couple of months, we could start feeling like we're running around without accomplishing anything.

God desires just one thing from his children: obedience. First John 5:3 says, "Loving God means keeping his commandments, and his commandments are not burdensome."

God doesn't ask us to run around without purpose. He simply wants us to keep his commandments. But to follow his commands, we have to know what he asks us to do. The only way to do that is to read his Word. It may take a little extra time now, but knowing God's Word can save us a lot of energy and make us more effective for him in the long run.

DADDY-*Daughter Time*

In Exodus 20, you can find a list of God's Ten Commandments to the people of Israel. Then in John 15:10-17, Jesus tells us what he commands us to do. Look at those two lists. What are some similarities? What's different? Write down a couple of ways that you can follow God's commandments every day:

_____

_____

WHAT'S THE WORD?
Loving God means keeping his commandments, and his commandments are not burdensome. 1 JOHN 5:3

THE BEST MEDICINE

QUIZ time. Don't worry, this one's fun.

    1. True or False: Kids laugh more than adults.

That's true. Researchers found that children laugh an average of three hundred to four hundred times a day, while an adult may laugh twenty or fewer times.

    2. True or False: Boys laugh more than girls.

False. Surveys have discovered that girls laugh more than boys.

    3. True or False: This is a good time for a tickle fight.

True. Is there ever a bad time?

Okay, the quiz is over. Not too bad, right? But there is one more question: do you like to laugh? Hopefully, you do. The Bible says that laughter is good medicine (Proverbs 17:22). Doctors have done research and found the Bible is correct. According to medical professionals, laughter can lower blood pressure, increase the amount of oxygen in the blood, give you an abdominal workout, reduce stress, defend against respiratory infection, decrease the frequency of colds, and increase memory and learning ability. One study found that people remember 80 percent more of what they hear when they're laughing. So try to laugh a lot at school!

As you can see, laughter is a good thing. And laughter comes from God. It's true. Back in Genesis, God promised a man named Abraham that he'd have more descendants than he could count. Just one problem: he and his wife, Sarah, didn't have any children and they were really old. Do you know what happened? God did a miracle and Sarah had a son they named Isaac, which means "laughter." When Isaac was born, Sarah declared, "God has brought me laughter. All who hear about this will laugh with me" (Genesis 21:6).

Isn't it cool that God brings laughter?

DADDY-*Daughter Time*

It's time to laugh. Go to your computer and search for "Tim Hawkins on Bad Candy." You should end up on Christian comedian Tim Hawkins's GodTube page. Watch his video on bad candy and a few other ones if you want. When you're done laughing, thank God that he brings you so much joy.

WHAT'S THE WORD?

Sarah declared, "God has brought me laughter. All who hear about this will laugh with me." GENESIS 21:6

THE CORNERSTONE September 18

MORE than two hundred years ago, George Washington proved he was more than a good president and strong military leader. He could also build. On this day in 1793, he laid the cornerstone to the United States Capitol Building. Before this time, the United States didn't have a permanent capitol, so Congress met in various cities, including New York, Philadelphia, and Baltimore. It took nearly one hundred years to complete the construction of this amazing building, which houses the legislative branch of American government.

Today, the US Capitol covers approximately four acres in Washington, DC. Its distinctive dome and pillars make it one of the most recognizable buildings in the world. Every year nearly five million people from around the globe visit the Capitol.

When Washington laid the cornerstone, he placed the most important stone in the Capitol. Every other stone was set using the cornerstone as a reference point. In the Bible, Jesus is called the cornerstone. It's first referenced in the Old Testament. Then in Acts 4:11 Peter says, "Jesus is the one referred to in the Scriptures, where it says, 'The stone that you builders rejected has now become the cornerstone.'"

Everything in the Christian faith is based on Jesus. He existed before the universe was formed. And when God's Son came to earth, he was rejected and killed for our sins. His sacrifice makes it possible for us to be forgiven and have a personal relationship with God. When it comes to your faith, all you have to do is look at your cornerstone to know how you should line up your life.

DADDY-*Daughter Time*

Do you have any old blocks lying around the house? If so, go get them and build a tower together. Notice how important it is to perfectly place the cornerstone. If the cornerstone is crooked, the whole foundation will be messed up.

When you build your life on Jesus Christ, you have a firm foundation. With him as your cornerstone, you can't go wrong. What are you building your life on? Friends? Money? Good grades? Career? Sports? Talk with each other and be honest about what seems to be your cornerstone. Then commit to each other to build your lives on Christ.

WHAT'S THE WORD?

Jesus is the one referred to in the Scriptures, where it says, "The stone that you builders rejected has now become the cornerstone." ACTS 4:11

HISTORY-MAKING VICTORY

WHEN Lexi Thompson woke up on this day in 2011, she was the same fresh-faced sixteen-year-old she'd been the day before. But there were some differences. Her bank account had an additional $195,000 in it because she'd become the youngest golfer to ever win a Ladies Professional Golf Association (LPGA) event. By shooting a 17-under 271, Lexi won the Navistar LPGA Classic in Prattsville, Alabama.

Heading into the final round on September 18, the teenager led by five strokes but had to deal with a ton of pressure and a talented field trying to catch her from behind. Lexi bogeyed a couple of holes on the back nine as her lead over Tiffany Joh shrunk to three strokes, but birdies on holes sixteen and seventeen gave Lexi a comfortable victory. As Lexi walked up the eighteenth fairway, her father, Scott (who was also her caddie), had to move to the side because he thought the emotion might make him cry. He barely held it together and was the first person to hug his daughter after she sunk her history-making putt.

The relationship between golfer and caddie is an important one. Not only does a caddie carry a player's clubs, but he or she also gives advice, provides encouragement, and helps a player overcome obstacles and challenges. A good caddie can be the key to victory, because of his or her knowledge of the sport and what's best for a particular golfer. For Lexi, her dad and her caddie were the same person, so she got a double benefit.

Actually, when you think about it, dads and caddies serve a similar role. Sure, there's no Bible verse that says, "honor your caddie." But King Solomon wrote, "Get all the advice and instruction you can, so you will be wise the rest of your life" (Proverbs 19:20). That isn't written directly for golfers, but it would serve a person well on the course. Those words will also serve you well in life. When you listen to your parents, pastor, and other trusted adults and then get the proper instruction, you're bound to be a success.

DADDY-*Daughter Time*

Gather a broom, a tennis ball, and a small bucket—you're about to have a putting contest! Place the bucket across the room and see how many times you have to whack the ball to get it in. Take turns to see who gets the lowest score. While you play, talk about why it's so important to get good advice from people you trust (and to make sure that advice lines up with what it says in the Bible).

WHAT'S THE WORD?

Get all the advice and instruction you can, so you will be wise the rest of your life.
PROVERBS 19:20

THE GUMBY PRINCIPLE

GUMBY, a dark green superstar made of clay, would be a senior citizen now. So it's a good thing that clay ages well. Gumby was created in the 1950s, but we can learn a lot from this star of more than 250 TV shows and movies. Gumby reminds us it's good to be kind to talking horses (he had an orange horse named Pokey) and not to be a Blockhead (the name of Gumby's nemesis). But seriously, Gumby's greatest characteristic is something we should all possess: flexibility.

You must stay bendable, because life is filled with twists and turns. You forget a homework assignment. You don't make the school softball team. Your best friend ditches you for the new girl. Unfortunately, unlike on TV, it often takes more than thirty minutes to solve situations that come our way. Instead of fighting problems using our own power, we need to bend to God and trust him.

In Paul's letter to the church in Philippi, he reminded the believers of Jesus' position in heaven. After the Lord came to earth and died on the cross, God elevated him to a place of high honor. In fact, one day "at the name of Jesus every knee should bow, in heaven and on earth and under the earth" (Philippians 2:10).

Sometimes it's easy to forget how powerful our Lord is. We fall into a pattern of self-reliance, instead of calling on the powerful name of Jesus. Maybe we feel like we're the only one who can get something done, but eventually we realize that we're not omnipotent and omniscient. God is both. He knows everything that's going to happen, and he's all-powerful.

Often God uses the challenges in our lives to bend us into being more like him. When tough times come your way, don't stiffen your neck and try to fight through. Loosen up and turn toward God. By bending your knee and bending to God's will, you'll be better able to handle life's twists and turns.

DADDY-*Daughter Time*

Life is unpredictable. Change is one constant you can rely on. So embrace change, don't fear the unknown, and stay flexible.

Speaking of flexibility, find out who's more flexible. Can you or your dad

- bend at the waist and touch your toes?
- put a foot behind your head?
- do the splits?

Don't hurt yourself as you find out who's the most flexible. When you're done, remember to trust in God and his plan for your future.

WHAT'S THE WORD?

At the name of Jesus every knee should bow, in heaven and on earth and under the earth. PHILIPPIANS 2:10

GASTON'S FOLLY

BOB loved the Disney classic *Beauty and the Beast*. He'd seen it a dozen times, and he was excited to share the experience with his three-year-old daughter for the very first time. They pulled the movie off the shelf, hit Play, and settled in for the opening musical number. As a sweet, bookish girl strolls through town, villagers exchange opinions of Belle, the main character. One of the locals, a conceited lout named Gaston, tells his sidekick that he intends to marry Belle because she's "the most beautiful girl in town. That makes her the best."

Whoa, wait a minute. Bob hit Pause. Wondering if his little girl absorbed Gaston's skewed emphasis on physical beauty, Dad felt he needed to set the record straight. "Sweetie, Gaston is wrong. Belle is the best because she has a good heart. Being pretty is just a bonus." Bob gave his daughter a kiss and got a smile in return. Then they enjoyed the rest of the movie.

Seizing that teachable moment paid off. In the months and years that followed, whenever the *Beauty and the Beast* sound track played during tea parties or puzzle time, Bob's daughter would respond to Gaston's infamous line by whispering, "No, Daddy, it's her heart." More than a decade later, "cute's just a bonus" remains a family catchphrase.

Unfortunately, most of the world thinks like Gaston. Young women are assaulted with images and messages suggesting that their worth begins and ends with how they look. You can probably think of examples. But God's Word is clear that obsessing over our appearance is a dead end. For one thing, physical beauty doesn't last (see Proverbs 31:30). And although it's tempting to waste a lot of time, energy, and money chasing the world's notion of attractiveness, we're much better off cultivating inner beauty (see 1 Peter 3:3-4). It's available to everyone. And it never fades!

DADDY-*Daughter Time*

Discuss the challenges of living in a superficial, image-based culture. What's a healthy balance between looking your best and buying into "Gaston's Folly"? Parents do a lot of teaching. Lessons often float in and out of our brains, but others really stick. Can you each recall one that stuck for you? Write them on slips of paper and tie them to helium balloons. Release your balloons and pray that your words of wisdom bless those who find them.

WHAT'S THE WORD?

Don't be concerned about the outward beauty of fancy hairstyles, expensive jewelry, or beautiful clothes. You should clothe yourselves instead with the beauty that comes from within, the unfading beauty of a gentle and quiet spirit, which is so precious to God.
1 PETER 3:3-4

I REALLY REALLY REALLY
REALLY REALLY . . . LOVE YOU *September 22*

CAN we hear "I love you!" too many times? In offices around the world, dads display little notes in their work spaces from their kids. Like little time capsules of a child's love, these treasures are often written in crayon and have misspelled words, unsophisticated drawings, and stickers. But to a dad, they're masterpieces. Because when a dad looks at these drawings, he doesn't read the words. All he sees is "I love you, Dad." Sometimes that's all these little notes say. One dad proudly displayed a letter from his daughter, Leah, on his desk for years that read (misspellings included):

> *Dir Dade*
>
> *I Really Really*
> *Really Really Really*
> *Really Really Really*
> *Really Really Really*
> *Really Really Really*
> *Really Really Really*
> *Really Really Really*
> *Really Really*
> *Really Really love You*

That dad certainly knows he's loved! And it doesn't bother him one bit that there are twenty-four "Reallys" and not one comma in that note. He loves being loved. To answer the earlier question for dads everywhere, no, we can never hear "I love you" too many times, especially from our daughters. The same is also true for daughters. They can never hear "I love you" too many times from their dads.

Our heavenly Father is like that too. Nowhere in the Bible will you find God saying, "Enough already, I get it . . . you love me!" God delights in our love. David was said to have a heart after God. When he was saved from Saul, David knew exactly what to do—he sang a love song to God: "I love you, LORD; you are my strength" (Psalm 18:1). Think that was too much for God? Probably not.

Love is powerful. When the apostle Paul talks about gifts that last forever, he says the greatest is love (see 1 Corinthians 13:13). So tell your dad (or your daughter) and God that you really really really really really love them today!

DADDY-*Daughter Time*

Survey ten dads and ask how many times they hear "I love you" from their children each day. How often would they like to hear those precious words? Discuss the results. What does this show you about the need to express your love to each other? Share some ways besides hearing "I love you" that make you feel loved (actions, gifts, time together, etc.).

WHAT'S THE WORD?

If I could speak all the languages of earth and of angels, but didn't love others, I would only be a noisy gong or a clanging cymbal. . . . Three things will last forever—faith, hope, and love—and the greatest of these is love. 1 CORINTHIANS 13:1, 13

NIFTY NETMINDER

HOCKEY has been called the "coolest game on earth." Huge athletes fly around the ice at speeds in excess of twenty-five miles per hour. The high-speed collisions and pinpoint shooting make professional hockey one of the most exciting sports on the planet. Plus, hockey players are tough. A missing tooth is a badge of honor. Hockey players don't think twice about blocking pucks with their bodies, dropping their gloves for a fight, or getting stitches during a game and jumping back on the ice. All things considered, the National Hockey League seems like a man's world. But on this day in 1992, a woman laced up her skates and played an exhibition game for the Tampa Bay Lightning.

Manon Rheaume was the first woman to play in the NHL. Competing against the opposite gender was nothing new to the talented goaltender. At age five, Manon first put on the pads and goalie mask to block shots from her brothers. She played on boys' teams coached by her father and always earned her spot as goalie. By eleven, Manon was making national headlines in Canada by becoming the first girl to play in the International Pee-Wee Hockey Tournament in Quebec. After her brief stint with the Lightning, Manon played four seasons for different men's professional minor-league teams, compiling a 7–6–2 record. She also did well in women's hockey, leading Canada's national team to world championships in 1992 and 1994.

It's a goalie's job to make saves. Hall of Fame goalie Patrick Roy (pronounced "wah") won four Stanley Cup trophies during his eighteen-year career with the Montreal Canadiens and the Colorado Avalanche. As Patrick helped the Avs win their first championship, fans often held up signs that said, "Only God Saves More Than Roy." While meant to be funny, it's actually very true. According to experts, more than eighty thousand people make the decision to accept Jesus as their Savior every day. That's a lot of saving! Maybe Psalm 68:20 says it best: "Our God is a God who saves! The Sovereign Lord rescues us from death."

DADDY-*Daughter Time*

Get a feeling for what it's like to play goalie. Roll up a pair of socks or find a Nerf ball. Take turns standing in front of a door while the other person throws the ball at you. Keep your shots low (because you won't be wearing a mask). Goals only count if they're shoulder level or below. Take ten shots each and see who makes the most saves. Then thank God for his amazing saving power!

WHAT'S THE WORD?

Our God is a God who saves! The Sovereign LORD rescues us from death.
PSALM 68:20

A LOOSE USE OF SEUSS

DEEP in the hollow of Snibbity Snooks
Lived a man with a talent for rhyming kids' books.
He coined silly words and drew funny creatures
Like Yertle the Turtle, The Lorax, and Sneetches.
And don't forget Whoville (that Grinchy yule scam),
The Cat in the Hat, and Green Eggs and Ham.
Through whimsical stories, Ted Geisel became
An author known better by his other name.
But on this same date in the year '91,
The life of our dear Dr. Seuss was all done.

Think of the books you enjoyed as a child. Were any written and illustrated by Theodor Geisel (aka Dr. Seuss)? Odds are you can recall at least one. Were you aware that twenty-nine different publishers rejected his first book before it released in 1937? And yet Geisel went on to launch Beginner Books, win a Pulitzer Prize, and have his forty-seven stories translated into twenty languages. It just goes to show, never give up on a dream!

As we take a moment to celebrate the life of Dr. Seuss, it's worth noting how one of his books has been used to celebrate life in general. *Horton Hears a Who!* is about an elephant who sacrificially protects a microscopic city on a dust speck that's resting on a clover. Horton values each tiny life because, as he puts it, "a person's a person, no matter how small." Although the author never intended his persevering pachyderm to speak for unborn children, over the years God has used Horton to do precisely that. Cool, huh?

Pro-choice advocates argue that a baby isn't really a baby until it's born. But Psalm 139, modern ultrasound technology, and a selfless elephant all testify to the truth: even in the womb, a person's a person, no matter how small.

DADDY-*Daughter Time*

Discuss the sanctity of human life and how you feel about the ongoing debate over abortion. How should a Christian respond? It's probably been a few years since you've shared a bedside, lights-out tale by Dr. Seuss. If you own a copy of *Horton Hears a Who!*, read it together tonight. You may also enjoy watching the 2008 animated film and discussing its rich subtext (for talking points, search the "Movie Nights" page at pluggedin.com).

WHAT'S THE WORD?

You made all the delicate, inner parts of my body and knit me together in my mother's womb. Thank you for making me so wonderfully complex! Your workmanship is marvelous—how well I know it. You watched me as I was being formed in utter seclusion, as I was woven together in the dark of the womb. PSALM 139:13-15

THE EMPIRE THAT DIDN'T STRIKE BACK

PICTURE a lifesaving act of heroism. What does yours look like? Perhaps you envisioned a caped crusader making a last-second rescue, a lifeguard reviving a swimmer, or a firefighter pulling a child from a burning building. But how about a man sitting in a chair and doing nothing? It's hard to imagine that story leading the evening news. Yet that's precisely how Stanislav Petrov saved the world.

On this date in 1983, Americans went about their business, unaware that a Soviet early-warning system was signaling Moscow that the United States had launched five ballistic missiles at Russia. It was a false alarm. Nevertheless, with Cold War tensions already high, Lt. Col. Petrov watched that panel of flashing lights from his secret bunker, and it was up to him to decide whether to push "the button" and launch a devastating counterstrike. Instead of retaliating, the coolheaded Soviet officer weighed the facts and suspected a system malfunction. It turned out he'd guessed right. *Whew!*

God was looking out for humanity that day, and in the process gave us a great illustration of why we shouldn't be quick to strike back at our enemies. When we suspect someone has said or done something to hurt us, it's easy to overreact. We grow defensive. We want to get even. However, retaliation can have devastating consequences—and not just for the target of our anger. There's almost always collateral damage.

Romans 12:17-19 tells us to leave payback to the Lord, because his anger is righteous. He knows all the details. He has no sinful motives or hidden agendas. And his timing is perfect. On the other hand, our judgment is often clouded by pain, hatred, impatience, and pride. So the next time it seems like missiles are flying in your direction, resist the urge to retaliate. Pause. Take a deep breath. Then pray for the wisdom to make the right move . . . which may mean doing nothing at all.

DADDY-*Daughter Time*

According to Matthew 5:38-48, how should Christians respond when wronged? Have emotions ever led you to push "the button" and cause more damage? If you're struggling with a situation right now, pray about it together.

Nations' early-warning systems are far more sophisticated than they were in 1983, but it's still easy to feel anxious about global conflict. Share your feelings about that.

WHAT'S THE WORD?

Never pay back evil with more evil. Do things in such a way that everyone can see you are honorable. Do all that you can to live in peace with everyone. Dear friends, never take revenge. Leave that to the righteous anger of God. ROMANS 12:17-19

NOT ON MY LAND

SUPPOSE a world-famous pop singer wanted to shoot a music video in your back-yard. Would you let him or her do it? Maybe you'd want to ask a few questions first. For instance, "Will you be keeping your clothes on?" On September 26, 2011, a humble farmer in Northern Ireland was wishing he had asked that question before granting Rihanna permission to film a video in his wheat field.

Since Alan Graham wasn't familiar with the singer, he had no way of knowing just how skimpy her wardrobe would get once the cameras started rolling. But pretty soon, traffic stopped to watch the spectacle in his field. Alan drove up on his tractor and politely explained that, if the artist didn't cover up, she and her production crew would have to leave.

"I requested that they stop filming, and they did," he said. "I wish no ill will against Rihanna and her friends. Perhaps they could acquaint themselves with a greater God."

As you might have guessed, Alan is more than just a gentleman. He's a Christian. Yet while many people applauded him for taking a stand, not everyone appreciated it. Gawkers from the highway resented him for stopping the show. And some of his neighbors got angry because they'd expected to make money from tourists visiting the site of this racy video. Alan might have profited too. But he didn't care. It was worth more to do the right thing.

What happened with the music video? It was completed on schedule, shot a few miles down the road. Alan had no control over that. All he knew was that God didn't want him taking part in it. We live in a fallen world. And we can't always keep people from making bad choices. But no matter what happens on somebody else's farm, we need to stand strong and say with confidence, "As for me and my household, we will serve the LORD" (Joshua 24:15, NIV).

DADDY-*Daughter Time*

Have you ever had to take an unpopular stand? What happened? What would you say if a film crew wanted to set up in your yard . . . or living room? Did you know that you invite the entertainment industry into your home every time you download music, rent a movie, or watch TV? Is anyone dancing inappropriately in your field?

WHAT'S THE WORD?

If serving the LORD seems undesirable to you, then choose for yourselves this day whom you will serve, whether the gods your forefathers served beyond the River, or the gods of the Amorites, in whose land you are living. But as for me and my household, we will serve the LORD. JOSHUA 24:15 (NIV)

DON'T EXPECT GOD TO SHOUT

"HEY there, Kristen."

Kristen couldn't hear a thing with her earbuds in and the volume cranked up, but out of the corner of her eye she saw her youth pastor circling his desk to sit down. "Oh, hey Pastor Nick. Thanks for offering to help me," Kristen said as she kept one foot tapping along with the tune on her iPod. "This may sound strange, but I'm having a hard time hearing from God."

"Um, maybe not so strange. Would you mind?" Nick motioned to the iPod, and Kristen turned off the music. "Thanks. Can I ask you a few questions?" She nodded. "What do you do first thing in the morning?"

"Well, the alarm goes off, and the radio comes on. I time myself in the shower by listening to two or three songs, then a few more while I do my hair and get dressed. Usually I eat breakfast at the computer so I can catch up on Facebook posts until it's time for school."

"How about after school?"

"Once my homework is done—which takes forever because of all my friends texting me—I watch a little TV before dinner. After we eat, I check Facebook again." She thought for a second. "Most nights I get Eliza on the phone so we can hunt for funny videos on YouTube. Then I pretty much text people until Dad says 'lights out.' So anyway, how come God isn't talking to me?"

"Are you sure he's not?" Nick asked. "You may just be having a hard time hearing him with all the distractions competing for your attention. He's probably getting drowned out. If you could add some quiet time to your day, you might be surprised how much easier it is to hear his still, small voice." Kristen's pained expression spoke volumes. "It won't be easy," Nick added. "But it'll be worth it."

DADDY-*Daughter Time*

Can you relate to Kristen's situation? What do you think of Nick's advice? Do you think it lines up with how God spoke to Elijah in 1 Kings 19:11-13? For a week, log any time you spend with electronic media. Break it down by type. Pray about ways you can cut back and spend more time with God and each other.

WHAT'S THE WORD?

The LORD was not in the wind. After the wind there was an earthquake, but the LORD was not in the earthquake. And after the earthquake there was a fire, but the LORD was not in the fire. And after the fire there was the sound of a gentle whisper. . . . And a voice said, "What are you doing here, Elijah?" 1 KINGS 19:11-13

LOST, BUT MAKING GOOD TIME

HAVE you ever known someone whose unique perspective on the world spawned odd sayings that caught on and got repeated by others? New York Yankees catcher Yogi Berra played on ten world championship teams and was inducted into baseball's Hall of Fame in 1972. But he has become just as well known for his quirky quotes—head scratchers that have themselves become legendary: "It ain't over till it's over"; "When you come to the fork in the road, take it"; "It's déjà vu all over again." Classic Yogi.

One day, while driving to the Baseball Hall of Fame with his wife and three sons, Yogi somehow strayed off course on his way to Cooperstown, New York. There was no GPS to get him back on track. So after traveling in the wrong direction for a while, he turned to his wife and announced, "We're lost, but we're making good time!"

That Yogi-ism could describe a lot of people's lives these days. Swept up in activity, they're racing to keep pace in a twenty-first-century society obsessed with doing more things faster. To what end? For what purpose? It's easy for Christians to lose track of God amid all the busyness and stress. And people who don't yet know Jesus can easily be so distracted by the hustle and bustle that they never realize how much they need him as their Savior. In short, many people are not sure where they're going, but they're making great time.

Are you a Christ follower on the road that leads to heaven? As Jesus points out in Matthew 7:13-14, the path is narrow and difficult, but it leads to eternal life. As destinations go, that path leaves Cooperstown, Mount Rushmore, and Disney World in the dust! Yet many people are missing it. They're lost. Perhaps God wants you to be the spiritual GPS that helps them get on track.

DADDY-*Daughter Time*

Describe the road you're traveling. How have you sensed God directing you? If you feel that others are making better time than you are, remember that God's timing is perfect (see Habakkuk 2:3). When was the last time your family planned a road trip? Maybe it's time for another! If you live in the northeast United States, you might enjoy visiting baseball's Hall of Fame in Cooperstown, New York.

WHAT'S THE WORD?

You can enter God's Kingdom only through the narrow gate. The highway to hell is broad, and its gate is wide for the many who choose that way. But the gateway to life is very narrow and the road is difficult, and only a few ever find it. MATTHEW 7:13-14

AS SEEN ON TV

EVERY year at about this time, US television networks unveil their new fall line-ups. Many of these shows will be gone by Christmas. But others will find a home and could become world-changers. Here are several examples of American TV's global influence:

- The seventies' police series *Kojak* was so big in Brazil that criminals in Rio de Janeiro coined the phrase "I won't give a chance to Kojak," meaning they'll be diligent not to leave any clues for the police.
- Romania's Nicolae Ceausescu let his people watch the prime-time soap *Dallas* in the 1980s, expecting them to reject capitalism after seeing that drama's corrupt oil and cattle tycoons. The communist dictator's plan backfired. *Dallas* is credited with encouraging the Romanian revolution of 1989.
- *Beverly Hills, 90210* was such a hit in Sweden in the early 1990s that Dylan and Brandon (names of main characters) suddenly became huge baby names in that country, even though they're hard to pronounce in Swedish.

Equally amazing is how the mere introduction of television can impact a culture. Did you know that the South Pacific nation of Fiji didn't get TV until 1995? For generations, its women took pride in their plump, robust figures. No one dieted. But television changed that. Once shows such as *Melrose Place* and *Friends* flickered into their lives, islanders noticed a sharp rise in eating disorders among girls. A study just three years later found that 74 percent of young women said they felt too fat.

Anthropologists believe those girls saw TV as a guide for making it in the modern world. It skewed their view of reality. Sadly, the same thing happens all around us; we just don't notice because it's been going on for decades. Our view of family. Of religion. Of romance. Therefore, as the networks compete for your attention, be selective. Don't let televised images shape your sense of what's right, healthy, and normal. Instead, see what the Bible has to say, and let the truth set you free.

DADDY-*Daughter Time*

The contrast between our sinful nature and the fruit of the Spirit is dramatic, much like the difference between many TV shows and how Christians are called to live. Read Galatians 5:16-26 together. Which current shows exploit the worst in human nature? Which attempt to celebrate positive virtues? What have you learned—good or bad—from things you've seen on television?

WHAT'S THE WORD?

Those who belong to Christ Jesus have nailed the passions and desires of their sinful nature to his cross and crucified them there. Since we are living by the Spirit, let us follow the Spirit's leading in every part of our lives. GALATIANS 5:24-25

DO you know which Bible verse is the shortest? It's John 11:35: "Jesus wept" (NIV). Two little words. His friend Lazarus had died and been in the tomb for four days. Some of the mourners accused Jesus of being late. But he was right on time. That's because God's bigger plan involved helping Lazarus and proving that Jesus had power over death.

Beyond the resurrection of Lazarus, something else is interesting about this passage. In John 11:39, Jesus instructed the people to move the stone blocking the tomb's entrance. Why didn't he just do it himself? Jesus was about to raise a man from the dead. That would have been an awesome opening act, wouldn't it? Picture this: The Lord extends his hand, and the heavy stone rolls away. The wailing crowd's jaws drop open. Then, once he has their attention, he calls for Lazarus to come out.

We know Jesus could have done it. He'd already proven his power over nature. He'd walked on water. He'd calmed the wind and the waves. Moving a big rock ten feet would've been a cinch, right? So why didn't he do it? The Bible doesn't tell us. But for whatever reason, Jesus chose to involve people in the process. It's as if he were saying to the crowd, "Cooperate with me. You move the obstacle; I'll perform the miracle."

Is there an obstacle in your life that needs moving? Maybe you've sensed God prodding you to make a change that's keeping you from becoming everything he wants you to be. An attitude. A habit. How you're spending your time or your money. The entertainment you're choosing. The friends you're hanging out with. God may be waiting to do something amazing in you that first requires an act of obedience or a step of faith. If so, move that stone and watch God work!

DADDY-*Daughter Time*

Can you think of other times in the Bible when God worked a miracle only after someone followed specific instructions? How does it feel to know that God can function without us but wants us to be his partners? For example, God will turn bulbs into beautiful flowers, but someone needs to plant them. Why not do that together this week and see God work? You'll have a colorful reminder of his faithfulness in the spring.

WHAT'S THE WORD?

Jesus, once more deeply moved, came to the tomb. It was a cave with a stone laid across the entrance. "Take away the stone," he said.   JOHN 11:38-39 (NIV)

WHERE'S THE FIRE?

THE drive home from school was short. The conversations that fourteen-year-old Hannah and her mom usually had were simple—about school, how her sisters were doing, or what was planned for dinner—and not deep stuff. But today, Hannah wore a troubled look.

"Do I *have to be* 'on fire for the Lord,' Mom?" she suddenly blurted.

"That's a curious question for a girl who gave her heart to Jesus years ago," Hannah's mom replied, then responded with one of her own: "Why do you ask that?"

"Well, Amy told me that she is *so* on fire for the Lord that she's going to be a missionary someday. She's going on a missions trip to South America this summer. I want to be on fire for the Lord, too, but I'm not sure I'm ready to be a missionary, or if I'll ever be. What if I'm never ready to be on fire for the Lord?"

"Hannah, you may very well become a missionary," Mom said. "Then again, maybe not. I remember something that was important to me when I wrestled with the same question. Being a missionary isn't the only way to be on fire for the Lord. In Colossians 3:17, Paul explained how important *everyday living* for God is, in big and small ways. He said 'whatever you do, whether in word or deed, do it all in the name of the Lord Jesus.' Remember those three words, 'whatever you do,' when you're wondering how to be on fire for him."

Hannah considered this well into the night. Only God knew what she'd be doing in five, ten, or twenty years. But she realized she wanted to be serving and glorifying God. The fire was already there.

DADDY-*Daughter Time*

Maybe you've wondered how deep into the jungle you would have to go or how boldly you would have to preach to a hostile crowd to really, truly demonstrate that you're "on fire for the Lord."

Being on fire for Jesus isn't just for missionaries and evangelists. It means you're excited to know him, to serve him, and to live for him. You can do that anytime, at any age, anywhere.

The word *whatever* means just that . . . everything! Every day and in every choice we make, we have an opportunity to show a life on fire for God. What are some small and big ways you can show you're on fire for him?

WHAT'S THE WORD?

Whatever you do, whether in word or deed, do it all in the name of the Lord Jesus, giving thanks to God the Father through him. COLOSSIANS 3:17 (NIV)

THE COWARDLY MAN *October 2*

WHAT would you do if you and your dad were at a baseball game and a foul ball came flying right at you? If you had a glove and a keen sense of hand-eye coordination, you'd probably try to catch it.

But how would you feel if your dad ran away as the ball zoomed closer . . . and it hit you?

A dad is supposed to be a girl's first line of defense in life. Later, perhaps, a husband will step into that role to protect and care for "daddy's little girl." Every dad hopes his daughter will find a stand-up guy, someone who will catch a dangerous foul ball or get hit trying.

That's not what happened on August 9, 2010, at a Houston Astros game. A young dating couple was watching the action when a foul ball came screaming right at them. Instead of trying to catch it, the boyfriend darted away and let his girlfriend get hit by the ball. He quickly earned a nickname from the television crew broadcasting the game: *Bo the Bailer*.

Unfortunately for "Bo," the scene was caught on camera, went viral on the Internet, and was watched hundreds of thousands of times. The embarrassed couple was repeatedly interviewed and talked about on TV and radio for the next several days. Before the week was over, the young woman decided to end the relationship.

"Bo" isn't the only man in history to duck away when difficulties come. Sometimes men in the Bible were just as cowardly. Not once, but twice (in Genesis chapters 12 and 20) Abraham asked his wife Sarah to pretend to be his sister so the ruler of the land wouldn't kill him to take her. And both times God stepped in to protect Sarah and expose the truth.

As your relationships deepen, don't be surprised if your dad is highly interested in the courageous-or-cowardly makeup of your friends. Decide now that you won't settle for friends or fiancés who will not seek to protect you and put your interests above their own.

DADDY-*Daughter Time*

What are some of the qualities you and your dad agree are important in your friends or in a future husband? What verses can you think of that highlight those traits? Ephesians 5:25-33 is a good place to start. Make a promise to each other to keep that list of godly traits in mind through the years. Your heavenly Father, your daddy, and you will be pleased if you wind up with a spouse or friends who meet these high standards.

WHAT'S THE WORD?

Each man must love his wife as he loves himself, and the wife must respect her husband. EPHESIANS 5:33

AUTOCORRECTING GOD

IT happens when you're texting or typing on a computer. You begin to spell a word, or you inadvertently hit the wrong letters in a word, and the software tries to guess what you want to say. Before you're even done typing, an alternative word pops up on the screen.

This can be pretty humorous when you're trying to type "Dinner done at seven" and it comes out "Dimmer food at peter." But it can also be really, *really* frustrating.

We can be that way with God. We jump to a conclusion about what God is trying to say or do in our lives, without letting him "finish the sentence," so to speak.

Job's friends thought they knew exactly why he was suffering and told him all about it. They argued with Job for days before God arrived and silenced them. In the New Testament, Peter acknowledged that Jesus was the Messiah, then minutes later argued with him about his coming death. Jesus rebuked Peter for his foolish presumption.

But, in the book of Ruth, there is a beautiful example of someone understanding God's intentions. After losing her husband and two sons, Naomi is a bitter woman living in a faraway land. She's ready to go home and insists that her daughters-in-law, Orpah and Ruth, go back to their families since their husbands are now dead.

Naomi assumes she knows what God's story and purpose is when she says, "No, my daughters, return to your parents' homes. . . . Things are far more bitter for me than for you, because the LORD himself has raised his fist against me" (Ruth 1:12-13).

Orpah reluctantly leaves. But Ruth refuses to accept this. She must have learned a lot about God's faithfulness and provision through Naomi's family. She tells Naomi, "Wherever you go, I will go; wherever you live, I will live. Your people will be my people, and your God will be my God" (Ruth 1:16). Ruth, as the story turns out, was right to trust God and stick with Naomi.

DADDY-*Daughter Time*

Sometimes our circumstances make us quick to judge what God is doing or going to do. Think about some examples in your family when an unexpected event happened that brought something good out of something bad. Make a quick list together of some examples in Scripture. Are you currently going through a difficult time? Ask God to help you now, and in the future, to trust him and not jump to conclusions about his will in your life.

WHAT'S THE WORD?

Wherever you go, I will go; wherever you live, I will live. Your people will be my people, and your God will be my God. RUTH 1:16

CALL HER BLESSED!

PROVERBS 31 is held up for women and girls in churches around the world as an ideal to aim for. Young men are taught to seek these qualities when they think about sharing the rest of their lives with someone.

Noble. Good. Hardworking. Strong. Industrious. Wise. Caring. Frugal. Nurturing. Dignified. That's a daunting list to live up to!

A dad named Brad was reading this chapter one day as he thought about these qualities and how he could help develop them in his daughters. He came across two verses in the chapter that changed his whole perspective: "Her children stand and bless her. Her husband praises her: 'There are many virtuous and capable women in the world, but you surpass them all!'" (Proverbs 31:28-29).

The Proverbs 31 woman was helped by her husband and children. They had a role to play that, very likely, encouraged this incredible woman when she needed it most. This revelation energized Brad. It dawned on him that as his wife strove to live out those wonderful qualities, he and his daughters owed it to her to encourage her and not take her for granted.

Brad talked with his daughters, and they decided to be more deliberate about demonstrating their appreciation for their mom. They even took turns that night going around the table to thank Mom for something specific that she did regularly. They also shared one blessing of hope they had for their mom's future. By doing this, Brad and his daughters lived out Proverbs 31:31: "Reward her for all she has done."

And it wasn't even Mother's Day!

DADDY-*Daughter Time*

What are some things that you and your daddy appreciate about the moms and grandmas in your lives? Have you ever thought about how difficult her days can be sometimes? What are some ways you can show your appreciation and love? Write them down:

- _____

- _____

- _____

Put these ideas into action soon. It's never too early or too late to let someone know how much you love, respect, and appreciate them. Be an encouragement for her as she keeps doing the difficult daily work of family life.

WHAT'S THE WORD?

Charm is deceptive, and beauty does not last; but a woman who fears the LORD will be greatly praised. Reward her for all she has done. Let her deeds publicly declare her praise. PROVERBS 31:30-31

STRONG ROOTS

COASTAL redwoods are the tallest trees on earth. The largest one grew to 367 feet and was 44 feet around at its base. That's longer than a football field and almost as big around as a house!

But these mammoth trees have surprisingly shallow roots that grow only about four to six feet under the earth. So why aren't coastal redwoods easily toppled by heavy rains and strong winds? The answer is simple: they get support from their friends.

While the roots go down only 6 feet, they can spread out as far as 125 feet. Redwoods are able to live thousands of years by intertwining their roots and supporting each other underground. By locking roots and strengthening each other, redwoods thrive together to become the mightiest of all trees.

Just like God designed redwoods to support one another, he created families and friends to help one another through life. Ecclesiastes 4:9 says, "Two people are better off than one, for they can help each other succeed."

As individuals it's easy to get blown over by the storms of life. But when we have family and friends supporting us, we can stand up to anything. Standing firm with the people closest to us not only makes life more enjoyable, but it can make us stronger in our faith. Have you ever asked an older Christian to talk about a time when Jesus made a big difference in his or her life? If you haven't, you need to. Connecting with other strong believers makes us more firm in our faith. So put down your roots over a wide area and grow a life that stands out for Christ.

DADDY-*Daughter Time*

Families are most healthy when members support one another physically, emotionally, and spiritually. Try this activity. Sit back-to-back on the floor. Bring up your feet until your knees almost touch your chest. Now push back against each other and try to stand up. By working together and supporting each other, you'll be able to stand tall. (Sometimes the size difference between fathers and daughters makes this more difficult, but give it a try!)

Did you learn anything? The fact, is we all need to support each other to thrive in life. Dads, always try to be there to listen to and support your daughter's dreams. Daughters, keep talking to your dad—he cares about you more than you could ever know.

WHAT'S THE WORD?

Two people are better off than one, for they can help each other succeed.
ECCLESIASTES 4:9

WHERE IS THE MOUNTAIN? *October 6*

THE scenery near Colorado Springs, Colorado, can be stunning. On average, the sun shines more than three hundred days a year. One of the best benefits of clear skies? On over 82 percent of days, the residents of this region can see Pikes Peak, rising majestically to an altitude of 14,115 feet.

In July 1893, the mountain inspired a woman who had traveled to its summit to pen the words of what would become the song "America the Beautiful." Her words captured the imagination of the nation, and the grandeur of the mountain: "O beautiful for spacious skies/For amber waves of grain/For purple mountain majesties/Above the fruited plain!"

On rare days, fog, rain, low clouds, and snowstorms hide the "mountain majesties." The mountain seemingly disappears. After the weather passes and the mountain comes back into view, the residents get to *ooh* and *aah* over it as if they're seeing it for the first time.

When Pikes Peak can't be seen, you'll never hear a Coloradan ask, "Is the mountain gone? Will it be there when the weather moves past?"

Of course they wouldn't ask that, you might be thinking. It seems silly to worry that a snowstorm might blow over a mountain, or that Pikes Peak might get up and walk away.

But sometimes we're tempted to think that about God, right? When life gets a little foggy, we wonder if God has gone away. If you ever feel that way, a great Psalm can help you understand how constant and faithful God is. In Psalm 121, the writer looked up to the mountains and said, "The LORD keeps you from all harm and watches over your life. The LORD keeps watch over you as you come and go, both now and forever" (vv. 7-8).

DADDY-*Daughter Time*

Think of a hill or a mountain that your family lives near. If your home is on the plains, picture a mountain you'd like to visit. God is more solid and unmoving than any mountain. Get out some paper and markers, and draw a "family mountain" together to remind you that God does not sleep or wander off. God stays true, providing shelter and watching over you now and forever. Encourage each other with your own drawing of a family mountain!

WHAT'S THE WORD?

The LORD keeps you from all harm and watches over your life. The LORD keeps watch over you as you come and go, both now and forever. PSALM 121:7-8

SAY *CHEESE*! . . . OR SAY *JESUS*?

October 7

GRANDPARENTS love them. Parents dread them. Children put up with them. They can be only one thing: family Christmas portraits.

These pictures, whether taken at home or in a portrait studio, are destined to be placed into cards, envelopes, and gifts to be sent to friends and relatives near and far.

While the settings for these photos may change, one thing is certain . . . every family wants the perfect picture. Many pictures will be rejected, which is why lots of families start early to get the right shot. "Everyone is smiling except Joe." "Why is Angela looking over there when everyone else is looking up?" "Max is waving to the photographer." "Laura is making that funny face again!" "Jackie's eyes are closed."

After looking at hundreds of photos, it can seem like the perfect family picture is impossible. But we still try, don't we? We try because we long to capture a moment when everyone is happy, everyone is unified, everyone is looking in the same direction and trying to accomplish the same thing.

Proverbs 15:30 says that "a cheerful look brings joy to the heart." Isn't that what we're trying to capture for ourselves, our family, and our friends? In the book of Hebrews, right after a list of "Hall of Faith" people who trusted God no matter what, we find a great "portrait" moment. The writer tells Christians to keep "our eyes on Jesus, the champion who initiates and perfects our faith" (12:2). So why is this important? Because Jesus is the perfect portrait to keep in the hallways of our hearts.

If we're honest, we know our families will never be perfect. But by keeping Christ as our focus, we can strive for his perfection. Our family portrait should reflect Jesus. Sure, we won't always get along in our family, but we should all be focused on Christ. So as family photo time rolls around again, will we "watch the birdie" and say *cheese*? Or will we put our eyes on Jesus?

DADDY-*Daughter Time*

If your family pictures are coming up, think together about a way your family can use this verse in the picture-taking process. Maybe you can come up with your own special word to say when smiling, like "Jeeeeeesus!" or "Christmas tree!" Talk about how your family portrait represents Jesus. Make it a family goal to get the best picture ever this year . . . even if it's not perfect.

WHAT'S THE WORD?

A cheerful look brings joy to the heart; good news makes for good health.
PROVERBS 15:30

AN APPLE FOR TEACHER October 8

FOR at least 150 years, apples and teachers have gone together like Father's Day and neckties. It's hard to picture one without the other. While nobody's positive how this tradition started, it stems in part from the practice of students giving an apple to their teacher during the frontier days. Teachers appreciated the gift, because their limited incomes often prevented them from buying fruit. Other teachers felt the apple was a symbol of the fruit of their labor to teach children— representing the planting of seeds of learning in young minds.

Whatever the origin, this tradition has been around for a long time. But even before kids gave apples to their teachers, there was a biblical mandate to honor teachers. The apostle Paul writes that Christians, as they are taught God's Word, "should provide for their teachers, sharing all good things with them" (Galatians 6:6). Paul's words encourage us to show how much we value those who help us understand what God is saying in the Bible. The act of sharing, of providing for their needs, shows not only how appreciated they are, but also how important their work is for God's people.

October is observed as Clergy Appreciation Month, sometimes called Ministry Appreciation Month. Maybe this month your family could consider some special ways to show your thankfulness for youth group leaders, Sunday school teachers, pastors, and family members. For homeschooling families, that might mean honoring Mom or Dad. Other families may consider honoring a grandparent or other relative who has invested time to teach God's Word.

DADDY-*Daughter Time*

Make a list together of the people who have influenced you and your dad the most in your growing knowledge of God's Word. Make sure the list includes those who are currently in your lives and those who have helped you learn in the past.

Come up with a special way your family can honor and thank them. Greeting card? Gift card? E-mail? Phone call? There are many options available. Have fun!

WHAT'S THE WORD?

Those who are taught the word of God should provide for their teachers, sharing all good things with them. GALATIANS 6:6

BE READY FOR AN ATTACK

EXPERTS say you're more likely to be struck by lightning than be attacked by a shark. Both happen rarely, but sharks have teeth—lots and lots of teeth. Most sharks go through around twenty to thirty thousand razor-sharp pearly whites in a lifetime. All those teeth and eight thousand pounds of biting pressure make for a dangerous combination. As the apex predator of the ocean, sharks are at the top of the food chain. Nobody eats them, and they eat nearly everything. Plus, sharks are amazing hunters. They can strike quickly, swim stealthily, and always find their next meal.

That sort of sounds like the devil. Although the devil is compared to a lion and serpent in the Bible, a shark could describe him as well. Sharks are the "king of the ocean," just like lions are called the "king of beasts." First Peter 5:8 says, "Stay alert! Watch out for your great enemy, the devil. He prowls around like a roaring lion, looking for someone to devour."

The best way to protect yourself from lions—or sharks—is to have a sturdy cage. You can build that cage with God's help. Think of the bars of the cage as God's Word. When you read the Bible and memorize Scripture, you protect yourself from the devil's schemes, because you know God's truth. The top of your cage is prayer. Confess your sins to God, and praise him for his power. At the bottom of the cage are your relationships. Make sure you have friends who build your faith, instead of tearing it down. Lastly, Jesus is the lock on your cage. Nothing and no one can pull you away from God when your life is locked by Jesus.

So don't fear the devil, but be aware that he's prowling about. He may be like the "king of beasts," but you belong to the King of kings.

DADDY-*Daughter Time*

Statistics show that a majority of shark attacks in the United States occur in August, September, and October. The devil prowls around all the time, so be aware of things that try to pull you away from God. It may be a relationship, friend, attitude, or entertainment choice. Those things could be the devil trying to get a foothold in your life. If you ever feel under attack, run to God and climb into his protective cage. Pray and thank God that he conquered the devil so you can have victory in your life as well.

WHAT'S THE WORD?

Stay alert! Watch out for your great enemy, the devil. He prowls around like a roaring lion, looking for someone to devour. 1 PETER 5:8

CLOSER THAN YOU THINK *October 10*

THE fear was understandable. A mom frantically calling 911, asking for help for her family. They were lost. It was dark. They didn't know which way to turn, and the night was filled with scary noises.

Before you get too worried for this family's safety, you should know they were in a seven-acre corn maze. The parents had entered the huge maze with their three children when the sun was still out, but then lost their way. The sun went down, and they couldn't escape. The mom called 911, hoping the police could help. When the police arrived, they were able to find the family in less than nine minutes. Why so quickly?

The family was only twenty-five feet away from the street. They were close to being out of the maze, but they were afraid and tired. They were unsure if they were near the end of the maze or lost in the middle of it.

Sometimes as we journey through life, we act like that family. We can feel like giving up when things look dark and we aren't sure where to go. But God often asks us to press on, especially when we're doing something good. Following the Lord's commands can bring a lot of teasing from people who don't know God. In Galatians 6:9, Paul encourages Christians to "not get tired of doing what is good." Doing what is right will bring a "harvest of blessing if we don't give up," he adds.

That's a great principle to guide you. Keep pressing on. Trust that God will honor your commitment to doing what's right, even when it's hard.

DADDY-*Daughter Time*

Ask your dad about some situations in his life in which he either pushed through (and was glad he did) or gave up (and wished he hadn't). Now think about some things that have been hard for you or your family to keep doing. If your family lives near a corn maze, make plans to visit and don't give up until you reach the end.

The temptation to give up can be pretty strong. Commit to praying together for perseverance. Write down those "hard to keep doing" things on a little piece of paper and put it on a mirror or somewhere you'll see it daily and can remember to pray for each other. And remember . . . don't give up doing what's good. The street might be only twenty-five feet away!

WHAT'S THE WORD?

Let's not get tired of doing what is good. At just the right time we will reap a harvest of blessing if we don't give up. GALATIANS 6:9

SIX HOURS OF LUXURY

THE man got his wish! He won the contest . . . and his prize was a brand-new Lamborghini, a luxury sports car worth an estimated $380,000! What would you do if you won that car or another similarly expensive vehicle in a contest? Would you take it for a joyride? Race it up and down the mountains? Go to your favorite drive-through and eat a big greasy burger?

Or would you take it for a slow, careful spin, then put it in storage where it would be safe from thieves, French fries, and the weather? For this man, the answer was simple. Joyrides with family and friends. Unfortunately for him, the joy lasted only six hours. That's how long it took for him to drive recklessly and crash his car. Thankfully, no one was hurt, but the damage was done. He quickly made another decision after that: fix the car and sell it.

There are many treasures in life. Some are given as gifts. Others are earned by hard work and sacrifice. A few can be won in contests. Once we have something important, we have to choose what to do with it. Will we protect it? Hide it? Be careless with it?

Joseph was given a treasure. After Joseph interpreted Pharaoh's dreams foretelling famine, the ruler of Egypt put Joseph in charge over all his land (see Genesis 41:41). After years of being a slave, a prisoner, and a forgotten man, Joseph had all the riches of Egypt available to him.

What would the rest of the story look like if he had squandered that responsibility? What if he had hoarded the grain and riches of Egypt for himself, or tried to overthrow Pharaoh? One can only imagine, but the consequences would've been much worse than a wrecked sports car. Joseph would have missed the opportunity to reunite with his father and brothers, and save a lot of people.

Joseph had a treasure, and he used it to the glory of God.

DADDY-*Daughter Time*

What treasures and responsibilities have been put in your hands? Dad's job? Family heirlooms? A savings account? Talk about the importance of being a good caretaker of these treasures and responsibilities. Imagine together how life would be different if you took better care (or stopped taking good care) of these parts of your lives.

WHAT'S THE WORD?

Pharaoh asked his officials, "Can we find anyone else like this man so obviously filled with the spirit of God?" . . . Pharaoh said to Joseph, "I hereby put you in charge of the entire land of Egypt." GENESIS 41:38, 41

KNOWN BY YOUR ACTIONS *October 12*

WHAT creates your reputation? How do people know who you really are? In Proverbs 20:11, we read that "even children are known by the way they act, whether their conduct is pure, and whether it is right." In other words, starting in our childhood people pay more attention to what we do than to what we say.

President Theodore "Teddy" Roosevelt spoke many famous words, but he's often remembered for saying, "Nobody cares how much you know, until they know how much you care." His point was that people want to see your actions and judge your character before they take what you say seriously. If your actions are rotten, nobody's going to care what you say. Similarly, even if your words are lacking, but you come through with your actions, then you'll be viewed positively.

Jesus told a story in Matthew 21:28-31 about two sons. The older boy told his dad that he wouldn't work for him at the vineyard. Later, he changed his mind and went to help. The younger son said he'd be there for his dad, but then blew it off. Jesus asked, "Which of the two obeyed his father?" (v. 31). Obviously, actions speak louder than words. The Bible is full of stories of people who hurt their reputation—and godly witness—when their actions didn't match their words.

Saul was a king who said he'd follow God's direction for the people of Israel. Then he disobeyed God's direct orders, consulted a medium for advice, and had the kingdom of Israel torn away from him (see 1 Samuel 10–31). Even Saul's son understood that Saul was not a worthy leader and accepted David as the new king. Ananias and Sapphira were a couple who sold their property to help out the early church. But they secretly held back some money for themselves. They paid for their lies with their lives, not because they didn't give God enough, but because their actions were a lie (see Acts 5:1-10).

When it comes to walking the talk, age doesn't matter. So make sure to always do what you say.

DADDY-*Daughter Time*

When have your actions not matched your words with someone? Was there a broken promise, or did you secretly say one thing and do another? Make a commitment to each other to gently and respectfully point out when your actions don't match your words. If we want people to know us better, and to know Jesus, we need to pay attention to always walk our talk.

WHAT'S THE WORD?

Even children are known by the way they act, whether their conduct is pure, and whether it is right.   PROVERBS 20:11

TAKING CARE OF FAMILY FIRST

AN elderly woman named Esther lived a long and fruitful life for God. Through decades of life, she had encouraged her family to follow God, prayed diligently for the needs of people she knew and had never met, and smiled no matter what came her way. When it came time for her to move to another state to be closer to family, Esther's home church sent over some families to help her pack the trailer that would carry Esther's belongings to a new home and a new life.

As the volunteers from church arrived at the nursing home, they were shocked to discover that Esther was already packed and ready to go. Sure, a few boxes and some hanging clothes needed to be carried to the trailer, but Esther's family had already taken care of her, carefully packing the tiny trailer with her treasures. After helping with a few remaining items, her family and friends shared a prayerful good-bye.

What a joy it was to see Esther's family taking such good care of her! It was a great testimony of their love for her and for God. Unfortunately, many elderly residents of similar facilities are neglected and forgotten by their own families.

Paul wrote to Timothy about the importance of Christians caring for their families. He didn't make it optional. He said, "Those who won't care for their relatives, especially those in their own household, have denied the true faith. Such people are worse than unbelievers" (1 Timothy 5:8). Paul's words remind us that God puts a high priority on family. If we neglect our family, we fail to follow one of God's key commands.

DADDY-*Daughter Time*

Think of some relatives with whom you haven't had much contact. Do you have any family members who are in need? Write a letter, send an e-mail, mail a card, or call them to check on how they're doing. If you know of a need they have, pray together about how you might meet it. But don't stop there. Look at your immediate family. What do they need that you can help with? Surprise them today in an unexpected way, and give God the glory for any good that comes of it.

WHAT'S THE WORD?

Those who won't care for their relatives, especially those in their own household, have denied the true faith. Such people are worse than unbelievers. 1 TIMOTHY 5:8

LAUGH IF YOU MUST

October 14

IT never feels good when people laugh at you. When they laugh *with* you, that's different. Laughter can be contagious, which is why laughing with others is more fun than laughing alone. Television comedy producers know this fact, so they often record their shows with a live audience in the studio. The immediate reaction of laughing people energizes the actors. Some TV shows even insert a laugh track, so viewers at home have "someone" to laugh with.

But when people laugh *at* you, well that stinks . . . and it always has. Thousands of years ago, a man named Job endured some very tough times. The Bible says he lost his family, his possessions, and his health. Like anyone who has gone through difficult times, he wrestled with questions like Why is this happening? But through all his hardship, Job continued to fear, trust, and love God. He expected that God would answer his questions, saying that "my friends laugh at me, for I call on God and expect an answer" (Job 12:4).

Job was in good company. People laughed at Jesus for what they thought was foolishness. Before Jesus healed Jairus's daughter, he told the mourners that she was just asleep (see Mark 5:38-40). That's when the laughter started. But Jesus had the last laugh. He went into the girl's room, held her hand, and said, "Little girl, get up!" (v. 41).

She did, and the people stopped laughing. They were simply amazed.

When we tell others about God—explaining to them why we follow him and believe in Jesus—we open ourselves to ridicule. If people initially laugh at you, be patient with them. They don't know God's power like you do. Just like Job, you can be confident that God will always do what he says . . . and that's no laughing matter.

DADDY-*Daughter Time*

Standing up for what you believe is not always easy. Have you been laughed at for your faith? Talk together about how you reacted, and how you should react to those who make fun of you in the future. Pray for each other to be strong in your faith and to keep telling others about Jesus Christ.

Or maybe you've been the one laughing when somebody said something you disagreed with or experienced an embarrassing moment. If you can, find the person you offended and apologize for laughing. Always strive to laugh *with* people, instead of *at* them.

WHAT'S THE WORD?

My friends laugh at me, for I call on God and expect an answer. I am a just and blameless man, yet they laugh at me. JOB 12:4

IRON WOMAN

HAWAII'S Ford Ironman World Triathlon Championship is known as one of the most difficult athletic competitions in the world. Consisting of a 2.4-mile swim in the ocean, 112-mile bike ride, and 26.2-mile run, it tests the planet's best athletes every year. And on this day in 2005, Sarah Reinertsen established herself as one of those elite athletes. Her time of fifteen hours and five minutes didn't place her at the top (although she did finish ahead of four hundred other competitors). But by completing the grueling course, Sarah became the first female amputee to finish the Hawaii Ironman.

Sarah has never let the loss of her left leg slow her down. You may have seen her climb the Great Wall of China on the TV show *The Amazing Race* in 2006. Well before that, Sarah was flying around tracks. At age eleven—four years after her leg was amputated above the knee due to a bone-growth disorder—she realized she could run relays. And by sixteen, she was competing at the Paralympic Games in Barcelona, Spain. However, after falling at the starting line in one of her races, she gave up running for a couple of years. In time, she missed running and took up marathons. Pretty soon she turned her athletic talents to swimming, biking, and running in triathlons. Sarah said she wanted to show everyone that challenges can be overcome with passion and hard work.

King David had a similar message for his son Solomon in the Bible. As Solomon went to finish God's great Temple, David encouraged him to "be strong and courageous, and do the work. Don't be afraid or discouraged, for the LORD God, my God, is with you" (1 Chronicles 28:20). Solomon, like Sarah, was willing to do the work, and the results were amazing.

DADDY-*Daughter Time*

Do you have any obstacles that you have to overcome? You might not have to deal with the difficulty of missing a leg, but maybe you're extremely shy or tend to worry a lot about what people think of you. Share your struggles with each other and pray that with God's help—and some hard work—you can overcome them.

Watch *Soul Surfer*, a movie about professional surfer Bethany Hamilton, who had to conquer her fear and physical limitations after a shark bit off her arm. Check out the Father-Daughter Movie Nights appendix for more information.

WHAT'S THE WORD?

Be strong and courageous, and do the work. Don't be afraid or discouraged, for the LORD God, my God, is with you. He will not fail you or forsake you.
1 CHRONICLES 28:20

EITHER WAY
WE HONOR HIM

THE football coach knew his team needed to take their performance to the next level. The Christian high school team was about to play its biggest game, and the coach wanted to introduce a new philosophy: their play on the field wasn't about them anymore; it was about God.

"We gotta give [God] our best in every area," the coach said. "And if we win, we praise him. And if we lose, we praise him. Either way, we honor him with our actions and our attitudes."

In the 2006 film *Facing the Giants*, Coach Taylor's new approach to football is really nothing new. His players may not have known it, but the coach was sharing something that Jesus taught in his even more famous "speech" known as the Sermon on the Mount. In Matthew 5, Jesus wasn't talking to football players, but to thousands of people who had come to hear him teach. After encouraging the poor, the meek, the grieving, the humble, and the oppressed with the promise of a better future, he told everyone who was listening to be salt and light. More specifically, Jesus said they needed to be "salt of the earth" and "the light of the world" (verses 13 and 14). He told them—and us—to be like a lamp that "is placed on a stand, where it gives light to everyone in the house" (v. 15).

Cool! Ask anyone who is stumbling around in the dark how important light is. Jesus went on to say, "In the same way, let your good deeds shine out for all to see, so that everyone will praise your heavenly Father" (Matthew 5:16). Jesus didn't say we have to win at everything, accomplish great things, or be perfect. He said that our good deeds should point people to our heavenly Father.

That goal is what is so great about Coach Taylor's team philosophy. Lots of athletes praise God on TV after winning a game. What about when they lose? We live in a world that closely watches the actions of those who claim to be followers of Jesus. We can be a light or a distraction. Which will it be?

DADDY-*Daughter Time*

As your family watches sports together, keep track of which athletes honor God after games or during interviews. Notice how many take credit for their victories. Talk about what it might sound like if a player praised God when his team lost. Discuss what this attitude might say about the athlete's understanding of God. Together, ask God to show you how to let your light shine.

WHAT'S THE WORD?

Let your good deeds shine out for all to see, so that everyone will praise your heavenly Father. MATTHEW 5:16

ASKING A TOWN FOR FORGIVENESS

AS a young man, Elwin Wilson hated people who didn't look like him. Back in 1961, Elwin, a white man, led a group into a bus-station waiting room in Rock Hill, South Carolina, to attack civil rights protesters who were on the "Freedom Rides" to test segregation laws in the South. A black man named John Lewis became their main target, with Elwin leading the attack.

But a remarkable thing happened in recent years. Elwin, certain that he was bound for hell for the many sins of his life, found the forgiveness that comes only through salvation in Jesus. Once Elwin discovered true forgiveness in Christ, he began to seek out the many people in his town whom he had harassed, beaten, and threatened. He had a simple message for them; he asked for their forgiveness.

It's humbling to ask one person to forgive you and admit your wrongs. But Elwin had to ask practically a whole town of people who'd known him for his hate for decades. The apology that was noticed around the world, however, was the one he gave to John Lewis, who had since become a US Representative in Congress. The two hadn't seen or spoken to each other since that horrible day in 1961. Nearly fifty years later, John accepted Elwin's apology and offered forgiveness, and love. "Maybe," he said to Elwin, "others will come forward because there needs to be this healing."

In 2 Samuel 19, King David heard a similar confession. Shimei, a man from King Saul's family, had despised, attacked, and cursed David as he left Jerusalem. But as David returned, Shimei went out to greet him, confessing his sin and asking for mercy. Though he was advised to kill Shimei, David forgave him and spared his life.

It takes courage to humble yourself and ask for forgiveness. Whether days or years go by, it is never too late.

DADDY-*Daughter Time*

Is there some unresolved sin that you've committed against someone in your family, church, school, or neighborhood? Discuss together what's needed to make things right. Ask the Lord to give you the same courage that Elwin and Shimei had. When you say, "I'm sorry; will you forgive me for what I've done?" you won't regret it.

WHAT'S THE WORD?

"My lord the king, please forgive me," [Shimei] pleaded. "Forget the terrible thing your servant did when you left Jerusalem. May the king put it out of his mind. I know how much I sinned." 2 SAMUEL 19:19-20

A CALL FOR HELP

HAVE you ever been in an emergency? If there was a fire in your house, an accident in the car, or a medical emergency, would you know what to do? A five-year-old girl named Savannah knew what to do when her father needed help. And her quick thinking, courage, and grace likely saved her dad's life.

When Savannah's dad suddenly had difficulty breathing, the little girl became a lifeline for help. Using her dad's cell phone, she called 911 and calmly spoke to the operator for over ten minutes while help sped to the rescue. Savannah explained that her dad couldn't breathe well and was shaking. She carefully repeated the address that her dad gave her, answering every question and encouraging her dad that everything would be okay. Since they were on a cell phone, the operator couldn't trace their location immediately. Savannah's information shaved precious minutes off the response time, and she was credited with saving her father's life.

When we find ourselves in the middle of an emergency, God should be first on our list of "calls" to make. Though crying out to God doesn't guarantee that we will get what we want, it's not something we should be reluctant to do. King David in the Bible understood this truth. In Psalm 31, David writes a beautiful and powerful sort of 911 call to God. David is in a time of despair and danger, surrounded by enemies who have plans to kill him. David shows two important qualities during his emergency: he asks God for help, and he trusts God for whatever he sees as best.

When we're in trouble or our hearts are heavy, we can call on God for help. Like David, we can trust that God knows what is best and holds our future in his hands.

DADDY-*Daughter Time*

Does your family have plans for different types of emergencies? Discuss together how your dad would want you to handle a fire, a medical emergency, or other dangerous situations. Remembering not to panic and knowing where to go for help can be the difference between life and death.

What about emergencies of the heart? Look at Psalm 31 together and talk about how David's prayer applies to your family. Be prepared to take your emergencies to God at any time.

WHAT'S THE WORD?

I am trusting you, O LORD, saying, "You are my God!" My future is in your hands. . . . In your unfailing love, rescue me. PSALM 31:14-16

MONEY AND HAPPINESS

HOW would you feel if someone walked up and handed you $1,000? How about $100,000? Or maybe one million dollars? You might assume that you'd start jumping around and doing your happy dance. Maybe you'd think, *I can finally do what I've wanted to do,* or *Now I can help the ones I love with all that money!*

Money is not evil. The Bible says that the *love* of money, however, is "the root of all kinds of evil" (1 Timothy 6:10). Though many people believe that wealth creates happiness, one man realized something very different. Money made him miserable. A millionaire in Austria named Karl Rabeder decided to give away everything he owned. He hadn't always wanted to do that. Though Karl had grown up very poor, he eventually amassed a great amount of wealth. He was driven to work hard to acquire more money and things.

"For a long time, I believed that more wealth and luxury automatically meant more happiness," he said. "I was working as a slave for things that I did not wish for or need."

While on a luxury vacation in 2010, he was shocked to realize "how horrible, soulless, and without feeling the five-star lifestyle is." That's when he decided to sell all of his belongings, move to a simple mountain hut, and donate everything to charity. By making this huge lifestyle change, Karl said he now feels "free."

Solomon, the wise king of Israel, understood the emptiness of wealth. Whatever he wanted, he could get. In addition to being wise, he had wealth beyond compare. In Ecclesiastes 5, however, he lets us in on one of his greatest nuggets of wisdom: it's wrong to think that wealth will make us happy. Seems like Karl realized that too. While Karl doesn't judge others for what they do with their money, he came to the conclusion that any happiness he might find would have to come from something other than material possessions.

DADDY-*Daughter Time*

Make a list of your most prized possessions together. What emotions do those things stir in you? How long do they provide you with joy? What do you expect them to do for you?

What motivates you, your dad, and your family and friends? If money or things are your heart's passion, ask the Lord to help you have a different expectation for things in life. It takes wisdom to know how to use what you have for God's glory. Now, just for fun, get up and practice your happy dance.

WHAT'S THE WORD?

Those who love money will never have enough. How meaningless to think that wealth brings true happiness! ECCLESIASTES 5:10

A FATHER'S JOY

MANY things bring dads joy. Often it's something that most men like (and sometimes girls don't always understand):

- the beauty of a newborn baby . . . especially our girls!

- the satisfaction of a job well done, and the praise of our peers

- the respect of the women in our lives

- the thrill of victory by our favorite sports teams and athletes

Sometimes, though, dads can be pretty serious. The challenges of a job, pressures of financial matters, burdens of protecting their family, and speed of time can distract dads from the joy in life. There are times for seriousness, but girls enjoy seeing their dads joyful.

Truly joyful moments make for sweet memories. Can you recall a time when your dad showed genuine joy? The kind that comes with a big ear-to-ear smile, a hefty cheer, or a hearty laugh. Tell that story and see if it doesn't make you smile too. Maybe it's a memory from an unexpectedly humorous family situation or an action he wouldn't normally do.

But do you know what brings a dad the greatest joy? The Bible gives us some important clues in two verses. The first comes when John the Baptist baptized Jesus. The heavenly Father's voice boomed, "You are my dearly loved Son, and you bring me great joy" (Mark 1:11). God let everyone know that Jesus' obedience at the start of his ministry made the Father really happy! The second is found in 3 John. The apostle was commending his dear friend Gaius for his faithful living. As Gaius's spiritual father and mentor, John wrote to him, "I could have no greater joy than to hear that my children are following the truth" (v. 4).

Both of these examples remind us that knowing and following God is the most important thing in life—and the thing that brings the most joy. So . . . follow the truth and you'll spread true joy.

DADDY-Daughter Time

Talk together about what makes you most joyful. Explain to your dad how it makes you feel when you see him full of joy. Dads, tell your daughter how it makes you feel when you see her make godly choices. Daughters, as you make more of your own decisions with each new year, think about how your choices can bring joy to your dad and to your heavenly Father.

WHAT'S THE WORD?

I could have no greater joy than to hear that my children are following the truth.
3 JOHN 1:4

REACTING TO THE LIGHT

WHAT happens when you come out of a dark theater on a sunny day? Do you squint your eyes and quickly put on a pair of sunglasses? Maybe you sneeze.

Some people do automatically. They can't help it. Their first reaction is . . . *a-a-a-choo!* Scientists call this phenomenon "photic sneeze reflex" or ACHOO (autosomal dominant compulsive helio-ophthalmic outbursts of sneezing—try saying that five times fast). Doctors have discovered this condition gets passed genetically from generation to generation. An estimated 18 to 35 percent of the population has it. Those with ACHOO can count on sneezing a specific number of times, typically two or three, when they go from dark to light.

What exactly causes these sneezing outbursts? Scientists don't know. Does it have to do with changing light intensities? Do the eyes water and affect the sinuses? No one has figured that out. Light and dark affect us in many other ways too. We blink and our pupils get smaller when it's light, but we open our eyes wide when it's dark.

The Bible tells us that light and dark reveal a lot about our character. Jesus once said, "All who do evil hate the light and refuse to go near it for fear their sins will be exposed" (John 3:20). Those who don't follow God will often seek dark places to do their dirty deeds. Proverbs has another take on light and dark: the deeds of righteous people shine brightly, while the actions of the wicked cause darkness (see Proverbs 4:18-19).

Someone once said that you display integrity by what you do when no one is watching. What we choose to do, and how we do it, in the dark or quiet places shows ourselves and our family a lot about who we truly are. Do our actions gleam like the morning sun or cause us to stumble in the dark?

DADDY-*Daughter Time*

Has anyone ever discovered that you were doing something wrong when you thought no one knew? Talk about some examples and how you felt. It's not always fun, but it can be a relief to be found out and to make things right.

Discuss the importance of integrity—being consistent when the lights are on or when nobody's around. Share how you can pray for each other to lean on God's Word in those times.

WHAT'S THE WORD?

The way of the righteous is like the first gleam of dawn, which shines ever brighter until the full light of day. But the way of the wicked is like total darkness. They have no idea what they are stumbling over. PROVERBS 4:18-19

EXPECTING A PROMISE KEPT

FAITH takes many forms. When Joseph (the kid with a really colorful coat) was dying in Egypt, he gave his family a command that showed just how much he trusted God's promises. He told his brothers that God would someday lead them out of Egypt. When that happened, he wanted to go with them. He asked them to take his bones on the journey into the Promised Land (see Genesis 50:24-25). Joseph was a ruler, second in command to Pharaoh. His leadership and godly wisdom helped Egypt survive during a massive famine. He could have commanded that a great tomb be built to honor his leadership. After all, he had saved many people. But Joseph had the wisdom to remember God's promise of a new land— first promised to Abraham, then Isaac, then to Joseph's father, Jacob. Joseph chose, even in death, to trust God and go with his people to this new land.

Contrast Joseph's desires with another famous person, or at least the inventor of a famous container. Dr. Fredric J. Baur was a chemist and a food storage specialist. He invented the now-famous container for Pringles potato chips. And he must have been quite proud of his invention, because he wanted to be buried in it. When the eighty-nine-year-old doctor died in 2008, his children honored his request. Dr. Baur was cremated, and part of his ashes were placed in a Pringles can and buried. He joined many people throughout history, famous and not-so-famous, who wanted to celebrate their personal accomplishments through their death.

Joseph, on the other hand, chose to celebrate God's promises and remind his family that they should expect even greater things to come. Now that's great faith.

DADDY-*Daughter Time*

Talk about some famous people who died this year. How were their lives celebrated? Did people focus more on their accomplishments, their families, or maybe their faith? Do you think they focused on important things?

Now discuss some of God's promises that are important to your family. Talk about how your life can remind your family and friends of those promises.

WHAT'S THE WORD?

"Soon I will die," Joseph told his brothers, "but God will surely come to help you and lead you out of this land of Egypt. He will bring you back to the land he solemnly promised to give to Abraham, to Isaac, and to Jacob." Then Joseph made the sons of Israel swear an oath, and he said, "When God comes to help you and lead you back, you must take my bones with you." GENESIS 50:24-25

THE STRENGTH OF LOVE

A popular song says, "Love makes the world go round." Scientists might disagree with that assertion, but storytellers in literature, music, and Hollywood seem captivated by it. In the movie *The Princess Bride*, Westley finds his long-lost love and wryly tells her, "Death cannot stop true love; all it can do is delay it for a while." Their true love binds them together as the credits roll. On the flip side, in Jane Austen's classic novel *Sense and Sensibility*, John Willoughby professes his love for Marianne Dashwood (and leads her to believe they will marry someday). But his dishonorable choices show he loves himself more than he loves her. In the end, John dashes Marianne's hopes and her heart. Love stories can stir anger, joy, happiness, and sorrow, because love is powerful.

But there's no love more powerful than Christ's love for us. In the New Testament, Jesus tells the story of the Prodigal Son, who deserted his father and wasted his inheritance. When the son comes crawling home feeling worthless, his father celebrates his return and loves him unconditionally. Then in Romans 8:35 Paul asks, "Can anything ever separate us from Christ's love?" Some things may make it feel like God's love is far away. Maybe we're persecuted or hungry or overwhelmed. Paul answers his question with a stunningly simple and thrilling no. "Nothing can ever separate us from God's love," he writes (v. 38).

It's in our nature to want to earn God's love. Movies and books often show that love must be earned. But when it comes to God, we don't need to live in fear of unexpected rejection, or tragic circumstances, or of some powerful force ripping us away from him.

DADDY-*Daughter Time*

No power in the universe is greater than God's love. How does that truth make you feel? Discuss what true love looks like in both a nonromantic and romantic way. Make a list of the traits that characterize true love. First Corinthians 13 can give you some ideas.

Discuss the difference it makes when we're convinced of someone's love versus when we are uncertain of it. Consider how freeing the never-failing love of Christ is when we go through difficult times.

WHAT'S THE WORD?

Nothing can ever separate us from God's love. Neither death nor life, neither angels nor demons, neither our fears for today nor our worries about tomorrow—not even the powers of hell can separate us from God's love. No power in the sky above or in the earth below—indeed, nothing in all creation will ever be able to separate us from the love of God that is revealed in Christ Jesus our Lord. ROMANS 8:38-39

WHEN SPECIAL TREATMENT IS ORDINARY

DO you ever feel as though "important" people get treated better than everyone else? Maybe a political leader receives special favors or gifts because he has power and influence. Maybe you've read about a celebrity who avoided consequences for breaking the law because she had high-powered lawyers and fans in the jury box. Or perhaps you've seen in school that the more popular or athletic kids get preferential treatment. And sometimes, sadly, favoritism happens in churches when people who give a lot of money or lead a lot of activities are treated like they're more important than the rest of us. The truth is, none of us like it when someone gets preferential treatment.

But if we're honest, we have to admit that sometimes we treat certain people better than others. We want to be friends with the popular kids, so we find ourselves making the mistake of treating them better than other students. The problem of prejudice has been going on for thousands of years.

James, a self-described servant of Jesus, warned the early church about favoring some people over others. In those days, a church might give special attention and seating to the people who looked wealthy. On the other hand, a poor person might be mistreated and seated in the back. God inspired James to condemn this practice (see James 2:4). When you show preferential treatment, it's often because you have selfish motives. God says that everyone should receive special treatment instead of some people being honored over others. "It is good when you obey the royal law as found in the Scriptures: 'Love your neighbor as yourself.' But if you favor some people over others, you are committing a sin" (James 2:8-9). In other words, special treatment should be ordinary.

DADDY-*Daughter Time*

Do you think we treat everybody the same in our neighborhoods, schools, and churches today? Have you been treated poorly while someone else got special treatment? Discuss how that felt.

Now think about some times when you or your family have been somewhere, maybe church, and ignored some people while showing more attention toward others. What do you plan to do next time you see that happening in yourself or others at church or school?

WHAT'S THE WORD?

It is good when you obey the royal law as found in the Scriptures: "Love your neighbor as yourself." But if you favor some people over others, you are committing a sin.
JAMES 2:8-9

BOLDLY TO THE THRONE

WHAT do you think it would be like to enter a royal palace and approach the king or queen? Would you be nervous? excited? scared to do or say the wrong thing?

History is filled with kings who demanded order. They'd make rash decisions if a certain protocol wasn't followed. One of those kings was Xerxes the Great of Persia. You can read about his reign in the book of Esther. And you may have read about him in this book a couple of times already (see July 21 and September 11). Xerxes was a bit of a control freak. If someone came into his presence without being invited, he might order him or her killed. Or maybe, if he was in a good mood, he might extend his scepter to show mercy. No pressure, right?

King Xerxes took Esther to be one of his queens about five hundred years before Jesus was born. Esther was beautiful, but she'll always be remembered more for her courage. In order to save her people, she went before the king . . . uninvited. *Yikes!*

Esther's story is a great read. The lives of the Jews hung in the balance, so Esther resolved to do what almost no one else in the kingdom would dare: to see the king without an invitation. She had to do something. Too many lives were at stake. In one of the most courageous statements ever made in history, Esther said, "Though it is against the law, I will go in to see the king. If I must die, I must die" (Esther 4:16).

If that's how dangerous approaching a human king could be, how safe is it to go to the throne of God? After all, he's the King of all kings. When we have a question or a concern, do we have to take our chances and hope for mercy? Not at all! Hebrews 4:14-16 tells us that, because of what Jesus has done, the separation between us and God is gone. We can approach God's throne boldly, knowing that we'll find grace, help, and mercy when we need it most.

So don't think twice about approaching the one true King. Esther's king is long gone. Our King reigns forever!

DADDY-*Daughter Time*

Talk about how you feel when you pray to God about your concerns, questions, or struggles. Are you ever afraid? Make a list of some issues that you have been reluctant to take to God. Spend time praying together with courage, thankful you can approach God without fear.

WHAT'S THE WORD?

Let us come boldly to the throne of our gracious God. There we will receive his mercy, and we will find grace to help us when we need it most. HEBREWS 4:16

COMPARED TO HER . . .

I wish I were like her. I wish I looked like her. I wish I had her family, her friends, her possessions, her talents, her personality. I wish I were her.

Every daughter struggles with the temptation to compare herself to other girls. It's actually a natural temptation for all of us. King Saul couldn't rejoice with the nation of Israel at David's success. Saul thought the praises being heaped on both of them were actually comparing him to David . . . and not favorably (see 1 Samuel 18). When the disciples argued about who would be the greatest in the Kingdom of God, Jesus turned the whole question upside down: the servant is the greatest. Jesus even told a parable of a Pharisee and a tax collector in the Temple. The self-righteous Pharisee thanked God in his prayers that he wasn't like sinners, including the nearby tax collector. The tax collector wasn't comparing himself to anybody; he simply asked God to have mercy on him (see Luke 18:9-14).

In C. S. Lewis's classic book *The Voyage of the Dawn Treader* from the Chronicles of Narnia series, the character Lucy struggles with the temptation to read an enchantment that would grant her beauty beyond any living woman. As she considers saying the spell, Lucy imagines her older (and more beautiful) sister, Susan, seeing her new beauty and being struck with intense jealousy. Only intervention from the Christlike lion, Aslan, keeps Lucy from giving in to the desire.

On and on it goes. We all struggle with comparing ourselves to others. We all battle with jealousy. The Bible has a lot to say about jealousy, but the book of Galatians has a particularly helpful message: Stay focused on what is in front of you and do a good job; you don't need to compare yourself to others, because you're only responsible for your own actions (Galatians 6:4-5). Those are wise and helpful words, no matter our age!

DADDY-*Daughter Time*

Ask your dad to whom he compared himself when he was young. Share with him the struggles you might be having in this area.

Come up with a phrase that you can use to encourage each other in this part of your life, such as "Be aware. Don't compare." or "Do your best. Pass the test." When you notice the other comparing himself or herself with someone else, write or say that phrase as a gentle reminder of how we should respond.

WHAT'S THE WORD?

Pay careful attention to your own work, for then you will get the satisfaction of a job well done, and you won't need to compare yourself to anyone else. For we are each responsible for our own conduct. GALATIANS 6:4-5

FOR fans of the St. Louis Cardinals, October 27, 2011, was a night to remember. No, the Cards didn't win the World Series (that would happen a day later). But in game six of the World Series, St. Louis claimed victory after twice being one strike away from losing and going home.

The first time came in the bottom of the ninth inning when the Texas Rangers led 7–5 and were just one strike away from winning their first World Series. But Cardinal third baseman David Freese hit a triple to score two runs and send the game into extra innings. Then in the tenth inning, down two runs (and again one strike away from defeat), Lance Berkman got a hit to score two runs and keep the game going. The unthinkable happened in the eleventh. With the score tied, Freese hit a home run to end the game. Sports reporters called it the best World Series game of all time. The edge-of-your-seat, nail-biting drama of game six will be something Cardinals fans remember for the rest of their lives.

Funny thing about that kind of drama, though: When future replays of the game happen, fans won't be thinking, *Oh, I sure hope he hits a home run this time too!* They already know the ending, and that gives them peace, without all the drama.

As Christians we may experience moments of great drama in life, wondering what will happen next. But ultimately, we also have the security of knowing *the end of the story* already: God wins, Satan loses, and everybody on Jesus' team will live with him forever. When you have a strong team praying for you, it helps keep you safe in God's love (see Jude 1:20-21) . . . just like Freese was safe at home plate to win the game.

DADDY-*Daughter Time*

Have you experienced some "moments of drama" this year? Do you recall how it felt to wait and see what would happen? Share together how it feels to look back on it now? Did you have friends and family praying for you and building you up?

Get some blank note cards and write "We Know the End of the Story!" inside them. When someone in your family experiences a rough stretch, write a note of encouragement alongside that message and share it with him or her.

WHAT'S THE WORD?

You, dear friends, must build each other up in your most holy faith, pray in the power of the Holy Spirit, and await the mercy of our Lord Jesus Christ, who will bring you eternal life. In this way, you will keep yourselves safe in God's love. JUDE 1:20-21

MOST BEAUTIFUL
WOMAN IN NEW YORK

SHE'S not your typical beauty. She stands over 111 feet tall and weighs 450,000 pounds. Her skin doesn't just glow like copper—it is copper. And even though she lives on an island, millions visit her every year. Can you name this beautiful New York City woman?

She's the Statue of Liberty, of course. On this day in 1886, President Grover Cleveland officially dedicated this dazzling gift of friendship from France. For generations the Statue of Liberty has stood as a beacon to immigrants, meaning new beginnings, new opportunities, and freedom.

But erecting the statue wasn't easy. The Americans who worked with France to receive and build the statue lacked the money needed for construction. Citizens rallied, sending what little they could afford. Even children offered their pennies, giving their scant savings in order to make Lady Liberty stand tall.

An American poet, Emma Lazarus, wrote a sonnet titled "The New Colossus," which was engraved on a plaque at the statue's base:

> *"Keep, ancient lands, your storied pomp!" cries she*
> *With silent lips. "Give me your tired, your poor,*
> *Your huddled masses yearning to breathe free,*
> *The wretched refuse of your teeming shore.*
> *Send these, the homeless, tempest-tost to me,*
> *I lift my lamp beside the golden door!"*

With these beautiful words, Lazarus captured the same hope that Jesus shared with those who were considered undesirable. Jesus offered hope and love to those who yearned to be free. Even children.

One time, parents were bringing their children to see Jesus. The disciples didn't want children to bother him, so they tried to get the parents to take their children home. Jesus not only prevented this, but he was angry. He said simply, "Let the children come to me" (Mark 10:14). He still says that today . . . to everybody. He offers the greatest freedom of all: freedom from death and sin to anyone who comes to him!

DADDY-*Daughter Time*

Can you or your dad recall a time when, as a child, you weren't made to feel welcome at church, school, or in a store? That's how the kids felt at first when they came to see Jesus. Consider getting involved in your church with your dad to help out some aspect of children's ministry. Help them come to Jesus.

WHAT'S THE WORD?

One day some parents brought their children to Jesus so he could touch and bless them. But the disciples scolded the parents for bothering him. When Jesus saw what was happening, he was angry with his disciples. He said to them, "Let the children come to me. Don't stop them! For the Kingdom of God belongs to those who are like these children."
MARK 10:13-14

MARATHON DELIVERY

PREGNANCY has been called a marathon. A nine-month race to the finish line that results in a new life. But can you imagine running an actual marathon while you're pregnant? Racing twenty-six miles just hours before giving birth seems impossible.

Amber Miller didn't set out to accomplish two amazing feats in one day, but that's what happened. The avid runner signed up for the Chicago Marathon in 2011 before she knew she would be having a baby. As the marathon approached, she realized it was only days before her baby's due date. Amber and her husband decided to join the forty-five thousand other runners at the starting line, but had no intention of finishing the race. They expected to run for a while, take a break, and rejoin the marathon at the end just for fun. But then something amazing happened. The couple ran some, walked some, and finished the race! Sure, it took Amber twice as long as it normally would, but she was running for two . . . literally. After she crossed the finish line, Amber headed to the hospital and hours later gave birth to a baby girl.

If you've ever run track, you know running one lap is hard enough. A marathon is like 125 laps! To keep going that long, you have to have a lot of endurance. And to run while you're pregnant . . . well that takes a massive amount of endurance.

The word *endurance* pops up a lot in the Bible. In the New Testament, it's used over a dozen times to encourage and instruct early Christians. Just like runners, followers of Jesus Christ need a lot of endurance. In Romans 5, Paul explains that endurance can result in strong character and hope.

As you get older, you'll encounter difficult days. During times when you feel like quitting, remember that with God's help you can endure. And after you make it through those hard situations, you'll be able to look back and see that your faith and hope grew stronger.

DADDY-*Daughter Time*

What are some hard times you've had to endure? Ask your dad about times he worked through something when he wanted to quit. What did he learn from that experience?

If you live near a school, go to the track and jog a lap with your dad. You can also run around your block. The next time you're tired and feel like giving up, think about how God might be using this situation to strengthen your character and give you hope.

WHAT'S THE WORD?

Endurance develops strength of character, and character strengthens our confident hope of salvation. And this hope will not lead to disappointment.   ROMANS 5:4-5

HENCE, THE SHABU October 30

THE two friends entered an acclaimed restaurant with their taste buds watering. They'd heard amazing things about the Asian-influenced dishes and couldn't wait to eat. As the waiter listed the evening specials, he mentioned a "Seafood Shabu." The friends nodded knowingly, as if they completely understood. They were both in the mood for some seafood.

When the waiter left, they considered other menu options. But when it came time to order, they couldn't get the *shabu* out of their minds. Their curiosity overwhelmed them, and they asked the waiter to explain the special. While giving the explanation, the waiter concluded with the statement "in the end, the broth can be mixed with the remaining vegetables and rice; hence, the shabu." Again, the friends nodded. The waiter apparently thought the explanation was adequate and the meaning of the dish was evident. Unfortunately, it was not. Even so, they both ordered the special and enjoyed the meal immensely. But later that night, they had to go online and research the meaning of the Japanese cooking term *shabu*.

This story ended well, but it illustrates a bigger point: sometimes we need to admit that we don't know something or that we don't understand what we just heard. A wise person once said the only dumb question is the one that's not asked. As Christians we need to remain curious about the world around us and about the Creator who made it all. Proverbs 1:5 says, "Let the wise listen and add to their learning, and let the discerning get guidance."

So don't be afraid to admit that you don't understand something, whether you're at school, in church, or at a restaurant. It's better to ask for an explanation than to end up eating monkey brains. The wise—not the foolish—say, "Can you explain that to me? I still don't get it." That's exactly what God wants us to do with him and his Word.

Hence, the shabu!

DADDY-*Daughter Time*

Is there something that you've pretended to understand but really don't quite get? Share these things with each other. Then pick something (maybe "shabu-shabu" cooking) that you would like to learn more about. Studying God's world or his Word is always a good use of time. Spend a few minutes doing research and sharing with each other what you're learning!

WHAT'S THE WORD?

Let the wise listen and add to their learning, and let the discerning get guidance. . . . The fear of the LORD is the beginning of knowledge, but fools despise wisdom and discipline. PROVERBS 1:5, 7 (NIV)

October 31

BEING an Old Testament prophet was not an easy job. Sure, they had a good boss, but the hours were long, travel could be rough (just ask Jonah), and they often had to confront people with their sinful behavior. God had lots of messengers, including Ezekiel, who warned the people, "Don't let [your sins] destroy you!" (Ezekiel 18:30).

Many cities, such as Sodom and Gomorrah, as well as the nation of Egypt, didn't heed God's message. Sometimes God's prophets were killed for telling people they needed to change. Other times they were just ignored or ridiculed. And every once in a while, people listened and stopped their evil practices—like what happened in Nineveh—so God "changed his mind and did not carry out the destruction he had threatened" (Jonah 3:10). The truth is, people don't like to hear that they're wrong. So even if you're doing the right thing by sharing God's warning, you probably won't receive a pleasing response.

On this day in 1517, a man dared to tell his church that it needed to change. His name was Martin Luther. Luther had dedicated his life to studying God's Word. He became convicted that some church practices went beyond, if not against, biblical teaching. One tradition that concerned him was that some churches sold God's forgiveness of sins through the purchase of "indulgences." Luther knew that only God could forgive sins and that forgiveness could not be bought with money when "the debt" was already paid by Jesus. Hoping to encourage church leaders to examine what was right and wrong, Luther wrote out his concerns and nailed his Ninety-Five Theses to the door of All Saints' Church in Wittenberg, Germany.

For years after, Luther was an outlaw, his life in jeopardy. But hundreds of years later, his ideas inspire debate as Christians wrestle with understanding God and the Bible.

DADDY-*Daughter Time*

Make a list of some things that you see in your family, school, work, neighborhood, church, state, country, or the world that you believe are wrong. Find verses in the Bible that support your opposition to these practices. Now print these out and post them somewhere in your home as a declaration of things that "gotta change" someday. Commit to praying as a family that people will be bold enough, and humble enough, to turn to God and repent, asking for his forgiveness and help.

And if you see a friend or family member making bad decisions, resolve to have the courage to say, "That's gotta change."

WHAT'S THE WORD?

When God saw what they had done and how they had put a stop to their evil ways, he changed his mind and did not carry out the destruction he had threatened.
JONAH 3:10

AS LONG AS YOU LOVE ME   *November 1*

ON this date in 1997, the Backstreet Boys' hit single "As Long As You Love Me" debuted on the Billboard pop chart, where it would remain for a whopping fifty-six weeks! Even more impressive is how some Christian teens used lyrics from that popular love song to share Jesus with their friends.

In the chorus, the Backstreet Boys reassure a girl feeling a little inadequate: "I don't care who you are, where you're from, what you did, as long as you love me." Sweet. But if you think about it, that's also a loose paraphrase of what Jesus tells a certain Samaritan woman he met at a well. If you're not familiar with that encounter, take a minute to read about it in John 4:1-30. In that passage, the woman is shocked that a man would talk to her at all, much less a Jew addressing a lowly Samaritan. It simply wasn't done. And Jesus does it despite knowing her checkered past. But the Lord wants this thirsty soul to know that he is the Messiah, the living water that will satisfy her deep spiritual need. By the end of the conversation, Jesus has essentially told her, "I don't care who you are [a woman], where you're from [Samaria], what you did [moral failures], as long as you love me [as Messiah]."

That chorus's similarity to Scripture made the song a nonthreatening way for girls in particular to chat with fellow Backstreet Boys fans about the "living water" we all need.

A lot of people want to tell their friends about Jesus but don't know how to begin. One way is to follow Paul's example in Acts 17:28, and use the artists of the day as a starting point for talking about bigger spiritual truths. What "artists" are impacting your friends? Songwriters are probably pretty high on the list. If you listen carefully, a line from a hot new single (or golden oldie) you both enjoy could provide the perfect common ground for talking about the greatest love of all.

DADDY-*Daughter Time*

Has God ever used a secular song to make a spiritual impression on you? If so, talk about that. Have you felt led to share Jesus with someone? Who? Find out which "songwriters" have that person's ear. Then, as father and daughter, explore how those artists' lyrics could be a springboard for conversation about eternal truth.

WHAT'S THE WORD?

Jesus replied, "Anyone who drinks this water will soon become thirsty again. But those who drink the water I give will never be thirsty again. It becomes a fresh, bubbling spring within them, giving them eternal life." JOHN 4:13-14

IF you enjoy game shows such as *Jeopardy!* or *Wheel of Fortune*, you should get to know Charles Van Doren. Never heard of him? Well, his name means a great deal to the millions of Americans who, in 1957, sat glued to their television sets, eager to see how long the thirty-year-old Columbia English professor and son of a Pulitzer Prize–winning poet could remain champion of the popular quiz show *Twenty-One*.

Quiz shows were the hottest thing on TV in those days. And Van Doren's amazing run on *Twenty-One* made him a pop-culture icon as big as the biggest reality stars today. He even graced the cover of *Time* magazine. Then it all came crashing down. You see, after Van Doren's impressive streak ended, bitter former contestants exposed the show as a fraud. It turned out the producers had fed answers to the more popular competitors in advance and then coached them for dramatic effect (furrow brow, stroke chin, wipe sweat from forehead) to earn higher ratings.

A grand-jury investigation led to Congressional hearings . . . and public outrage. Do you know who ended up as the blushing face of the quiz-show scandal? You guessed it: Charles Van Doren. On this date in 1959, he admitted to Congress that *Twenty-One* was fixed. He may have "won" $129,000 and instant celebrity on that program, but he lost something far more valuable: his reputation. And not just his own. Even though his father had earned a Pulitzer, his mother was a novelist, and his uncle was a noted historian, their once-sterling family name suddenly became associated with cheating and deception.

Proverbs 22:1 reminds us that there's nothing more precious than the respect that comes with a good reputation. So when you're tempted to compromise by cheating on a test, cutting corners at work, or fudging on your income taxes, remember Charles Van Doren. Then pray for the strength and wisdom to make choices that will honor not only your name, but the name of Jesus as well.

DADDY-*Daughter Time*

On a scale of one to ten, how would you rate your family name? Why? What are you doing to preserve (or perhaps restore) a solid reputation? Have you ever been tempted to cheat? How did you handle that situation? If you have a favorite game show, make a date to watch it together sometime this week.

WHAT'S THE WORD?

A good name is more desirable than great riches; to be esteemed is better than silver or gold.   PROVERBS 22:1 (NIV)

PAPER, RIBBONS, AND BOWS

GETTING the curls right was always the hardest part. *Drag the scissor blade across the grainy side of the ribbon,* Dot reminded herself. *Tighter thumb, tighter curl. There. Perfect.* She was taping the last beautiful coil onto an already stunning package when her sister Annie walked into the room.

"Whoa, nice job. Who's that for?" she asked.

"Mary," Dot replied. "Her birthday party's Saturday."

"What's inside?"

"Stuff I picked up at the dollar store." Dot was distracted by a rogue ribbon that was losing its ideal corkscrew-like spiral. "The important thing is that this looks amazing next to all the other presents."

"Are you serious?" Annie had often told her sister that she worried too much about appearances. "Don't get me wrong, Dot, the wrapping's gorgeous. But isn't it more important for Mary to like what's inside? You've spent all your time on paper, ribbons, and bows that will get thrown away. You hardly gave any thought to what will be around after the party's over."

Obsessed with her project, Dot heard nothing, then declared, "I think it needs pine cones!"

Y'know, it's easy to fall into the trap of wanting to look good. Some people even turn it into a competition. The clothes they wear. The car they drive. The house they live in. But the Bible warns that investing in external things is a dead end—especially when it comes to our spiritual lives. Jesus reserved some of his harshest criticism for the Pharisees, pious religious leaders who cared more about their image than about developing godly character (see Matthew 23:27). He called them "whitewashed tombs," attractive on the outside, nasty on the inside. If our top priority is having a heart for Christ, then we'll glow amazingly on the outside, too.

DADDY-*Daughter Time*

Like Dot, do you ever find yourself overemphasizing the "wrapping"? How? If you were Mary and opened Dot's gift, how would you feel? Do you think Jesus feels that way when our image becomes more important to us than our character?

Think about people you know whose inner beauty shines through. Write notes of encouragement using blank postcards. Include your name, or send them anonymously.

WHAT'S THE WORD?

What sorrow awaits you teachers of religious law and you Pharisees. Hypocrites! For you are like whitewashed tombs—beautiful on the outside but filled on the inside with dead people's bones and all sorts of impurity. MATTHEW 23:27

THOSE CHATTY ANIMALS

HAVE you ever seen a grown man lose his temper with a talking animal? If you're a fan of classic cartoons, of course you have! Elmer Fudd and Yosemite Sam fly off the handle with Bugs Bunny all the time. Ranger Smith is constantly yelling at Yogi Bear. And who can forget Shrek bellowing at Donkey? But don't assume that sort of thing only happens between animated characters. It also happened in the Bible.

After fleeing Egypt, the Israelites—a huge nation—reached the plains of Moab. Their arrival intimidated the rulers there. So those rulers sent for a man named Balaam and offered him money to come curse these powerful Israelites. After consulting God, Balaam had no plans to curse Israel, but he still agreed to make the trip. During that journey, his donkey acted up. It saw a sword-wielding angel of the Lord standing in the way, so the beast bolted off the road. Balaam beat the animal and turned it back onto the path. But it saw the angel again, and this time it tried to squeeze through a narrow opening, squashing Balaam's foot against a wall. Balaam whacked the donkey again. The third time it saw the angel, the poor beast lay down, which led to more abuse.

Suddenly, the Lord opened the donkey's mouth. "What have I done to you that deserves your beating me three times?" it said (Numbers 22:28). Imagine Balaam's shock. A talking donkey! He was totally speechless, right? Actually, no.

Have you ever seen someone so enraged and irrational that the person started shouting without thinking? Red face. Little blue vein bulging in the forehead. Balaam must have been that mad, because he proceeded to argue with the donkey! Imagine how ridiculous he looked. Balaam probably felt even sillier when God finally allowed him to see the angel himself. You can read all about it in Numbers 22.

The Bible warns us to "stop being angry! Turn from your rage! Do not lose your temper—it only leads to harm" (Psalm 37:8). Chances are you won't end up screaming at a talking animal; you'll be unleashing your wrath on a precious human being made in God's image. And that's bad news.

DADDY-*Daughter Time*

Seeing cartoon characters blow their tops (sometimes literally) can be humorous. In reality, however, the Bible says numerous times that losing our temper is a sign of foolishness. Why do you think that's true? Has your fuse ever burned down to the point where you exploded? What are some ways Christians can keep that from happening?

WHAT'S THE WORD?

Stop being angry! Turn from your rage! Do not lose your temper—it only leads to harm.
PSALM 37:8

LADIES' FIRSTS

HOW do you feel about Election Day? The campaigns leading up to it can be exhausting for everyone, but the right to vote is a true privilege. In fact, Susan B. Anthony devoted more than fifty years of her life to securing that right for women in the United States. She was even arrested for casting an illegal ballot in protest on this date in 1872. We've seen a lot of girl-power progress since then. Here are a few notable female firsts:

- 1903—Physicist Marie Curie is the first woman ever to win a Nobel Prize.
- 1910—In Los Angeles, Alice Wells becomes America's first policewoman.
- 1932—Amelia Earhart soars into history as the first woman to fly solo across the Atlantic.
- 1977—Janet Guthrie breaks the gender barrier by racing at the Indianapolis 500.
- 1981—Sandra Day O'Connor becomes the first female judge appointed to the US Supreme Court.
- 1983—Sally Ride lifts off on the space shuttle *Columbia*, making her the first woman in space.
- 1987—Aretha Franklin gets a little r-e-s-p-e-c-t as the first female artist elected to the Rock and Roll Hall of Fame.
- 2010—Filmmaker Kathryn Bigelow becomes the first woman ever to win the Oscar for Best Director.

With accomplishments like these, it's hard to imagine a time when women had to battle for respect and equal opportunity, isn't it? Yet in many cultures, women are still treated as second-class citizens. That's how it was in Jesus' day. Nevertheless, when we find the Lord interacting with women in Scripture, he always honors them and preserves their dignity, even when other men don't (see Luke 7:36-50; John 4:4-27; 8:3-11).

Jesus cast another vote for "girl power" when he chose to appear first to Mary Magdalene after his resurrection (see John 20:10-18). In a society that devalued the testimony of women, the Lord entrusted one who had a less-than-sterling reputation to tell men about the most important event in human history. Now that's a fabulous female first!

DADDY-*Daughter Time*

Can you think of other famous ladies' firsts? Of those listed, which do you find most impressive? What does Jesus' attitude toward women tell you about God? about women? about you? Read Isaiah 1:17 together and discuss practical ways you can help oppressed women around the world.

WHAT'S THE WORD?

Just then his disciples came back. They were shocked to find him talking to a woman, but none of them had the nerve to ask, "What do you want with her?" or "Why are you talking to her?" JOHN 4:27

WISDOM: A REAL GEM

YOU'VE heard it said that a dog is man's best friend and that diamonds are a girl's best friend. So if a golden retriever wearing the De Beers' Marie Antoinette Necklace were to walk into the room right now, today's devotion would be over. But barring such a distraction, think about the most beautiful gemstones you've ever seen. Perhaps you're partial to jewels of a certain shape, size, or color. Maybe you like the way the cut catches your eye, light dancing among its facets. Actually, the God who created jewels thinks they're pretty special too.

In John's vision of the New Jerusalem in Revelation 21:19, we read that "the foundations of the city walls were decorated with every kind of precious stone" (NIV). He proceeds to list a dozen by name. And in Exodus 39:8-14, God tells Moses to adorn Aaron's priestly breastplate with a specific arrangement of twelve jewels. Clearly, some stones are more than mere rocks.

Throughout history, however, people have given greater spiritual significance to these gems than God ever intended. They've become associated with signs of the zodiac. Some folks even believe they possess magical powers that can influence the cosmos, ward off evil spirits, or cure disease. Along the way, we've also designated specific birthstones for each month of the year. And while most people innocently wear them in jewelry to represent the month they were born, others can get downright superstitious about their birthstone's mystical qualities.

In chapter 28 of the Old Testament book named for him, Job describes man's descent into the earth to mine its treasures. Onyx. Sapphires. Jasper. Rubies. He mentions these valuable jewels simply to say that none of them is worth as much as *wisdom*. Indeed, while certain minerals sparkle with exceptional majesty, the ability to know God's heart, discern truth, judge wisely, and live well outshines them all.

DADDY-*Daughter Time*

Discuss how wisdom is valuable in your daily life. Who do you consider wise, and why has that person earned your respect? Like Job, King Solomon valued wisdom above riches (see 1 Kings 3:1-14). Take a moment to follow his example by asking the Lord for wisdom. Do you know your birthstone? If you have a November birthday, it's topaz. Together, learn more about these and other precious gems.

WHAT'S THE WORD?

Coral and jasper are not worthy of mention; the price of wisdom is beyond rubies.
The topaz of Cush cannot compare with it; it cannot be bought with pure gold.
JOB 28:18-19 (NIV)

HERO OF THE FAITH

WILLIAM often rolled out of bed before 3 a.m. He uttered his first good mornings to a barn full of cows. (When your dad owns a dairy farm, chores start early.) As much as he loved the smell of hay and enjoyed playing with the goats, he had no desire to take over the family business. Like lots of boys, he dreamed of becoming a big-league baseball player.

Boundless energy often landed William in trouble. Overturning egg baskets. Throwing rocks at cars. He even pushed a dresser down a flight of stairs once, just to see what would happen. Nevertheless, he was a happy, likable child, which is why the victims of his practical jokes had a hard time staying mad at him. He was also an avid reader who gravitated to biographies of preachers and missionaries in far-off lands. Mom taught him Bible verses. Dad led family prayers and devotions. However, the boy known as Billy Frank had yet to invite Jesus into his heart.

As a teen, William arrived home from school one day to find dozens of local farmers in his pasture, praying for relief from financial woes and preparing for a series of revival meetings. A friend asked William why there were so many cars on his property. "I guess they're just some fanatics who talked Dad into letting them use the place," he replied. Little did William Franklin Graham know that, during those revival meetings, he would surrender his life to Jesus Christ and begin a journey as remarkable as any he had read about.

Born November 7, 1918, Billy Graham has devoted his life to sharing the gospel. His stadium crusades, radio sermons, and television broadcasts have reached more than 2.2 billion people worldwide. He personifies Christ's command in Matthew 28:19 to "go and make disciples of all the nations, baptizing them in the name of the Father and the Son and the Holy Spirit." Billy's sincerity and integrity have even earned him seventh place on Gallup's list of the most admired people of the twentieth century. God turned a mischievous young dairy farmer into a renowned evangelist, a prolific author, a pastor to numerous US presidents, and a true hero of the faith.

DADDY-*Daughter Time*

What surprised you most about Billy Graham's humble origins? How are heroes of the Christian faith different from Hollywood heroes? Do you admire any high-profile believers? What is it about them that earned your respect? If you've never heard Reverend Graham preach, watch one of his messages together on YouTube.

WHAT'S THE WORD?

Go and make disciples of all the nations, baptizing them in the name of the Father and the Son and the Holy Spirit. MATTHEW 28:19

HAVE MERCY!

AS best friends go, you can't beat a teddy bear. Those cuddly little buddies are soft, warm, and always ready with a hug. Plus, they're excellent listeners! But have you ever wondered how the teddy bear got its name?

In November 1902, the governor of Mississippi, Andrew H. Longino, invited US president Theodore "Teddy" Roosevelt on a bear-hunting trip. Roosevelt was an avid hunter. And a good one. But even the best marksmen have bad days. When it looked as if the president would go home empty-handed, someone reportedly captured a black bear and suggested that Roosevelt shoot the tethered animal as his trophy. Not very sporting, right? That's what the president thought too! He refused to fire on such a helpless target, and his act of mercy was quickly immortalized in a *Washington Post* cartoon.

Well, that cartoon inspired Morris Michtom and his wife, Rose, to create a sweet, innocent-looking stuffed bear to honor the president's noble choice. They called it "Teddy's Bear" and propped it up in the window of their candy and stationery store. Suddenly, everybody wanted one. So the Michtoms founded the Ideal Novelty and Toy Company and became the first teddy-bear manufacturers in the United States.

The next time you see a teddy bear, let it serve as a reminder that God wants us to show mercy to others (see Zechariah 7:8-9), much the way a powerful president elected not to harm a helpless bear. Oh, and if you need another example of mercy, look no further than God himself. In Ephesians 2:4-5, the apostle Paul writes, "God is so rich in mercy, and he loved us so much, that even though we were dead because of our sins, he gave us life when he raised Christ from the dead. (It is only by God's grace that you have been saved!)"

If that doesn't make you feel all warm and fuzzy, nothing will.

DADDY-*Daughter Time*

Share a memory of a favorite teddy bear, then search online together for Clifford Berryman's famous editorial cartoon, "Drawing the Line in Mississippi." Can you recall a time when you've shown mercy to someone or something? How is mercy different from compassion, and why do you think it's so important to God? Can you think of a worship song that describes the Lord's mercy?

WHAT'S THE WORD?

This message came to Zechariah from the LORD: "This is what the LORD of Heaven's Armies says: Judge fairly, and show mercy and kindness to one another."
ZECHARIAH 7:8-9

WHY NOT NOW?

DO you ever procrastinate? Psychologists say everybody does now and then, but about 20 percent of Americans qualify as true procrastinators. They make it a habit to look for distractions (and needn't look far these days) in order to delay difficult or unpleasant tasks. Some even decided to establish International Procrastination Day, though you won't find it on the calendar—they keep putting it off.

All kidding aside, God's not a fan of procrastination. We often read in the Bible that he wants us to respond to him immediately, because he knows how stuff can creep in when we delay being obedient. We can easily forget what we have heard. We get distracted. Also, it's easy to come up with lame excuses for waiting until . . . tomorrow. Are you prepared to drop everything when the Lord wants you to do something? Jesus described one of those drop-everything moments in Matthew 5:23-24. He said if we're worshiping and happen to remember that someone has a grievance against us, we should leave our gift at the altar, make things right with that person, then come back and present our offering.

When responding to the nudging of the Holy Spirit, may we all be as enthusiastic as the Ethiopian treasurer in Acts 8:26-39. There he was, riding along in his carriage, reading aloud a prophecy about Jesus. Philip overheard him and offered to explain it. So Philip climbed aboard, shared the gospel, and led the man to faith in Christ. Then they saw something shimmering in the sunlight. The Ethiopian said, "Look! There's some water! Why can't I be baptized?" (v. 36). This brand-new believer seized the very first opportunity to obey God through the act of baptism.

Maybe the Lord has been urging you to do something. Don't procrastinate. The Bible says we can be confident that we know Jesus when we obey his commands (1 John 2:3). It's not enough to know what we should do. We need to develop the discipline to take action, *pronto*. Forthwith. Posthaste. And just to be clear, those aren't fancy words for "tomorrow."

DADDY-*Daughter Time*

What do you think of the old saying "Never put off until tomorrow what you can do today"? If you struggle with procrastination, what steps can you take to develop better habits? Have you been ignoring a chore that needs attention? Perhaps together you can help each other clear those hurdles. Or maybe reading Jesus' command about healing a relationship makes you realize that you need to go to someone and work things out. Why not now?

WHAT'S THE WORD?

We know that we have come to know him if we obey his commands.
1 JOHN 2:3 (NIV)

WIN ONE FOR THE GIPPER

"SOME time, Rock, when the team is up against it, when things are wrong and the breaks are beating the boys, ask them to go in there with all they've got and win just one for the Gipper."

Notre Dame senior All-American George Gipp reportedly shared those now-famous words with his college football coach, Knute Rockne, shortly before pneumonia took Gipp's life. On this date in 1928, Rockne quoted his former player's deathbed request in one of the most inspirational locker-room speeches of all time. The underdog Fighting Irish rallied to beat undefeated Army, 12–6.

God's people faced a pretty formidable army themselves in 2 Chronicles 20. The war-minded Moabites and Ammonites (along with some Meunites) were marching on Judah. When King Jehoshaphat heard this, he and his people went straight to God. Judah couldn't win without divine intervention. God told Jehoshaphat to go out, meet the enemy, and stand firm. They wouldn't even have to fight (see verse 17). So early the next morning, the king mustered his troops and positioned singers ahead of the army to praise God. ("Tenors, you go first.") His people trusted that God would deliver them, just as he had promised.

Sure enough, Judah's army watched as their would-be conquerors destroyed one another. Every last man. And Jehoshaphat didn't even have to deliver a "Win one for the Gipper" speech at halftime! Would you believe it took three days for them to collect the plunder? On the fourth day, everyone gathered to honor God. Neighboring kingdoms heard about Judah's miraculous victory and feared the Lord, which led to a season of peace.

Are you faced with an unwinnable battle? long odds? Those are God's favorite kind, because he's sure to get the glory when the final whistle blows.

DADDY-*Daughter Time*

Have you ever experienced an amazing victory that just had to be God? What happened? Did he get the glory? Psalm 20:7 says, "Some nations boast of their chariots and horses, but we boast in the name of the LORD our God." What do people (or nations) boast of today? Why are those things less reliable than faith in God? To see and hear the story of George Gipp, search for "Notre Dame vs. Army - 1928 - Win One for the Gipper" and watch the video.

WHAT'S THE WORD?

You will not even need to fight. Take your positions; then stand still and watch the LORD's victory. He is with you, O people of Judah and Jerusalem. Do not be afraid or discouraged. Go out against them tomorrow, for the LORD is with you!
2 CHRONICLES 20:17

METTLE OF HONOR

ON Veterans Day, we honor military men and women who have fought for the United States. We host parades. We sing songs. And not just for high-ranking officers or Purple Heart recipients. We thank everyone who has defended America, at home or abroad. But if you scan the Old Testament, you'll see that not all courage in battle received equal recognition.

For example, in 1 Samuel 14, King Saul's brave son Jonathan quietly slips away from his troops and, along with his armor bearer, takes on an outpost of twenty Philistines. The duo not only wipes out the entire detachment, but their attack creates such confusion that the rest of the Philistine army fights one another, giving Israel an easy victory. Jonathan gets a big parade, right? Wrong. The next thing you know, Saul is ready to kill his son for eating honey in violation of an oath Jonathan didn't even know his father had taken. How's that for gratitude?

Just a few chapters later, an unknown shepherd boy named David knocks out a giant with a rock, and everyone in the kingdom goes wild. He's an instant celebrity. If they'd had Wheaties back then, David's face would have shown up on a cereal box. As it was, he received a high position in the army and moved in with the royal family. Women even gathered from all over to dance and sing David's praises.

You could understand if Jonathan had protested, saying, "Whoa, wait a minute. This rookie slays one Philistine and gets his own song? I led a two-man offensive that had their entire army on the run! Where's my pop hit?" But he didn't do that. Rather, he made a vow of friendship with David (see 1 Samuel 18:3) before giving him his own robe, tunic, belt, sword, and bow. The two became best friends, in large part because Jonathan refused to give in to jealousy. He chose to be humble. The king's son cared more about a relationship than winning a popularity contest. Now that's uncommon valor.

DADDY-*Daughter Time*

How important are popularity and applause to you? Have you ever expected praise, only to watch someone else get the spotlight? What happened? Why is it easier for people to overcome jealousy if they redirect glory to God instead of seeking it for themselves?

Take a few moments to discuss what Veterans Day means to you and your family. If you know someone who has served in the military, do something to thank that person.

WHAT'S THE WORD?

Jonathan made a solemn pact with David, because he loved him as he loved himself.
1 SAMUEL 18:3

MIGHTY WINDS OF CHANGE

CAROLINE'S family had been on the road nearly ten hours when she saw it. Was it a freak of nature . . . or something else? As their SUV motored across the wide-open plains of Texas, she glanced out the window and noticed all of the trees along the interstate were leaning in the same direction at an identical sharp angle. But where was the wind? Any gust capable of bending mature trees that violently should have been buffeting their car. Caroline lowered her window. Nothing. Yet those trees kept leaning.

"Daddy, why are the trees bent over even though there's no wind?" she asked.

Caroline's father knew this stretch of highway well. "It may be calm today, honey, but it's not usually like this," he explained. "Most days, a mighty wind sweeps across these plains. It's been such a powerful force for so long that even when the wind subsides, you can see how its influence has changed the character of the trees."

Caroline had observed in nature something that can happen to us if we're not careful. As we seek to grow straight, tall, and strong for Jesus Christ, a lot of forces in this world could blow us into leaning a different direction. Irresponsible friends. Bad entertainment. The list is long. And while an occasional blast from one of those forces may simply rattle our branches a bit, constant exposure will bend us away from God just as surely as those powerful Texas winds leave dozens of trees growing at odd angles.

The apostle Paul understood that growing into a mature Christian is a daily challenge. In fact, he warns us about worldly winds in Ephesians 4:14. Take your orders from the Bible. Pray for strength to make wise choices. Then your godly character will stand as a testimony to the holy forces shaping it.

DADDY-*Daughter Time*

What "worldly winds" have impacted people you know or celebrities you've read about? Have you ever felt pressure to bend in a direction you knew you shouldn't? What happened? Consider the following progression, based on Galatians 6:7: "Sow a thought, reap an act. Sow an act, reap a habit. Sow a habit, reap a character. Sow a character, reap a destiny." What does that say to you? Take a moment to list the positive influences shaping you right now.

WHAT'S THE WORD?

We will no longer be immature like children. We won't be tossed and blown about by every wind of new teaching. We will not be influenced when people try to trick us with lies so clever they sound like the truth. EPHESIANS 4:14

CHEAP IMITATION
OR THE REAL THING?

POSERS. Don't you hate it when people pretend to be something they're not? That bugged the apostle Paul, too. In 2 Corinthians 13, he told the church at Corinth to take a long, hard look in the mirror to see if they were real believers in Jesus. He wanted them to mature in Christ, not be a bunch of phonies. Sometimes it can be hard to tell a counterfeit from the genuine article . . . unless you know what you're looking for.

That brings to mind the Plaza Hotel robbery of 1925, in which jewel thief Arthur Barry robbed Mrs. James P. Donahue, the daughter of F. W. Woolworth. Barry was a bold criminal. He pulled the heist in broad daylight. In fact, he lifted a $450,000 string of pearls from a dressing table while Mrs. Donahue was taking a bath just a few feet away! The drawer actually held five pearl necklaces. He left behind four imitations the police deemed "good enough to fool an oyster." With so little time to study the goods, how did Barry tell them apart? He later revealed that he rubbed the pearls gently across his teeth, aware that fakes are slippery and smooth, while real pearls create a slightly rough, grating sensation.

Pearls are valuable, but not nearly as precious as our salvation in Jesus Christ. Have you ever wondered if your faith is genuine? Here's how you can tell: Authentic faith begins with repentance. That means truly being sorry for your sin and turning to Christ for forgiveness. Why Christ? Because as God's sinless Son, he was uniquely qualified to pay the price for our transgressions and restore our relationship with our holy Creator. Jesus was born in a manger, died on a cross, rose from the grave, and lives in us today. Is his lifesaving sacrifice where your hope comes from? Is it where you've placed your trust? If so, then like pearls that feel slightly rough when rubbed across the teeth, your faith is the real thing!

DADDY-*Daughter Time*

A counterfeit faith can be slippery, just like fake pearls. But when you whole-heartedly pray to Jesus and ask him to forgive your sins, you know that your relationship is real. Just like it says in 2 Corinthians 13:5, you'll see Jesus in your life when your faith is genuine. Talk to each other about ways that you see Jesus in your lives. Thank God for the confidence you can have for eternal life with him.

WHAT'S THE WORD?

Examine yourselves to see if your faith is genuine. Test yourselves. Surely you know that Jesus Christ is among you; if not, you have failed the test of genuine faith.
2 CORINTHIANS 13:5

November 14

ONE of the most successful movie trilogies of all time is The Lord of the Rings. Based on novels by J. R. R. Tolkien, it's a tale of elves, dwarfs, men, and hobbits joining forces to vanquish evil and rescue Middle-earth. One of the stars of this big-screen epic is Liv Tyler. During an interview with *Plugged In*, she talked about a valuable lesson she learned while playing the role of elf princess Arwen.

"I learned about patience and trust more than anything, because it was such a long experience," Tyler explained. "Obviously we had all of this great material, and we were quite clear, yet we also weren't a lot of times. We'd shoot a scene, and a couple months later they would completely change it and shoot a scene with other characters and give them those same words. There's so much in the movie that would happen like that. So I learned to be patient and trust [the director] to use the best material and do what was right."

Since all three films earned Oscar nominations for Best Picture, it's safe to say that the director knew what he was doing.

"It's hard to trust somebody that much," Tyler added. "I think that can be relevant to school with a teacher. You sort of think you have all the answers. I felt on this movie there were a couple times I made mistakes, and I wish I had listened more. It has definitely made me more aware of that."

It's easy to get impatient. To assume we know best. Not just with a parent, teacher, boss, or Hollywood director, but even with God. How silly is that? Instead of trusting the loving, all-knowing Creator of the universe and waiting on his perfect timing, we rush to do things our own way and miss God's best. Abraham blew it in that department. So did King Saul. But you don't have to. Psalm 37:3-7 and Proverbs 3:5-6 promise that when you let God direct, you'll always get the best picture.

DADDY-*Daughter Time*

Do you have a hard time being patient or trusting someone? Why do you think that is? Before praying about these challenges together, write down as many words as you can that not only describe God's character, but reinforce that he is indeed worthy of your trust. If you've never read Tolkien's novels, check out book one of the trilogy, *The Fellowship of the Ring*.

WHAT'S THE WORD?

Trust in the LORD with all your heart; do not depend on your own understanding. Seek his will in all you do, and he will show you which path to take.   PROVERBS 3:5-6

FIGHTING THE
URGE TO FIX IT

STEPHANIE'S day had gone from bad to worse. Late for school. Misplaced homework assignment. Then, in an attempt to defend her best friend against some gossipy girls, she spilled personal information obtained in confidence. Part of Stephanie wanted to crawl into a hole and hide. But another part of her needed to talk to Dad. She found him in his workshop, repairing her bicycle.

"Hey, Steph, just in time," he said, wiping oil from his hands and giving her a hug. "Bad caliper. That's why the hand brakes were sticking. But you're ready to roll now." Then, sensing that something was obviously wrong, he asked, "What's up, kiddo?"

"Dad, some girls were saying mean things about Robin, so I stuck up for her."

"That's my girl. Way to go!"

"No, that's not it," Stephanie explained. "While defending her, I slipped and said something I shouldn't have. Robin trusted me with a secret, and—"

"Oh, honey," he interrupted, "you and Robin have been friends a long time. I'm sure if you just explain what happened and ask her to forgive you, she'll understand. Why don't you give her a call? Your bike's fixed, so you can ride to the store together, treat her to ice cream—it's on me."

"Dad, this isn't a bike." She sighed, tears welling up in her eyes. "I don't need you to fix it. It's been an awful day, and I just need someone to listen."

Fathers tend to be fixers, don't they? It's in the DNA. And it's a wonderful trait. It's what keeps life from stalling when the sink backs up or a computer glitch threatens to wipe out a research paper. Dads also get rewarded for solving problems at work, so it's easy to understand how they can default to the same skill set in relationships—even when the best solution is to listen quietly. If that sounds like a dad you know, be patient with him. He's probably a world-class troubleshooter at heart.

DADDY-*Daughter Time*

Have you ever felt like Stephanie or her father? What happened? Realize that solving problems is often dadspeak for "I love you." But sensitive fathers have learned there are times for listening without offering advice, and they practice the wisdom of James 1:19. The challenge is knowing the difference. Designate a sofa in your home as the "talking couch." Had Stephanie begun with "Dad, can we spend a minute on the talking couch?" she would have sent a signal to her father that what she needed most was a listening ear.

WHAT'S THE WORD?

Understand this, my dear brothers and sisters: You must all be quick to listen, slow to speak, and slow to get angry. JAMES 1:19

MY FAVORITE THINGS

HAVE you ever had a day when things didn't go so well? *When the dog bites. When the bee stings. When you're feeling sad?* What did you do to send those blues packing? For a young woman named Maria in the award-winning Rodgers & Hammerstein musical *The Sound of Music*, it was as simple as singing about a few of her favorite things, such as raindrops on roses and whiskers on kittens.

That's not a bad idea. It's always helpful to replace negative thoughts with positive, uplifting ones. Of course, sometimes life's challenges require more than sentimental images of warm, woolen mittens and crisp apple strudel.

A godly man named Nehemiah knew all about that. Heartsick to learn that the walls of Jerusalem lay in ruins, he wasn't content just to recall happier times. Nehemiah took action by organizing a huge rebuilding effort (see Nehemiah 1–6). Unfortunately, the difficult days kept coming, and even more trials greeted him at the construction site. Bullies mocked the workers and threatened to attack them. Nehemiah also had to manage a food shortage, strife among his people, death threats, and enemies spreading lies about them. But amid all the fear and frustration, one of Nehemiah's favorite things was prayer. He prayed for God's favor. He prayed for strength. He trusted the Lord to guide and protect everyone in his care. And less than two months after the project began, it was finished, and everyone realized that God had helped them (see Nehemiah 6:15-16).

Are you in the middle of a big assignment at work or school? Perhaps, like Nehemiah, you feel as if every time you overcome an obstacle, another one pops up. You may be struggling with anxiety or opposition. Take a deep, cleansing breath. Then turn your thoughts to some of your favorite things, making sure God is at the top of that list. Keep in mind that he loves you, cares about your challenges, and wants to be part of the solution.

DADDY-*Daughter Time*

The Sound of Music made its Broadway debut on this date in 1959. Listen to the song "My Favorite Things" and talk about some of your favorite things. If you're feeling creative, each of you can write a new verse that puts your list to the song's melody. If you enjoy attending the theater together, see if a nearby high school is having a show. Many of them happen in November.

WHAT'S THE WORD?

The wall was finished—just fifty-two days after we had begun. When our enemies and the surrounding nations heard about it, they were frightened and humiliated. They realized this work had been done with the help of our God. NEHEMIAH 6:15-16

CRYING CROCODILE TEARS

November 17

CAN you name ten professions mentioned in the Bible? Give it a try. Okay, you probably got the obvious ones, such as fisherman, shepherd, carpenter, and king. And maybe you dug a little deeper for centurion, scribe, governor, or tent-maker. But odds are, "professional mourner" didn't make your list.

Did you even know there was such a job? It was a custom for many years. Women, mostly, would be hired by relatives of the deceased to amp up the intensity of mourning (see Jeremiah 9:17-18; Amos 5:16). These drama queens would cry. They'd wail. They also had a knack for verse, which they would recite on the fly, peppering their poetry with family references and praise for the departed.

If you've read the story of Jesus raising Jairus's daughter from her deathbed in Mark 5, you may have wondered how grief could turn to laughter so quickly when the Lord told the wailing crowd, "The child isn't dead; she's only asleep" (vv. 39-40). Anyone truly torn up over losing the little girl wouldn't have been in any mood to laugh at the one person offering them hope. Many experts believe these mockers were professional mourners.

Are you familiar with the expression "crying crocodile tears"? It's used to suggest a sadness that's insincere, hypocritical, or manipulative. The phrase came about because God gave crocs special glands that secrete moisture into their eyes when they've been out of the water awhile. They're located near the throat muscles. So when a ravenous reptile is eating its prey, those muscles will sometimes put pressure on the glands and force liquid out of the beast's eyes, making it appear to be weeping for its victim. But we know better.

God wants us to live lives of integrity, to value truth, and to be sincere (see 1 Corinthians 5:8). Not that we're likely to run away and become professional mourners, but every day we must decide to deal genuinely with those around us. Are we different people in different situations? Or are we ambassadors for Christ where we worship, work, and play?

DADDY-*Daughter Time*

We've all seen movies or TV shows with duplicitous characters who shed crocodile tears, secretly enjoying someone else's suffering. Do any come to mind? What does "living a life of integrity" mean to you? If you enjoy nature videos (and don't get emotionally attached to wildebeests or gazelles), browse online for clips of feeding crocs—and see if you can catch them crying.

WHAT'S THE WORD?

Let us celebrate the festival, not with the old bread of wickedness and evil, but with the new bread of sincerity and truth.   1 CORINTHIANS 5:8

ATTITUDE OF GRATITUDE

DID you hear about the silent order of monks allowed to say only two words every ten years? After his first decade at the monastery, brother Eli uttered, "food bad." He served in silence ten more years, after which he said, "bed hard." Then, on his thirtieth anniversary, he appeared again before the elderly abbot and used his two words to proclaim, "I quit." The wise old leader leveled his gaze at Eli and replied, "I'm not surprised. You've done nothing but complain since you got here."

Seriously, though, it's easy to find things to complain about. "I have too much homework." "My Internet connection is slow." "Gas went up another nickel." "My favorite team lost again!" Yet when we count our blessings, we realize how much there is to be grateful for. For instance, if those gripes hit home, it means you receive a decent education, enjoy online access, own transportation, and . . . well, there's always next season!

Frankly, two people could look at many situations, and one will complain while the other finds a reason to give thanks. Wouldn't you rather be the second person? It's totally up to you. The key is developing an attitude of gratitude.

In Nehemiah 12, God's people were ready to dedicate the wall of Jerusalem. Singers and musicians came from all over the region. In verse 31, Nehemiah notes that he assigned two large choirs to give thanks, positioning one on top of the wall toward the Dung Gate. Do you think there might have been some grumbling from that choir? "Thanks, Nehemiah. Nothing like the smell of manure to inspire songs of thanksgiving!" But wait. Verse 43 says, "Many sacrifices were offered on that joyous day, for God had given the people cause for great joy." If there was a stench, it didn't matter because this was a day to celebrate. They didn't let the little things bother them when there was so much to be joyful about.

DADDY-*Daughter Time*

Take turns reading lines from Psalm 100, and share what you're grateful for. Then use modeling clay, paper, or other items to craft a turkey body, neck, and head. Mount it on a half side of a paper plate. Cut tail feathers out of construction paper so that guests can write down what they're thankful for. On Thanksgiving Day, distribute the feathers (and pens). When your guests are finished, tape them to the front of the plate and display your bird.

WHAT'S THE WORD?

Many sacrifices were offered on that joyous day, for God had given the people cause for great joy. The women and children also participated in the celebration, and the joy of the people of Jerusalem could be heard far away. NEHEMIAH 12:43

YOUR whole family is watching TV. Even the cat. Suddenly, an edgy commercial sends Mom scrambling for the remote control. The cat goes flying. Whoa! Where did *that* come from?

Been there? Believe it or not, at one time television networks actually employed people called "censors." And sometimes those censors would ban risqué commercials rather than risk offending viewers. One of the more historic examples occurred on November 19, 1980, when CBS refused to air a racy Calvin Klein jeans spot featuring fifteen-year-old actress Brooke Shields. Kudos to CBS! Unfortunately, the fashion designer capitalized on the controversy, and scandal soon became part of Calvin Klein's advertising strategy. As all media lowered its standards in the years that followed, everyone from fashion labels to fast-food chains has been testing—and redefining—the bounds of decency.

We often make the mistake of assuming that God's standards shift and creep the way society's do—that what was inappropriate decades ago is somehow okay today since it has become more socially acceptable. However, God won't adjust his view of right and wrong simply because people relax their standards. How do we know? Because our heavenly Father is the model for it. Right and wrong are reflections of God's character. And his character doesn't change.

The apostle Paul knew that a pure mind leads to a pure heart. That's why, in Philippians 4:8, he reminded the believers to focus on things God would deem pure, honorable, lovely, and praiseworthy. And he issued that warning even though no one was being distracted by inappropriate television commercials.

In the book *All God's Children and Blue Suede Shoes*, author Kenneth Myers writes, "Every generation of Christians faces unique challenges. . . . The challenge of living with popular culture may well be as serious for modern Christians as persecution and plagues were for the saints of earlier centuries." All the more reason to heed Paul's advice and make God's standards your standards.

DADDY-*Daughter Time*

What do you think of Kenneth Myers's statement? Do you agree? In your lifetime, how have you seen the line of decency move in a certain area? Talk about ways the Lord has impressed upon you that certain messages from the media might not be healthy, even though many people don't seem bothered by them. Can you think of something positive you've seen that reflects the qualities listed in Philippians 4:8?

WHAT'S THE WORD?

Dear brothers and sisters, one final thing. Fix your thoughts on what is true, and honorable, and right, and pure, and lovely, and admirable. Think about things that are excellent and worthy of praise. PHILIPPIANS 4:8

CUTS LIKE A KNIFE

WHEN you reach for a knife, do you prefer one that's sharp or dull? Unless you plan to spread butter on a muffin, you're probably looking for a razor-edged blade with the strength and precision to cut through just about anything. A classic TV commercial from the late seventies advertised one that could carve through a tin can and still slice a tomato. It hacked wood, then cleanly split a piece of paper. Now that's a useful tool! *But wait, there's more. . . .*

Did you know we are God's instruments? When he opens his knife drawer, you can bet he reaches for a sharp one. Not necessarily the person who's strongest, smartest, or most talented. Rather, he simply wants in his hand an available, well-prepared individual who's ready for service. Maybe that's why he chose a lowly shepherd boy as Israel's second king, a reluctant stutterer to be his spokesman to Pharaoh, and a Jewish orphan to save her people as Persia's queen.

Do you want to be used by God? Sadly, some Christians are content just to sit in the drawer, dull and idle, watching as sharper knives see the real action. That's a shame, because the Lord wants to use each of us and has forged us for different tasks. The key is staying sharp. That requires prayer, a passion for truth, an openness to the Holy Spirit's leading, and the support of other believers who are eager to develop Christlike character. In fact, Proverbs 27:17 tells us that godly people can keep each other sharp!

If you visit Mexico City, you might see *El Afilador de Cuchillos* riding his bike through town, plying his trade as a knife sharpener. He blows a whistle to let folks know he's passing through. If a customer waves him down, he puts his rear wheel on a stand and pedals backward to rotate the gritty sharpening stone. Now, if you've ever sharpened cutlery, you know there's friction involved. Sparks fly. But it's all good. In the master's hand, the result is a finer, more useful blade, sure to see plenty of action.

DADDY-*Daughter Time*

What does it mean to "stay sharp" for God? Name things that can cause us to lose our edge—as well as healthy habits to prevent that from happening. Does someone in your life care enough to, like *El Afilador de Cuchillos*, apply a little pressure to keep you sharp? If you have a whetstone, carefully use it to sharpen household knives and scissors. Talk together about some of the similarities between sharpening knives and sharpening your spiritual life.

WHAT'S THE WORD?

As iron sharpens iron, so one man sharpens another.   PROVERBS 27:17 (NIV)

NO THANKS TO WIKIPEDIA *November 21*

THERE'S gospel truth, and then there's Wikipedia, the free online encyclopedia that anyone can edit. Have you visited that popular site lately? On one hand, it can be a helpful starting point for general information and research, though by itself it's not a very reliable source. Even the folks at Wikipedia warn readers that postings may contain incomplete or inaccurate information, not to mention opinions, rumors, or the writer's own slant on a subject.

For example, at one point the entry for Thanksgiving stated, "The event that Americans commonly call the 'First Thanksgiving' was celebrated to give thanks to Native Americans for helping the Pilgrims of Plymouth Colony survive their first brutal winter in New England."

Huh? If that sounds a bit off, it should. The truth is, the Pilgrims celebrated with their new neighbors, but the point of their feast was to give thanks to God, who sustained them through their first year in a strange new land . . . and inspired their trip in the first place.

In September 1620, 102 Pilgrims set sail from Plymouth, England, in search of religious freedom. They were crammed below deck in the *Mayflower*'s cargo hold for a stormy, sixty-six-day voyage before landing at Cape Cod and establishing Plymouth Colony. Soon after, they signed the Mayflower Compact, which stated their purpose to "the glory of God and the advancement of the Christian faith." Even though half of them died from terrible sickness that first winter, the colonists found plenty of reasons to thank God with a harvest feast, including the bountiful crop they learned to farm with help from friendly Native Americans.

As your family celebrates Thanksgiving this year, take a moment between the football and pumpkin pie to acknowledge the holiday's distinctly Christian roots. Discuss ways that you can follow the commands of Psalm 105:1-2 and "tell everyone about his wonderful deeds."

DADDY-*Daughter Time*

What does Thanksgiving mean to you? Do you have a favorite family tradition at this time of year? What are you thankful for? In 1863, President Abraham Lincoln passed a Thanksgiving resolution that quoted Psalm 33:12 and said, "It is announced in the Holy Scriptures and proven by all history, that those nations are blessed whose God is the Lord." Do you believe that America's god is still the God of the Bible? Why or why not?

WHAT'S THE WORD?

Give thanks to the LORD and proclaim his greatness. Let the whole world know what he has done. Sing to him; yes, sing his praises. Tell everyone about his wonderful deeds.
PSALM 105:1-2

WE BELONG TO HIM

WHEN you were little, did you have one special doll or stuffed animal that meant everything to you? You talked to it. You slept with it (and maybe even had a hard time sleeping without it). You gave it a name like Soft Doggy, Big Dolly, or Sleepy Puppy. You loved it so hard that it got holes in it. And even though it probably would have been easier to replace it after several years of wear and tear, Mom took the time to stitch those holes. More than just a plaything, it was a precious friend. You cherished it, not because it did anything to deserve your affection, but simply because it was yours.

Did you know that's how God sees you? Sometimes we make the mistake of thinking of God as some kind of heavenly boyfriend. In other words, if we do and say all the right things that prove our love for him, then he might just love us back. But that's not how our heavenly Father operates.

First John 4:10 reminds us that God loved us first with the purest love there is: "This is real love—not that we loved God, but that he loved us and sent his Son as a sacrifice to take away our sins." We're special to God simply because we belong to him.

If you've seen the *Toy Story* movies (the first of which was released on this date in 1995), you know what that sort of bond is like. Andy's favorite toy is his pull-string cowboy, Sheriff Woody. They're inseparable. In fact, Andy scrawls his name on the sole of Woody's boot. Even though things happen in those movies to make Woody and his toy-box buddies question where they belong, Woody never forgets whose they are. He's been branded. Andy's name is written on him. And just as Woody bears Andy's name, we bear the name of the one who loved us first.

DADDY-*Daughter Time*

Do you remember loving a particular toy as a child? What was it? Why was it so special to you? How does it feel to know that the Lord loved you first? Have you invited Jesus to write his name on your heart? Why not follow Andy's example and write his name on the sole of your shoe? Big or small, those letters can be a daily reminder that you belong to the Lord.

WHAT'S THE WORD?

This is real love—not that we loved God, but that he loved us and sent his Son as a sacrifice to take away our sins. 1 JOHN 4:10

FROM THE LOOK
OF THINGS

HAVE you ever misjudged someone based on appearance? Blame your brain. It takes a picture, then tries to file it in a familiar place. *Cowboy with a white hat? Good guy. Scowling dude with a hook for a hand?* Bad guy. Well, unless you saw the Disney film *Tangled*, which surprised us by flipping those expectations upside down. Interestingly, something similar happened in the Bible.

God had a mission for Samuel: go to Bethlehem and find Israel's next king among Jesse's sons (see 1 Samuel 16). Samuel sized up those strapping young men and concluded, "It must be Eliab, right Lord?" Nope. "Um, how about Abinadab?" Nope. Pretty soon, Jesse was running out of sons, and God still hadn't given Samuel the green light. So they called the youngest boy from the fields where he was tending sheep. At first glance Samuel must've thought, *Hmm. Not exactly king material.* But sure enough, the Lord chose David, reminding Samuel that, while men judge by appearance, God looks deeper (see verse 7).

For a modern example of how appearances can be deceiving, look no further than the reality show *Britain's Got Talent*. In 2009, a dowdy middle-aged woman named Susan Boyle strode onto the stage with ambitions of becoming a professional singer. The crowd murmured, and eyes rolled. Contemptuous judges humored her. Then she sang. Just seconds into her rendition of "I Dreamed a Dream" from the musical *Les Misérables*, members of the audience leaped to their feet and cheered. In the days that followed, Boyle's performance got more than 120 million YouTube views, shaming a cynical, image-conscious world too often governed by first impressions. This viral sensation reminded us all that it's what's inside that counts. In fact, her debut CD, *I Dreamed a Dream*, arrived on this date in 2009. It immediately soared to number one and outsold every other album released that year.

David would endure the taunts of a giant named Goliath. Susan Boyle had to impress a snickering crowd that had already written her off. And both knocked 'em dead.

DADDY-*Daughter Time*

If you witnessed Susan Boyle's shining moment on *Britain's Got Talent*, how did it make you feel? If you haven't seen it yet, watch it together on YouTube. Has anyone ever been too quick to judge you? What happened? How can you avoid making snap judgments of others and try to see them through God's eyes?

WHAT'S THE WORD?

The LORD said to Samuel, "Don't judge by his appearance or height, for I have rejected him. The LORD doesn't see things the way you see them. People judge by outward appearance, but the LORD looks at the heart." 1 SAMUEL 16:7

WHERE CREDIT IS DUE

SARAH dreaded opening the mailbox. *What if it's another bill?* she thought. At first, having a credit card seemed like a great idea. She could go out with friends without wondering if she had enough cash in her purse. It made refueling the car and buying gifts online a snap. But she got carried away, and now her part-time job barely covered the minimum payments. With spiraling interest, the sixty-dollar shoes she bought last month could end up costing three times that much. Just thinking about it made her head hurt.

Credit-card companies would like us to believe that carrying a piece of plastic is a sign of status or a rite of passage into adulthood. "Got your card? Swipe away!" But a growing number of people like Sarah are paying a heavy price. That's because anytime we spend money we don't have, we run the risk of having others exert control over our lives—control that Christians have already surrendered to Jesus.

God's people encountered this problem while rebuilding Jerusalem's walls in Nehemiah 5. Wealthy nobles and officials were taking advantage of fellow Jews struggling to make ends meet during a food shortage. Poorer families with more mouths to feed had to borrow against their fields, vineyards, and homes. Several cried out, "We have already sold some of our daughters, and are helpless to do anything about it, for our fields and vineyards are already mortgaged to others" (v. 5). Upset that the rich lenders were also charging interest, Nehemiah insisted that they return what belonged to their countrymen.

Unfortunately, Nehemiah isn't around to shame the bank into cutting Sarah some slack. She'll have to pay her debt. Afterwards, she might want to cut up her credit card, investigate what God's Word has to say about managing money, and learn to be more content with what she already has (1 Timothy 6:6-8). It's an investment guaranteed to pay dividends.

DADDY-*Daughter Time*

How do you feel about credit cards? If you had a friend in Sarah's very expensive shoes, what advice would you offer? Maybe it's time for a family discussion about buying on credit, interest rates, and the dangers of debt. Why should it bother us to hear that some indebted fathers were forced to sell their daughters in Nehemiah's day?

WHAT'S THE WORD?

True godliness with contentment is itself great wealth. After all, we brought nothing with us when we came into the world, and we can't take anything with us when we leave it. So if we have enough food and clothing, let us be content. 1 TIMOTHY 6:6-8

LOST IN TRANSLATION

IF you've ever studied a foreign language, you've probably translated sentences from one tongue into another. It can be a real challenge. Just one little slip and instead of saying "I'm hungry," you're offering to cook a huge dinner. *Oops!* But at least you weren't one of the marketing gurus responsible for these messages getting lost in translation:

- The name Coca-Cola in China was read *Kekoukela* which, depending on the dialect, means either "Bite the Wax Tadpole" or "Female Horse Stuffed with Wax."
- General Motors couldn't figure out why its Chevy Nova automobile wasn't selling well in South America. Then it realized that, in Spanish, *nova* means "it won't go."
- Beverage maker Bacardi came up with a fruity drink, calling it Pavian to create a sense of French chic. It worked until they tried to market it in Germany, where *pavian* means "baboon."
- In the 1960s, PepsiCo ran the campaign "Come Alive! You're in the Pepsi Generation!" In Chinese, however, their slogan promised, "Pepsi Brings Your Ancestors Back from the Grave." Imagine the excitement (and then disappointment) in Shanghai.

With translations being so tricky, you might wonder how reliable the Bible is. After all, thousands of manuscripts have been discovered and translated over the years. Couldn't copies or translations from one language to another become just as corrupted as these ad slogans? That's a fair question, though the incredible number of carefully preserved copies actually strengthens the case for Scripture by giving us a solid basis for comparison. As radio host and Bible answer man Hank Hanegraaff explains, "If you start checking them out, you find out that there are differences in style, but no difference in substance. So we know that over time, God has indeed preserved his word with great authenticity." The next time you pick up your Bible, you can have the confidence of Isaiah: "The grass withers and the flowers fade, but the word of our God stands forever" (40:8).

DADDY-*Daughter Time*

Do you ever struggle to communicate clearly with each other? Have you tried to choose words carefully, only to wind up misunderstood? If so, you're completely normal. Talk about that a bit. How might you work together to avoid that frustration in the future? Since 1942, Wycliffe Bible Translators has played a part in converting God's Word into more than seven hundred foreign languages. Visit wycliffe.org to learn more about this remarkable organization, as well as the history of Bible translation.

WHAT'S THE WORD?

The grass withers and the flowers fade, but the word of our God stands forever.
ISAIAH 40:8

November 26 **EXPLORING THE UNKNOWN**

HOWARD Carter wiped sweat from his brow. *This could be it,* he thought. Most archaeologists had given up hope that any tombs remained undiscovered in the Valley of the Kings, but this British Egyptologist had faith. He also had money, thanks to his benefactor, Lord Carnarvon. After seven years of searching, the men watched as workers broke through a final, sealed, mud-brick door. Carter's hands trembled. A rush of hot air caused his candle to flicker. He peered into the blackness.

"Can you see anything?" Carnarvon asked.

"Yes," an astonished Carter managed, his eyes slowly adjusting, "wonderful things."

On November 26, 1922, these men entered a treasure-filled antechamber that had been sealed for more than three thousand years. The tomb was dark and eerily silent. Footprints of its builders were still visible on the dusty floor. Carter's team tested the air for noxious gases and stepped cautiously, wary of pitfalls. Passages led from room to room and, eventually, to the resting place of the boy-king himself, Tutankhamen. Can you imagine the mix of anxiety and wonder those men must have felt while exploring King Tut's tomb for the first time? Each step in the dark was rewarded with more excitement. More history. More gold.

Choosing to follow Jesus is also an adventure. We step with him into the unknown, keenly aware of the darkness in the world around us. Yet we can be confident that, having discovered the one true King, heavenly treasures await—and not just at the end of our quests. As we walk with Christ, we'll find spiritual riches at every turn. You may ask, "How can we see them and avoid stumbling?" Great question! Psalm 119:105 notes that God's Word is a "lamp to guide my feet and a light for my path." We couldn't ask for better illumination. By walking in his light—step-by-step—you too will see wonderful things.

DADDY-*Daughter Time*

What does it mean to walk in the light? Share some of the wonderful things you've witnessed since deciding to follow Christ. Have you ever seen the relics from King Tut's tomb? Together, search for those images online. Then read Mark 16:1-7 and 1 Thessalonians 4:14. Why do you think some people would rather marvel at the contents of a dead king's tomb than stand in awe of the empty tomb of the risen King?

WHAT'S THE WORD?

Your word is a lamp to guide my feet and a light for my path. PSALM 119:105

SETTING THE RECORDS STRAIGHT

DO you enjoy singing in church? Whether you prefer classic hymns, modern praise choruses, or a combination of the two, something special happens when we lift our voices to God in song. Psalm 96:1 (NIV) tells us, "Sing to the LORD a new song; sing to the LORD, all the earth." For some folks, creating a "new" song has involved giving a familiar one a spiritual face-lift. For instance, did you know that the tune for the beloved hymn "O Sacred Head Now Wounded" ("Passion Chorale") first appeared as "My Heart Is Distracted by a Gentle Maid," a German love song from the early 1600s? No kidding! And the practice didn't stop there.

Beginning in the late 1800s, members of The Salvation Army changed the words to popular music-hall songs in hopes of appealing to unchurched men and women attending its meetings. More than one hundred of those anthems are still in that ministry's *Tune Book*, including melodies borrowed from "Buffalo Gals," "Here's to Good Old Whiskey," and "Where Is the Merry Party?"

As for today's Top 40 hits, since 1992 the Christian parody band ApologetiX has spoofed hundreds of songs from the rock era, overhauling the lyrics of each track with a strong biblical statement. Part Billy Graham, part Weird Al Yankovic, writer and lead singer J. Jackson redeems the hottest radio hits by applying a clear grasp of God's Word and a clever sense of humor.

"When we do a concert for a youth group, kids know right away that the words coming out of our mouths aren't the same as what they're used to," he told *Plugged In*. "Even music from their parents' generation. And they love it." As a result, families are studying lyric sheets together, digging into Scripture, and singing new songs to the Lord. How is your family attempting to honor God with your music? Are you following the encouragement of Colossians 3:16 and letting the word of Christ dwell in you "as you sing psalms, hymns and spiritual songs with gratitude in your hearts to God" (NIV)?

DADDY-*Daughter Time*

How do you feel about Christians using secular tunes for holy purposes? Talk about possible pros and cons. To learn more about the ministry of ApologetiX and to see which songs the band has parodied, visit apologetix.com. On the flip side, can you think of a catchy tune ruined by lousy lyrics? Rewrite 'em! Then schedule a date to have dinner and attend a Christian concert together.

WHAT'S THE WORD?

Let the word of Christ dwell in you richly as you teach and admonish one another with all wisdom, and as you sing psalms, hymns and spiritual songs with gratitude in your hearts to God. COLOSSIANS 3:16 (NIV)

RED-AND-BLUE lights flashed rhythmically in the twilight. The squad car drove off with a guilty passenger in the backseat as other officers monitored crackling walkie-talkies. Eager reporters leaned in to hear young Matthew and Emily explaining to Lieutenant Shaw how they solved their latest small-town mystery.

"The limping chauffeur who supplied her alibi was also lying," Matthew stated confidently. "The suit, the shoes, the carburetor—"

Emily interrupted, "And we found this bit of shoe leather near the gas pedal. This was handmade. See the edge? It was cut with scissors. No scuff marks. It's not even discolored!"

The lieutenant smiled and shook his head. "You two are amazing. I'll add it to the evidence." He noticed streetlights coming on. "It's getting pretty late, kids. You'd better head home."

Emily was in no hurry to get home. Not tonight. Solving mysteries with her friend was a lot more fun than working through conflict with her brother. They'd had an argument that morning, and things were still unresolved. Both had said things they shouldn't have. For her part, Emily knew she needed to apologize, but she just didn't feel like it. Ephesians 4:26 pricked at her heart. *Too late,* she thought, *the sun has already set on my anger. Besides, he should apologize first. Definitely.* The scowl on her face caught Matthew's eye.

"What's that look for?" he asked. "We just solved one of our biggest cases ever. What could possibly be wrong?" As they walked, she told him the whole story—well, her side of it anyway. When they stopped in front of her house, the junior detective told his partner, "Sometimes when I fight with my sisters, Dad reminds me of 1 Corinthians 13:2. It says solving mysteries is great, but if I don't love other people, I'm the one who's busted. Or something like that."

Emily stared at the path to her front door. Matthew had a point, of course, but swallowing her pride was going to be harder than cracking a case. Much harder.

DADDY-*Daughter Time*

Read Ephesians 4:26-27 and discuss why you think God wants us to overcome anger quickly. Is it within your nature to resolve conflict this way? As Christians, love should be our compass. Share a time when you felt like Emily, and how things worked out. Do you enjoy a good mystery? If you have the board game Clue, play it together.

WHAT'S THE WORD?

If I have the gift of prophecy and can fathom all mysteries and all knowledge, and if I have a faith that can move mountains, but have not love, I am nothing.
1 CORINTHIANS 13:2 (NIV)

UNNECESSARY ROUGHNESS *November 29*

AT six feet five inches tall and three hundred pounds, professional football players are expected to knock heads on the field. But some have been tackling violence off the field. In 2010, the NFL Players Association published *NFL Dads Dedicated to Daughters*, a collection of thoughts from rough-and-tumble guys raising girls in a culture that often disrespects women. Here's what several said about the fathers they try to be, and the kind of young men they hope their daughters will admire:

- "Too many men feel like they have to be rough and tough all the time. . . . Stern or aggressive behavior is easy for us. But being gentle, loving, and compassionate is a sign of maturity." —Kevin Mawae, Tennessee Titans
- "I love her unconditionally, and I make it a point to keep the lines of communication open between us so that she knows she can talk to me about anything." —Darren Sharper, New Orleans Saints
- "Leaders have to challenge the messages on TV and the music lyrics that use demeaning language to talk about women, . . . [who] should be treated and talked about with respect." —Chris Kelsay, Buffalo Bills
- "My job is to be there for her, to help guide her in the right direction, and to give her the confidence to know that she can do anything." —David Diehl, New York Giants
- "I want her to see in me a man of integrity who is loyal and loving, so that she knows what to expect from other men when she gets older. I want to protect her from anything and anybody who may hurt her." —DeMarcus Ware, Dallas Cowboys

If dads seem overprotective at times, it's because boys can be knuckleheads. And who knows better than men, who used to *be* boys? Ideally, fathers want their daughters to find a guy like Boaz, who honored, protected, and provided for Ruth with no romantic agenda. Or the patient, diligent Jacob, who was willing to labor fourteen years for the hand of Rachel. Then there's Joseph, the humble carpenter who stood beside Mary and raised God's Son. All of those men exemplify Paul's words in Ephesians 5:25. Young ladies need to guard their hearts and demand respect. Having high standards doesn't hurt.

DADDY-*Daughter Time*
Which of the players' statements stood out to you? Why? How did Jesus show uncommon respect to women? Tell your dad how you've seen him modeling these virtues. Dad, tell your daughter why she—as your child and a child of God—is worthy of deep love and respect.

WHAT'S THE WORD?
For husbands, this means love your wives, just as Christ loved the church. He gave up his life for her. EPHESIANS 5:25

November 30

WHAT are the odds of being hit by a rock from space? Well, if you consider that there are seven billion people in the world today, and there has been only one scientifically documented case of someone being hit by a meteorite in all of human history, you can probably rest easy. The one woman who didn't rest easy was thirty-four-year-old Elizabeth Hodges of Sylacauga, Alabama.

On this date in 1954, Mrs. Hodges was asleep on her living-room sofa when an eight-pound sulfide meteorite crashed through the ceiling, bounced off a console radio, and left a nasty bruise on her left hip (not to mention some emotional scars). But the good news is, she survived! Can you imagine how it must have felt to be the only one ever to be hit by space junk?

At times you may feel like the only person in the entire world hurting in a particular way or struggling with certain emotions. It's a very real, very intense situation. You're on a planet inhabited by seven billion people, yet you couldn't feel more alone. If you're working through a challenge like that, here are two things to keep in mind: Like Mrs. Hodges, you're going to make it. Also, Jesus genuinely understands. You see, while visiting earth, the Lord lost loved ones. He bore heavy burdens. He experienced excruciating physical pain and was tempted, misunderstood, and betrayed. He can relate to what you're going through.

Isaiah 53:3 tells of the grief and rejection Jesus would experience. If you ever feel alone staring down a fiery temptation, take comfort in Hebrews 4:15, which reminds us that Christ was tempted in every way, just as we are, but never sinned. That's right, Jesus lived a sinless life—another very exclusive club. Can you imagine how it must have felt to be the only one ever to have that unique experience?

DADDY-*Daughter Time*

When did it seem as if no one could relate to a trial you were facing? What role did God play? How might you help each other through similar challenges in the future? Several major meteor showers occur every year, including the Geminids, which generally peak in mid-December. Learn more and make plans to watch them together. Also, for an estimate of the world's population at any moment, visit census.gov and search "US & World Population Clock."

WHAT'S THE WORD?

He was despised and rejected—a man of sorrows, acquainted with deepest grief. We turned our backs on him and looked the other way. He was despised, and we did not care. ISAIAH 53:3

GET ON THE BUS

ONE day can change a life . . . and change history.

On the morning of December 1, 1955, Rosa Parks was a relatively unknown seamstress for a department store in Montgomery, Alabama. But that evening, Rosa did something that put her in the history books. She refused to give up her seat on a city bus. It was the custom in Montgomery that the first four rows of seats were reserved for white passengers. African American riders had to sit farther back. If the white section was filled and more white passengers got on the bus, the driver would ask black passengers to give up their seats and move to the back of the bus. After working all day, Rosa climbed on a bus and sat just behind a fully filled white section. When three more white passengers got on the bus, the driver asked Rosa and three other African Americans to move. Three moved, Rosa didn't. Her arrest and conviction sparked the Montgomery bus boycott, which brought national attention to the poor treatment of blacks in the southern United States.

The boycott lasted 382 days, and Rosa eventually won a Supreme Court decision that outlawed racial segregation on public transportation. Many experts look at this day as the beginning of the civil rights movement. When Rosa died in 2005, her casket was placed in the rotunda of the United States Capitol for two days—an honor normally reserved for presidents.

It's hard to imagine that in the middle of the twentieth century all Americans didn't enjoy equal rights. In God's eyes, we've been created equally for thousands of years. Galatians 3:28 (HCSB) says, "There is no Jew or Greek, slave or free, male or female; for you are all one in Christ Jesus."

Jesus is a uniter, not a divider. He doesn't see race, age, or gender. When we commit our lives to him, all God sees are his children.

DADDY-*Daughter Time*

Think about your friends. You probably know people with different backgrounds. How do you pick your friends? You probably want people who treat you nicely and are loyal and honest. Skin color doesn't matter. Dr. Martin Luther King Jr., who helped organize the Montgomery bus boycott, said in his famous "I Have a Dream" speech that he dreamed his children would not be "judged by the color of their skin but by the content of their character." Strive to live with high character that does not judge by skin color. And thank God that all people can come to him and find forgiveness.

WHAT'S THE WORD?

There is no Jew or Greek, slave or free, male or female; for you are all one in Christ Jesus. GALATIANS 3:28 (HCSB)

A CHILD IS BORN

THE world's population has surpassed seven billion. That's a lot of people. According to the United States Census Bureau, more than 350,000 people are born each day. If you do the math, that means 14,709 babies are born every hour, 245 babies come into the world every minute, and 4 arrive every second.

Can you count to four in just one second? Get a watch and try. *One, two, three, four!* Wow, that's fast.

But on December 2, 1952, TV producers were saying "three, two, one," as the first human birth was televised to the public. Records don't say how many people watched the first birth on KOA-TV in Denver, Colorado. It definitely wasn't billions. But God saw that birth—along with the billions that have happened since then.

It's hard to imagine that God sees everything and is intimately involved with every life, but that's the truth. God knew you and had a plan for your life even before you were born. In Jeremiah 1:5, the Lord spoke to the priest Jeremiah and said, "I knew you before I formed you in your mother's womb. Before you were born I set you apart and appointed you as my prophet to the nations." From before the time that Jeremiah was born, God knew he would use him to speak to the people. Jeremiah warned the people of Judah to repent of their wicked ways. They were following idols instead of God. They lived immorally instead of by God's laws. Jeremiah had a tough job, but God gave him the strength—and the words—to do it well.

DADDY-*Daughter Time*

Do you know what God is calling you to do? Chances are you know a basic direction, but not all the details. It takes faith to put one foot in front of the other to follow him. But you can be confident that God will equip you with the skills, talents, and courage to accomplish what he wants you to do.

Dad, go find some photos of your daughter when she was a baby. Look at them together. Tell your daughter about the day she was born. What do you remember? What were your dreams for her? What are your dreams for her now?

WHAT'S THE WORD?

I knew you before I formed you in your mother's womb. Before you were born I set you apart and appointed you as my prophet to the nations. JEREMIAH 1:5

WHAT GIVES?

THE teacher stood in front of the classroom and announced that the school's annual canned-food drive was about to begin.

"As you know, the needs are greater this year than any other," she said. "The food banks are really low, so I'm asking each one of you to bring in at least five items. And remember, if our class brings in the most food, we get an extra hour of recess."

Lindsay barely heard what the teacher was saying. *Wow, five cans of food,* she thought. *With my dad being laid off, I don't know if my family can spare that much.*

At the same time, Kayla thought to herself, *I love recess. I bet if I ask my mom really nicely, she'll let me bring in a whole bag of food!*

Two weeks later, Lindsay sneaked into the room and dropped three cans of food into the box. She had talked with her parents about what they could give, and they all agreed that they wanted to help as much as they could.

Later that day, Kayla's mom knocked on the classroom door. She burst in carrying two large shopping bags overflowing with cans.

The teacher stopped what she was doing and clapped with excitement. "Thank you, Kayla, for donating so much."

DADDY-*Daughter Time*

Who do you think gave more, Kayla or Lindsay?

God doesn't look at the size of the gift. He looks at the heart and motivation of the giver. In Luke 21:1-4, Jesus watched as people put their gifts into the offering box. At one point, a widow dropped in a couple of small coins and Jesus said, "I tell you the truth, this poor widow has given more than all the rest of them" (vv. 3-4).

The widow, like Lindsay, gave all she could. The rich people gave a greater amount, but they could afford to do it.

God uses people to give perfect gifts and provide for the needs of others. Whether it's your time, talents, or money, make yourself available to be used by God. You may end up giving the perfect gift to someone else.

WHAT'S THE WORD?

"I tell you the truth," Jesus said, "this poor widow has given more than all the rest of them. For they have given a tiny part of their surplus, but she, poor as she is, has given everything she has." LUKE 21:3-4

WHAT A TEAM!

DO you think Peter Pan could've defeated Captain Hook without Tinkerbell? Could Luke Skywalker have beaten the evil empire without Princess Leia? And do you think Frodo Baggins would've had a bunch of books and movies made about him without Samwise Gamgee? Frodo probably never would've made it to Mount Doom without his best friend and the others in his fellowship.

The fact is, people accomplish greater things and are more effective when they work as a team. Want to know why? God made us that way. We're designed for relationships—with God and with other people. We're created for community.

Jesus proved this when he came to the earth. He could've achieved his mission of dying for our sins to provide a way to heaven all by himself. But he chose twelve ordinary guys to travel and fellowship with him. Jesus used his time with the disciples to teach them about God's Kingdom and prepare them for when he would ascend back into heaven. They probably also created a lot of memories together: sharing dreams around the fire, discussing their families during a boat ride, helping each other in difficult situations, watching Jesus perform miracles.

In a lot of ways, Jesus and the disciples model the church. Many of today's churches strive to help people understand God's teachings, place members in areas where they can serve, and provide a place where they can fellowship with other believers. Hebrews 10:25 says, "Let us not neglect our meeting together, as some people do, but encourage one another." When followers of Jesus join together in a church, we can accomplish more by using our collective strength—and we will grow closer to him individually, as well.

DADDY-*Daughter Time*

What are your favorite parts of going to church? Do you like the worship? Is it fun to see your friends? Do you have a really good teacher? Write down the top three things you enjoy about your church:

Daughter	Dad
_____	_____
_____	_____
_____	_____

Every week, encourage each other to go to church and build deep relationships. After all, even the Lone Ranger needed Tonto to make him great. (Ask your dad about that one.)

WHAT'S THE WORD?

Let us not neglect our meeting together, as some people do, but encourage one another, especially now that the day of his return is drawing near. HEBREWS 10:25

ALL THAT GLITTERS . . .

PLINY the Younger (don't you just love the name *Pliny*?) was born forty years after Jesus' death and resurrection. This Roman senator said many wise things, but maybe the wisest words to come out of his mouth were "an object in possession seldom retains the same charm that it had in pursuit."

Do you get what he's saying? The anticipation of owning something is often better than actually possessing it. Have you ever acquired something that you really, really, really wanted and then felt let down? The smartphone isn't really that intelligent. The dress you thought would be supercute ends up puckering in a weird place. The iPad you saved to buy doesn't feel that cool once you hold it in your hands.

We've all felt that before. The "thing" doesn't make us happy and improve our lives. As you get older, you'll discover more and more that possessions don't bring happiness. A lot of people try to jam a lot of stuff in the hole in their lives that can be filled only by God.

In the book of Haggai, the prophet walked up to the governor and high priest and called them out on their wrong motivations. The Lord had seen that the people were more concerned about living in big houses than building a temple for him. As a result of their actions, Haggai said to them, "You eat but are not satisfied. You drink but are still thirsty. You put on clothes but cannot keep warm. Your wages disappear as though you were putting them in pockets filled with holes!" (1:6).

Only God satisfies. Only God can totally quench. God can bless you and stretch your resources further than you thought possible, and he can take away great riches in a blink of an eye.

DADDY-*Daughter Time*

It's easy to get caught in the trap of materialism, especially this time of year when you're making out a list of gifts you want for Christmas. But when we put "stuff" over God, we find only disappointment. Share a time in your life with each other when you really wanted something and eventually got it. Did it live up to your expectations? Did you stay satisfied? Chances are, the glitter of the object eventually wore off.

Our relationship with Christ never gets dull. There's always something new to learn about him. And when we get closer to God, we'll be truly satisfied.

WHAT'S THE WORD?

You eat but are not satisfied. You drink but are still thirsty. You put on clothes but cannot keep warm. Your wages disappear as though you were putting them in pockets filled with holes! HAGGAI 1:6

MIND YOUR MANNERS

HOW good are your manners? Take this quiz to find out.

   1. A woman with her arms full of packages is walking out of the mall, so you
   a. hold the door open for her.
   b. zip around her to get into the stores faster.
   c. think, *Boy, are her kids lucky.*

   2. There's only one Christmas cookie left, and it's your brother's favorite. You
   a. grab the last cookie before anyone notices.
   b. cut the cookie in half.
   c. decide to eat a piece of chocolate instead.

   3. Your mom asks for the salt at the dinner table, so you
   a. say, "Can't you reach it?"
   b. hand her the salt.
   c. hand her the salt and the pepper.

   4. You're in the room when a family friend who's a single mom says she's
      having difficulty finding time to buy her kids presents. You
   a. pop in your earbuds and pretend not to hear.
   b. offer to babysit her kids for free, so she can get gifts.
   c. say, "I babysit and only charge nine dollars an hour."

     Now check your answers. Number one is easy—it's *a*. The answer to questions two and three is *c*. (Manners experts say to always hand the salt *and* pepper when either is asked for.) Finally, go with *b* for question four. How'd you do?

     The holidays are supposed to be a time of joy, peace, and happiness. But those often aren't the character qualities many people display. Instead, some people come off as rude, selfish, and greedy. The Bible has simple advice when it comes to manners. Jesus says, "Treat others just as you want to be treated" (Luke 6:31, CEV). Try not to get caught up in the busyness of the holidays. Treat people with kindness.

DADDY-*Daughter Time*

Come up with a plan to help your mom during the holidays. Dads, maybe you could hang up Christmas lights, unload the dishwasher, or help with baking cookies. Daughters, you could watch your younger siblings or address Christmas cards. And be sure to always use your best manners, even when the people around you may get rude.

WHAT'S THE WORD?

Treat others just as you want to be treated.   LUKE 6:31 (CEV)

UNDER ATTACK

THE morning of December 7, 1941, started out normally for the nurses stationed at Pearl Harbor on the Hawaiian island of Oahu. Nurse Ruth Erickson had worked from 3 p.m. to 10 p.m. the previous evening and was enjoying a late breakfast. Then she heard them—hundreds of low-flying planes. Ruth ran outside to check what was happening when a plane flew right overhead with an image of the rising sun under its wing. Pearl Harbor was being attacked by the Japanese!

More than 2,400 Americans died that morning as the United States was drawn into World War II. An additional 1,200 people were wounded. The casualties could have been higher if not for the efforts of more than one hundred brave nurses. Military and civilian doctors and nurses worked nearly twenty-four straight hours treating the injured in the aftermath of the attack. Ruth Erickson was one of those heroic nurses. Chief nurse Annie G. Fox was another, and she received a Purple Heart (given to those wounded or killed in military service) and Bronze Star (awarded for bravery). Many more nurses would receive medals during the war. Although no nurses died on this day in 1941, more than two hundred died during World War II.

Jesus tells his followers that "no one has greater love than this, that someone would lay down his life for his friends" (John 15:13, HCSB). Thousands of servicemen laid down their lives for their country during the war. And as we get closer to Christmas, we can't help but remember that Jesus gave his life for us. That's a huge sacrifice and a ginormous display of love. You may never be asked to give your life for your friends, but you can show your love for your friends by serving them—just like the nurses did for people at Pearl Harbor.

DADDY-*Daughter Time*

Military families sacrifice a lot for their nation. Even during recent years, many military personnel have laid down their lives for their country. Do you know anybody in the military? Maybe you know a family who won't be together at Christmas because somebody is serving overseas. During this Christmas season, decide to do something kind for a military family. You can bake cookies, buy presents, or even make a thank-you card. Websites exist that allow you to send a care package or Bible to someone in the military.

Take time right now to pray for God's protection over military families. Thank Jesus that he laid down his life for you.

WHAT'S THE WORD?

No one has greater love than this, that someone would lay down his life for his friends.
JOHN 15:13 (HCSB)

BRAY FOR JESUS

WHAT sound does a camel make? Experts at San Diego Zoo say camels make a variety of sounds, including high-pitched bleats, loud bellows, a sort of roar, and a moaning-groaning sound. Camels can also create a low-pitched *nuuuurrrr* sound. Some people have heard these "ships of the desert" make a braying noise.

A youth choir at a Springfield, Oregon, church doesn't make braying noises at all. Instead it creates beautiful harmonies every holiday season by hosting a concert to help raise money for charity. Over the years, this choir has collected donations to send soccer balls to orphans in Mexico. They've also helped stock their local food bank with canned goods and sent blankets to refugees in Sudan. But several years ago, the choir members decided to buy a camel for a poor family in the Middle East. Camels come in really handy in hot, arid climates. They can haul supplies, carry people, even provide wool, milk, meat, and leather. The Oregon choir had just one problem: buying a camel cost more than $500.

Choir members sacrificed by bringing in their allowances, washing cars, and doing yard work. Pretty soon they'd collected $520! When the larger church body learned about the project, it got excited, too, and donated that same amount. So instead of one camel, the church sent more than $1,000 to World Vision to purchase two camels for needy families who might not know about Jesus.

The kids in the choir did everything they could to help families in need. In 1 Chronicles 16:9, David says to "sing to [the Lord]; yes, sing his praises. Tell everyone about his wonderful deeds." That's exactly what the members of the youth choir did. They sang, and they spread God's Good News to a part of the world that needs to hear about Jesus' wonderful deeds.

DADDY-*Daughter Time*

Think of Christmas carols that tell about God's wonderful deeds. "Santa Claus Is Coming to Town" doesn't work. But songs such as "Away in a Manger" and "Hark! The Herald Angels Sing" could be good choices. Write down a few more:

_____

_____

_____

If you know the words, sing a couple of those carols together. You can also find the lyrics or cool Christmas carol videos on the Internet. And if you want to help needy families around the world, look at websites for World Vision, Compassion International, or Heifer International. Many good organizations exist to help families at Christmas and all year round.

WHAT'S THE WORD?

Sing to [the Lord]; yes, sing his praises. Tell everyone about his wonderful deeds.
1 CHRONICLES 16:9

COMPUTER CREATOR

HAS your family's computer ever gotten a bug? Maybe some files were wiped out by a virus, or it just started to run slowly and mess up. Well, more than sixty years ago, Grace Murray Hopper's computer had a bug—literally.

Grace, who was a rear admiral in the US Navy, was a computer pioneer. In 1944, she became the first programmer of the Mark I computer. But don't picture a sleek laptop. The Mark I stretched fifty-one feet long, eight feet high, and eight feet wide—sort of like a doubly long semitrailer. Despite its huge size, the computer could store just seventy-two words and perform three additions every second. (Modern processors can do millions of additions per second.) Grace worked on subsequent Mark II and Mark III computers. Plus, she designed the first large-scale computer called the UNIVAC I, and she coinvented the COBOL language that allowed computers to respond to letters and not just numbers.

It was Grace who experienced the first computer bug. The Mark II kept getting errors as it tried to process a command. Grace carefully checked everything and discovered that a moth had been trapped inside the giant computer. She removed the bug and everything worked perfectly. Computer errors are still called "bugs," thanks to Grace.

Rear Admiral Grace Murray Hopper had an amazing work ethic. She went to the best colleges and worked with the most cutting-edge technology. God wants you to have a similar work ethic with the skills and talents he's given you. Colossians 3:23 (NIV) says, "Whatever you do, work at it with all your heart, as working for the Lord, not for men." You may not become a famous computer programmer (then again, you might), but you should always put your heart into everything you do.

DADDY-*Daughter Time*

Go to your family's computer. It doesn't fill a whole room, does it? Think about how far technology has come in the last seventy years. If you have time, play a short game against the computer. Computers are pretty smart now, huh?

Thank God for the creativity he gives engineers and that he shows in his creation. Pray and tell him you're going to work at everything you do for his glory.

WHAT'S THE WORD?

Whatever you do, work at it with all your heart, as working for the Lord, not for men. COLOSSIANS 3:23 (NIV)

MINT QUALITY

WHAT flavor comes to mind when you think about Christmas? Sure, there are the flavors of Christmas dinner—turkey, stuffing, cranberries, and potatoes. But if one flavor truly feels like Christmas, it has to be mint. Just the scent of mint refreshes, like a crisp winter morning. And, of course, mint makes us think of candy canes, a uniquely Christmas candy. Statistics say that more than 1.7 billion candy canes are produced each Christmas. That's enough candy canes for every man, woman, and child in the United States to enjoy five-and-a-half of them this holiday season.

Many legends surround the candy cane. Hard, sugary candies cropped up around Christmas in the 1600s. But the candy cane didn't get its unique shape until much later. The most popular story of the candy cane says an Indiana candy maker added peppermint oil to the candy in 1870. Then he formed them into the letter *J* to represent Jesus. Flipped around, a candy cane looks like a shepherd's staff in honor of Jesus, our Good Shepherd. Before this time, candy canes had been generally white, so the candy maker added red stripes as a symbol of Christ's blood. The thickest stripe symbolizes the blood Jesus shed on the cross to pay for our sins. As it says in Isaiah 53:5, "He was wounded for our transgressions . . . by His stripes we are healed" (NKJV).

DADDY-*Daughter Time*

When something is "mint quality," it's perfect; it doesn't have any blemishes. That's exactly what Jesus was. He never sinned. He was the perfect Lamb of God, sacrificed for our sins.

If you don't have any candy canes in your house, go out and buy some to hang on the tree. A candy cane may look simple, but its design contains so much meaning. Enjoy a couple of candy canes together. When you taste the minty flavor, think about Jesus being mint quality. When you look at the white of the candy cane, remember that he was sinless. And when you see the candy cane's stripes, thank God that by Jesus' stripes we are healed.

WHAT'S THE WORD?

He was wounded for our transgressions, He was bruised for our iniquities; the chastisement for our peace was upon Him, and by His stripes we are healed. ISAIAH 53:5 (NKJV)

FORGIVENESS IS
A DECISION

FORGIVENESS can be a four-letter word: H-A-R-D. It's also G-O-O-D. Not only does God command us to forgive people who wrong us, but forgiveness actually has health benefits. Researchers have studied the effects of forgiving others versus holding on to grudges. Growing evidence shows grudge holders have numerous long-term health problems. On the other hand, people who embrace forgiveness enjoy

- lower blood pressure and heart rate;
- less hostility and stress;
- more friendships;
- healthier relationships;
- greater spiritual well-being.

Who doesn't want more friends, less stress, fewer angry outbursts, and a healthy heart? Forgiveness is key to all of those. Plus, being forgiven feels great. Knowing that the God of the universe sees us as holy and righteous allows us to live free. But as we enjoy that freedom in Christ, we should also follow his example. When Jesus taught the disciples how to pray, he included the words "forgive us our sins, as we forgive those who sin against us" (Luke 11:4). Jesus wants us to act like him by forgiving "those who sin against us."

The word *those* can be a tricky one. In the original Greek, *those* means "everyone" (okay, maybe that's a loose translation). But God wants us to forgive everyone, even people we don't like. We should forgive those who do mean things to us over and over again. We also need to forgive our sister for borrowing our sweater without asking. God never said forgiveness would be easy, and often we can't forgive with our own strength.

At times when the hurt is too deep to let it go on your own, ask for supernatural help from God's Holy Spirit. Follow God's example of forgiveness as you forgive others. When God forgives, he doesn't bring up past sins when we mess up again. You'll know God is helping you truly forgive when you feel the hostility and bitterness you have toward a person replaced with feelings of compassion and peace. And that's a much healthier way to live.

DADDY-*Daughter Time*

Are you holding on to a grudge? You don't have to go into much detail, but share a time with each other when it was hard to forgive. How did you get through that time? Pray about those situations and thank God for giving you the strength to show forgiveness. Jesus knew what he was talking about when he said to forgive . . . so follow his advice.

WHAT'S THE WORD?

Forgive us our sins, as we forgive those who sin against us.   LUKE 11:4

QUEEN OF MEAN

WOULD you like to be known as the "Queen of Mean"? That's a nickname to steer away from, right? But in the late 1980s, newspapers in New York City gave that title to Leona Helmsley. Leona and her husband, Harry, owned billions of dollars of property—including the Empire State Building, apartment buildings, and twenty-three luxury hotels around the United States. The couple lived in an amazing penthouse apartment that overlooked Central Park, and they bought an $11 million mansion in Connecticut to use as a weekend retreat.

But all that money and high living didn't make Leona a nice person. People who worked for her said she was a tyrant. Stories surfaced that she screamed mean things at workers, fired people for little mistakes, and didn't pay bills on time. Then in 1988, the Helmsleys and two of their associates were indicted on tax evasion charges. Harry's health was declining, so Leona faced the court hearing alone. During the trial, one former employee said she heard Leona say, "We don't pay taxes. Only the little people pay taxes." Leona denied saying this, but those words stuck with her. On this date in 1989, Leona was sentenced to a four-year prison term, 750 hours of community service, and $7.1 million of tax-fraud fines.

In the Bible, the Pharisees tried to trick Jesus into saying something negative about paying taxes to the government (see Mark 12:13-17). But Jesus followed the law. He looked at a silver coin and asked whose picture was on it. The people said, "Caesar's." So Jesus replied, "Give to Caesar what belongs to Caesar, and give to God what belongs to God" (v. 17). God expects us to live by the government's rules. As Christians, we're not above the law; we should follow the law.

DADDY-*Daughter Time*

We may not understand the reasons behind all government laws, but God wants us to follow them anyway (see Romans 13:1). Pray and thank God for your government officials. Ask him to give wisdom to people in the government to do the right things and follow biblical principles.

Then talk about how you should treat other people. You definitely don't want to earn the nickname "Queen of Mean." By the way, after Leona got out of federal prison, she became more charitable. She donated $5 million to help families of New York firefighters after the 9/11 attacks. When she died in 2007, she gave most of her wealth—over $4 billion—to her charitable trust to benefit animals and other people.

WHAT'S THE WORD?

"Well, then," Jesus said, "give to Caesar what belongs to Caesar, and give to God what belongs to God." MARK 12:17

SECRET SANTA

ARE you a secret Santa at school? Some dads take part in secret Santa gift exchanges at work. The idea is to do something nice for somebody—usually in the form of little gifts—in the weeks leading up to Christmas. But for more than twenty-five years, Larry Stewart was Kansas City's secret Santa all year round.

For a quarter of a century, Larry quietly handed out one-hundred-dollar bills to people who looked like they needed it. He would visit Laundromats, diners, bus stations, homeless shelters, and thrift stores. When he saw someone who he felt needed a pick-me-up, he'd walk up, hand over one hundred dollars, and say, "Merry Christmas." Larry gave away money all year, but said giving at Christmas brought him the most joy. In all, Larry gave away more than $1.3 million.

Larry died in 2007, but his spirit of generosity lived on. Larry dreamed of every city having a secret Santa. And a new secret Santa took his place in Kansas City. Larry hadn't always had a lot of money. He grew up poor and failed in a couple of jobs. Once he earned his millions, he knew he wanted to give them away and help people.

The Bible talks a lot about helping the less fortunate. But God doesn't guilt people into giving money. "Don't give reluctantly or in response to pressure, 'For God loves a person who gives cheerfully,'" writes the apostle Paul in 2 Corinthians 9:7. And nobody gave more cheerfully than Kansas City's secret Santa.

DADDY-*Daughter Time*

You can be a secret Santa to the people in your life. Do you know a family who needs some encouragement this Christmas? Your church may have a list of people who need extra help during the holidays. See if you can do something anonymously to help them. Maybe you can bring a bag of groceries and homemade cookies to somebody's doorstep, ring the doorbell, and run away. Part of being a secret Santa is that nobody knows who you are. Larry never gave away his identity as secret Santa of Kansas City until shortly before he died. For him the joy came in the giving . . . not in being famous.

WHAT'S THE WORD?

You must each decide in your heart how much to give. And don't give reluctantly or in response to pressure. "For God loves a person who gives cheerfully."
2 CORINTHIANS 9:7

LOVING CORRECTION

WHEN you think about it, parents have a piece of advice for just about every situation.

- "Don't run with scissors."
- "Look both ways before crossing the street."
- "Put on a coat before you catch your death of cold."
- "If all your friends jumped off a cliff, would you jump too?"
- "Be good or Santa won't bring you any presents."
- "A penny saved is a penny earned."

(Okay, that last one came from Benjamin Franklin.)

As ridiculous as some of that advice sounds, parents have been quoting those statements for generations in an attempt to protect their children from life's pitfalls. Do you know why? Because parents love their kids. (No surprise, right?) That love makes parents want to keep their kids safe, hence the reason for most of the strange things that come out of their mouths. If you think about it, parents give nearly all of their advice to help their children avoid pain.

Sure, growing up requires a bit of pain. There will be broken friendships, possibly broken bones, broken hearts, and occasional bumps in the road. And when children ignore their parents' advice, they're bound to face some discipline. Like it says in Proverbs 3:12, "The LORD corrects those he loves, just as a father corrects a child in whom he delights."

So fathers, remember to discipline your daughter in a loving spirit with the Lord as your example. And daughters, remember that when you receive punishment, it's because your parents love you and want the best for you.

That's good advice, and so is this: "If you keep crossing your eyes, they're going to stick that way."

DADDY-*Daughter Time*

Fathers, take a few minutes to share some words of wisdom that your dad told you. Maybe it's something funny or something that meant a lot and helped you become the man you are today. Is there something your dad told you that you can pass along to your daughter to keep her safe?

Daughters, can you remember something your mom or dad told you that really helped you through a situation? What was it?

Can either of you cross your eyes? Try it. Then give each other a hug and promise to show each other love when you're giving—or receiving—correction.

WHAT'S THE WORD?

The LORD corrects those he loves, just as a father corrects a child in whom he delights.
PROVERBS 3:12

BUDDY the elf in the movie *Elf* knew something about Christmas. After all, he grew up at the North Pole. In the movie, Buddy says, "The best way to spread Christmas cheer is singing loud for all to hear."

That may be true. But another good way to spread Christmas cheer is with a good joke. Try out some of these:

Q: What is a rooster's favorite Christmas carol?
A: "God Rest Ye Merry Gentle Hen."

Q: What does Mr. Claus use to wash his hands?
A: Santa-tizer.

Q: What famous singer lives at the North Pole?
A: Elfish.

Q: Why did Joseph and Mary sleep in the *O*?
A: There was no room at the *N*.

Q: What food do angels like best?
A: Peas on Earth.

Q: Why do shepherds always know the correct time?
A: They keep *watch* over their flocks.

Are you rolling around in laughter? Probably not. But hopefully you chuckled a little. Laughter is good for you. Studies show you can burn over one hundred calories an hour by laughing. That's about the same number of calories you'd burn walking for sixty minutes. And which sounds like more fun, walking or laughing?

Plus, laughing makes you feel good. The holidays can be a difficult time for some people. The stress of extra expenses can weigh heavily. And those who have lost a loved one during the year will miss them even more at Christmas.

So when you see someone down in the dumps this time of year, spread a little cheer by singing loudly . . . or telling a good joke.

DADDY-*Daughter Time*

During the Old Testament days, King Solomon was considered one of the wisest men in the world. In Proverbs 17:22, he wrote, "A cheerful heart is good medicine, but a broken spirit saps a person's strength." When you're sad, your whole body can feel rotten. Sometimes it's even hard to get out of bed. But when you're laughing and cheerful, everything can feel right with the world. Be a lighthearted light for Jesus this holiday by spreading Christmas cheer.

Before you go to bed tonight, spread a little cheer in your own family by telling each other your favorite jokes. Laughter is a good thing and draws people together.

WHAT'S THE WORD?

A cheerful heart is good medicine, but a broken spirit saps a person's strength.
PROVERBS 17:22

A GOOD REPORT

IF you haven't received your report card yet, you soon will. Do you look forward to seeing your grades, or is it a little scary? If A is the most common letter in your report card, you probably can't wait for your parents to see it. If your grades are in the C or D range, you might hope it gets lost in the mail.

Have you ever thought about what a report card represents? Basically, it's a reflection of your work at school. Teachers give you a grade based on set standards. If you exceed expectations, you might receive an A. If you need improvement, you could get a D.

Aren't you glad God doesn't look at you this way? He's not in heaven grading each one of our thoughts and actions. Sure, he knows everything we do and say. But he doesn't look at us and give us a grade with all the A-students earning the right to go to heaven and the F-students (well, you know where they'd go). The fact is we could never do enough to earn our way into God's presence. God is perfect and holy. If we sin just once (and we all sin a lot more than that), then we could never get into heaven on our own merits.

The good news is we don't have to be perfect, because we have a perfect Savior. Jesus lived a sinless life and died in our place so we could be seen as sinless in God's eyes. The apostle Paul describes it well in 2 Corinthians 5:21: "God made Christ, who never sinned, to be the offering for our sin, so that we could be made right with God through Christ." If you want to put a big word on this concept, it's called justification. Our report card doesn't earn us a spot in heaven, just like being a good volleyball player or helping the homeless won't earn God's adulation. But when we ask Jesus to be our Savior, he justifies us in God's eyes. And that's better than any straight-A report card.

DADDY-*Daughter Time*

To better understand justification, watch the movie *The Chronicles of Narnia: The Lion, the Witch and the Wardrobe.* Pay particular attention to the scene where Aslan lays down his life. Why did the mighty lion give himself up so willingly? Turn to the Father-Daughter Movie Nights appendix and look at the questions for that movie. Aren't you glad you live in a world where it's not always winter and Christmas comes every year?

WHAT'S THE WORD?

God made Christ, who never sinned, to be the offering for our sin, so that we could be made right with God through Christ. 2 CORINTHIANS 5:21

TAKE FLIGHT

TODAY, nobody thinks twice about jumping on a plane and flying across the country . . . or around the world. But for thousands of years, people just looked up and dreamed of flying like the birds. Even just over a hundred years ago nobody could have imagined what it felt like to fly.

The dream of flight started to take shape on this day in 1903 when Orville and Wilbur Wright successfully tested a self-propelled aircraft. You've probably seen photos of the fragile-looking gas-powered biplane on the sand dunes near Kitty Hawk, North Carolina. Before this time, engineers had designed gliders to soar through the air. But the Wright brothers' plane was propeller driven. Although the flight lasted just twelve seconds and covered only 120 feet, it opened the door to future developments and let the world know that it was possible to create flight.

Orville and Wilbur were an interesting pair. They built printing presses and owned a bicycle shop. Because they made enough money with these endeavors, they had the resources to pursue their dream of building an airplane. In 1901, the Wright brothers experimented with almost two hundred different designs for wings and airplane frames. In 1902, they flew a glider with a rudder that allowed them to steer it. Then in 1903, all their hard work paid off.

During their hundreds of experiments and years of tests, the Wright brothers probably got tired. But in the end, they soared like eagles. In the Bible, God promises his followers that they will fly too. "Those who trust in the LORD will find new strength. They will soar high on wings like eagles. They will run and not grow weary. They will walk and not faint" (Isaiah 40:31).

Isn't that awesome? As Christians, we can be confident that when we trust in the Lord, he gives us strength—strength enough to soar!

DADDY-*Daughter Time*

Gather a bunch of paper and have a paper-airplane-flying contest. Experiment with different designs. You can find fun ideas on the Internet. Fly them down the stairs or across the room. You can also take out markers and stickers to decorate your planes. Give awards to the airplane with the best design, longest flight, and craziest twists.

After your flying contest, thank God for giving you strength. Even when you're tired, God can give you strength that you didn't know you possessed and help you fly like an eagle.

WHAT'S THE WORD?

Those who trust in the LORD will find new strength. They will soar high on wings like eagles. They will run and not grow weary. They will walk and not faint.
ISAIAH 40:31

POWER IN THE NAME

WHAT are the most popular names in your school or youth group? For boys it might be Jacob, Ethan, or Matthew. You probably also know a lot of Sarahs, Madisons, and Emmas.

What's your name? Do you know what it means? You're probably known by a lot of other names, too: student, daughter, sister, young lady, Christian, friend, musician, athlete. Dads may be known as provider, friend, coworker, or husband. But your list of names is nothing compared to Jesus Christ's. Scholars have uncovered more than seven hundred titles or names for Jesus in the Bible. All of them reveal a different aspect of his character. Even the name *Jesus* has special meaning. When Mary was pregnant, an angel of the Lord appeared to Joseph in a dream and told him that Mary "will have a son, and you are to name him Jesus, for he will save his people from their sins" (Matthew 1:21). The name Jesus literally means "Jehovah is salvation."

Sending Jesus to earth was God's plan to save a sinful people once and for all. But saving us wasn't easy. During the joy of Christmas, we shouldn't forget the sacrifice of Easter. After all, Jesus came in order to be the Lamb of God (see John 1:29). He died and rose again so we could be forgiven. He is our Redemption (see 1 Corinthians 1:30, NIV). He is the Way (see John 14:6) to heaven. By eating of the Bread of Life (see John 6:35), we will live forever. We can trust the Good Shepherd (see John 10:11) to lead us and protect our families. While we may struggle to live up to our various names, the Rock (see 1 Corinthians 10:4) never comes up short.

DADDY-*Daughter Time*

Jesus certainly lived up to his name . . . uh, make that names. Which one of Jesus' names has special meaning to you? If you want more names to choose from, check out

- Isaiah 9:6,
- Matthew 1:23,
- Revelation 1:8, and
- John 15:5.

Can you think of ways that Jesus embodies each of his names? Thank God that there's power in his names.

WHAT'S THE WORD?

She will have a son, and you are to name him Jesus, for he will save his people from their sins. MATTHEW 1:21

THE church leader had a problem. Too many people were focused on gift giving at Christmas, instead of on the awesome miracle of Jesus Christ's birth. What could he do? Instead of laying on a guilt trip with a convicting sermon, this wise man of God decided to bring the Christmas story to life. He asked a few friends to dress up like Joseph, Mary, and the shepherds. He gathered some farm animals, found a small cave, and brought in some hay. Then he staged Jesus' birth scene and invited people to view the "living nativity."

Sounds like the obvious solution, right? But consider this: it happened nearly eight hundred years ago!

St. Francis of Assisi created the first living nativity in 1223 in Greccio, Italy. Using the Bible as a blueprint, he re-created the manger scene in a small cave and used a doll for baby Jesus. As it says in Luke 2:16, the shepherds "hurried to the village and found Mary and Joseph. And there was the baby, lying in the manger." When people saw the simplicity of how Christ came to earth, they were reminded of God's great sacrifice.

Less than one hundred years later, nearly every church had a nativity scene at Christmastime. Soon after that statues replaced the human actors, with the scenes becoming more elaborate and decorative. Over the years, nativity scenes have come in a variety of sizes and been made from a number of different materials. But these visual reminders help us all focus on the true meaning of Christmas.

DADDY-*Daughter Time*

Go look at Christmas lights as a family. You can often find displays close to you by typing "Best Christmas lights in [fill in your city]" in an Internet search. As you drive around to look at different homes, count the number of nativity scenes that you see. You can also search for "living nativity" scenes in your area and visit those displays. If your church does a living nativity, maybe you could volunteer to take part in some way. By focusing on the nativity and baby Jesus, you'll be able to get back to the true meaning of Christmas.

WHAT'S THE WORD?

They hurried to the village and found Mary and Joseph. And there was the baby, lying in the manger. After seeing him, the shepherds told everyone what had happened and what the angel had said to them about this child.   LUKE 2:16-17

PERFECT BABY

BABIES cry.

It's a fact. Don't believe it? Just ask your dad if you cried when you were a baby. (He probably cried *waaaay* back when he was a baby too.) Doctors say most newborns cry for one and a half hours a day. At six weeks old, it's normal for a baby to cry three hours per day. And babies will cry for any number of reasons. They're hungry. They need a diaper change. They're overtired. They're bored. They're overstimulated. They're teething. They're sick. *Yikes!*

With that in mind, has it ever bothered you to sing the popular Christmas carol "Away in a Manger"? You know the line: "The cattle are lowing, the poor Baby wakes, but little Lord Jesus, no crying He makes."

Really? No crying? But Jesus was fully God *and* fully human. Certainly, a baby who's wrapped in strips of cloth, lying in a food trough, and surrounded by smelly farm animals would be crying.

The truth is some people are uncomfortable thinking about the God of the universe crying . . . or getting his diaper changed. But instead of ignoring the human side of Jesus, we should appreciate it. By coming to earth as a baby and growing into an adult, God's Son knows all the hardships of being human. Jesus understands how it feels to cry, to get zits, or to hurt when friends let you down.

Jesus is the King of kings. He could've been born in a palace surrounded by a host of angels, but God chose that he would be "wrapped snugly in strips of cloth, lying in a manger" (Luke 2:12). Jesus can relate to us more—and us to him—because he came to the earth as a baby. Now that's something to sing about!

DADDY-*Daughter Time*

A lot of families go to church only at Christmas. These families may not know Jesus as their Savior. They simply visit a church this time of year because everybody else does, so a lot of church nurseries are more busy now than ever.

As a way to serve those families, ask your church if it could use some extra help in the nursery on Christmas Eve. By volunteering to be with the children, you might help somebody be introduced to Jesus Christ for the first time. Plus, you could find out firsthand that babies *do* cry.

WHAT'S THE WORD?

You will recognize him by this sign: You will find a baby wrapped snugly in strips of cloth, lying in a manger.   LUKE 2:12

DREAMING OF
A SNOWY BIRTHDAY

DO you know someone who has a birthday that's close to Christmas? Some people love getting to celebrate their birthday during a time when we honor Jesus' birth. Others don't like it because they feel their birthdays are overshadowed by Christmas festivities.

Alicia loved her December 21 birthday. When she was little, she thought her birthday meant two things: snow and Christmas. Before she totally understood calendars, Alicia would look out the window, see an early snowfall, and exclaim with glee, "It's snowing! It's Christmas. It's my birthday!" She truly dreamed of a white Christmas and a snowy birthday every year.

Many people dream of a "White Christmas," thanks to the popular Irving Berlin song. After Bing Crosby sang it, it became the bestselling single of all time—topping 50 million copies in sales. "White Christmas" is also the most recorded Christmas song, with more than five hundred versions in numerous languages. Deep inside, we *all* must long for glistening treetops.

As Christians we can live with that same longing, watching, and anticipation of celebrating Jesus throughout the year. Plus, we have eternity with the Lord to look forward to with excitement. The Bible says the Lord Jesus will come again to take his people home to heaven. We don't know the day or the hour it will happen (Matthew 24:36), but it's surely something we can hope for!

So while Alicia continues to dream of a white Christmas and snowy birthday, we can look forward to a time of eternal love and joy with Jesus and other believers. Like it says in 2 Timothy 4:8, Jesus will give us a crown when he comes back, "and the prize is   for all who eagerly look forward to his appearing."

DADDY-*Daughter Time*

Discuss what you've learned through God's Word about eternal life. It's hard to imagine what it will be like, but God does offer some great clues. If you're really interested, look for a good book with your dad about heaven.

If you know some people who have a birthday near Christmas, figure out something special you can do for them. Even in the busyness of the season, they need to know they're celebrated and not forgotten.

WHAT'S THE WORD?

I have fought the good fight, I have finished the race, and I have remained faithful. And now the prize awaits me—the crown of righteousness, which the Lord, the righteous Judge, will give me on the day of his return. And the prize is not just for me but for all who eagerly look forward to his appearing. 2 TIMOTHY 4:7-8

CRAVING BRAVERY

WHAT comes to mind when you think of the word *bravery*? Maybe you picture an ol' cowboy walking into the middle of a dusty street to defend his town against Black Bart's gang. Or maybe it's a soldier who risks his life by running into enemy fire to save a friend. Hollywood idolizes the hero who comes to the rescue.

But what about the girl who stands up in class and says she believes in Jesus Christ when the teacher claims the Bible is just a bunch of fairy tales? Is she brave? Or how about the girl who refuses to make fun of the new student when everybody else is doing it? Is that bravery?

Bravery is a difficult concept to fully grasp. Some people think it's not being afraid of anything. Others might say being brave means facing and overcoming your fears. But the girl who stands up for her beliefs and does the right thing—even when it's not popular—also shows bravery.

You don't have to run into a burning building to prove your courage. God created you to be brave. The apostle Paul encourages you to "be alert, stand firm in the faith, act like a man, be strong" (1 Corinthians 16:13, HCSB). Bravery means standing up for God in a culture that puts him down. It means being a leader among your friends. It means being aware of what's going on in your life and around you—and then stepping out to solve problems and live for God. By being brave in this way, you'll make God's day.

DADDY-*Daughter Time*

In 1967, the government of Canada created three official Bravery Decorations:

- The Cross of Valour is the highest civilian award for bravery.
- The Star of Courage is given to members of the military.
- The Medal of Bravery is awarded to any person who risks his or her life to save or protect Canadian interests. The recipient doesn't have to be Canadian, and the event doesn't have to take place in Canada.

Grab some paper, a pair of scissors, and some markers. Make each other official Decorations of Bravery. How does your father show courage? What actions show that your daughter is brave? Once you've created your honors, cut them out, then present them to each other in front of your family as you say how you see the other living out bravery.

WHAT'S THE WORD?

Be alert, stand firm in the faith, act like a man, be strong.   1 CORINTHIANS 16:13 (HCSB)

GIFT OF CHRISTMAS

IT'S not just kids who love Christmas. Pets love it too!

Dogs are barking happily about Jesus' birth, because studies show that 56 percent of them will receive a Christmas present. In fact, more than half of pet owners say they plan on buying their pet a present. Sadly, these same studies reveal that only 48 percent of cats are getting a gift. (Maybe our feline friends should be more grateful . . . they always act like they're *purrr*-fect.)

The truth is, for most people—and most pets—Christmas is all about presents. But looking back, the first Christmas had very little to do with giving gifts to each other and everything to do with God giving us a gift. God's Son, Jesus Christ, came to the earth as a baby so we could be forgiven our sins and live forever in heaven. As Romans 6:23 says, "The free gift of God is eternal life through Christ Jesus our Lord."

When we give presents at Christmas, it's a reflection of God's generous nature. Just as God showed his love by sending his Son, we show love to our family and friends when we give them gifts. This holiday season look for real ways to share the Good News of Jesus with others through your gifts.

DADDY-*Daughter Time*

Have you received God's ultimate gift of Jesus Christ? Have you prayed to ask Jesus to forgive your sins so you can live with him forever in heaven? Opening God's gift is the most important thing you can ever do.

If your immediate family already knows Jesus, can you think of an extended family member or friend who doesn't know God? Write his or her name here: _____. Talk it over as a family and decide if you want to use some of the money that'd normally be spent on presents to show this person the love of Jesus Christ. You could prepare a special meal or buy a little gift. And when you give it, let the person know that God loves him or her and wants to forgive his or her sins. That's the best gift anybody could receive this time of year.

WHAT'S THE WORD?

The wages of sin is death, but the free gift of God is eternal life through Christ Jesus our Lord.   ROMANS 6:23

FOLLOW THE WISE MEN

NO nativity scene is complete without them. But many experts agree that the wise men didn't see Jesus lying in the manger. By the time the wise men arrived in Bethlehem, Jesus may have been a toddler. He certainly wasn't staying in a stable anymore.

No matter when these robed visitors met the Christ child, we can learn a lot from their actions. They risked their lives on a long journey to bring treasures to the new King. And "they entered the house and saw the child with his mother, Mary, and they bowed down and worshiped him. Then they opened their treasure chests and gave him gifts of gold, frankincense, and myrrh" (Matthew 2:11).

Look closely at the wise men's gifts: gold, myrrh, and frankincense. By giving God our gold, we help fund his work. Monetary gifts to churches and various ministries help spread God's truth around the world. In Jesus' day myrrh was used to anoint the dead. Jesus came to give his life for us. How can we give our life to him? Maybe we can spread his love to our city or another country. Finally, frankincense was incense used for worship. God desires our worship at Christmas and throughout the year.

DADDY-*Daughter Time*

Christmas carols are fun songs to sing, but they can also be much more. You can worship God when you sing songs that celebrate Jesus' birth.

John H. Hopkins Jr. wrote "We Three Kings" as part of a Christmas pageant more than 150 years ago. His nieces and nephews performed in the show. Today, it's the best-known Christmas carol about the wise men:

> We three kings of Orient are;
> Bearing gifts we traverse afar,
> Field and fountain, moor and mountain,
> Following yonder star.

Go onto the Internet or pop in a CD and listen to this song. What are some other things you can learn from the wise men? Write them down:

1. _____
2. _____
3. _____

Not only should we be willing to risk everything for Jesus and fall to our knees in reverence to the one true God, but we should act like the magi when we give gifts to the King.

WHAT'S THE WORD?

They entered the house and saw the child with his mother, Mary, and they bowed down and worshiped him. Then they opened their treasure chests and gave him gifts of gold, frankincense, and myrrh. MATTHEW 2:11

YOU may have noticed that all of your friends don't believe the same things as you do about Jesus Christ. Some probably don't know who he is. Others might say Jesus did some cool things, but he wasn't God's Son.

Even back when Jesus walked the earth, many folks didn't know what to think about him. One day Jesus asked the disciples what people were saying. A lot of different ideas were floating around, but only one was true and Peter knew it. In Matthew 16:16, Peter said to Jesus, "You are the Messiah, the Son of the living God."

Those were powerful words. For hundreds of years, the Israelites had been waiting for the Messiah. Prophecies predicted intimate details of the Messiah's birth, life, and death. Jesus' life fulfilled more than three hundred prophecies written hundreds of years *before* his birth. Those details included where Jesus was born, the miracles he performed, and his rising from the dead after three days.

Two professors estimated the scientific probability of any one man in history fulfilling just eight of those prophecies. The chances were incredibly small. The professors found that the odds were one in 100 quadrillion! (That's one followed by seventeen zeros.)

A French mathematician went a step further by calculating the chances of a person fulfilling just forty of those prophecies and found the odds are one in octodecillion, or 1 in 1,000,000,000,000,000,000,000,000,000,000,000,000, 000,000,000,000,000,000. Wow, that's a big number!

In other words, there's just no way that someone could "accidentally" fulfill all those prophecies. Jesus defies the odds, so we don't have to feel odd when we say we're 100 percent sure that he's the Son of the living God. The numbers back us up

DADDY-*Daughter Time*

Take a few minutes to look up these verses and write down the prophecy that Jesus fulfilled:

- Isaiah 7:14 and Matthew 1:20-21 _____
- Isaiah 11:10 and Matthew 1:1-6 _____
- Micah 5:2 and Matthew 2:1 _____
- Isaiah 29:18 and Luke 7:21-22 _____

Now pray together and thank God for sending his Son so we could know him personally and be confident about spending eternity with God in heaven.

WHAT'S THE WORD?

Simon Peter answered, "You are the Messiah, the Son of the living God."
MATTHEW 16:16

December 26 THANKS FOR EVERYTHING

TWO heads are better than one, so put your minds together to answer this question: Which of the following is nearest in size to the three-car garages that are built in many homes today?

a. a Chick-fil-A restaurant
b. a basketball court
c. the average home in the 1950s
d. an Olympic-sized swimming pool

The answer is *c*. Today's three-car garages often reach 960 square feet. Homes in the 1950s averaged between 1,000 and 1,200 square feet.

Think about that fact. The same amount of space that we use to store our stuff (and maybe our cars . . . if there's room) was all a family needed to live in the middle of the last century. And here's another fact: according to research, more Americans identified themselves as "very happy" in 1957 than in 1987, 1997, and 2007. Obviously, bigger isn't better when it comes to creating happiness.

If we want to be truly happy, we have to look to God. The apostle Paul figured out that fact around two thousand years ago, and we can learn from his wisdom today. He writes, "I have learned how to be content with whatever I have. I know how to live on almost nothing or with everything" (Philippians 4:11-12).

DADDY-*Daughter Time*

What did you get for Christmas? Chances are you didn't get everything you wanted. And that's okay. Instead of wanting, dreaming, and desiring more, we should look around and be thankful for what we have. God promises many times in the Bible that he'll meet our needs—not necessarily our wants.

But sometimes it's hard to be content. We see our friends get everything they want or think other people have an easy life. If you need help feeling content, try this: Take a few minutes to write down everything you're thankful for. You can write down your favorite possessions, family members, fun memories, or talents God has given you. Hang that list on the refrigerator. Any time you go to the fridge for something to eat or drink, let that list remind you of everything that God has given you. And be content.

WHAT'S THE WORD?

I have learned how to be content with whatever I have. I know how to live on almost nothing or with everything. I have learned the secret of living in every situation, whether it is with a full stomach or empty, with plenty or little. PHILIPPIANS 4:11-12

THINK about your friends. What do you enjoy doing together? Maybe it's shopping, playing sports, dancing, watching movies, or just hanging out.

Now think about your parents. What do you enjoy doing with them? Maybe it's playing games, talking, going to the mall, or doing vacations together. Research shows that building close family relationships requires family members to be near each other (sounds obvious, right?). Being close in proximity creates closeness.

When John recorded the events of the Last Supper, he wrote, "One of His disciples, the one Jesus loved, was reclining close beside Jesus" (John 13:23, HCSB). This disciple was close enough to whisper into the Lord's ear. Some experts believe that John may have even rested his head on Jesus' shoulder. The physical proximity of Jesus and John demonstrated the love they shared for each other.

In the same way, fathers and daughters can show their love for each other by being close. They can hang out on the couch and watch a movie or go on a Daddy-Daughter date (see the appendix at the back of the book for ideas). Often it's the little things that make the biggest difference in relationships. Family is forever, so work together to keep your daddy-daughter relationship up close and personal.

DADDY-*Daughter Time*

Many fathers struggle with wanting to be good parents, when the truth is good parenting can be simple. Studies show good parenting activity often doesn't look like parenting at all. Engaging in small talk, watching TV together, eating at the dinner table, and participating in hobbies build and maintain a strong relationship.

Dads, plan a fun family dinner this week. Make sure everybody eats together at the table without distractions from the TV or cell phones.

Daughters, tell your dad what you need most from him. Maybe it won't be easy to put this into words. You might want his advice with boys (when that time comes), his wisdom on how to follow God, his assurance that he'll love you no matter what, and his time so the two of you can talk. Perhaps you want a quick hug every night and his prayers.

In the coming years, life may get busier and more complicated for both of you. Instead of pushing each other away, remember to stay close and connected.

WHAT'S THE WORD?

One of His disciples, the one Jesus loved, was reclining close beside Jesus.
JOHN 13:23 (HCSB)

IN THE CARDS

IT'S easy to be thankful for the Christmas gifts we wanted. The fashionable scarf. The iPod. The digital camera. But what about the homemade sweater that your great-grandma knit for you? You know, the one with the reindeer on the front and a fluffy poof tail in the back. How can you be thankful for something that makes you itch and looks awful? (*Doesn't Great-Grandma know that red and brown aren't my colors?*)

The Bible doesn't tell us that we have to be thankful for every gift, but it does say to "be thankful in all circumstances, for this is God's will for you who belong to Christ Jesus" (1 Thessalonians 5:18). And the words "all circumstances" mean that you should be thankful when you open up a gift that doesn't live up to your expectations. With that in mind, it's good to have a plan on how to write a thank-you card for the gifts you don't love. (Just so you know, adults love getting thank-you cards in the mail.) Try this suggestion:

> *Dear Great-Grandma,*
> *How did you know that I love reindeer? Thank you. I'm so glad you didn't get run over by one on Christmas Eve.*

Okay, that's not very good. How about this?

> *Dear Great-Grandma,*
> *Wow, what a present! And the wrapping paper. The box! I loved the box. And then what was in it . . . it made me gasp for a moment. Thanks for such a unique gift.*

Uhhh, that doesn't quite work either. One more try.

> *Dear Great-Grandma,*
> *Thank you for the Christmas sweater. It looks like it took a lot of time to knit. Whenever I look at it, it'll remind me of all the cool memories we've had together. Thanks for thinking of me.*

Yeah, now that shows an attitude of gratitude.

DADDY-*Daughter Time*

Sit down to write thank-you notes together. Maybe you were able to thank some relatives in person for your gifts. For those who weren't able to see you open gifts, write them a personal thank-you card. You can buy thank-you cards at the store or make them together. You don't have to write a book to each person, but try to put down a few sentences that express your gratitude for the gift you received. Writing thank-you notes will help you feel more thankful and also brighten the day of the people who receive them.

WHAT'S THE WORD?

Be thankful in all circumstances, for this is God's will for you who belong to Christ Jesus.   1 THESSALONIANS 5:18

COLD-WEATHER CRUSADER

PICTURE your church. Can you imagine your church building being eaten by a pack of wild dogs? That's exactly what happened to the Reverend Edmund Peck's church. When he moved to Blacklead Island in northeastern Canada in the mid-1890s, the local people helped him build a church out of whalebone and seal hide. But one night when temperatures plunged to twenty degrees below zero, Rev. Peck awoke to the sound of hundreds of dogs tearing apart his church. After the initial shock, Rev. Peck didn't allow himself to get discouraged. He knew God had called him to this part of the world to share Christ with the Inuit people. By 1897, a new wooden church had been built. And five years later, he opened the first hospital in the area with the help of other missionaries. Rev. Peck taught the Inuit an alphabet and helped them learn to read and write. Then he translated the books of Matthew, Mark, Luke, and John into their language called *Inuktitut*. Hundreds of Inuit dedicated their lives to Christ because of Rev. Peck's love and courage.

Most people wouldn't give up a nice life in England to live on a cold island in the Arctic Ocean. But Rev. Peck wanted to carry God's Word to the remotest parts of the world. He learned the Inuit language and told the native people about his mighty Savior. Zephaniah 3:17 says, "The LORD your God is living among you. He is a mighty savior. He will take delight in you with gladness. With his love, he will calm all your fears."

Rev. Peck probably held on tightly to the truth in verses like that. There were plenty of times—including when his church was eaten—when he was afraid. But he knew that God was with him and would calm his fears.

DADDY-*Daughter Time*

God may not call you to share his Word in the farthest corners of the world. But you can pray for those who do. If you have a globe or atlas, go get it. You can also look at a world map on the computer. Take turns closing your eyes and pointing to the map. Wherever your finger lands, pray for the missionaries in that country. Pray that God keeps them safe and helps them be effective in telling others about the lifesaving truth of Jesus Christ.

WHAT'S THE WORD?

The LORD your God is living among you. He is a mighty savior. He will take delight in you with gladness. With his love, he will calm all your fears. He will rejoice over you with joyful songs. ZEPHANIAH 3:17

THE STREAK IS OVER

FOR nearly two and a half years, the University of Connecticut women's basketball team was perfect. The Huskies won ninety straight games—the longest winning streak ever in Division I college basketball—and two consecutive NCAA national titles. Not only was UConn's number of victories impressive, but how it won was equally amazing. The Huskies won each game by an average of thirty-three points! Plus, during the streak, they were behind on the scoreboard for just over 130 minutes, while they were ahead for 3,470 minutes. Talk about dominance.

But on this day in 2010, UConn's amazing streak ended in a 71–59 loss at Stanford. Strangely enough, it was the Cardinal who beat the Huskies just before the streak started in a game on April 6, 2008.

Stanford used its size advantage inside to score and get rebounds, while point guard Jeanette Pohlen sank five three-pointers and scored thirty-one points. After the game, UConn coach Geno Auriemma joked at first, saying, "This losing stuff is getting old, man; I hate it." But later he added, "I think winning that many games in a row is unheard of, just unheard of."

The UConn coach was right. A ninety-game winning streak *is* unheard of. No team is perfect, but for thirty-two months the Huskies were as close as you could get.

When it comes to perfection, you aren't going to find it on Earth. You might see a perfect sunset, play a song perfectly on the piano, or find the perfect shoes. But those are just moments of perfection. Between the perfect moments, you're going to experience a lot of mess ups and disappointment. There's only one way to find perfection on this planet, and that's to follow God. Second Samuel 22:31 says, "God's way is perfect. All the LORD's promises prove true." This side of heaven the only perfection you're going to experience is in God.

DADDY-*Daughter Time*

We can't be perfect, but we can follow one who is. Play a quick game of indoor basketball together. Get an empty trash can or bucket and roll up a pair of socks. Put the trash can against the wall and you're ready to go. Play a game of H-O-R-S-E or P-I-G. Or see who can make a shot from the farthest away. Whenever one of you misses a shot, say, "I'm not perfect, but God is. Praise God!"

WHAT'S THE WORD?

God's way is perfect. All the LORD's promises prove true. He is a shield for all who look to him for protection. 2 SAMUEL 22:31

HAVE A BALL

WHO doesn't love a good party on New Year's Eve? Playing games and enjoying time together with family and friends creates lasting memories. One of the biggest parties will take place in New York City. Around one million people will gather tonight in Times Square to ring in the new year. They'll huddle together for warmth and watch the famous New Year's Eve Ball drop as two thousand pounds of confetti are released into the night sky.

The first big New Year's Eve party in Times Square happened in 1904. Three years later, organizers created the original New Year's Eve Ball that descended from a flagpole in Times Square. The first ball was made of iron and wood, weighed seven hundred pounds, and was lit up with one hundred 25-watt lightbulbs. Today's ball, which was unveiled in 2008, is twelve feet in diameter and weighs nearly twelve thousand pounds. Every year new Waterford crystals are added to the magnificent round creation. In 2009, 1,728 crystals were added that featured tiny etched angels with their arms uplifted.

Angels are mentioned a lot in the Bible. Around three hundred verses talk about these spiritual beings, created for specific purposes by God. Some people think we become angels when we die, but that's not what the Bible teaches. The Bible says that angels protect us. Like David writes in Psalm 91:11, "He will order his angels to protect you wherever you go." Angels can provide for physical needs, like they did for Jesus (see Matthew 4:11) and the prophet Elijah (see 1 Kings 19:5-6). They also carry out God's judgment (as described in Revelation) and proclaim God's truth (like they did to the shepherds and will do when Jesus comes back to earth). And when Jesus returns again . . . now that will be a reason to party!

DADDY-*Daughter Time*

Stay up together and watch the ball drop in Times Square. As you see the giant ball ring in the New Year, think about the 1,728 angels etched into the crystals with their arms raised in praise to God. As you begin the new year, take time to honor God for his blessings and comfort in the past year. Then thank him for providing for you in the coming year and protecting you with his angels.

WHAT'S THE WORD?

He will order his angels to protect you wherever you go.   PSALM 91:11

Appendix A:
Father-Daughter Movie Nights

Bob Smithouser

DO YOU ENJOY fixing a snack and settling in with a good movie? The best films entertain while challenging us to think about ourselves and our world a little differently—especially when we look at what's happening on-screen from God's perspective. Jesus recognized the power of stories to communicate truth and touch people in a deep, meaningful way (see Mark 4:33-34). That's why he taught with parables. And movies are modern parables.

In fact, Robert K. Johnston, a professor at Fuller Theological Seminary, told *Time* magazine, "Film, especially for those under thirty-five, is the medium through which we get our primary stories, our myths, our read on reality. . . . As the culture has moved from a modern to a postmodern era, we have moved from wanting to understand truth rationally to understanding truth as it's embedded in story."

Since families already enjoy watching movies together, why not check out a few Hollywood hits sure to lead into new areas of discussion and discovery? In this appendix, you'll find fifteen G or PG features chosen for their appeal to dads and daughters alike.

In each case, you'll find several conversational spark plugs to get the dialogue started. You're sure to come up with additional interesting areas of discussion. Also, consider these general questions, which could apply to any film: (1) What's the main point of this movie? (2) What do the filmmakers appear to believe is true? Do you agree or disagree? (3) Which character do you admire most? Why? In what ways is that character like you? (4) How does the behavior on-screen compare with the values you've learned at home, at school, or in church? (5) Do the themes in this story reflect reality? Do they reflect *truth*?

Of course, very few mainstream movies are perfect, and no one knows better than a parent about which ones would be a good fit for his family. That's why we strongly recommend that, before popping the popcorn and icing the drinks, you learn more about these or other movie-night options by visiting Focus on the Family's popular media-review website, pluggedin.com. That way you're sure to have a great time together with *no* unpleasant surprises.

Have fun at the movies!

ALICE IN WONDERLAND

PG

2010
WALT DISNEY
109 MINUTES

STARRING:
Mia Wasikowska,
Johnny Depp,
Helena Bonham Carter,
Anne Hathaway

DIRECTOR:
Tim Burton

THIS VIVID RETELLING of Lewis Carroll's classic tale packs a few fresh twists. Eager to step into adulthood and make her dreams come true, Alice feels suffocated by others' plans for her life. After tumbling into a rabbit hole, she lands in a bizarre world inhabited by strange creatures who believe that it's her destiny to slay the Jabberwocky and end an evil queen's oppressive reign. Alice just wants to go home. Despite the urging of the Mad Hatter and others, only she can decide if *their* cause is *her* calling.

1. What do you think of Alice's father's advice: "The only way to achieve the impossible is to believe it *is* possible"? Consider Matthew 17:20 and Luke 1:37. If it were possible to visit Underland, what part would you explore further, and which of the locals would you hang out with?

2. In some ways, Alice's frustrations in the room of locked doors (and being too big or small to pass through) symbolize the awkwardness adolescents feel as they transition into adulthood. Is there a door you need to walk through that's forcing you to change in uncomfortable ways? Discuss that together.

3. Why do you think members of the Red Queen's court secretly wore prosthetics to exaggerate certain body parts? How do people in our society do the same thing today?

4. Read Proverbs 3:5-6. Why must each of us catch God's unique, heroic vision for our lives personally, rather than being *told* who we are or what we should become? What was the turning point for Alice, and how can you relate to her predicament?

BEAUTY AND THE BEAST

G

1991
WALT DISNEY
90 MINUTES

STARRING:
Paige O'Hara,
Robby Benson,
Angela Lansbury,
Richard White

DIRECTORS:
Gary Trousdale,
Kirk Wise

A SPOILED PRINCE and his servants have fallen under a curse due to his selfishness. To return them to human form, the beastly young man must love someone *and* earn her love in return before his twenty-first birthday. Time is running out. So when a sweet girl wanders into their dreary, remote castle in search of her missing father, everyone rallies to win her heart and break the spell. Well, *almost* everyone. Nominated for a Best Picture Oscar in 1991, this delightful animated musical also became a huge hit on Broadway.

1. Belle willingly gave up her own freedom to spare her father (see John 15:13). What does that say about her?

2. Talk about the selfishness and prejudice that got the prince into trouble in the first place. Read 1 Peter 5:5, and discuss our need to show kindness and humility to everyone—including strangers. Who do you know who does that really well?

3. Was Gaston good, evil, or somewhere in between? What did he do or say that made you feel that way? Specifically, what did you think of his shallow focus on physical attractiveness, which is a big problem in our culture today? While Belle is pretty, what was it about her character that made her truly beautiful? (See Colossians 3:12-14; 1 Peter 3:4.)

4. What was Belle's first impression of the Beast? Somehow, she still managed to believe the best of him and see his gentler side. What can we learn from Belle's example? Does someone in your life need extra grace or patience?

★ FATHER-DAUGHTER MOVIE NIGHTS ★

presents

BECAUSE OF WINN-DIXIE

PG

2005

20th Century
Fox
104 minutes

STARRING:
AnnaSophia Robb, Jeff
Daniels, Cicely Tyson, Dave
Matthews

DIRECTOR:
Wayne Wang

NAOMI IS A sleepy little town with a new preacher. The minister's lonely young daughter, Opal, yearns for companionship and finds it in a stray mutt with a gift for making messes . . . and friends. Playful girl-and-her-dog high jinks give way to melancholy moments as Opal and her furry sidekick connect with solitary townsfolk plagued by sadness, mistakes, and brokenness. They find themselves gathering human strays. By learning to see the best in people, Opal also manages to draw closer to her father, a good man carrying a burden of his own.

1. Opal called Winn-Dixie "a dog who knew how to be a friend." What did he do to deserve such praise? What do you value most about *your* friends? See what the Bible says about friendship in Proverbs 17:17 and 27:9.
2. Among other things, James 1:19 tells us we should be "quick to listen." What makes that hard sometimes? Opal was impressed with Gloria's interest in her story ("I could feel her listening with all her heart, and it felt good"). Who do you know who's a good listener? How does listening show that we value someone?
3. Opal's mom and Gloria both struggled with alcohol. Has this issue touched your family at some level? If so, talk honestly about that, and discuss healthy boundaries in this area. Glean wisdom from Proverbs 20:1; 23:31-33; and Ephesians 5:18.
4. Which character's sad history touched you most deeply? Why? Read Jesus' words in Matthew 11:28-30. Can you recall three specific ways during his ministry that he showed grace to broken people? How can we model 2 Corinthians 1:3-4 and do the same?

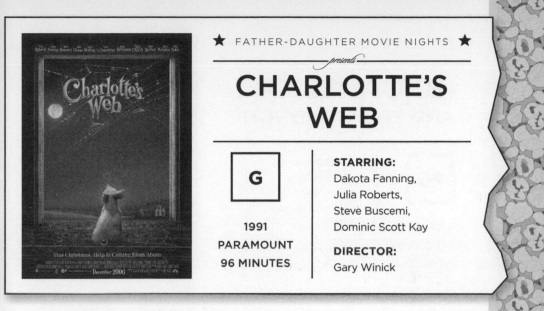

presents

CHARLOTTE'S WEB

G

1991
PARAMOUNT
96 MINUTES

STARRING:
Dakota Fanning,
Julia Roberts,
Steve Buscemi,
Dominic Scott Kay

DIRECTOR:
Gary Winick

THIS LIVE-ACTION REMAKE of the classic cartoon once again finds a young girl rescuing a helpless piglet from the farmer's ax. The barn's cliquish animals aren't very welcoming to Wilbur, a friendly pig who strikes up a relationship with a "creepy" spider named Charlotte. But Wilbur sees Charlotte's inner beauty and is rewarded when she saves him from becoming Christmas dinner by spinning words in her web—a miracle that inspires people to treat Wilbur as the main event rather than the main course. How's *that* for a web sight!

1. Fern saw no difference between a human life and that of a barnyard animal. Although all life has value, what's the distinction according to Genesis 1:24–28 and Matthew 6:26? Also, address Fern's harsh tone with her dad in that opening scene, and why children should respect their parents (see Ephesians 6:1-3).

2. What did Wilbur mean when he told the sheep, "I'm not sure being in the same place is the same as being friends"? Compare friendships of *proximity* (neighbors, classmates, or playmates whose parents are friends) to deeper relationships, like the one described in 1 Samuel 18:1-3. How are true friends different, both in what they offer us and what they expect of us?

3. The doctor was amazed at the "miracle" that spiders could spin webs at all. Read Romans 1:20, and point to evidence of God's fingerprints elsewhere in nature.

4. Just for fun, check your animal knowledge. A collection of sheep is called a flock. What term is used for a group of (1) dogs, (2) chicks, (3) bees, (4) crows, (5) lions, (6) butterflies, (7) ants, (8) otters, (9) geese, (10) hyenas? [Answers below]

Answers: (1) pack, (2) clutch, (3) swarm, (4) murder, (5) pride, (6) flutter, (7) army, (8) romp, (9) gaggle, (10) cackle

THE CHRONICLES OF NARNIA:
THE LION, THE WITCH AND THE WARDROBE

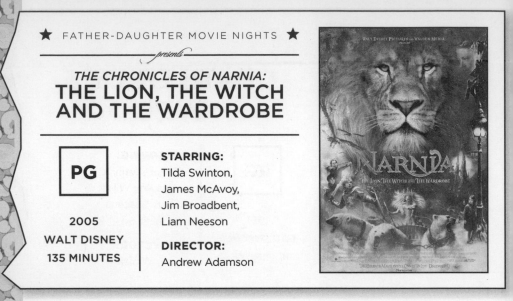

PG

2005
WALT DISNEY
135 MINUTES

STARRING:
Tilda Swinton,
James McAvoy,
Jim Broadbent,
Liam Neeson

DIRECTOR:
Andrew Adamson

FROM THE MIND of C. S. Lewis comes a timeless tale of four children who step into an enchanted wardrobe and emerge in a magical kingdom blanketed by snow. They meet talking animals and mythic creatures oppressed by the evil White Witch, who has set herself up as their queen. But the land's true rulers turn out to be the young visitors themselves, bickering siblings who must accept their royalty and rescue Narnia from the queen's icy clutches with the help of a noble lion willing to lay down his life to redeem them.

1. Peter and Susan told the beavers, "We're not heroes, we're from Finchley," as if heroes needed to come from someplace special. Read John 1:43-46 to see how people were just as shortsighted in Jesus' day. Do you ever feel not special enough because of where you come from?
2. Read Isaiah 14:12-15; 2 Corinthians 11:14; and 1 Peter 5:8-9. How many ways is the White Witch like our spiritual enemy, Satan? For example, she promised Edmund more than she delivered. How does the devil tempt people, then leave them imprisoned and wanting more?
3. How did Edmund's impulsiveness (like the apostle Peter's) get him into trouble? When did it serve him well? Discuss how our personalities are neither right nor wrong, but something we need to understand and submit to God. Which of your dominant traits could be both a strength *and* a weakness? How?
4. Aslan couldn't save Edmund by force or by rewriting the law. Why not? Examine God's commitment to play by the rules he set in motion, and how he rescued us (see John 3:16; Romans 6:23; Hebrews 9:22).

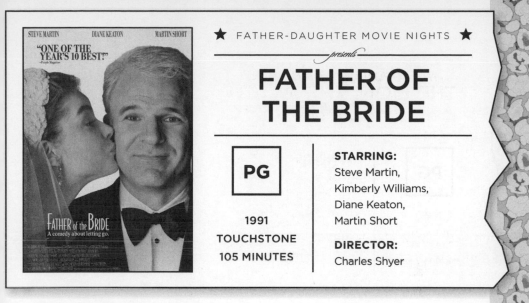

presents

FATHER OF THE BRIDE

PG
1991
TOUCHSTONE
105 MINUTES

STARRING:
Steve Martin,
Kimberly Williams,
Diane Keaton,
Martin Short

DIRECTOR:
Charles Shyer

RELEASING A DAUGHTER into adulthood and seeing a young man capture her heart can be tough on a dad. Just ask George Banks. In this sweet comedy, Annie, his little girl of twenty-two, returns from Europe with a fiancé. As wedding plans kick into high gear (and get increasingly expensive), George mourns the passage of time and the end of an era. Even Annie sees that their special bond is about to change. Best appreciated by dads and teens, it's a tender reminder that each passing day is one less we have to call the same house a *home*.

1. Write down five words each that describe Annie and George's relationship. Then compare your lists. What about their connection did you admire most? Did anything in the film remind you of *your* relationship?
2. Daughters: What frightens you about the thought of leaving home someday? What appeals to you? Read Ephesians 5:21-33 for a timeless description of love, service, and submission designed by God to strengthen marriages.
3. George promised, "I will try to remember my daughter's feelings, and how with every roll of my eyes I am taking away a piece of her happiness." How can we disrespect each other even without using hurtful words? Do you ever do that? Discuss those behaviors and how you might communicate more respectfully.
4. Playing basketball was a bonding activity for the Banks family. Do you have memories of a favorite father/daughter pastime you've shared? If so, plan to do it this week. If not, there's still time to make memories, just the two of you.

★ FATHER-DAUGHTER MOVIE NIGHTS ★

presents

FLY AWAY HOME

PG

1996
COLUMBIA/
TRISTAR
107 MINUTES

STARRING:
Anna Paquin,
Jeff Daniels,
Dana Delany

DIRECTOR:
Carroll Ballard

AFTER HER MOTHER'S tragic death, a child of divorce moves in with her estranged father, a scruffy inventor/artist eager to connect with his now-teenage daughter, but unsure how. What eventually breaks the tension is young Amy's devotion to a nest full of goose eggs displaced by a bulldozer. Once they hatch, the goslings bond with Amy and view her as their "mother." Together, father and daughter bond as they help the birds learn to migrate by outfitting Amy in an ultralight plane and charting a course from Ontario to North Carolina. Inspired by a true story.

1. What did the filmmakers want you to think of nature? of land developers? What lines or images said so? What's a healthy balance between *using* the land and *preserving* it? Discuss ways a movie can manipulate what we root for.
2. How did it feel to see Amy flying? Were you more nervous or envious? Do you think it was responsible of Tom to put her in a plane like that? As you watched the father/daughter relationship evolve, what were key turning points? Note how each found healing by modeling 1 Corinthians 10:24.
3. How did Amy, like the geese, need someone to show her the way? Why is it important to be careful who we follow? (See Proverbs 12:26.) According to Scriptures such as Joshua 1:8; Psalm 119:9-11; and 2 Timothy 3:16-17, why is it wise to make the Bible our primary guide?
4. As you heard in the movie, baby geese are called goslings. What do we call baby (1) deer, (2) whale, (3) eagle, (4) goat, (5) kangaroo, (6) horse, (7) seal, (8) turkey, (9) beaver, (10) fly? [Answers below]

374

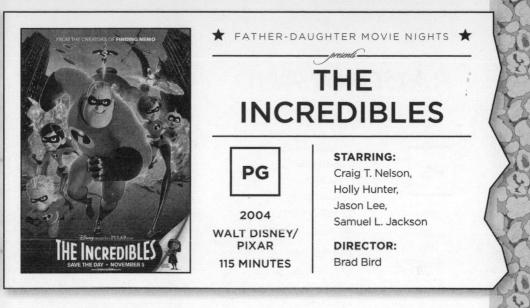

presents

THE INCREDIBLES

PG

2004

WALT DISNEY/
PIXAR

115 MINUTES

STARRING:
Craig T. Nelson,
Holly Hunter,
Jason Lee,
Samuel L. Jackson

DIRECTOR:
Brad Bird

AFTER BEING FORCED into retirement, two of Metroville's top superheroes marry and start a family. Among its members are a mighty dad weakened by the kryptonite of midlife, as well as a brooding teen who protects herself with invisibility and force fields. Targeted by the evil Syndrome, who is eager to rid the world of true champions, this otherwise typical family makes good use of its special talents, overcomes domestic squabbles, and saves the world.

1. At first, Mr. Incredible took pride in working alone. Read Exodus 17:8-16, and imagine the result if Moses had refused help from others. Discuss the Parrs' ability to accomplish more together than alone, and list your own family members' unique gifts.

2. In the film's production notes, the director said, "Violet is a typical teenager, someone who's not comfortable in her own skin and is in that rocky place between being a kid and an adult. So invisibility seemed like the right superpower for her." Would you agree? Have you experienced that feeling? If you could have any superpower, what would it be?

3. What did Elastigirl mean when she told the children, "Your identity is your most valuable possession. Protect it"? Read Proverbs 22:1. How can you protect *your* identity?

4. Aware that she expected too much of Violet on the plane, Mom reassured her that her gifts would develop in time. Have you ever felt pressured to grow up too soon or step into a role before you were ready? Explore that together in light of Ecclesiastes 3:1-11 and 1 Corinthians 13:11.

Answers: (1) fawn, (2) calf, (3) eaglet, (4) kid, (5) joey, (6) foal, (7) pup, (8) poult, (9) kit, (10) maggot

RAMONA AND BEEZUS

G

2010
20TH
CENTURY FOX

103 MINUTES

STARRING:

Selena Gomez,
Joey King,
John Corbett,
Josh Duhamel,
Ginnifer Goodwin

DIRECTOR:

Elizabeth Allen

A STRONG-WILLED FOURTH grader with a vivid imagination, Ramona Quimby loves to spend her days inventing "terrifical" words and having make-believe adventures. That is . . . until life muscles in on her fun. When Dad loses his job, Ramona sets out to save the house, though her best intentions usually end in messy mishaps—sometimes at the expense of her teenage sister, Beezus. More than just a playful comedy, this charmer based on Beverly Cleary's children's books introduces us to a loving, functional family meeting life's challenges head-on.

1. Describe a healthy balance between letting your imagination run wild and following rules. Which comes more naturally to you? If you could eliminate certain rules from your life, what would they be? How might those irritating regulations actually serve a purpose? See what Romans 13:1-5; Ephesians 6:1-3, 5-8; and Hebrews 13:17 say about submitting to authority.

2. Has your family been impacted by change or loss? Can you think of ways that even "good" change might be traumatic? If any of the Quimbys' challenges seemed familiar, discuss your feelings, how God took care of you, and the promises of Proverbs 3:5-6 and Romans 8:28.

3. Which of the warm moments shared by Ramona and her dad were most special to you? We learned that her artistic father was willing to crunch numbers for the good of the family. How have people in your home made personal sacrifices for one another?

4. Ramona complained about being the middle child. Where did you land in your family's birth order? What have been some of the advantages and disadvantages of that?

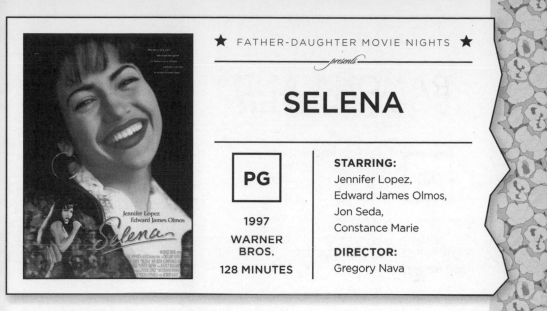

SELENA

PG

1997
WARNER
BROS.

128 MINUTES

STARRING:
Jennifer Lopez,
Edward James Olmos,
Jon Seda,
Constance Marie

DIRECTOR:
Gregory Nava

FROM A YOUNG AGE, beloved Tejano singer Selena Quintanilla had a musical gift and a father desperate to nurture it. In this bittersweet story, based on the singer's real life, one family overcomes racial prejudice and financial ruin in pursuit of a dream. Then Selena develops a sweet romance with a member of her band, and her star keeps rising. Concerts. Hit singles. A Grammy. But as in real life, the film ends tragically when the twenty-three-year-old's life is cut short by a disturbed associate. Despite its sad conclusion, this is a warm, life-affirming father-daughter story.

1. Abe tried to live out his unfulfilled dreams through Selena. How else do parents sometimes attempt to live through their children? At what point can a father's healthy encouragement of his child stray into being *too* pushy? Come up with a few examples.
2. Abraham got upset at Selena's dancing in skimpy outfits. Mom defended her. Who was right according to 1 Peter 3:3-4? Is it easy for young women to dress modestly in our culture? Why or why not? Why is it better for everyone that they do? (See 2 Samuel 11:2-5 and Matthew 5:28.)
3. What did you admire about the romance between Selena and Chris? How did you feel when Abe tried to end their relationship? Put yourself in Abe's place, then Selena's. How does Ephesians 6:1-4 apply to this situation?
4. Read Philippians 2:3. Then name several ways Selena handled fame well and treated others with respect. Can you think of a celebrity who seems to have a similar attitude? Have you observed others who don't? Does their behavior influence your feelings about entertainers?

SOUL SURFER

PG

2011

SONY PICTURES

106 MINUTES

STARRING:
AnnaSophia Robb,
Dennis Quaid,
Helen Hunt,
Carrie Underwood

DIRECTOR:
Sean McNamara

THIS INSPIRATIONAL TRUE story of competitive surfer Bethany Hamilton—a Christian teen who lost her arm in a shark attack—celebrates her faith, family, and fight to reclaim her dream. Bethany's courage is amazing. Forced to relearn the simplest tasks, she manages to adjust and trust that God has a plan. She even gets back on her surfboard with Dad's help. But can she still *compete*? It's a great story made all the better by an excellent cast and surfing footage that puts us right in the middle of the action.

1. Have you experienced a loss or faced a challenge that changed how you did things? In what ways can you relate to Bethany's struggles? How did God work in your situation? Talk about Sarah's message to the youth group about stepping back in order to gain perspective (see Isaiah 55:8-9).
2. To catch the best waves, surfers must first navigate the "impact zone," where waves break hardest, pounding and tossing athletes about. Endurance is rewarded. How is this a metaphor for life in general and the Christian life in particular? Read Psalm 138:7; 2 Corinthians 4:8-9; and 1 Peter 4:12-13.
3. What did you like most about Bethany's relationship with her father? Both parents loved her, yet they had different strategies for helping her bounce back. Discuss that tension. Which approach made the most sense to you?
4. Bethany turned a corner when, on the missions trip, she took her eyes off her own problems and reached out to others. Why do you think that helped? Has a problem been consuming you? Look for a way to meet someone else's needs.

SPELLBOUND

G

2002
WARNER
BROS.

97 MINUTES

STARRING:
Ted Brigham,
Ashley White,
Harry Altman,
Angela Arenivar

DIRECTOR:
Jeffrey Blitz

REGIONAL SPELLING BEES. Dictionary memorization. Boring stuff, right? Just wait until you see *Spellbound*! As compelling as any sporting event or reality TV show, this Oscar-nominated documentary follows eight bright young people from diverse backgrounds as they prepare for and compete in the National Spelling Bee. Win or lose, they're all champions at heart. Whether you're driven to excel at academics, athletics, or the arts, this wholesome, entertaining nail-biter contains valuable lessons for students and adults alike.

1. Which spellers did you root for, and which parents did you admire most? Why? In what ways did the parents support their kids? Dads, ask your daughter, "On a scale of one to ten, how well do you feel *I'm* supporting *you*? What would it take to reach a ten?"
2. How do the filmmakers' attitudes toward their subjects differ from producers of the typical reality TV show? Name a reality show eager to exploit its subjects and shock the audience. Do any programs, like *Spellbound*, seek to inspire viewers by celebrating the best in people?
3. After being eliminated, one boy mentioned having set a series of goals, and his decision to focus on the ones he *did* reach. Why is this healthier than an all-or-nothing approach to competition? Another contestant blamed the official for mispronouncing his word. How did it feel to hear him make excuses?
4. Which do you think would be more stressful, competing in the bee yourself or watching helplessly while a loved one competed? Why? Read Philippians 4:6-7 and 1 Peter 5:6-7 for strength and comfort when the heat is on.

SPY KIDS

PG

2001
DIMENSION
88 MINUTES

STARRING:
Antonio Banderas,
Carla Gugino,
Alexa Vega,
Daryl Sabara

DIRECTOR:
Robert Rodriguez

IMAGINE THE SHOCK of learning that your boring, minivan-driving parents are actually semiretired secret agents. Disguises. Gadgets. A secret lair. That's what happens to squabbling siblings Carmen and Juni Cortez after Mom and Dad get captured by an old enemy out to enslave humanity. It's up to the kids to put aside their differences, face their fears, and save the world. In the end they decide, "Spy work? That's easy. Keeping a family together, that's difficult. And *that's* the mission worth fighting for."

1. Juni asked his dad, "What's so special about being a Cortez?" If someone asked what's special about being a [*your last name here*], what would you say? Read Proverbs 22:1 together and consider, "What choices can we make to protect *our* good name?"

2. One of the greatest stories a father can tell his daughter is how he met and married Mom. Share that personal tale of romance and adventure. What did Ingrid mean when she said, "The two most dangerous, trusting words you can say to anyone are *I do*"?

3. Ephesians 4:29 and James 3:9-12 warn us not to hurt people with unkind or careless words. In what ways did Carmen and Juni need to learn that lesson? Has anyone ever insulted you, even in a joking manner? How did it make you feel? Are you ever tempted to say something mean when *you* get angry?

4. Juni loved "Floop's Fooglies," but Dad thought the program was unhealthy. Has your family had similar disputes over a movie or TV show? Discuss the need for caution when choosing entertainment (see Philippians 4:8; Colossians 2:8).

TANGLED

PG

2010
WALT DISNEY
100 MINUTES

STARRING:
Mandy Moore,
Zachary Levi,
Donna Murphy,
Brad Garrett

DIRECTORS:
Byron Howard, Nathan
Greno

IN 2010, THIS bright, playful musical welcomed Rapunzel into Disney's collection of animated princesses. Stolen from her royal crib for the healing power of her hair, our plucky heroine is confined to a secluded tower and raised by the scheming Mother Gothel. Now a restless teen, Rapunzel longs to see more of the world, and gets her chance when a handsome young thief named Flynn Rider seeks refuge in her tower. Each has something the other wants, so they strike a deal that leads to adventure beyond their wildest dreams.

1. We rooted for Rapunzel to escape her prison, though she defied "Mom" by leaving the tower. Read Ephesians 6:1-3. Why is obedience important, and why is it just as vital that parents allow children to become more independent over time? Have you ever felt desperate to escape restrictions placed on you by someone, even if that person meant well?

2. In light of the Bible's definition of love (see John 15:13; 1 Corinthians 13:4-7), what did Flynn do or say that signaled a change of heart toward Rapunzel? Why should a daughter of King Jesus refuse to settle for less than true love from any man seeking her affection?

3. As we learned at the Snuggly Duckling, there's more to a person's story than meets the eye. Describe a time when your first impression of someone missed the mark.

4. How do you think Rapunzel's life changed after meeting her parents and discovering her true identity? As Christians, how can we experience greater power, confidence, and opportunity by embracing our royalty as children of the King (see 1 Peter 2:9)?

Appendix B:
Daddy-Daughter Dates

Leon C. Wirth

I am the dad of eight girls. Yes . . . *eight girls*! I honestly love having these precious little ladies in my life. God has used them to sharpen my thinking, soften my heart, and give me a better understanding of his love. As I once told a friend a long time ago, "Either God knows exactly what I can handle, or he knows exactly what I need to knock the rough edges off of me and make me who he wants me to be."

My friend replied with a chuckle, "I think it's the latter."

The journey of fatherhood with all these girls is a constant learning process. I am not a perfect dad—far from it. But I've learned from experience and the wise counsel of other dads that focused one-on-one time with our girls is absolutely necessary for the health of our relationship and for the health of our daughters.

I don't need to tell you that the time flies by. Before we know it, our opportunity to guide and impact our daughters' lives will be gone. We have to use the time well.

One of the most effective traditions we've established in our family is the Daddy-Daughter Date. It's a practice that accomplishes an awful lot of good for us, and it gives me the chance to understand and affirm each of my girls' unique personalities.

Why Do a Daddy-Daughter Date?

You are the very first man in your daughter's life.

I know you may be thinking, *I'll be the only man in her life until she's forty*! But seriously, whenever she develops a relationship with any other man, *you* will be the first one she'll compare him to. You shape your daughter's expectations in relation to the opposite sex.

If you want your daughter to be confident, comfortable with herself, equipped to avoid high-risk and destructive behaviors, and prepared to have healthy relationships with men, you'll want to build a good relationship with her now. Because our time with our daughters is short, and our lives are increasingly busy, make time to show your daughter how important she is. When you start doing regular daddy-daughter dates, she won't let you stop! My daughters are constantly looking forward to their next turn.

Here are some of the best reasons I've enjoyed doing daddy-daughter dates:

- You get to know her better. She's changing but you don't always realize how unless you talk to her.
- She gets to know you better. Your daughter needs to start learning how men think and approach life. You can help her with that.
- Your curiosity about her heart and her life communicate your love.
- You get to know her likes and dislikes.
- She feels loved.
- She knows you care about her.
- She feels important and valuable.
- She feels safe. You're giving her the gift of an opportunity to let you know how life is going in her world.
- She feels like a princess! Show her chivalry is not dead. Open car and building doors for her. Pull out her chair at restaurants. Tell her over and over again, "This is how a gentleman should treat a lady like yourself." She might giggle a lot when she's little, but deep inside, she'll love it.
- She will raise the bar for all future dates, boyfriends, maybe even a husband based on how you treat her. You get to set the standard. I say, "Set that bar high!"
- You lay a foundation for the future of your relationship. Want to improve those teen years before you get there? Spend time with your daughter regularly before she turns thirteen.
- You get to know what her dreams are for the future.
- You can both use the time to reconnect and smooth over any rough patches that may have cropped up.
- She feels beautiful. You can never tell her too often "I love you!" and "You are beautiful!"

What Is a Daddy-Daughter Date?

A daddy-daughter date is simply scheduled time to connect and have fun together. It doesn't have to be expensive, predictable, or complicated. The date can be anything you and your daughter make it. But it has to be regular. And, dads, if you schedule a date with your daughter—*don't break it.* She has to know that she can count on you and trust you to follow through on your word.

Here are some ideas to consider when planning daddy-daughter dates:

- Go to her favorite restaurant.
- Find a new restaurant.
- Let her pick an activity to do together.
- Surprise her with an evening all planned out.
- Flowers are always nice.
- Dress up! Give your daughter a chance to be glamorous.
- Dress down . . . be relaxed.
- Introduce her to a new activity: miniature golf, bowling, laser tag.
- Go sit in a mall with some ice cream and "people watch."
- See a movie together . . . but spend time after the film talking about the themes and how the movie did or didn't reflect a biblical perspective.

- Take a class together to learn a new skill.
- Go shopping for Mom or a sibling.
- Take a hike.
- Ride bikes.
- Let her buy something at your or her favorite store. You'll learn a lot about what's important to her and how well she's learning about money.
- Take some food to a park for a picnic. If it rains, eat in the car.
- Take an old family album with you and reminisce. Tell her stories of your childhood.
- Go to a sporting event together. If you're a sports fan, explain to her what made you love your favorite teams.
- Do a service project together.
- Go to a concert, museum, or art exhibit. Talk about what makes art effective or beautiful.
- Take a special evening to talk about the qualities she is looking for in a husband, if she were to get married. This is not just a question for the teen years. Asking this early on will give you an opportunity to shape those expectations.

Ask lots of questions on your date. Some girls talk easily, but others need coaxing and encouragement. Good questions will get the ball rolling.

- Ask "What if . . . ?" questions.
- Ask "Would you rather . . . or . . . ?" questions.
- Ask her who she most admires and why.
- Ask her what she believes and why. Give her room to ask hard questions—even about God. When you don't know the answer to one of her tough questions, assure her that you'll think about it, research it, and get back to her. Then . . . follow through! That builds her trust in you.
- Ask about her fears.
- Ask about her dreams.
- Ask about her friends.

And let her ask you lots of questions too!

Be creative. Be curious. Have fun!

May your daddy-daughter dates create wonderful memories for you and your young lady.

Scripture Index

Fiction series by Sandra Byrd, author of *The One Year Be-Tween You and God*

Join fifteen-year-old Savvy and her family as they adjust to the British way of life after moving from the States. Experience the high-fashion world of London and learn about life in England— all while journeying with an all-American girl and budding journalist.

Along the way, you'll probably learn the same lessons Savvy does: it's better to just be yourself, secrets can be complicated, and popularity comes with a high price tag!

Giving advice to others is one thing. It's another thing to find out that God expects you to live out those lessons yourself. . . .

Read the entire series!

Book #1: *Asking for Trouble*
Book #2: *Through Thick & Thin*
Book #3: *Don't Kiss Him Good-Bye*
Book #4: *Flirting with Disaster*